Henry Alsberg

Henry Alsberg

The Driving Force of the
New Deal Federal Writers' Project

Susan Rubenstein DeMasi

McFarland & Company, Inc., Publishers
Jefferson, North Carolina

LIBRARY OF CONGRESS CATALOGUING DATA ARE AVAILABLE

BRITISH LIBRARY CATALOGUING DATA ARE AVAILABLE

ISBN (print) 978-0-7864-9535-1
ISBN (ebook) 978-1-4766-2601-7

Front cover: photograph of Henry Alsberg (Library of Congress)

Printed in the United States of America

*McFarland & Company, Inc., Publishers
Box 611, Jefferson, North Carolina 28640
www.mcfarlandpub.com*

To Jack DeMasi, my love;
to our children;
and to our grandchildren,
with the hope that their world
will become the world
Henry Alsberg dreamed of

Table of Contents

Acknowledgments

When four years (and a lifetime) ago I decided to journey back in time and enter the world of Henry Alsberg, I could not have imagined how many people would come along with me. Now, with snow covering the ground as I near the end, I think about the Arctic languages and their many words for snow and find myself wishing for a multitude of words for "thank you."

My indebtedness begins in Palo Alto, Henry's last home. There, librarian/local historian Steve Staiger helped lead me to Anne Nevins Loftis, friend of Elsa Alsberg. She graciously met with me that very afternoon, regaling me with stories of Elsa and Henry. She told me about the "Alsberg" desk she inherited, and how she shipped off Henry's archival papers to the University of Oregon.

The courtesy and friendliness of everyone at the University of Oregon's Special Collections and University Archives department, as well as the beautiful setting, made for an unforgettable experience. I extend my gratitude to James Fox, Linda Long, Bruce Tabb, and their associates.

Columbia University's archivist Jocelyn Wilk and colleagues in the Rare Book and Manuscript Library helped me piece together Henry's college life. The American Jewish Joint Distribution Committee in New York provided unfettered access to important archives. I especially thank Misha Mitsel, who provided generous guidance and support. I also thank the JDC's Abra Cohen; Gunnar Berg and colleagues at the YIVO Institute for Jewish Research; Zachary Loeb and others at the Center for Jewish History in New York; Boni J. Koelliker, American Jewish Historical Society; and Elisa Ho, at the Jacob Rader Marcus Center of the American Jewish Archives in Ohio. There are many people to thank at the New York Public Library's Manuscripts and Archives Division, but I especially acknowledge Thomas Lannon, Tal Nadan, Weatherly Stephan, and Kyle Triplett, as well as Jeremy Megraw at the Billy Rose Theatre Division. I'm grateful to Spencer Howard and Craig Wright at the Herbert Hoover Presidential Library and Museum. Reference staff at the Library of Congress's Prints and Photographs and Manuscript Divisions offered friendly assistance during my visits. Ryan Reft and Jonathan Eaker were especially generous with their expertise and time. Staff members at other institutions provided similar support: Amy Hague, Smith College; Thomas L. Hollowak, University of Baltimore; Sharon Lehner, Brooklyn Academy of Music; Hannah Rainey, the Harry Ransom Center, University of Texas at Austin; Martha Tenney, Barnard College Archives; Melinda Wallington, University of Rochester Rare Books and Special Collections; and David Webster, Hoboken Museum. I am thankful to countless others at the Beinecke Rare Book & Manuscript Library, and Manuscripts and Archives, Yale University; the Central Zionist Archives in Jerusalem; the Tamiment Library and Wagner Labor Archives, New York University; Division of Archives and Research Collections, McMaster University; Smithsonian Archives of American Art; Louise Pettus Archives, Winthrop University; Hoover Institution Archives, Stanford University; the International Institute of Social History; University of Chicago Library; Bancroft Library, UC Berkeley; and the National Archives. I am also appreciative of support from Harvey Balopole, Dana Bell, Richard Caliban, my loving mother-in-law, Bernardine DeMasi Dawidziak, Sarah Palmor, Kayla Axelrod and Luke Connors at Congressman Steve Israel's office, James McGrath Morris and others at Biographers International, and Gabriel Milner and the Living New Deal organization.

It is tremendously practical to have librarians and other academic colleagues and friends to call on. I'm grateful to Sally Glasser (Hofstra University), and many at my home base of Suffolk County Community College (SCCC): Kerry Carlson, James Cassidy, Alyssa Kauffman, Mary Kim, Kevin McCoy, Carol McGorry, Lisa Melendez, Kevin Peterman, Gertrude Postl, Jason Ramirez, and Bruce Seger. My appreciation extends to the SCCC community, especially those who handle professional development programs, which supported this endeavor. I offer my thanks to Dr. Philip Christensen, Laurel Frey, Dr. James Keane, Steven Schrier, Marie Hanna, and the Faculty Association of Suffolk Community College. Victoria Pendzick acted, essentially, as my photo editor and deserves special mention for the photographic expertise she provided time and again. Her handiwork with reproductions of old college photographs was particularly appreciated.

I am indebted to Becky Bartlett for giving me the first opportunity to write about the Federal Writers' Project for *Choice* magazine, and to actors Richard Buley-Neumar and Simon Jones for their interpretations of Henry's character in two different dramatizations. Jerre Mangione's memoir of his time on the Writers' Project introduced me to Henry Alsberg, and for that I am thankful.

Meeting (in person or on email) the friends and relatives of people who knew Henry made him come alive for me. Thank you most of all to the Hanau and Bloch families: Richard Hanau (son of Stella Bloch Hanau), Christopher Lee Douglas, Meredith Briggs Skeath, Alison Bradbury, Carol and Sandy Briggs, and Suzanne Stella Bloch Sodergren. Edward Bloch, Stella's nephew, has been nothing short of a prince, as well as a great research assistant and new friend. To feel that Henry and I share a friend is a special experience.

Patricia Tool McHugh kindly shared her memories and artwork. I am appreciative of stories shared by Bryan Dunlap and Sarah Stephens, grandchildren of Henry's friend Philip Coan; Kellock family members Kate O'Brien, Peter Setlow, and Alan Kellock; Alan Frese of Hastings House; James Zetzel; Donald Harris; and Jean Kroeber. An email exchange with Ursula Le Guin, daughter of Alsberg family friend Alfred Kroeber, offered a brush with literary celebrity.

I am particularly grateful to have met the smart and kindhearted Elizabeth Alsberg Stoerk, who survived the Holocaust and moved to New York but never had the chance to meet her cousin Henry; she told me of the family's genealogical and geographical history. Doris Stiefel and Ernst Klein were also helpful. Mack and John Lipkin, and Austin Kessler, relatives of Henry's sister-in-law, Elsie Fraenkel Alsberg, also answered my call, displaying the familial traits of kindness and helpfulness.

I wish I could include a photograph to show the view from the waterside gazebo that Susan McGovern and Shel Lipsky bestowed upon me for those times when I needed a quiet writing place. Heather Forest and Larry Foglia offered a similar respite. Sylvia and Marty Lipnick and Naomi and Lew Serviss provided accommodations and fine company on extended research trips. Lee Caggiano, Amy Olander, and Brian P. Quinn were my saviors from the demons of inertia and insecurity. Ongoing support from others has been much appreciated.

I offer sincere thanks to my manuscript readers for agreeing to take on hundreds of pages and then actually reading them. David Quinn asked important questions and gave valuable advice. Richard Jay Hyman gave emotional support, editorial guidance, and provided ideas that I couldn't believe I didn't think of myself. Stephanie Sakson copy edited the book and made excellent suggestions. I appreciate her kind, supportive words and friendship.

There are no words for author Lawrence J. Epstein, my mentor, who taught me how to write a book. He deserves a place in the advisor hall of fame. During some very difficult days, his reassurance put me back on track. He answered at least a few hundred questions with grace and humor. I treasure his counsel.

I thank my late parents, Artie and Anita, for giving me an unending curiosity about the world; Joan Rubenstein, my aunt, for also being my big sister and cheerleader; and my late Uncle Phil Rubenstein, who showed me that it's okay to jump into new endeavors—whether it's acting or writing a book—at any age. I've been equally lucky to have the love of my brother Steve and my late brother, David.

My heartfelt gratitude and love go to my children and their spouses—Ariel and Nick Rodriguez and Alex and Rhijuta DeMasi—who never seemed to doubt that I would finish this long, involved project. While I gestated a book, they created the two new loves of my life, Michaela and Raphael.

I am beyond thankful for Jack, my husband and soul mate. He's been my editor for as long as I can remember, and we should share author credit. It couldn't have been easy to live in this sort of ménage a trois with Henry for the last few years. Jack spent hours upon hours reading and taking on the role as my on-call main editor, and I depended on his guidance. I am fortunate to share my life, and now, this project, with him.

Finally, to Henry: I felt your spectral presence next to me more than once. Thank you for letting me into your world.

Preface

In my imagination we agreed to meet at a coffee shop on Fifth Avenue, near the main branch of the New York Public Library. I thought he'd appreciate, all these years later, the ambience of caffeine-infused writers hunched over their keyboards.

Of course he hadn't been to New York in ages and wanted, he said, "to pace the streets, smell them, jump back into my memories." We had planned to do just that after our coffee; his tardiness, however, suggested that he couldn't help himself, getting detoured along the way, lured perhaps by a persuasive pretzel vendor. He'd certainly be in for some culinary shock with the vast, multicultural changes in street food over the time he had been gone. I wondered if perhaps he had found a protest to join, a picket sign to carry, a cause to support along the way. So many new causes have sprung up. That would be Henry, too exuberant and idealistic for his own good.

He finally loped in, flushed from his walk, excited as if he had seen wonders that couldn't be contained in mere words. I recognized him immediately; he matched the pictures I'd seen and the descriptions I'd read: "A great Newfoundland of a man," with a "proverbial twinkle in his eye," "a big man with a skyscraper brow topped by disheveled iron hair, deep-set eyes and a prominent nose above a small, sandy mustache."[1] The dashing good looks from his more youthful years still shone through. He wore an old-fashioned, charcoal woolen suit, with a necktie more colorful than I would have expected. But then again, I'd only seen him in black and white photographs. He looked as if he had stepped in from another time.

And, of course, in my imagination, he had.

Henry Garfield Alsberg, or at least the specter of him, came to me from 1938. And from 1925. And from 1903. He came to me from New York City, from Moscow, from Constantinople. He came to me with stories of revolution from his days in Russia with Emma Goldman and tales of misery from his time as a refugee worker aiding Jews in post–World War I Europe. He came to me from the famous Provincetown Playhouse, where he was a producer. More than anywhere else, he came to me from Washington, D.C., and the Federal Writers' Project.

This New Deal jobs program, which set out to tell "the story of America," existed for only four years but left a legacy that still reverberates throughout our culture today. From 1935 through 1939, Alsberg, as national director of the Federal Writers' Project (FWP), left his fingerprints on every document produced by that prolific and idealistic agency.

I knew for sure that the story of his stewardship of the Writers' Project needed to be told. It wasn't just the hundreds of titles published, or the now-legendary *American Guide* books still reprinted every year, or the dramatic battles with the House Committee on Un-American Activities. It wasn't merely the thousands of oral histories compiled by the FWP—first-person narratives from former slaves, newly arrived immigrants, and people of myriad ethnicities, regions, and occupations—that are now being mined by scholars, writers, and filmmakers.

All were fascinating. But what captivated me most was the realization that the FWP, in its efforts to promote social justice and racial equality, personified Henry Alsberg himself. Like Alsberg's life, the Project encompassed a compelling mixture of journalism, human rights, anthropology, folklore, publishing, politics, and theater. No field seemed untouched either by the Project or by Henry Alsberg. The man and the Project, intertwined and separate, still influence our literary and cultural landscape so many years later.

It drew me in so much that I spent hours, days, weeks in the serene spaces of the New York Public Library, my head deeply ensconced in the 1930s. When I left at last call—yes, that happens in libraries, not just bars—and those dusty folders had to go back to their secret library hiding places, I would almost see the world in black and white for a few hours. Walking the surrounding streets, I expected to see an automat, men in felt hats, women in smart skirt suits and white gloves, a Clark Gable movie on the marquee. I could hear the strains of Gershwin and Benny Goodman and Fats Waller struggling to seep through the general hum of 21st-century New York City. Making my way through adjacent Bryant Park, I would look for a tall man in a charcoal suit, hurrying past in one of his quests to save the world. The black and white faded, of course, and as the color returned, so did the city's full-blast, modern cacophony. But my search continued for my new friend, Henry Alsberg.

I indulged my obsession, writing a stage play and a radio play about his journey with the FWP. I saw and heard actors reciting the words I imagined Henry Alsberg saying. Always, I thought back to those ten thousand or so first-person narratives collected by the FWP. Former slaves, sharing memories from the days before freedom. Coal miners and factory workers, Native Americans and Western pioneers—all people who never dreamed their life stories would be preserved.

Henry Alsberg helped tell their stories. Now I want to help tell his.

Introduction

*He represented "the best that was in America—sincerity and easy joviality, direct-
ness and camaraderie."*—Emma Goldman

More than a century after he graduated at age twenty-two with a law
degree from Columbia University, more than eighty years since he trekked
around Bolshevik Russia with Emma Goldman and worked as a foreign correspondent and volunteer for Jewish refugees in Europe, more than seventy years
since the House Committee on Un-American Activities eviscerated his career
with Roosevelt's New Deal, and more than four decades since he died an old,
largely unremembered man, I met—and fell in love with—Henry Alsberg.

Like other love affairs, ours began serendipitously. I was at the New York
Public Library researching the Federal Writers' Project (FWP), one of Franklin
D. Roosevelt's Works Progress Administration (WPA) programs, and kept trip-
ping over the shadow of Alsberg's six-foot-plus frame. From 1935 through 1939,
Alsberg was national director of the FWP, so of course I was going to run into
him. I had already become fascinated with the Federal Writers' Project and its
against-all-odds, enthusiastic telling, through hundreds of guidebooks and
other publications, of the story of America. Henry Alsberg, the "guiding star,"
the passionate architect of this "freak enterprise,"[1] hovered like a ghost over
the dusty bins, in the underground warrens, in the miles of bookshelves of the
New York Public Library.

Thanks to WPA-smitten researchers and scholars, the significance of Alsberg's work has not gone unnoticed. But of the many people who contributed
their creative energies to the New Deal, Alsberg stands almost alone in being
overlooked by the critical lens of a biography.

Looking at the now-collectable *American Guide* books—that "self-portrait
of America" which became one of the enduring hallmarks of the FWP—along
with the literary works and ethnic-culture books produced under his guidance,

it becomes obvious that Alsberg helped change the very landscape of the twentieth-century literary and cultural scene. In fact, John Steinbeck, who owned a complete set of the *American Guide* books, praised the series in his autobiographical travelogue, *Travels with Charley*.

Moreover, these contributions have not yet ended. A revived interest in the cultural and historical legacy of the project has fueled the publication of multitudes of books, both popular and academic. Many of those make extensive use of the project's voluminous collection of primary materials, some of which never made it to print during the life of the program; the life-history and folklore collections, in particular, are still being actively mined by writers and filmmakers. The original FWP books published in the 1930s and 1940s continue to be reprinted.

Alsberg's Writers' Project, an evolving landscape of an agency, was inhabited by such writers as Ralph Ellison, Saul Bellow, Studs Terkel, and Zora Neale Hurston. Although most FWP writers worked mainly on the *American Guide* books, Alsberg pushed for the FWP to act as patron to a few writers, allowing them to pursue creative work. Most famous among these is Richard Wright, whose talent Alsberg quickly recognized; he wrote *Native Son* under its aegis.

Alsberg also cultivated a landscape that promised immigrants and African Americans the chance to help write their own history. His progressive leanings, as well as his interest in the work of leading anthropologists and folklorists, led to the establishment of programs promoting cultural and ethnic diversity. These programs, unprecedented in their undertaking, included gathering oral histories and folklore from immigrants and former slaves.

However, Alsberg's time steering the unwieldy boat that was the FWP was cut short by conservative lawmakers, most notably the zealous and media-savvy Congressman Martin Dies, Jr., chair of the House Committee on Un-American Activities (commonly known as HUAC). Alsberg's clashes with Dies' massive ego and HUAC became fodder for newspapers nationwide.

Although my original search was ostensibly for FWP documents, I soon discovered Henry Alsberg peeking around every research corner, whispering, luring me over to where he could tell me about his *other* work, too. It inevitably became a personal game of hide and seek. What I found was compelling—a passionate, compassionate man who was prominent and influential, over the course of his life time, in journalism, human rights, publishing, politics, and theater.

I found him in more places than I could have imagined. There are thousands of pages of his newspaper and magazine articles, short stories, plays, and books. Because he maintained close ties to the liberal intellectuals who defined twentieth-century thought and lived and worked among the cognoscenti in the artistic, political, and literary scenes, Alsberg also appears in countless biographies (e.g., Henry Morgenthau, Jr., Felix Frankfurter, George Gershwin, Emma Goldman, Roger Baldwin, Bertrand Russell). From the Reds to the Beats, his letters to and from these agents of change—now in archives across the United States and abroad—extend over half a century, from the early 1900s until shortly before his death in 1970 at age eighty-nine.

Alsberg and his contemporaries helped lay the groundwork for future social justice movements: civil liberties, human rights, peace studies, women's rights, racial equality, and other issues. With a primary focus on these struggles, this correspondence provides a looking glass into the vibrant world they shared in the first half of the twentieth century.

Who is to say *exactly* what lured me in to the life of Henry Alsberg? Was I attracted to the combination of idealism and restlessness that seemed to propel him? Who *is* this man who befriended Emma Goldman and Alexander Berkman in Russia, helping them ward off starvation? Who *is* this man, who as a theatrical producer, publisher, and editor, championed the careers and literary works of Richard Wright and E.E. Cummings, among others? Who *is* this man who was an eyewitness and participant in some of the most important historical events of the twentieth century? Who *is* this man, who as both a foreign correspondent and a refugee worker, helped focus America's attention on the plight of Jews in post–World War I Eastern Europe? Who *is* this man who wrote about the pogrom in the Ukrainian town my grandmother and her family fled from only a few years before?

Born in 1881 and raised in New York City, Henry Garfield Alsberg grew up in a secular German-Jewish family. After earning two degrees at Columbia by the age of twenty-two, he spent a few years practicing law, then a year pursuing postgraduate work at Harvard University, studying comparative literature with William James. But a staid life was not for him: Henry Alsberg's heart was drawn to journalism. And because he was deeply moved by transgressions against the poor and disenfranchised, it was mostly leftist and radical journalism. He was an editorial writer for the *New York Evening Post* while also contributing to *The Masses*. He lived alternately with his mother, on West 95th Street, and in Greenwich Village.

Politics and the call of exotic locales sent him in another direction in 1916 when he left for Turkey as private secretary to the United States Ambassador, seeing France, Germany, and Austria under wartime conditions. In that position, he worked with Ambassador Abram Elkus to provide aid to Armenians and Jews in Turkey. As a member of the diplomatic service he even brought a proposal for a peace settlement with Turkey to U.S. Secretary of State Robert Lansing, who in turn brought it to President Woodrow Wilson.

Alsberg completed his Foreign Service stint and returned for a time to his newspaper-writing career in New York. Whether because of journalistic pursuits or simply the desire to explore his "philosophical anarchist" beliefs and experience the historical changes in revolutionary Russia, he spent the next few years, pen in hand, crisscrossing that country and nearly every country in Europe as a foreign correspondent for *The Nation*. At the same time, he volunteered as a director for the American Jewish Joint Distribution Committee in its operations in Russia and Eastern Europe to save millions of starving and pogromized Jews. As a zealous defender of human rights with the necessary political acumen and foreign-language skills (he spoke German and French fluently, along with some Russian and Yiddish), it suited him well. So as the political and human rights situations deteriorated, he consistently put his life in danger.

Not much is known about his life as a homosexual in these repressive times, or even how early in his life that he self-identified as being gay. However, Alsberg cultivated close friendships with Goldman and Berkman, perhaps appreciating the acceptance that the anarchists accorded to homosexuals. He traveled with them on their famed museum expedition through the Ukraine. Ironically, he was the only one arrested by the Soviets and, according to accounts, got drunk with the arresting officer. He was with them as Goldman's fervor for the cause, as well as his own, turned to disillusionment over the realities of the fascist government. After years of reporting about the complex political conditions and war, and the attendant, uncomplicated atrocities; after years of helping feed and clothe and otherwise save millions of Jews; after a blossoming disillusionment with the Soviets, he returned home, bringing with him yet another cause: freeing jailed "politicals" in the Soviet Union. Working with American Civil Liberties Union founder Roger Baldwin and future Supreme Court Justice Felix Frankfurter, he maintained a resolute, years-long effort.

But what of his own literary pursuits during this period? If Henry Alsberg had to compile a modern-day resume, he would require a separate section just for his theatrical and literary ventures. When he returned to the United States— and after being investigated by the FBI for alleged Bolshevik activities—his translation and adaptation of S. Ansky's play, *The Dybbuk*, enjoyed critical accolades during a two-year Off Broadway run and in later revivals. His production also introduced this Yiddish masterpiece to the Western world. As a producer at the famed Provincetown Playhouse in New York City, he worked closely with Eugene O'Neill and E.E. Cummings. His role as a theatrical impresario and playwright/translator would continue, on and off, into the 1940s and 1950s.

How long would such a resume be? Alsberg's publications as both writer and editor, even apart from the Writers' Project, spanned his lifetime and ranged from left-wing and mainstream publications to acclaimed books. Left out of this resume, of course, would be his many unpublished works. His personal traits and frenzied lifestyle, the source of this vacuum, not only usurped his quest for literary prominence but also made for the chaotic timeline of his life.

The sheer number of activities he packed into the 1920s, for instance, is dizzying. Arguably his most active period, he energetically segued from journalism to refugee relief work to theatrical pursuits to political endeavors, shifting almost seamlessly. A personal daybook entry from a random calendar week in 1925 would have shown Alsberg submitting articles to various newspapers and magazines; strategizing to free international political prisoners; writing a book about Eastern European Jewry; directing operations at a downtown New York theater; and rewriting portions of his play (at a *different* theater). How Alsberg even kept to such a schedule is mind boggling. A graphic representation depicting Alsberg's completely nonlinear life during this decade would necessitate a series of color-coded, zigzag lines to follow his actions across time zones and continents, from Russia to California.

Because all of the aforementioned activities require contextual background—and to save the reader the feeling of ricocheting from event to event—Chapters 5 through 7, which cover this period, are structured more thematically.

Was Henry Alsberg a man who couldn't decide where to lay his hat as he labored in the diverse and distinct realms of journalism, theater, foreign affairs, and progressive social movements? What does his *specific* journey tell us about the interconnection of these movements? Why do his writings, prominently and widely distributed during his lifetime, still resonate so many years later?

The first half of the twentieth century was not a black-and-white world as we may imagine from photographs and films of the era. These were colorful and vibrant times, made so at least partially by this spirited and idealistic man and his counterparts. Henry Garfield Alsberg did not just live *within* the history of the period; he participated in and contributed to its evolving social, political, and literary activism. Understanding Alsberg's principled struggles for a more humanistic and pacifistic society and viewing his specific contributions—particularly the vast contribution and legacy left by the Federal Writers' Project—leads us to a deeper, more nuanced understanding of the times.

Although my desire to write about Henry Alsberg began at the New York Public Library, it was solidified in the place where he lived his final years and was laid to rest: Palo Alto, California. Writer Anne Nevins Loftis, eighty-nine-years old when I interviewed her, had met Henry Alsberg after he'd moved from New York to California to live out his last years with his sister, Elsa—far away in time and space from the engrossing world in which he had lived and worked. Despite his age and ill-health when Loftis met him in the 1960s, she noted that "he had this aura of having lived an adventurous life. There was something compelling about him."

What began for me as an intellectual query turned into a personal quest. When I visited the sun-drenched, plant-filled mausoleum where he is interred, I meditated on the life of a man who has been ashes in a niche 3000 miles away since I was twelve years old. Leaving no direct heirs, I was likely his first visitor in decades. After so many years, the name plaque over his niche had begun to fade, its letters getting fainter by the decade. I realized *he* too was getting fainter by the day.

Sitting in that mausoleum, I thought of the thousands of Jews he worked so hard to save after World War I and how he must have felt later when so many were likely murdered during the Holocaust. I thought of his theatrical success, *The Dybbuk*, where the wall between reality and the supernatural disappears, where the soul of a dead person lives on. I thought of his work with the Writers' Project, and the preservation of the life stories of thousands of people who otherwise would have disappeared into oblivion. I knew with certainty that Henry Alsberg's story was not yet ready to fade away.

CHAPTER 1

"The strangely gifted Henry G. Alsberg"
1881–1907

The icy mud pathways through the then–Romanian village of Ataki could hardly be called roads. For the passengers attempting the unforgiving route via a horse-drawn, springless carriage, it was, as Henry Alsberg wrote, "a terrible instrument of torture if applied to one's spine." The carriage ride was, perhaps, the most luxurious part of Alsberg's travels through this Eastern European region. Alsberg's goal was the town of Mohilev, which lay a mere two hundred yards across the river—and over the border—in Russia. The wrecked bridge, its steel beams twisted from years of war, was half submerged in the icy river. The travelers had no choice but to cross in a small boat. The river currents and thunderous collisions with ice floes battered the vessel, threatening to capsize it and drown its occupants.

Under the best of circumstances, January in Eastern Europe does not offer optimum travel conditions. For our travelers—two journalists, a soldier, and the boat's pilot—the weather was the least of it. In 1920, the magnitude of destruction resulting from both World War I and the Bolshevik revolution dominated the landscape. Turmoil and unrest, with different political and military factions alternately controlling a city on any given day, had rendered the region unstable and volatile. The area was much like that small boat given over to the vicissitudes of the Dniester River.

With Henry Alsberg at the bow, the group "bullied" their way across the river.

As a foreign correspondent for *The Nation* and an aid worker for the American Jewish Joint Distribution Committee (JDC), the indefatigable Alsberg felt relentlessly driven to cross into Russia. Waiting on the other side, as he wrote in his *Nation* dispatch, was "reigning anarchy." But cross he did. Mohilev had undergone twenty harsh regime changes in just a few years. For the residents, this meant pillaging and terror, starvation and disease; for the Jewish population, pogroms accompanied the other horrors. Once in Mohilev, Alsberg made his first order of business the distribution of a "large sum of money" entrusted to him by the JDC. He planned subsequently to travel to Kiev and Moscow to continue his reportorial duties for *The Nation*. However, soon after he dispersed those urgently needed funds to the beleaguered local Jewish residents, he discovered that his travel plans had become impossible.

Murderous robber bands had just taken over the city. The local Jewish council convened to warn Alsberg that he was in danger. So, dressed in Orthodox garb, he circumvented the robber bands and soldiers, taking refuge at the home of the poorest Jewish family in town. He hid there for four days, and as volleys of gunfire streaked the night sky, he made his way back across the Dniester to Romania. Eventually, he wound his way to Moscow.[1]

Alsberg, at age thirty-eight, was almost halfway through his life during those frigid months of 1920 when he wrote about that incident for *The Nation*. His dispatch included not just the harrowing ordeal, but also—with wry humor—the loss of his favorite hat while escaping the violent gangs. What confluence of character, temperament, and history—his own and the world's— had brought him to that wintry battleground?

Alsberg was most certainly a man driven by his ideals. Pacifism, human rights, and all those movements that we now place under the umbrella heading of "social justice" propelled him to action. He abhorred human suffering and could not merely expose the injustices he witnessed through his writing; he felt compelled to act on them. Intrigued by and with a keen eye for political and governmental machinations, he also could not help but direct his gaze toward the ever-present victims. Although he often concentrated on the welfare of his fellow Jews, his writings make clear that he was blind to race and ethnicity when it came to the torments inflicted by the powerful onto the powerless.

Alsberg, conscious of the dangers encountered on these trips, remained unruffled for the most part—at least as his letters and reportorial dispatches suggest. Whether he was truly fearless is unknown, but his creativity in getting through these situations was evident. Perhaps this was all fueled by his unusual amount of *schpilkes*—a word, likely to be in his Yiddish lexicon, that means, roughly, "ants in the pants."

The incidents in Ataki and Mohilev—risking his life to assist fellow Jews, reporting about the political and military and human rights situations, providing his readers with an understanding of the ever-changing regimes, even working in the anecdote about his hat—illustrate Alsberg in belief and action. The temperament and mindset that led him to those choices during that winter of

1920 came from somewhere. Indeed, the trajectory that landed him in Ataki began in New York City.

The Constellation of Family

Henry Garfield Alsberg grew up in a secular German-Jewish family on the Upper East Side of Manhattan. Born September 21, 1881, just two days after President James Garfield died of gunshot wounds suffered during an assassination attempt, and the youngest of four Alsberg children, he was the only one with a purely American-inspired middle name.

It may not have been pure patriotism that motivated his parents, Meinhard and Bertha Alsberg—née Baruch—to bestow their baby with this illustrious middle name. His liberal, intellectual parents most likely supported Garfield's political agenda. The twentieth president was an abolitionist, a civil rights proponent, and an advocate for universal education.

A different assassination on the other side of the world—that of Czar Alexander II—also made the news the year Alsberg was born and sparked events that would reverberate throughout his later life. The assassination brought murderous pogroms against Jews, who were scapegoated and blamed for the Czar's death. That wave of pogroms began in Russia's southwest provinces, in the same region and in some of the same towns that Alsberg would visit repeatedly as a reporter and refugee worker. The violence on that far-off continent was a long way from the up and coming New York City neighborhood where Henry joined siblings Carl, Julius, and Elsa.

The family's roots were in Germany; Bertha was born in New York of German-American parents, and father Meinhard in the town of Arolsen, Germany. Meinhard's intellectual talents qualified him for university; he studied under Friedrich Wöhler, the scientist who discovered aluminum, and Robert Bunsen, inventor of the Bunsen burner, and by age twenty two Meinhard earned a Ph.D. in chemistry. He arrived in America the following year, 1865— just a few months after the assassination of Abraham Lincoln and about a month before the ratification of the 13th Amendment abolishing slavery— debarking from the steamship *Saxonia* at the Castle Garden Immigration Center (which preceded the famous Ellis Island entryway).

Unlike later waves of Eastern European Jewish immigrants, Meinhard and other German Jews did not come to America to escape brutal pogroms. Nevertheless, wide-ranging constraints on Jews in German states restricted marriage, employment, and real estate acquisition. Although German Jews were granted some legal rights and had achieved professional status and prominence in many fields, deeply rooted anti–Semitism and accompanying discriminatory practices still provided sufficient incentive for young German Jews to emigrate to America. Whether Meinhard left Germany for better professional opportunities or due to discrimination, or both, is not known. His maternal uncle, a physician, preceded him to America, which may have added impetus to the move.

Meinhard initially headed to Philadelphia in search of an academic post but eventually found better, more commercial prospects, in New York. It didn't take long for him to establish himself. He pioneered the manufacturing of vermillion in 1868, prior to forming his own chemical company. Later, he became an assistant chemist at Columbia University, and Chief Chemist for the New York City Board of Health. During this period, the city ramped up its efforts and made great strides toward improving the metropolis' sanitary conditions, particularly in tenements and immigrant neighborhoods. Free vaccinations and safer milk, food, and water supplies were hallmarks of this effort.

In 1876, Meinhard married Bertha, ten years his junior, and became a naturalized citizen. As a founder of the American Chemical Society, Meinhard was also prominent in scientific circles, and able to provide quite well for his family. By 1880, with Meinhard Alsberg's own successful chemical company in operation, the family lived on the Upper East Side of Manhattan. Now a historic Landmark District and home to some of society's most affluent, in the late 19th century it was just beginning to lose what was left of its rustic character. The Alsberg's first home on 71st Street by Park Avenue was a handsome five-story masonry structure. Four families lived in the building, with the heads of households all in the professions.

Modernity came in waves, with streetcars joining the horse-pulled cars on Lexington Avenue. Mount Sinai Hospital and Central Park were just a few blocks away, and four synagogues—which would not be used by the secular Alsberg family—were within a short distance. In the mid–1880s, Meinhard, Bertha, and the four children moved a few blocks north to 146 East 74th Street. Two elevated railroad lines running up Second and Third avenues past the Alsberg's neighborhood led to rapid population increases. Germans represented 13 percent of New York City's population by 1883, with this particular area comprised of "middle class merchants and professionals, many of German, especially German-Jewish, and Irish descent."[2]

Much of what is known about Henry Alsberg's youth and family life is gleaned from accounts written about his older brother, Carl, and biographies of the prominent anthropologist Alfred Kroeber, a close family friend.

Firstborn Carl Alsberg was destined to become a renowned scientist, at least in part through his work as Chief of the United States Bureau of Chemistry, later renamed the Food and Drug Administration; much like his father with the New York City Bureau of Health, Carl helped ensure the safety of food and drugs nationwide. Julius and sister Elsa followed Carl's entrance to the family in short order. Henry came along just four and a half years after Carl. Four children under five years old made for a boisterous household. It was also a multilingual home, with English and German predominating. Later, Henry Alsberg also became fluent in French and knew some Yiddish and Russian.

Mother Bertha, vivacious, jolly, and easy going, came from a family of physicians, which included her brothers and her stepfather, Meinhard's uncle, Meyer Baruch. They were an educated but not a staid lot; one account portrayed Meyer Baruch as "the most eccentric member of the medical profession" who wore makeup in order to look younger.[3] Another story told of Baruch, an atheist, attending Yom Kippur services, eating candy and reading a novel in a back pew.[4]

Bertha wouldn't have been too troubled, then, by Meinhard's lack of religious convictions. Although Bertha was described as being "indifferent" to religion, Meinhard was downright aggressive in his agnosticism. Talk of religion in the Alsberg home was taboo. The children were encouraged to study Thomas Henry Huxley's scientific essays, not the Torah, a sharp contrast with Meinhard's own upbringing. He had come from a religious family in Germany where his mother kept a kosher home. As a youngster, he was forced to arise early every morning to study Hebrew.[5]

Meinhard was tenacious in pursuit of his profession, firm regarding his intolerance of religion in the home, and alternatingly stern and playful. At meals, the children had to place their hands in their laps while not eating. Disobeying would mean a slap on their hands. But he could also display moments of lightheartedness and wasn't beyond teasing his children and Alfred Kroeber, who was almost part of the family.

Alfred Kroeber described Meinhard as a man "who loved to lounge genially around the house in slippers and a very old coat; taciturn, but with sly jokes for the kids, or on them." Papa Meinhard was lenient when it came to the children's roughhousing, which included "battles with brooms up and down the stairs, water fights in the attic."[6]

Mother Bertha Alsberg wasn't just tolerant; filled with a vibrant spirit, she rejoiced in a house full of noisy children and encouraged them—her own and their visiting friends—by keeping them fueled with enough food that would befit the stereotype of any Jewish mother. "If there was a party," Kroeber wrote, "charlotte russes were pressed on us by Mother Bertha until we gagged. She loved seeing children eat." She also provided a balance to an atmosphere filled with the scientific predilections of Meinhard and his similarly-inclined older sons, Carl and Julius. Bertha filled the house with music, singing "Schubert with fervor."[7] Mastering the cello at a young age, Henry's development, like his sister's, was likely more in line with her artistic proclivities.

In the midst of what sounds like familial chaos lay a close-knit family and an ebullient, tolerant, liberal household filled with music, science, and literature. The family as a whole was also described as "cosmopolitan, cultivated, and above all, kind."[8] The culturally rich environment derived from scholarly traditions begun in Germany and continued in America, with both parents encouraging vigorous intellectual pursuits. Kroeber described a stream of scientists and artists from Germany visiting the Alsberg household on a regular basis. Henry, with all of this stimulation and encouragement, was precocious, and being the youngest, benefited from his siblings' pursuits. When Carl studied piano as a child, young Henry, who looked up to his eldest brother and probably thought him able to do anything, asked him at the dinner table if he could then "write a symphony?"[9]

Henry tagged along behind brothers Carl and Julius, Alfred Kroeber, and other boys on outings, with the wilds of New York City as their backyard. He almost giddily recalled those days to Alfred's sister, Elsbeth, many years later: "We used to go on immense trips together ... usually up to the Bronx Zoo or to Van Cortland Park or along the aqueduct up in Westchester, or played hare and hounds in Central Park."[10] As part of Carl's "gang," their boyhood wanderings included trips to the New Jersey marshlands, rural Staten Island, and parklands in the Bronx, "then largely open country, to collect beetles and butterflies."[11]

Where his older brothers tended more toward their father's scientific bent (brother Julius went on to become an engineer and patented a number of devices), Henry's interests veered toward the creative and literary. Like his brothers, during his youngest years he probably was home-schooled by his mother, with private tutoring augmenting her efforts. New York City did not yet have public high schools; Henry attended Mount Morris Latin School for his secondary education.

A visit to relatives in the "old country" also became part of Alsberg's childhood education and exposed him to the wider world of international travel and European culture. When Alsberg was thirteen, his mother took the children to Germany for a summer visit. Meinhard stayed home to tend to his business. Traveling first class on the Cunard Line's *Etruria*, Alsberg's premiere voyage foreshadowed the many transatlantic crossings he would make in his lifetime.

Summer retreats to Long Island and the Adirondack Mountains in upstate New York should have contributed to an almost idyllic childhood for Henry Alsberg. However, tragically, on one of these vacations to the Adirondacks,

Meinhard died suddenly at age fifty, just a few weeks before Henry's sixteenth birthday.

Because he lost his father at such a young age, Alsberg may not have had time either to rebel against or embrace Meinhard's values and attitudes. If there was rebellion, it hadn't yet reared up publicly. Far too little is known about the family dynamics, but it must be considered that Henry was the only son not to follow in his father's scientific footsteps and that rather than turn away from his Jewish heritage, he embraced Jewish causes—if not the religion.

Nevertheless, Alsberg wouldn't totally escape his father's influence. The character taking shape in the young man would be heir to the dry humor and the mischievous manner of his father. His father had possessed a charm that made him well liked in his world, and although they would live and work in very different professional realms, the youngest Alsberg demonstrated a good-naturedness that would similarly earn him loyal friendships throughout his life.

Henry Alsberg retained an exceptional position even without the steady presence of his father. From birth, he had been an integral part of a constellation of family and friends that inhabited the rarefied worlds of academia and government, law and the diplomatic service, medicine and science. It was an insular world, an extended family of sorts, somewhat limited to a secular professional class of German-Americans. According to Kroeber, although they didn't intermarry, Jews and Gentiles in this German-American community fraternized more with one another than with other groups, and mixed, for the most part, without rancor. This might not have totally been the case, evidenced by the fact that many of Alsberg's associations in his early adulthood aligned more closely to the German-Jewish community. This network of liberal intellectuals and professionals provided Alsberg with both a moral compass and a well-developed social conscience.

From the famous to the quietly prominent, they bolstered Alsberg throughout his life, even when his radical propensities would lead him to drift even further afield than their own leftward political boundaries. If research a century later would point to the youngest child being a radical non-conformist drawn to the creative, Alsberg would fulfill that psychological destiny.

This familial background, along with his classical education in natural sciences, classical languages, and literature, music, and art, simmered in a bouillabaisse of progressive political and cultural movements of the coming American century. Where his brothers adopted largely old-world sensibilities, taking more conventional intellectual paths, Henry would follow a meandering, non-conformist road of his own creation and more akin to sister, Elsa; both would be involved in creative arts and spend a considerable part of their lives working on behalf of the disenfranchised of the world.

Training for Rebellion

"I am more or less in revolt against everything that they would hold most sacred, and advocate causes that would be abhorrent to all their habits and fixed beliefs." A quarter century after graduating from Columbia University, Henry Alsberg, in a missive to former classmates preparing for their twenty-fifth college reunion (which he did not attend), noted the divergence of their paths, and his detachment from any sort of conventional lifestyle. "I am so completely out of touch with the point of view of the majority of them. They are leading the normal life of the average American middle class citizen. I am leading the life of a person out of touch with this point of view completely."[12] However, when he entered Columbia in 1896, he was not so different from his privileged classmates and, presumably, not yet radicalized enough to feel disconnected from the other ninety-seven freshmen.

Just fourteen years old when he sat for his entrance examinations and two weeks past his fifteenth birthday when his studies began in the fall, Alsberg was the youngest member of the class of 1900, self-named the "Naughty-Naughtians."[13] His older brothers, Carl and Julius, were already in attendance, and sister Elsa would start at Barnard in 1898. Entrance required both intellectual agility and scholarly preparation. Students were expected to be proficient in either French or German. Additionally, they had to be conversant with both Latin and Greek, with the ability to read prose and understand grammar, composition, and the rules of poetry in both ancient languages.

His youth might have hindered him—socially, not intellectually—at first. Alsberg's friend Melville Cane told the story of Alsberg's early months on the campus, when upper-classmen took advantage of his confusion and duped him into entering one of the women's buildings at Barnard College.[14]

Alsberg entered at the beginning of a new era for Columbia; his would be the last class to attend at the 49th Street buildings, and then, only during his freshman year. Columbia was in the process of moving to the Upper West Side area known as Morningside Heights, its present location. This area was still largely undeveloped, with open fields spread out into the landscape. Alsberg's sophomore year commenced at the new Morningside Heights campus. There were as yet no dormitories, and after Meinhard's death, the family moved to the Upper West Side, close to Columbia.

Other changes heralded this new age for Columbia besides the move uptown. Franz Boas, a newly hired professor who brought the study of anthropology to the school, later strongly influenced Alsberg during the Writers' Project years. Noted composer Edward MacDowell created the department of music, as well as the college's Philharmonic Orchestra.

During Alsberg's freshman year of 1896, his brother Carl, along with Alfred Kroeber, destined for fame in chemistry and anthropology, respectively, founded the school's literary magazine, *The Morningside*. This illustrated publication was created to "reflect the lighter and brighter side of Columbia life." As Carl Alsberg described it later, *The Morningside* was "unorthodox by undergraduate standards," owing to its role in attacking undergraduate and university affairs.[15]

Younger brother Henry (or "Hank," a nickname that would persist through his life, among old friends and family) embraced this undertaking. By the time he was a junior at age seventeen, and on through his graduation, he served as an editor of and regular contributor to *The Morningside*. Alsberg, along with Harold Kellock and John Erskine, consti-

Henry Alsberg, *middle row left,* **in a junior class photograph, circa 1899 (Historical Photograph Collection, Class Portraits; University Archives, Rare Book & Manuscript Library, Columbia University).**

tuted the triumvirate of editors on the masthead for a time. Both Kellock and Erskine would figure in Alsberg's future. Kellock, like Alsberg, went on to become an editor of the *New York Evening Post* and a writer for *The Nation*.

Erskine became a novelist and had a storied career as a Professor of English at Columbia and Amherst College. His presence in Alsberg's life seemed relatively minor; their most significant link, Erskine's inclusion of Alsberg in his autobiography, provides one of the few records of Alsberg's college literary activities. In *The Memory of Certain Persons* (1947), Erskine wrote about "the strangely gifted Henry G. Alsberg, poet and cello player." Erskine recalled a small group of "real scholars" and included Alsberg as one of their number, as well as part of the literary circle known as "Kings Crown." The nascent writers in this group met regularly to discuss literature and matters of current import with Professor George Woodberry, one of their favorite literature teachers. The meetings usually took place at the college tavern. With a keg of beer to perhaps set free their inhibitions, the young men would read their works to the group. Erskine described Alsberg taking a turn. "Hank always read his stories bashfully, but this one was superbly written, and its effect was powerful. Woodberry gave this accolade. 'I wonder how you sleep of nights, Mr. Alsberg!'"[16] It would later be published in *The Morningside*.

Other classmates in his circle of acquaintances included Simeon Strunsky and Melville Cane. Strunsky, Cane, and Alsberg had in common not only working for the *New York Evening Post* after college; they were also three of the minority of Jewish students at Columbia. Strunsky and Alsberg later became members of the Judaeans Society, an organization that sought to "promote and further the intellectual and spiritual interest of Jews."

A Literary Life Commences

Alsberg spent a considerable amount of time on both editorial duties and writing for *The Morningside*; the literary life seemed his vocation. His poems and short stories were numerous and popular.

In some ways, Alsberg's involvement in the birth years of this literary publication—one that now bills itself as the nation's oldest college literary magazine—foreshadowed, by more than thirty years, his work with the Federal Writers' Project, albeit on a much smaller scale. As part of the editorial board, he helped determine the direction and policies of the magazine, selected manuscripts, and wrote editorials.[17] *The Morningside*, besides giving him editorial responsibilities, was also an outlet for his evolving writing skills.

Alsberg's time at Columbia, save for his work on *The Morningside*, does not stand out as notable. But there were other activities in addition to his literary undertakings. He belonged to the Société Française. He joined Edward MacDowell's Philharmonic Society as a cellist alongside brother Julius, a violist, and performed with the Philharmonic and other groups, sometimes as featured soloist, throughout his years at Columbia.

But what of his interest in politics and social reform and human rights issues? Alsberg's active pursuit of the ideas that illuminated his life's work would commence in just a few years.

At that time, Ivy League college students were not, for the most part, interested in changing the mores that would lead to social transformation. *The Columbia Spectator* and other university newspapers told of football successes and pep rallies and scholastic awards; if students railed against the injustices of the day, the *Spectator* did not notice it. Columbia at the turn of the twentieth century, a place for the fortunate, favored few, did not mirror the Columbia of radical 1960s anti-war demonstrations.

It would be difficult to see how this environment fostered his future path and cultivated his empathy for the poor and disenfranchised. However, certain rigorous class assignments certainly helped students focus on some social issues of the day. The *Spectator* lists a number of debate topics students prepared for in the spring of 1899: "National factory laws should be enacted; Goods bearing the union label should be bought in preference of others; heavy progressive heritance taxes should be laid." Alsberg, ironically, was assigned to argue against the following supposition: "The growth of corporations is harmful." Of course, in light of his later predilections, this would have merely been an intellectual exercise.[18]

The institution's move to Morningside Heights and the family's move nearby may also have contributed to Alsberg's tilt toward the unconventional. Lionel Trilling, in a history of Columbia, wrote about the era when Alsberg lived and attended college there: "I do not know whether research has been done in local social history to substantiate my impression that the neighborhood was sought out by literary and artistic people and that it acquired something of the character of a respectable Bohemia."[19]

A few pieces of personal evidence do indeed point to his future path.

Alsberg presaged his future progressive political writings and disposition toward women's rights with a story he wrote for an 1899 issue of *The Morningside*. "A Homely Tragedy" told the story of an audacious young woman, Hepsibah Hopkins, who was forbidden by her father to fulfill her dream to escape her farm-family life, attend college, and become a teacher; her father also disdained her love of books.

> So Hepsibah bribed her brother Job or the hired man Jake, in order that, when he drove to town, he might buy her some novels in return for her hoarded savings; and then Hepsibah would steal away to the attic, after her day's work was done, where nobody could espy her, and sit all hunched together by the little attic window over a wild book of adventure; and the last rays of the setting sun would steal in and kiss her and bless her, while she, unmindful, would, with her eager, straining eyes, be chasing the story from page to page of the book. But lately, very lately, Hepsibah had even ventured (in an inspired moment, no doubt) to go further than this, and had scribbled some stories of her own composition on the unused pages of her old copy-books. These effusions of her soul, however, she hid guiltily away lest some Philistine hand should find them, bring them to light and her into ridicule and disgrace. Had ever the like been heard in the Hopkins family?[20]

The tribulations of Hepsibah would not have occurred in Alsberg's family, which encouraged his sister, Elsa, like other young women in their social circle, to attend college. He was surely paying close attention to the news of the day, where the struggle for women's suffrage made nationwide headlines.

Elsa, it should be noted, led a dynamic life. After graduating Barnard, she took post-graduate classes in Romance languages. Like many "uptown Jews" (the German-Jews whose assimilation preceded the arrival of Eastern European Jews), Elsa became active in working with her less fortunate coreligionists who emigrated to escape brutal oppression. Her later deep involvement in aiding immigrants of all ethnicities and denominations through education, literacy programs, and job training began on Ellis Island and continued throughout her long life.

That Alsberg expressed such empathy for Hepsibah and the women she represented may also have been part of the family tradition. Anne Nevins Loftis, who knew Alsberg when he lived with his sister during the 1960s, said: "All the Alsbergs seemed to share an equilibrium, a sense of confidence and the capacity to immerse themselves in the concerns of others without losing their own sense of values."[21]

His attraction to other causes and movements, particularly anarchism and its theories of a harmonic society, freed from government and other institutions, also entered the landscape. Peter Kropotkin, the Russian radical who espoused these anarchist ideals—and whom Alsberg would meet and support within the next few decades—visited New York on two lecture tours, one in Alsberg's junior year in 1897 and again in 1901 while Alsberg was in law school. Even if Alsberg hadn't attended these lectures, he most certainly would have been aware of the content of Kropotkin's speeches. They were publicized in the radical press as well as the popular newspapers of the day. *The Atlantic Monthly*, in fact, serialized Kropotkin's memoirs in 1897.[22] Liberal intellectuals would have tuned in. Alsberg's future friend, anarchist Emma Goldman, who helped arrange Kropotkin's lecture tour, was already a troublemaker of renown during the 1890s and early 1900s, lecturing in support of topics such as women's rights and trade unionism. The movement's overall philosophical ideas, with its calls for "unhampered human development, the cornerstone of true social progress and harmony,"[23] surely appealed to him, if not in 1900, then shortly thereafter. Alsberg may also have been personally attuned to the anarchist message because it questioned conventional sexual mores. Espousing the individual's right to choose whom and how to love without interference from society or government, anarchism was the only political movement to openly discuss homosexual love in this time period.[24]

At that time, other progressive movements flourished that Alsberg would eventually write about and participate in: civil liberties, free speech, the labor movement, women's rights, African American and immigrants' rights, and pacifism. Looking back from a twenty-first-century perspective, it's like a twisted timeline, with the 1960s happening more than a half century before they actually happened. It's as if Abby Hoffman and cohorts picked up where Emma Goldman left off after the "intermission" of World War I, the Great Depression, World War II, and the Cold War. Assaults on the status quo swirled in the ether. A young man with an open, curious mind, someone like Henry Alsberg who displayed a disposition toward "the concerns of others" would have been drawn in.

Perhaps Alsberg already self-identified as a "radical" on the eleventh day of June when the class of 1900 gathered for commencement exercises and Alsberg received his A.B. degree. A survey published in Alsberg's class book, *The Naughty Naughtian,* showed that in a class of fewer than 100 men, most were politically conventional, labeling themselves, for the most part, as Republicans, Democrats, or Independents. Only one student called himself "Radical." The ballots cast by the class of 1900 perished long ago, but as liberal as some of his classmates would turn out to be, none would go on, as Alsberg did, to participate in a lifetime of radical causes.

Not yet 19, Henry Garfield Alsberg graduated with an A.B. from Columbia College (the School of the Arts of Columbia University) in 1900, likely the youngest in his class. His satirical autobiographical sketch ("The great secret of my life is that I was born a day later than I was scheduled for") appears with this photograph in the privately published *Naughty Naughtian* Class Book. He did not sit for his yearbook photograph (author's collection).

His class book autobiography did not yield much more insight into his time at Columbia, but did disclose a whimsical, even facetious streak, mixed with a playful disregard for authority. Where others in the book proclaimed scholastic and athletic conquests and ambitious dreams for the future, Henry Garfield Alsberg wrote, somewhat proudly, about being late for classes on a regular basis.

"My reputation in this regard is wellnighed unsullied. Indeed, I remember having arrived promptly at a lecture, by an unforeseen accident, only once, from the shock of which mischance the department hasn't quite recovered yet. My friends have tried numerous plans with which to inveigle me into promptness, such as turning the hands of the City-hall clock backward or bribing Phoebus to retire earlier than usual; but none of these devices has succeeded. Whether, at the last day, I shall arrive late for my funeral is still, however, a bettable question."[25] (In a modern-day nod, *The Blue and White*, the undergraduate magazine of Columbia University, published an excerpt of his graduation piece in their "Curio Columbiana" section in 2008.)

His 1900 graduation photograph shows a sturdy young man—his tie askew, possibly from running late to the photography studio—handsome, with thick, somewhat unruly hair, intense brooding eyes, and a mustache that he'd sport for the rest of his life.

Although Alsberg's predilections leaned toward the literary during his undergraduate years, perhaps his decision to enroll in Columbia's Law School best evidenced his growing interest in the political. Or, despite spending much of his later life traveling and writing, at age nineteen he quite possibly wasn't ready to leave the family home. Like many young people, he may have chosen further education to postpone that entrance into the working world. Education, after all, was a family value, and for Alsberg, continuing on an academic path might have been a way to fulfill a cultural, family responsibility. His siblings either already had advanced degrees or were in the process of earning them. Bertha and her young adult children all lived on West 94th Street, a pleasant tree-lined street of brownstones less than two blocks away from Central Park, in an area populated by German-Jews. It was a mere half-hour walk to Columbia. Even if the atmosphere of Columbia College itself was too placid, Alsberg knew his way around. No upperclassman trying to bully him into entering the women's college could make a fool of him again.

On the Field and in the Courtroom

The cupboard that might once have held evidence of Alsberg's activities during his three years in law school is almost bare, historically marked only by his football exploits and his graduation. It seems somewhat unlikely, but Alsberg's extracurricular interest during this period was on the football field, joining the team as a student in the Columbia University School of Law. (In the realm of athletics, he was active to a lesser extent in baseball, wrestling, and fencing as an undergraduate). Perhaps by then, at age twenty-one, 178 pounds, and not quite the youngster anymore, he had grown physically large enough to compete.

He played fiercely for two seasons on both the college and the varsity football teams in the positions of guard and tackle. Alsberg's college football career is remembered in the newspapers of the day, with one account describing the five stitches near his eye that were necessary after he "had his head cut open."[26]

Alsberg's stint as a working lawyer lasted only slightly longer than law school itself. On graduation with an LL.B. from Columbia in 1903, the kinship that marked his community came into play, and the circle of Jewish professionals rallied to help the twenty-two-year-old lawyer get started.

Seated center, with his hair a bit longer than his classmates' and sporting a mustache, Henry Alsberg in the "Class of 1900, Arts and Mines, Senior Year" photograph (Historical Photograph Collection, Class Portraits; University Archives, Rare Book & Manuscript Library, Columbia University).

He was fortunate, of course, to have this circle, as most law firms denied entrée to Jews.

He worked "partly for [him]self, and partly as an employee of other lawyers." One of those attorneys, Nathan Bijur, eventually became a State Supreme Court Judge; another was Julius Henry Cohen, a long-time attorney for the Port of New York Authority. Both men were politically prominent and, although far from Alsberg's radical leanings, espoused at least some liberal values that he advocated.

Alsberg practiced law on and off over a ten-year period, and his discontent with this conventional lifestyle came quickly. One case he argued (and won)— in which he represented a gas utility being sued—illustrates the type of lackluster topics that may have led to his dissatisfaction.[27] By then he was already gaining entry into the world of writing about radical causes; representing a gas company and writing for *The Masses* just did not jibe.

Alsberg's first retreat from the profession came in 1906. Returning to his intellectual comfort zone, literary pursuits were back on the table and he went off to study comparative literature at Harvard's Graduate School of Arts and Science. He spent only a year at Harvard, a year that time would have committed to oblivion except for his encounters with two great American philosophers.

William James—philosopher, writer, psychologist, physician—was in his final semester of teaching at Harvard in the fall of 1906, just a few years after writing *The Varieties of Religious Experience: A Study in Human Nature*. Considering Alsberg's experiences at home with the vicissitudes of religious attitudes and his later interest in psychology, James' discussion of the psychology of religion seemed ready-made for Alsberg's consumption. The twenty-five-year-old graduate student, on his way to proclaiming a pacifist stance, would likely have been attracted to James' other ideas as well. James expressed a forceful belief in pacifism in his essay, "The Moral Equivalent of Law." So, in addition to comparative literature courses, Alsberg became a student of William James, who taught his last course, "General Problems in Philosophy," before retiring.

Although Alsberg's time at Harvard was short, one anecdote forever links him to William James and to James' friend, the noted American philosopher Charles Peirce. Alsberg lived in a three-room bachelor apartment in Prescott Hall, located in Cambridge. Peirce, sickly and destitute, stayed for a short time in Prescott Hall. According to Alsberg, the landlady asked him to check on a gentleman in the residence who seemed on the verge of death. Entering the room, Alsberg found Peirce, malnourished and ill. "In a wild confusion of emotions Alsberg and a friend went to find William James, and caught him coming out of class. James listened to their story. 'Why,' he said, his face changing, 'I owe him everything!' and he swung them into a cab to call for Peirce and take him home."[28]

Back into the Fold

After only a year, Henry Alsberg decided to change direction; he left academia and returned to New York, the graduate degree forever unfinished. Perhaps the New England culture at Harvard was not a good fit for him. Jerre Mangione, who worked closely with Alsberg in the Writers' Project, reported that Alsberg found Harvard "dull."[29] The bohemian lifestyle beginning to flourish at home in New York City certainly could have lured him back. This zigzag path, moving from law to the serious study of literature (and back to law again, for a short time) was not out of character for him. Alsberg would display this propensity for restlessness and abrupt changes in direction throughout his life.

Later, friends who were surprised at his appointment to head the Writers' Project would recall his tendency to leave projects unfinished.[30]

Looking ahead, however, he most likely wanted to explore his writing aspirations, while also getting closer to the political action centered in New York. His return there dramatically set his restless path in motion.

Whatever baggage he brought back with him on the train to New York was inconsequential to what Alsberg carried within. Endowments from his family and the community of his youth provided him with emotional sustenance, intellectual rigor, and connections to various social and professional networks. These early connections remained intact throughout his life, with some ties blossoming into personal friendships as well as professional liaisons. He enjoyed ongoing friendships with the Kroebers, still exchanging letters and visits with these childhood acquaintances through their elder years.

His discussions with childhood friend Allie (Alexander) Bloch provide insight into Alsberg's thinking. Allie was already working in the business world, but his real love was music. Alsberg convinced him to follow his dream. "He had studied law, but he didn't like it. He gave it up to go into writing ... that gave me the courage to throw over my job," said Allie, who went on to a prominent career as a conductor and composer.[31]

His adopted family to come would extend to include muckrakers, progressive reformers, anarchists and other political radicals, Jewish refugee workers, and, the most crusading of all vocations, writers. Everything mattered, and taken together, everything led him to the Writers' Project.

Alsberg, joining his college friends for an alumni reunion dinner in 1917, met up again with Erskine. Both were invited to give speeches. Erskine, by then a Columbia professor of English, discussed life there as compared with their own student days. Alsberg, who had recently returned from war-torn Europe after serving in the United States diplomatic corps, spoke on "Conditions in Europe, Particularly in Turkey." Though Alsberg would later tap his old friend Erskine to play a part in the Writers' Project, their paths from their days together in the college tavern and at the Morningside editorial offices had diverged exponentially.[32] Just a few years later, Alsberg would opt not to attend another reunion. By then, he'd spent many cold winters reporting from battle zones and working with refugees amid the harsh conditions in Eastern Europe, and years advocating for various leftist causes such as freeing international political prisoners. He was busy, he said, trying "to save the world from reactionaries."[33]

CHAPTER 2

The Wanderlust of a
"Philosophical Anarchist"
1907–1918

A loving, tolerant family; a liberal, classical education; associations with great thinkers of the time—all of these experiences, along with the swirling, churning waters of the progressive movements of the early 1900s came together in Henry Alsberg. He could have settled down in New York to practice law, to live a stable, sedate life. Old family friends and newer acquaintances from Columbia and Harvard were in high enough places to help, but he would not take the proscribed path. He could move comfortably *through* an elite world, but he would not live in it.

"Alsberg has turned from the practice of law to the writing of plays." This small update appearing in the 1907–8 *Columbia University Quarterly* had it almost right. In fact, although his intent may well have been to give up law altogether and devote his energies to writing, Alsberg still had a few remaining courtroom appearances before that could happen. So as the world rolled toward the first double-digit decade of the twentieth century, his meandering path headed toward full-time writing, political activism, and then, the marriage of the two.

It was as if he were finally entering his own life. The false starts of law and graduate school were worthwhile, in their own ways, but unfulfilling. For a man who in just a few years would act nearly fearlessly while reporting and living in war zones, arguing civil cases must have seemed both mundane and spiritless. Many years later, Alsberg described those years quite succinctly (in itself, decidedly uncharacteristic of him) to a 1943 congressional committee investigating communism. After law school, he explained, "I decided I wanted to study and took a year or more off and went to Harvard for a year, and traveled a little. Then I started writing. Some of my things were accepted in various magazines. Then I became editor of the *New York Post*."[1]

What he didn't say, of course, was that the creativity he enjoyed as a writer for *The Morningside* needed time and space to mature. College friend Melville Cane managed to practice law and also make a parallel career as a distinguished poet. However, for Henry Alsberg, law was too confining and he could not resist the pull into the writer's life. Or, as sister Elsa put it: "He was not particularly interested in lawyers fighting each other. He was interested in people and human relations."[2]

His forays into the professional world of literature began, as the alumni network reported, with playwriting. He lived at home with Bertha and Elsa on West 95th Street (after the family moved just another block uptown) but his network of friends extended far downtown to the theater district and Greenwich Village. He was introduced to the successful but somewhat reclusive novelist, poet, and playwright Paul Kester, who invited Alsberg to send a manuscript to him in 1910.

In an otherwise diffident letter to Kester, the twenty-eight-year-old Alsberg described his unnamed play as "pseudo-romantic, pseudo–Maeterlinckian."[3] Maurice Maeterlinck, the Belgian poet and playwright who later won the Nobel Prize, may have attracted the interest of Alsberg because of their similar backgrounds. Maeterlinck came from a well-off, educated family. He entered law at his family's urging, but left the field after only a few years to devote his time to writing. Maeterlinck was described as "absolutely unfit for the pettifogging quarrels and public counsel's speeches in the law court. He was attracted by literature."[4] This description could apply to Alsberg as well.

Alsberg's letters to Kester, for the most part, reveal an insecurity not often seen in his later political and journalistic writings. "It seems a rather presumptuous thing to send one's manuscript to someone who is innocent of all wrongdoing toward the sender ... the enclosed play was an experiment, and as such, of course, something of a failure, as the words, from act to act, shift and waver uncertainly,"[5] he wrote to Kester in early 1910.

Although Kester's replies are lost, he apparently liked Alsberg's work enough so that after some rewriting on Alsberg's part, he sent an introductory letter and recommendation to Bertha Galland, a popular actress who had starred in one of Kester's plays. Kester's approbation was an emotional boon for Alsberg, who wrote: "My contempt for it at first was vigorous. But now I imagine there must be something in it ... thank you so much for your kindness."[6]

The correspondence suggests that the two men had become friendly and that Kester acted as Alsberg's mentor. Alsberg admired the work Kester published in national magazines and commented thoughtfully on it. Alsberg, particularly enamored with those pieces that he considered unorthodox, asked Kester for advice on getting such work published.

Alsberg had the means to leave the potentially lucrative field of law for the uncertainties of writing. Meinhard's thriving business left Bertha with financial resources. Her two older sons, Carl and Julius, were doing well professionally; Elsa worked as a teacher, social worker, and writer. Henry may have contributed to the household, and likely did so while working in law, but he had no one to support but himself. He devoted a considerable amount of time to travel (including voyaging with his mother and Elsa to Europe) and writing from 1910 through 1912.

Another factor during this period may have been Alsberg's health. Throughout his life he complained of digestive problems, sometimes severe. (This could have been at least partially due to emergency abdominal surgery when he was younger. As a teen, he suffered a ruptured appendix in the middle of the night, but not wanting to wake his family, waited until morning to tell them of his pain. This surgery could have left enough scar tissue to plague him throughout his life.) In the spring of 1910, he suffered from typhus and needed time to recuperate. He wrote of stays in two seaside towns that year, Belmar on the New Jersey coast and Sea Cliff on Long Island. He recovered well enough to begin writing again by fall, though he expressed displeasure with the results. In a congratulatory note to Kester on the successful production of the latter's play in Europe, Alsberg wrote: "My own muse is at present on a strike. Just finished the worst thing I ever hope to do, so help me. It's a rotten play, if ever there was one."[7]

A four-day wintery "tramp" with friends out to the wilds of eastern Long Island may have helped him get his spirit back. Again writing to Kester: "We hoofed it along the beach, mostly between high and low tide, on the frozen sand, snugly sheltered from the north wind by the dunes. It really makes fine walking, and, with ocean endless on one side and the agitated sand heaps endless on the other, gives quite an adventurous mood to an excursion, without involving you in any real hardships; for the clams, clam chowder, and oysters and scallops, world famous, are always at hand for rescue. Moreover, most of the island went wet [against Prohibition] last election."[8]

In any case, with the family home as his base and the savings he realized during his law years, he could afford, at least for a period of time, a lifestyle that suited his character. It would be a lifestyle to which he would return, when he was able, at other times in his life. Material acquisitions seemed not to concern him; travel, writing, reading, and the company of close friends represented the good life. In any case, living with no discernible income did seem to bother Alsberg at least a little. Exaggerating his actual circumstances, he wrote to Kester in 1910 of being "giddy with starvation" and perhaps trying his hand at a more commercial kind of play, one with "the biggest outlay of fantastic romanticism and aerial moonshine I can lay my mind on."[9] Alsberg continued on this course, co-writing in 1911 a play called *The Hoodoo*. Neither *Hoodoo* nor the other plays that Alsberg so excitedly discussed with Paul Kester would see the stage; his playwriting plans would not be realized, at least in this decade.

Fireflies Out to Sea

Alsberg's other creative writing did take a turn toward commercial success, however, with the publication of his short story, "Soiree Kokimono," in 1912. This was a coup; *The Forum* was a well-regarded national magazine that, in addition to focusing on the intellectual, literary, and political topics of the day, also published poetry and short stories. Alsberg joined the company of his friend Paul Kester, as well as acclaimed writers Ezra Pound and Edna St. Vincent Millay.

In "Soiree," an unnamed narrator tells of an eccentric gathering at an ocean-side mansion in which the partygoers are drugged during a pseudo-Japanese tea ceremony. The narrator describes perhaps "a little somethin', dream-makin' stuff," being put into the tea and preserves. "Things did get to look sort of rosy an' intense an' glorified after that ...." During this hallucinatory state, partygoers observed thousands of fireflies as they were freed from cages for the dazed guests to chase and capture and put in their mouths and in their hair. "As for noise, only the distant, metropolitan roar of the ocean, and nearby, the glug-glug an' slurf-slurf of runnin' water, and the faint but most extraordinarily sweet chorus of cricket song, almost like a muted orchestra of hummin' birds playin' for the rise of the curtain."[10] *Soirée* was chosen for the book compilation *Forum Stories* the following year. In the preface, editor Charles Vale wrote that the stories represent "the best American work of to day." A puzzle remains: Just as fast as Alsberg gained entrée into the literary world, he left it. Did he turn away or was it just a pit stop on his way to his new pursuit—journalism? In any case, it is another example of Alsberg's tendency not to settle into one thing, either by choice or by temperament. Perhaps a shortcoming for some, but for him it led to broader avenues of endeavor.

One of the first mentions of his work as a reporter comes from Abram Elkus, the future U.S. Ambassador to Turkey, who would play an important role in Alsberg's life. Elkus, a prominent lawyer, was known for his work as chief counsel of the New York State commission which investigated the tragic Triangle Shirtwaist Factory fire that killed 146 workers, mostly young immigrant women. Elkus was also active in Jewish causes and a stalwart Democrat.

As a Wilson campaign strategist, Elkus recalled contacting the thirty-year-old Alsberg. Part of Wilson's campaign platform rested on the notion that Republican-imposed tariffs caused American-made goods to be found cheaper abroad than at home. Elkus asked Alsberg to travel to London to gather proof.[11]

Alsberg sailed on the *Lusitania* in September 1912. Traveling first-class, he had access to the verandah café and the men's exclusive smoking room, as well as the opulent two-deck dining room topped by a magnificent gold-leafed dome. On arrival in England just a few days after his thirty-first birthday, he went shopping.

"I was to buy everything in London that an American family buys—I looked over my lists—everything from shoe polish and tooth powder to stockings and bedsteads." Returning in October, the resulting article in the *New York Sunday World* about his London shopping spree became a promotional piece for the campaign. "Our English cousin may pound his thumb with an American hammer which costs him less in London than it does here," he wrote in his typical droll manner.[12] Whether Alsberg worked for the Democratic Party or the newspaper, which supported Wilson, is not made quite clear, but the machinations of that era of journalism would not have precluded both.

His next foray into journalism proved both more professional and long standing. He landed a position at the *New York Evening Post*, joining his college friend Simeon Strunsky. Alsberg no longer called himself "lawyer." He listed himself on official documents as "editor and writer" or, in the case of his most recent passport, said he followed "the occupation of literature." His former law office on William Street was less than a mile from the *Evening Post*'s striking Art Nouveau building on Vesey Street. But they were worlds apart.

The politics of newspaper owner Oswald Garrison Villard made it a good fit for Alsberg. Villard was an advocate of women's rights and birth control, a founding member of the NAACP, and a pacifist. Villard also owned *The Nation*, the *Post*'s sister publication. Alsberg wrote news articles, features and editorials for both. The *New York Evening Post*, besides being the oldest continuous American newspaper, was also one of the most influential. It was considered both liberal and intellectual, and with the legacy of journalism legends Horace White and William Cullen Bryant, Alsberg couldn't have fallen into a better placement.

In some ways, the concerns of the day that Alsberg covered for the newspaper were strikingly familiar to those fought for by liberals in the 1960s and now in the twenty-first century. An article in an Alsberg-era issue of the *Post* reported on Jane Addams and women activists who petitioned Congress to divert $14 million from building battleships to funding child welfare programs. It heralded the 1960s saying, "It will be a great day when our schools have all the money they need, and our air force has to have a bake-sale to buy a bomber."[13]

Newspaper work was harried enough for Alsberg's quick and restless mind; the newspaper atmosphere melded the intellectual with the practical, providing a good grounding for his work twenty years' hence with the Writers' Project. At about the same time, Alsberg became involved with the more radical writers in Greenwich Village. While the *Evening Post* might have been liberal, *The Masses* was the epitome of radical.

The Great Storm of 1914

After a winter of record cold, with thermometers dipping below zero Fahrenheit, temperate weather finally returned to New York City in late February. It only took a few days of forty-degree temperatures to lull residents into hopes of an early spring. So the raging blizzard that battered the city on the first day of March was a surprise assault, awakening New Yorkers to a heavy and blinding snow. With winds topping 80 miles per hour and plunging temperatures, the storm left over a foot of snow, overwhelming the city and making most streets impassable. Coal and milk supplies ran low; at least a dozen people died. And as in most natural disasters, the poor and homeless suffered most.

The *New York Times* devoted its column space over those few days to comprehensive coverage of the storm. Reportage from the *Evening Post* took a slightly different tack; its first edition after the blizzard provided readers with general coverage, while also spotlighting the plight of the homeless.

In the midst of the storm and in the days following, unemployed men and women, led by Industrial Workers of the World (IWW) organizer Frank Tannenbaum, paraded through lower Manhattan looking to churches for food and places to sleep; the city homeless shelter, they said, wasn't fit for a dog. Some churches, like St. Mark's, accommodated the "army of the unemployed." Others, like St. Alphonsus' Roman Catholic Church, did not. When the protestors' "army" entered the church anyway, Tannenbaum and nearly two hundred of his followers—considered menacing gangs by some and crusaders by others—were arrested.

Alsberg's growing politicization caused him to enter the fray with an article in Max Eastman's famously radical publication, *The Masses*. The magazine devoted a sizable portion of its April issue criticizing the churches that turned away the homeless. Alsberg's article, "Was It Something Like This?" was the showpiece of the issue. A satirical allegory written in the form of press reports and editorials from Jesus' era, it mocked churches, newspapers, and public officials for their treatment of the unemployed protestors. This from Alsberg's *Tribuna Diurnalis* (Daily Tribune) of Rome, with the dateline, Jerusalem, and the headline, "Riots of Unemployed in Judea Continue; Jesus of Nazareth Leads Hobo Army on Jerusalem":

> Yesterday the army of the unemployed, under the leadership of Jesus of Nazareth, reached the outskirts of this city camping in Mt. Olive Park. The army is composed of a miscellaneous assortment of hoboes, ragamuffins and weak-minded enthusiasts, who have left devastation in their wake among the olive-plantations of the country-side. Their leader has himself set the example by destroying fig trees. This afternoon a crowd of loiterers, tramps, hoodlums and idle-curious, together with a few worthy unemployed of this city, streamed out of town, along the upper boulevard, to Mt. Olive Park, where the hobo general made a highly incendiary address, urging his followers not to work for a living, to despise the virtues of frugality and thrift, and to look to the king, the property owners and capitalists for sustenance in ease and idleness.[14]

Alsberg's article was a triumph for him, and announced his entrée into Greenwich Village's radical movement.

Bohemian Rhapsody

Home to artists, writers, and social reformers, Greenwich Village, known as the Ninth Ward by Italian immigrants living in the area, was New York City's answer to Paris' Left Bank. Broadmindedness nurtured the unconventional citizens of this radical nation within New York City proper, supporting the advocates of women's suffrage, birth control, free love, social experimentation, and all forms of nonconformity.

Representing the political, social, and cultural hub of the left, both nationally and in New York City, stood "Red" Emma Goldman. While Alsberg's friendship with her would not begin until 1920 on the other side of the world, they shared some political stances, as well as friends and acquaintances such as future American Civil Liberties Union (ACLU) founder Roger Baldwin. Goldman also may have at least partially contributed to Alsberg's anarchist leanings. During his time with the *Evening Post*, Goldman stumped the lecture circuit, often in New York, speaking on such topics as birth control, feminism, labor issues, and pacifism. All of these would have been of personal, if not professional, interest to Alsberg.

Her lectures on homosexuality in 1915 and 1916 likely resonated most significantly with him. Goldman followed the teachings of Magnus Hirschfeld, a German physician and early gay rights activist. According to Terence Kissack, her lecture circuit speeches (including, "The Intermediate Sex: A Discussion of Homosexuality") "were part of her effort to educate about the nature of homosexual desire and to inform the public about what life was like for homosexual men and women."[15]

Same-sex love may not have been universally accepted by the anarchists, but it was the only American movement of its time to address the existence of homosexuality and sexual diversity.[16] Goldman's beliefs on sexuality were ingrained in her anarchistic politics, which promoted the freedom for men and women to use their bodies as they saw fit, and her speeches defending homosexuals reflected this.

Anarchist Alexander Berkman, who would also become Alsberg's lifelong friend, had recently published his *Prison Memoirs of an Anarchist*, with its acceptance of homosexual love. Goldman and Berkman numbered among the founders—with Alsberg a later supporter—of the Ferrer Modern School in Greenwich Village, a counterculture educational and cultural center. There, lectures on same-sex love were often presented, apparently to no great outcry.[17] If Alsberg was looked for acceptance, Greenwich Village and the anarchists were his best bets, at least in America.

Alsberg's circle of compatriots in the Village would later be among the people he would bring into the Federal Writers' Project when the Great Depression hit. These included the "vagabond Bohemian" poet Harry Kemp, *Masses* editor Floyd Dell, free speech and same sex love advocate Leonard Abbott, and birth control activist and childhood friend Stella Bloch Hanau. Although Alsberg still lived at the family home on the Upper West Side of Manhattan, the Village was where he worked and played. If it was true that the Bohemians of the era thought that "Greenwich Village is a state of mind, it has no boundaries,"[18] then Alsberg was a citizen.

Approaching his mid-thirties, Henry Alsberg seemed to have no desire to settle down; his nomadic path contrasted with his siblings' more conventional professional routes. Elsa, like Henry, had a bit of the reformer in her. Making her way as a social worker and writer after college, she promoted educational opportunities for immigrants. Soon she was working on a national level with the Council of Jewish Women, organizing programs to provide housing, education, and vocational training for young immigrant women.

Although Julius and Carl pursued more orthodox trajectories, their careers were neither mundane nor inconsequential. Middle brother Julius, studious and straightforward, became a successful mechanical and chemical engineer. By 1912, he had registered two patents. His marriage also brought a new dimension to the family; wife Elsie Fraenkel came from an accomplished, socially conscious, liberal intellectual family. Her brother Osmond Fraenkel served as chief counsel to the ACLU for more than twenty years and advocated for free speech and other progressive causes. Eldest brother Carl, biochemist and physician, was in many ways the star of the family, eminent in academia, government service, and science. In 1908, he left a teaching position at Harvard for a government post in Washington, D.C. Within a few years, as Henry struggled with his writing career, Carl was appointed Chief of the U.S. Bureau of Chemistry (later renamed the Food and Drug Administration), remaining there until 1921. He was the youngest man ever to head the bureau.

    Carl was described by one co-worker as amiable, "leisurely, cosmopolitan,

Henry's oldest brother, Carl, in 1912, after being named Chief of the U.S. Bureau of Chemistry, which later became the Food and Drug Administration (FDA). Carl, the youngest chief of both agencies, was a prominent scientist who eventually co-founded Stanford University's Food Research Institute (photograph by Harris & Ewing; Library of Congress, Prints & Photographs Division).

cultivated, and above all, kind."[19] Friends and colleagues would describe Henry similarly. Carl and Henry, the eldest and youngest siblings, both possessed insatiable curiosity—a characteristic, according to Carl, inherited from their father—and a propensity to follow their curiosity down diverse paths. Carl succeeded immensely in his professional ventures, though later in life he described himself as "a Jack of many trades, a master of none…. I suppose I didn't have a sufficiently consuming desire to be famous. But I've had more fun."[20]

Henry Alsberg, Diplomat Abroad

In 1915, Europe was already being torn apart by war. Despite President Woodrow Wilson's initial response of neutrality, the country began military preparations. On May 7, a German U-boat fired on the *Lusitania* (the same ship Alsberg took to London a few years earlier), killing nearly 1,200 people, including 128 Americans. The U.S. entry into the war seemed inevitable. Although the extent of Alsberg's involvement in the anti-war movement is not known, his friend Vincent McHugh later said he was "mixed up in the [pre-war] pacifist agitation."[21] During this period, peace activists and anti-war groups protested against the war and conscription, with many arrested and jailed. Alsberg at thirty-four, was too old to be drafted.

Alsberg had spent the previous few years moving amid diverse circles of people—the intellectual German-Jews from his youth, Wilson Democrats, anarchist Russian Jews, nonconformists of various stripes in Greenwich Village, artistic bohemians, liberals at the *Evening Post*, radicals at *The Masses*. The Alsberg characteristic of equanimity allowed him safe passage among these very different realms. And as unlikely as it would probably seem to the people in his circle, he soon added the U.S. diplomatic service to his resume.

It happened quickly. In the summer of 1916, he was still writing for *The Nation* and the *Evening Post*. The request to join the diplomatic mission landed on Alsberg's desk August 8. He said yes, was appointed two days later, and sailed the following week for Turkey as personal secretary and press attaché to Abram Elkus, the newly named Ambassador to the Ottoman Empire.[22]

One of Alsberg's last *Nation* articles before leaving for Turkey reviewed American artist R.A. Blakelock's otherworldly landscapes, then on exhibit in New York. Alsberg could never ignore the artists' call; even later when he was face to face with the daily violence of war, he seemed to need the refuge that art provided. So before setting sail toward the horrors of Europe, he wrote about Americans and their art forms. For him, it was also a form of patriotism,

Henry Morgenthau, left, and Abram I. Elkus, 1916. Elkus followed Morgenthau as U.S. Ambassador to the Ottoman Empire, both men working to help persecuted peoples under the harsh regime. This photo was likely taken aboard the ocean liner *Oscar II* as Elkus prepared to leave for his new post. Henry Alsberg sailed with Elkus, serving as his secretary in Constantinople. A few years later, Alsberg advised Morgenthau on the dire conditions of Jews in Poland after World War I (Library of Congress, Prints & Photographs Division).

one that would similarly obsess him later as head of the Writers' Project. But artistic sensibilities and the beauty of this painter-poet's scenes would have to be left behind.

This time Elkus' call to him went well beyond the London shopping spree/ Wilson campaign stunt from four years back. In his letter to the State Department, Elkus, a family friend who knew Carl from Harvard and Washington, outlined his reasons for requesting Alsberg's appointment. Elkus wrote of his desire to have "at least one man whom I knew personally and in whom I have entire personal confidence from close acquaintanceship." Of course, Alsberg's fluency in German and French supported his candidacy. And even though, officially, Alsberg would be hired as a clerk, Elkus certainly valued Alsberg's writing skills. "I have no doubt if he went there that the publicity end of anything that affects the interests of the United States would be carefully taken care of by him—he would know how to do it and do it in the right way."[23] What Elkus and even Alsberg did not realize then was how crucial a role the younger man would play in the Embassy's efforts to provide sustenance and safety to Armenians, Jews, and other minorities in the Ottoman Empire. Like the artist Blakelock, who Alsberg described as triumphing "over the limitations of his medium," Alsberg would move beyond the responsibilities of a clerk.[24]

When Alsberg joined Abram Elkus, Elkus' family, and other members of the diplomatic staff on the ocean liner *Oscar II*, bound for Copenhagen en route to Constantinople, he knew he would encounter a horrific wartime landscape. Ottoman lands ran with the blood of the Armenian genocide. Whatever social justice and human tragedies Alsberg observed as a reporter in New York City paled, to say the least, compared with what he would witness in Turkey.

In the Light of the Golden Horn

Elkus' predecessor was the powerhouse Henry Morgenthau, who had returned to America to work on Woodrow Wilson's reelection campaign. As Ambassador to Turkey from 1913 through 1916, Morgenthau remains well known for his entreaties and massive relief work on behalf of the Armenians both during and after his ambassadorship. "My failure to stop the destruction of the Armenians had made Turkey for me a place of horror," he said of his leaving.[25]

The horror wasn't close to over when the new diplomatic mission arrived. Said Elkus of the Ottoman dictators: "Their ideal was Turkey for the Turks and the suppression, if possible, of all other races and nationalities in Turkey."[26] Although the American Embassy's job was to protect the lives of Americans living in the Ottoman Empire, the assistance it provided went well beyond that mission, with relief to remaining Armenians "an all essential element in the rescue of these people from utter destruction."[27]

Various American groups contributed to Armenian relief efforts, including Protestant missionary and American Jewish relief organizations. Large sums were placed at the disposal of the Embassy staff to use as they saw fit to feed and otherwise support the needy. Soup kitchens were established, and embassy staff visited prisoner-of-war camps and hospitals to deliver medical supplies to the poor and sick of all ethnic groups.

Alsberg's new title could not begin to describe the responsibilities he assumed. Officially a clerk, and unofficially the Ambassador's personal secretary and press attaché, he was also charged with supervising the embassy's aid efforts, including working with Jewish groups as an intermediary for Jewish relief work throughout Turkey and later Palestine.[28]

Jews living in the Ottoman Empire, while they did not experience the indescribable horrors borne by their Armenian neighbors, nonetheless suffered food deprivation and were "sadly in need of help ... they touched a new depth in poverty," according to Elkus. "Because I had come from a country that had rallied so whole-heartedly to the relief of the Armenians, I was deluged with appeals from Armenian individuals and groups; because I was a Jew, the Jews of the Ottoman Empire looked to me as a special patron and friend."[29]

The Turkish government, hostile toward those they deemed Zionists, kept them under tight surveillance and restricted their movements. In fact, there were even fears that the Jewish population would face the same fate as the Armenians. Jews in Palestine who chose not to become Ottoman subjects were forced to leave, resulting in the deportation or arrest of thousands. The Embassy worked frantically to help American Jews depart Palestine; for those Jews who remained in Palestine and other areas of the Ottoman Empire, the Embassy provided desperately needed food and medical supplies. There was reason to worry. In less than a year, relations became markedly more hostile. The thousands of Jews who lived in Jaffa were forcibly deported without their belongings or any provisions. Looting and death, under the watchful eyes of military authorities, was reported. According to a State Department telegram, "the roads to the Jewish colonies north of Jaffa are lined with thousands of starving refugees."[30]

Relief work for the Jewish population extended from Constantinople to Jerusalem, with much of the funding provided by the American Jewish Joint Distribution Committee (JDC). This was a pivotal point for Alsberg; his work to help allocate this money and manage the relief efforts brought him to the attention of this efficient, important, and well-funded group, and led to a decade-long association.

The marble floors and grand frescoes of the Palazzo Corpi—the distinctive building occupied by the United States Embassy in Constantinople—starkly contrasted with the poor quarters Alsberg visited to survey the needs of those facing hunger and homelessness. It was in Constantinople, with its view of fabled sunsets over the Golden Horn (the inlet off of the Bosporus Strait), that Alsberg learned the art of relief work. If not for war, political tyrants, massacres of Armenians, and poor conditions of the Jews and other civilians, it might have been a grand adventure. Constantinople's placement at the crossroads of continents made it an exotic mosaic of East and West. Alsberg was fascinated by the foreign Jewish culture. He could speak German and get by in Yiddish, but many of the Jews there spoke and sang in the unfamiliar tongue of Judeo-Spanish (also known as Ladino). They played strange Sephardic Turkish music, using instruments such as the fretted *baglama*. Their dishes featured eggplant and leeks. This seasoned German-American traveler was a long way from Schubert and sauerbraten.

The various local Jewish groups did not present a united front when Elkus and Alsberg arrived in Turkey in 1916. Alsberg reported that "the Sephardic element clashed with the German-Austrian groups," the Zionists with the non–Zionists.[31] At least some of the conflict stemmed from the dire war conditions and the Jewish community's difficulties keeping up with its own needs. There were Jews whose homes were destroyed by Allied bombardments, refugees from Palestine who were deported from Jewish colonies by Ottoman authorities, orphans and invalids, victims of military and political persecution, destitute families, and above all, the hungry and the starving. Alsberg and Elkus adamantly insisted that salvation could come only if the factions worked together. After securing funds from the JDC, their first order of business was to organize a committee that included representatives from every Jewish group. This influx of money, wrote Alsberg, created "a new spirit of hopefulness and harmony among the divided Jews of Constantinople."[32]

Alsberg's stint as a Foreign Service officer in Turkey, brief as it was to be, gave him the personal satisfaction of contributing to an important cause. It ignited his desire to work on behalf of his coreligionists, setting the stage for his future involvement with Jewish causes at home and relief activities in Russia and Eastern Europe. He learned that he could turn his idealism and visions of social justice into action, while also being drawn to camaraderie he'd not seen before. The Jews of Constantinople had impressed him. Although he'd witnessed various factions at odds with one another, when they were on the verge of starvation, they came together as one. "It is hard to convey to an American Jew who has never been in a country where this racial unity exists," he said, "the feeling of comfort derivable from such brotherhood."[33]

He also experienced a Jewish pride that had been absent in his youth. He wrote of a group of Jewish boys from Palestine forced into cruel conscription with Turkish forces during World War I. Despite scarce food and unfit lodging, the boys represented "a new type of Jewish physique and temperament, sturdy bodies, bright minds, a passionate patriotism and love of the home country."[34]

Desperation for All

Since starvation affected noncombatants of all ethnic and religious heritages, Alsberg's exhaustive report on the food conditions in the Central Powers, written in March and April of 1917 for the U.S. Department of Agriculture, illuminated the desperation faced by millions in the Ottoman Empire. Written with a journalist's clear eye and a humanitarian's compassion, this account combined hard facts with an insider's perceptions. Alsberg reported on what he directly witnessed; additionally, because his affability brought him acquaintance with everyone from leading Zionists, suffering Armenians, German and Austrian diplomats, and foreign correspondents, he gleaned eyewitness testimony. His disturbing, yet comprehensive take on the situation remains an important historical snapshot.

Of the belligerent powers (Germany, Austria-Hungary, Bulgaria, and Turkey), those living in the Ottoman Empire, Alsberg wrote, suffered the most. (Of course, he hadn't yet traveled to the other war-torn areas.) In Constantinople, "200,000 persons, and this is a conservative estimate, are starving." In Jerusalem, with a population of about 56,000, "probably at least 40,000 are starving."[35] Beirut, he reported, "is worse off than Jerusalem. The people were actually dropping in the streets of starvation."

Country districts suffered equally, "ravaged by war ... deportation of the Armenians and the consequent destruction of life and property." Rampaging typhus in the winter and cholera in the summer multiplied the miseries. In Syria, he noted the persecution of Arabs and the deportation of Greeks. Lack of medical supplies, unreliable transportation, unemployment, fuel shortages: Alsberg's report was full of dismal circumstances. His outrage emerged as he described government corruption and policies that prohibited the transfer of food between provinces. "Instead of contributing to the public comfort, the corruption of the officials merely increased the general misery."

After the United States declared war on Germany, entering World War I in April 1917, the Turkish government broke off diplomatic relations. Alsberg and other embassy officials had to evacuate Constantinople and head home to the United States.

Alsberg's experiences in Turkey represented a turning point for him and left him with deep, lasting impressions and a wealth of knowledge about conditions in the Middle East and Europe. They introduced him to unfathomable human suffering due to unstable political situations and ethnic and religious prejudices. They brought him into close contact with those involved in international relief efforts. The human rights work that he would dedicate himself to in one form or another for much of his life began here, serving as his entrance into the fight, as both a journalist and a relief worker, against human suffering at the hands of political despots.

A Separate Peace

After landing in New York and spending time with his mother and sister, Alsberg headed to Washington, D.C., for a personal meeting with Secretary of State Robert Lansing in May 1917, just a month after returning to the United States. According Carl Alsberg, Elkus specifically sent Alsberg to visit Lansing in order "to explain by word of mouth the situation in the Near East."[36] What's astounding is the content of the meeting: Alsberg proposed to Secretary Lansing a plan to separate the Ottoman Empire from the German Alliance, thereby bringing about peace with at least one of the belligerent nations.

Early in their meeting, Alsberg gave Secretary Lansing a passionate and comprehensive overview of the dismal state of affairs in Constantinople. Alsberg's innate reporter's instincts gave him the ability to gather information, synthesize it, and then communicate it; the thirty-five-year old Alsberg impressed Lansing. Alsberg's affable, if not magnetic, personality and his comfort with people from all stations of life no doubt played a part in Lansing's attentiveness. Lansing transmitted Alsberg's in-depth assessment to President Wilson:

> He [Alsberg] said that even the [Turkish] government was becoming irritated at the arrogance of the Germans and feared German control after the war; that they did not want to become a vassal of Germany; that they saw in American capital the only hope of rebuilding their ruined fortunes and desired to remain on friendly terms but were compelled by the Germans to break off relations, which increased Turkish ill-feeling toward the German government.[37]

When Alsberg offered his plan to advance a separate peace with Turkey, Lansing reported that to the President as well. (That Lansing and later Wilson listened seriously to Alsberg itself seems almost far-fetched. After all, just a few years previously, Alsberg had written the centerpiece article for an issue of *The Masses*.)

Alsberg said that he believed the Turks would listen to terms of a separate peace if they dared. I asked him what prevented them, and he replied the GOEBEN and BRESLAU [German battle cruisers], which were anchored before Constantinople with their guns trained on the city, and that to the Turks the preservation of Constantinople was the all-important thing, that he believed that they would give up Palestine, Syria and Armenia in order to hold Constantinople ... he believed that it was possible, on account of the attitude of Turkey toward the United States, for us to approach the Turkish government with suggestions for a separate peace, and that it might be brought about if the German cruisers could in some way be destroyed by bombs or other means.[38]

Whether by coincidence or design, former Ambassador Morgenthau also called upon Lansing later that same day, offering a similar plan. The following day, Lansing wrote to President Wilson about the Alsberg and Morgenthau proposals. This spawned a mission to deliver a peace proposal to Turkey's leaders. Bigger names than Alsberg's, however, would be called upon, with Morgenthau ultimately leading the undertaking, and a reluctant Felix Frankfurter, future Supreme Court Justice and then an assistant to the Secretary of War, accompanying him. Alsberg played a vital role as an advisor to both men.

Morgenthau and Frankfurter did not get along from the outset, evolving into enemies by the end of what would turn out to be an unsuccessful and somewhat ill-fated mission. Although at odds with each other, they each approached it, thanks to Alsberg, armed with enough background information necessary to sound out the possibility of a peace plan. Former Ambassador Morgenthau had much of this already at hand, but he called on Alsberg for updates. Frankfurter, on the other hand, needed to "study up" exhaustively on Turkey.

Again, Alsberg's older brother entered the picture. Carl Alsberg and Felix Frankfurter, friends from Harvard, had become close in Washington. "Carl Alsberg had a younger brother, Henry, a Harvard man, who was a literary, cultural fellow," wrote Frankfurter. "I asked him to brief me about the personalities in the Turkish government, who was who, and what was what.... I spent a whole day being pumped full of knowledge." Alsberg stayed up through that night, preparing a thirty-page, handwritten "critical and analytical" briefing for Frankfurter.[39]

Alsberg himself had reached yet another juncture where he could have chosen a more mainstream career. After all, he had performed his government service exceedingly well. He had gained key connections with people in high places who could open doors for him to the public and private sectors in either Washington or New York. Carl championed his younger brother's talents and would have welcomed his presence in Washington.

But Alsberg was still not ready for that mainstream life. Whether lured by the tumultuous times or following his own restless disposition, he was drawn back to New York. There, he returned to the company of friends in Greenwich Village, and even taught a course at the Rand School on the socialist-inspired cooperative movement.[40] More importantly, he jumped back into the world of journalism headfirst, his expanded worldview now pouring through his pen. For the next year, he wrote for both the *Evening Post* and *The Nation*.

In an article following the February 1917 Russian Revolution, Alsberg profiled the head of the provisional government, Alexander Kerensky, providing an analysis of the country's first democratically elected government before the Bolsheviks wrested power from them in October.[41] The following year he entered the political fray when the U.S. government released documents purporting to show that Germany was financing the Russian Soviets. The so-called *Sisson Documents*, accepted as truth by most newspapers, caused a political uproar. Alsberg wrote editorials for the *Evening Post* disputing the documents as forgeries, a position later confirmed by many historians.[42] His interview with Tomas Masaryk, newly elected President of the newly formed Republic of Czechoslovakia, led to a front-page magazine article for Alsberg.[43]

Ever the adventurer, and taking a break from world events, Alsberg did not hesitate when invited, along with eight other newspaper reporters and a filmmaker, to take a test flight aboard the new Caproni biplane. After donning leather helmets, cotton earplugs, and heavy army coats, the men climbed a twenty-two-foot ladder to the cockpit where they wedged into an open compartment between the two pilots. In a record-breaking flight with twelve civilians reaching an altitude of 8885 feet, the three-engine plane with a seventy-foot wingspan lifted off from a Long Island field, passed over the Statue of Liberty, and gave the dizzied, virgin flyers views of the Hudson River. "I thought I saw Coney Island and Asbury Park at one and the same time, while I was having the sensations of all the amusement parks in the world in the pit of my stomach," Alsberg wrote. Reaching a speed of 110 miles per hour, the Italian pilots (one, the son of Italian poet Gabriele D'Annunzio) descended to 600 feet over Manhattan Island, buzzing Broadway at 110th Street, and "leaping air-pockets as if in a steeplechase." Describing to *Evening Post* readers the flying acrobatics that set the "world awhirl," Alsberg wrote of the sun "rolling at their feet" and the views and sensations of being carried "through clouds and over them, into a sort of heavenly amphitheatre, ringed in by white satin cushions shot with aurora borealis, and looking through the roof of a vague world."[44]

"Eh, bene, were you frightened?," asked one of the pilots after landing.

"A little dizzy, yes. Frightened, no," answered Alsberg.

A Haunted Worldview

Although Alsberg returned to the same job, the same friends, the same milieu following his time in Turkey, his experiences there changed him immeasurably. Alsberg may have left Turkey, but Turkey didn't leave him. As an eyewitness to the genocide's aftermath, he was sensitive to the suffering faced by the innocents caught in the cross-fire of disputes based on ethnic and racial prejudices, on jousts over political power, on the zeal and greed of the powerful. He would be forever haunted. His need to bear witness fueled some of his most powerful writing.

In the newspaper feature article "It Happened in Armenia," Alsberg told the story of an American woman from Massachusetts married to an Armenian-American.[45] She, her husband, and seven-year-old son were in Turkey visiting the husband's family when the first wave of atrocities descended on the Armenians. Written from Alsberg's experience as an Embassy official, he related the brutalities she'd lived through: the loss of her husband, most of his family, and their son. The juxtaposition of Istanbul's grand beauty and this American refugee's unexpected life circumstances was powerful. Describing the view from his embassy window: "The further distance rose up, majestically, tier on tier, to the Mosque of El Ghazi, and, above all, a crown of sunset melodrama not to be seen elsewhere than over Stambul." The woman, "monopolized by a great grief" and dressed in near-rags, "made the veriest contrast of deprecatory shabbiness to all this opulence, this splendor of the fabled East." Alsberg delivered her story to the readers of the *New York Evening Post* mostly in her own words, concluding: "The sun had set by the time she'd finished. El Ghazi and the roofs of Stambul were shadows on a faded, pastel sky, by now as unreal as the back drop of a Persian pantomime."

The New Maccabaeans

Besides reestablishing his journalism career, Alsberg added a wholly different venture to his life, one directly linked to his time overseas. The Zionist movement was not new in 1918 but had gained a fresh urgency, aroused by the decimation of Jewish colonies in Palestine and the continued suffering of Jews in Central and Eastern Europe. In addition to cultivating relationships with Elkus and Felix Frankfurter, he crossed paths with American and Palestinian Zionist leaders. Soon, Alsberg would work with Dr. Stephen Wise, future president of the Zionist Organization of America (ZOA), and Eugene Meyer, Jr., a wealthy investor and future publisher of the *Washington Post*. (Meyer was the father of Katharine Graham, the *Post's* publisher for thirty years.) In late 1917, the ZOA organized the Palestine Restoration Fund Campaign, which sought to raise one million dollars for restoration of the Jewish colonies crippled by the war, educational institutions in Palestine, and the establishment of a Jewish state in the Holy Land. When called on, Henry Alsberg readily volunteered. By January 1918, he was secretary of the Restoration Fund's National Finance Commission.[46]

Not all American Jews fell so easily into the Zionist camp. To meet criticisms that the movement suggested disloyalty toward America, Zionist leaders encouraged supporters to show that they remained steadfast, patriotic Americans. At rallies in support of the funding campaign, American flags were displayed and orchestras played both "The Star Spangled Banner" *and* "Hatikvah." As described by Rabbi Wise: "I am a Jew and an American. Within the Jewish life I am a Jew and nothing but a Jew, but I am not a Jewish-American. I am an American American."[47] This was in line with Alsberg's views. He considered himself a Jew, and just as he would later identify with anarchist political philosophies, he also knew he was wholly American. (Alsberg was aware of the difference between being a Jew in America and being a Jew in most of the rest of the world. From a later writing about Eastern European Jews on the run from atrocities in their home countries: "Despite their patriotism and devotion to the countries of their birth, they were friendless, both in their own homes, and in their places of refuge."[48])

He saw the future Palestine through a utopian lens, dedicated to social justice, and took on the cause with the words of a zealot. Writing in *The Maccabaean*, which billed itself as the official organ of the ZOA, he displayed a flair for public relations when he exhorted readers to dig deeply into their pockets. Every Zionist's "sole aim in life, for the next twenty-eight days, should be to make come true ... the two-thousand year old dream of his people," he wrote.[49] Newspapers of the day recorded his travel throughout the Northeast to stir enthusiasm and encourage donations.

Preparing for the New Decade

Henry Alsberg seemed to live several lives simultaneously as he progressed through the end of the decade into the 1920s. All of his recent experiences converged so that his advance became a multipronged attack on the evil forces of the world.

Over the last few years, Henry Alsberg's reportorial toolbox had expanded to include a deep understanding of international affairs. His front-page articles explicating military and political events showed that he possessed a rare ability to see the components of complicated situations and understand their inner workings. He was akin to a master watchmaker staring at the works of a pocket watch and understanding how the turning gears connected with each other. He could peer in to study the mechanism closely and step back again to see the cohesive whole. And then he could write about it.

With the signing of the Armistice in November 1918, Alsberg was pulled in another direction. When Oswald Garrison Villard sold the *Evening Post* that same year, he kept the *Nation,* with plans to expand its political reporting. To do that, he needed to augment his cast of foreign correspondents. Villard didn't have to search beyond Alsberg's desk in the newsroom.

In the fall of 1918 Alsberg put his affairs in order and took time off to spend with his family. Mother Bertha and sister Elsa were in New York. Carl still lived in Washington, where his work as Chief of the Bureau of Chemistry had supported the war effort. Julius, too, who had moved to Chicago with wife, Elsie, and their two children, also contributed to the war effort as a volunteer with the U.S. Food Administration. One of his charges in that role was to increase the production of glycerin, a chemical used to make explosives.[50] After spending a traditional Christmas in New York (one can only imagine the dinnertime conversations between Henry the pacifist and his two more conventional brothers), Henry, the youngest Alsberg at age thirty-seven, prepared for adventure on the other side of the Atlantic.

Alsberg's departure for Europe marked his 1918 end-of-the-year calendar. His restlessness and taste for foreign travel; his commitment to progressive politics and journalism; his desire to provide aid and comfort to beleaguered, innocent victims of war; his own emotional attachment to saving his fellow Jews—this mix was a prelude to a frenzied, adventurous, dangerous time. The next decade would find Alsberg energetically immersed in the worlds of reporting, human rights, and even theater. When the train heading for the 1920s roared out of the station, Henry Alsberg jumped aboard, carrying his idealism and, as always, his pen.

CHAPTER 3

"Our people are suffering in a terrible way"
December 1919–May 1920

Henry Alsberg—a born rover, to his mother's consternation—headed for Europe after Christmas, traveling across the North Atlantic through New Year's Eve and New Year's Day. The frigid winter crossing would barely prepare him for the coming year's journeys.

Alsberg arrived in London carrying a letter from *Nation* editor Oswald Garrison Villard as his calling card. It attested to his appointment as "special traveling correspondent of *The Nation* with special instructions for France, Italy, Great Britain and Switzerland."[1] Alsberg jumped into his reportorial duties, filing stories on British labor unions and the political and cultural climate in London, and becoming a freelance contributor to *London Daily Herald* in the process. He interviewed a British politician and diplomat who called for the United States to rule Ottoman lands until an Armenian nation "could stand alone." To that, Alsberg editorialized on such a "disastrous move," saying, "In fact, we may fairly claim to be the only country free from the hypocrisy attached to the 'white man's burden' nonsense."[2] While reporting on widespread labor strikes in Belfast and the subsequent interruption of gas and electricity, Alsberg wrote of reading, writing, and eating by candlelight in Belfast.[3]

One article he wrote about the lack of coal strayed into a humorous "American abroad" anecdote. He grumbled: "The other day, on what Londoners call only a reasonably misty day, when I blew into my unheated room, in my unheated hotel, in my unheated metropolis of London, I swear by all the gods of Mark Twain that so thick lay the fog in my room I had difficulty in distinguishing the bed from the wardrobe until I bumped my shins on the former; and I began to brush my teeth with my shaving brush."[4] As a cure, he cajoled a doctor to prescribe two lumps of coal with which to heat his room.

Meanwhile, across the English Channel, the Peace Conference had convened in the Paris suburb of Versailles. Both London and Paris teemed with diplomats, reporters, and the multitudes attached to them for this international summit. Alsberg stayed in London for a time where he had been elected as a delegate to the Zionist Conference held there in February, although it is unlikely that he attended.[5] He wanted to be where the real action was, across the channel in France, but post-war disorder and bureaucracy delayed his effort to obtain a visa. Eventually, a member of the Zionist delegation to the Peace Conference helped secure his documents. Alsberg checked out of the chilly Carlton Hotel in London and headed to Paris.

There, Alsberg was appointed as an attaché to the Zionist delegation.[6] Records are sparse regarding his activities with the group, but he did fulfill his writing obligations for *The Nation*, filing a story from Paris about politicians from Czechoslovakia, Poland, and Lithuania haggling for mineral rights and land. He also wrote about his interviews with Jewish refugees from Poland who escaped pogroms and the Polish official who denied this terrorism.

Alsberg did not hold back in his vehemence against the Polish government and the Polish people: "I think Europe will rue the day that it allowed this vast amorphous mass of Poland to coagulate into rank imperialism." His editorializing exposed his own bias and critiqued the governments of both Poland and the United States: "Most unfortunately the Poles, who have the personal charm of all oppressing races, have captured the American officials who have been visiting Poland ... they have been captured by the idea that Poland and the reactionary virtuoso government can prove a bulwark against the hoodoo of Bolshevism: the old delusion that you can defend yourself against one bad thing by use of something equally wicked."[7]

While in Paris, Alsberg connected with Jewish Joint Distribution Committee (JDC) officials; the organization sought volunteers to enter Central and Eastern Europe to assess and provide relief to destitute Jews. This appealed to Alsberg, who not only wanted to travel, but also *needed* to focus his indomitable energies on a cause he believed in. So, as if being a roving reporter wasn't enough, Alsberg readily agreed to take on this much more dangerous role as a soldier in the JDC's army of mercy.

Living in a Gentile World

Every Jew, I am sure, or at least every Jew who, like myself, has been half swallowed by the boa-constrictor of his western surroundings, loves to imagine that he is the great exception to the general rule, that he has no Jewish peculiarities at all, and can therefore stand back and note the peculiarities of his fellow Jews with an indulgent smile. If he has remained a Jew at all, it is by a sort of noble magnanimity, because he does not want to desert the racial ship in the face of prejudice. —Henry Alsberg[8]

A look back at Alsberg's own relationship to his Jewish identity could help explain his growing compulsion to devote a portion of his life to rescuing his coreligionists in battle-scarred areas across the globe. Records paint a picture of his involvement in Jewish causes for at least ten years. Despite his upbringing in an assimilated, secular family, he considered himself Jewish. This sentiment did not begin with the ritual *bris* (circumcision ceremony) on his eighth day of life, nor a Bar Mitzvah on his thirteenth birthday. He had neither. In fact, every year, wax candles festooned a Christmas tree, illuminating the parlor of the Alsberg home in New York City. Friends and family—young Henry and other children in their circle—gathered not to celebrate the Christian holiday, but rather to enjoy the traditional German festivities of food, drink, and merriment. Whatever circumstances turned Henry Alsberg toward Jewish causes and cultural roots, it didn't happen at home. Nonetheless, Jewish roots run deep, even in someone like Alsberg, who most likely espoused agnosticism, and perhaps even atheism. He saw himself, despite his rearing, as one of the tribe. Perhaps it began when, as a wide-eyed boy, his religious grandmother brought him—against his father's wishes—to the stately Temple Emanu-El on Fifth Avenue.

It's difficult to say when Alsberg first encountered anti–Semitism, or, as he put it, "the gentile world reacting toward us as it does."[9] Biographical accounts left by friends and contemporaries Alfred Kroeber and James Rosenberg give glimpses into Alsberg's world. From these reports, it seems plausible that Alsberg escaped overt bigotry as a child, only to encounter it at college.

Kroeber, of Christian German heritage, described the religious—or rather, nonreligious—milieu of the boys' childhood: "The relation of Gentile and Jew of German extraction in New York ... was really quite extraordinary, at least for the middle and professional classes. One knew the difference, but assumed it did not matter.... None of the German families I knew were church members. None of the Jewish families went to synagogue."

James N. Rosenberg, a friend from adolescence who later worked closely with Alsberg in the JDC, first became aware of anti–Semitism as a boy, and felt it again when he attended Columbia. Rosenberg, a member of Carl's tight-knit circle of friends, was only a few years ahead of Henry Alsberg at Columbia. Rosenberg's exclusion from fraternities and some athletic clubs left a bitter memory: "It is from that time that I date my full Jew-consciousness ... the Gentile youths not only thought us different, but wanted to keep us out of things. Did they dislike us? I saw the Jewish boys at college making friendships with their Christian classmates, but somewhere, as in a grey mist, an invisible and impenetrable wall existed. We were on one side of it; they were on the other."[10] Rosenberg also wrote of "the cold shoulder of contempt and disdain which the Columbia University Club turned upon me."[11] The bastion of higher learning was apparently not yet so enlightened as to prevent minority students from feeling the sting of intolerance. (On the other hand, the university had named Professor Richard Gottheil, an active Zionist, to the endowed chair of rabbinical literature in 1887.) It's impossible to say whether or not Alsberg suffered as Rosenberg did, but Alsberg may have felt somewhat estranged as part of the Jewish minority. In a 1964 letter to Melville Cane, Alsberg, then eighty-three years old, wrote that he was "indignant" that Cane, by then a prominent poet, had been excluded from a recent Columbia publication on alumni authors. Alsberg called the omission anti–Semitic, but there is no evidence that Cane agreed with him or that there was any basis to his grievance.

So, notwithstanding Meinhard's "aggressive agnosticism" and despite growing up in a neighborhood where "the lines between German-Gentile and German-Jew had not [yet] been drawn,"[12] Henry Alsberg still found himself "pushed into the spiritual ghetto" both at home and abroad. "Our gentile friends take great delight in this subtle flattery of assuring us that they never would have guessed we were Jewish at all," he wrote. Later in Russia, on learning Alsberg was Jewish, an acquaintance traveling with him said: "You know, Comrade Alsberg, I always thought you were a regular American, you had such perfect manners and such nice ways." His Russian-language teacher there criticized his accent: "You mustn't pronounce like that. That is the Jewish pronunciation of Russian, and considered very bad in good society." It also may have been dangerous; Alsberg related the story that when bandits held up trains in the Ukraine they "would make all of the passengers pronounce the Ukrainian word for corn, *Kukuruza*, and would incontinently massacre all that pronounced the word with a Jewish accent."

In America, Jews were often excluded from hotels, country clubs, and other venues. Alsberg spoke of friends on a trip upstate New York. Seeking overnight lodging, they could find only a hotel "that made it a point of not taking any of our people. It was a rainy night, no other hotel in sight, and my friends became Gentiles for that one occasion."[13]

His own encounters with bigotry, coupled with witnessing acts of cruelty against fellow Jews, roused a dormant force within him. His very near future would find him traveling on unheated, pestilence-ridden trains through obliterated Jewish Eastern European towns as he accepted the JDC's call in 1919. Perhaps as he rode one of those cold trains, wrapped in his camel-hair blanket to retain whatever body heat he could muster, he thought back to the German-American Christmas feasts of his childhood.

A Player on the Bloody Stage

For the Jewish population of these regions—the Ukraine, Poland, Hungary, Czechoslovakia, Romania, Russia—war, pogroms, and famine marked the era. World War I and the Russian Revolution, along with ongoing anti–Semitic persecutions, had wreaked havoc and left millions dead, homeless, starving, orphaned, or destitute. Bloody conflicts raged even post Armistice. Combatants in war frenzy—the Red and White armies of Russia, and Ukrainian and Polish forces—caused the populace, Jews and non–Jews, even more despair.

Alsberg later characterized the period as being marked with "the emergence of many minor nationalities, all imbued with grand imperialistic passions, fighting for their independence in a condition of economic wretchedness and moral degradation.... Human life lost its value." Talking about the JDC's efforts, he wrote,

> Had the armistice brought peace to the world as was anticipated, the task of the JDC would have been merely one of reconstruction and rehabilitation.... To the invalids of war, were added scores of thousands of people maimed and crippled by pogroms. To the widows and orphans of soldiers fallen on the field of battle, there was now joined an army of fresh widows and orphans—the crop of innumerable massacres. The large numbers of wartime refugees were now dwarfed by the vast hordes of Jewish wanderers whose sole purpose was to find a safe shelter and bread. The horrors of the World War paled against the terrors of unbridled anti–Semitism [14]

So in addition to the conditions borne by all segments of the population, the Jews suffered from unrelenting anti–Semitism. Those who had fled or had been deported from their homes languished in limbo, seen as the enemy on whichever side of the border they found themselves. Sometimes, returning home held even more danger than staying, unwanted, in another nation.

In late February 1919, Alsberg headed into this maelstrom. The Great War was over, but he was a soldier in a different battle, and essentially, these were his war years. His new emergency passport issued by the American Embassy in Paris listed his occupation as "food relief" for the American Relief Administration (ARA), the United States humanitarian organization headed by Herbert Hoover that provided post-war famine relief in Europe. The JDC worked, at times, in conjunction with the ARA.

A JDC report described the work of volunteers and staff: "Special commissioners visited the zones of operations, some conducting investigations and reporting their findings to the home office, others remaining for periods of weeks and months at particularly vital points to organize and supervise the distribution." Alsberg did all of that over a span of over four years in various countries, including the "bandit-ridden Ukraine."[15]

The JDC was happy to have Alsberg. He not only was sensitized to the plight of Jews but also came armed with the knowledge and insights gained in Turkey as part of the diplomatic mission and as a foreign correspondent. Well versed with the changing political situations and the tribulations of war victims and refugees, he was such a valuable asset that there was some dispute over where to best deploy him. A letter from Lewis L. Strauss, Hoover's secretary and the ARA liaison to the JDC, described Alsberg as "anxious to come to Poland for relief work."[16] However, the JDC had other plans for Alsberg. The organization had no one in Czechoslovakia. His first deployment would be there.

Alsberg caught a steam locomotive at the Paris train station bound for Prague. Soldiers heading off to new battles or retreating from defeat, diplomats making return trips to their respective European cities, civilians returning to their home regions—the crowd, as well as a border skirmish that rerouted the train, made for an intriguing trip. Arriving on the afternoon of March 1, he was ready to start his tour of duty as the JDC's first commissioner in the new nation of Czechoslovakia.

The Conscientious Observer

He didn't waste any time. After just a few days in Prague, Alsberg provided, if not an in-depth assessment, a preliminary budget request so that he could commence relief efforts. He relayed his request by courier service to Lewis Strauss at his Paris headquarters, saying, "The situation of the Jews in Czechoslovakia is unbelievably bad." It had to be quite a shock for Alsberg; he was not naïve, but living amid this oppression differed greatly from writing about it from afar.

His early letters delineated the critical situation of the nation's Jewish population: 7000 hungry, homeless, and destitute refugees from Galicia about to be deported by the government; hundreds of war orphans; plundering and looting of Jewish shops and homes; Jewish government officials and army officers being forced out of their positions; refugee students cut off from their families; and multitudes of malnourished and sick children and old people.

Alsberg's first budget request of $60,000 also came with an appeal for shoes and clothing.[17] In the Subcarpathian region, he wrote, "practically the entire population was in rags."[18] Conditions did vary throughout the country, with some regions and populations left more intact. Lewis Strauss, who had high regard for Alsberg, called him a "conscientious observer" and forwarded his request to New York JDC officials.[19] The funds were granted almost immediately.

Alsberg cabled Strauss his first impressions of the new nation. He told of one pogrom and multiple assaults. "The anti–Semitism, whatever its causes, is quite beyond belief. It happens frequently that Jews are stopped on the streets by soldiers from France and Russia, and insulted and beaten up. Jews have been chased out of cafes and beaten up by the crowds awaiting them."[20] Later that week he wrote again: "My job here, as you may have imagined, is not an enviable one. Nobody loves the Jews in Prague, at the present time, but myself."[21]

Alsberg also felt compelled to ease the pervading dread felt by Jewish inhabitants. His assurances that American Jews would stand by them allayed some of their anxieties, but there was plenty of bad news to agonize about. A local organization formed to boycott all Jewish businesses helped fuel anxieties. This boycott, along with new economic legislation, panicked wealthy Jews and caused a domino effect that exasperated him: Whereas affluent Jews had previously funded local Jewish institutions caring for the poor and the sick, they "were in such a state of uncertainly that they refused to risk any of their liquid assets for further support."[22] Despite their fears, he insisted that they contribute more.

Alsberg faced another frustrating situation. The two main local Jewish charity agencies in Prague slated to disburse JDC money worked chaotically and disliked each other. He had experienced similar obstacles in Constantinople and eventually cajoled the groups into working together. In addition to his usual factual reportage to Strauss, he couldn't resist adding a little tongue-in-cheek about his "grand premiere" bringing together the various factions. The toughest of the group was a woman with "true Yiddish *chutspa* who threatened the integrity and continuity of the proceedings. However, I quietly ignored her desire to run the whole shooting match and she subsided, out of awe for the unknown American."[23]

Alsberg's goal in Prague was to create one well-organized, permanent charity group, and to do it as soon as possible, because, as he put it, "I don't want to live out my life in this beautiful but poisonously anti–Semitic city."[24] His frustrations were myriad and he must have suffered some homesickness. In one letter to Strauss, he offered fervent thanks for English language newspapers—"a mental lifesaver." But he did have good news—or at least news that didn't involve atrocities of one sort or another—to report. The ARA's famine relief did not discriminate against Jews; the organization provided food for the general population, particularly undernourished children, and "made it quite clear that it considered the Jewish population entitled to the same treatment in its work as the non–Jewish."[25] Even the Czech government—despite its many faults and almost bipolar attitude toward the Jews—occasionally cooperated. Alsberg proudly reported that after his intervention with Prague authorities, they were "fairly decent" in providing "*mazoth* flour during the Passover Festival."[26]

During that spring in 1919, Alsberg headed south to assess the situation in Slovakia. Alarmed by what he found, he wrote from Pressbourg, a city situated at the corner of Austria, Hungry, and Czechoslovakia: "Just returned from a trip to Slovakia. The Jewish situation there is beyond description lamentable. Almost all of the Jewish families were totally robbed and plundered, many synagogues ruined or wrecked during the riots that followed the Czechoslovakian revolution ... the government has given out an order permitting the local authorities to expel or inter practically anyone they chose. This order is being used against the Jews. Those who fled from their old homes are now being forced to return home, where they cannot live, on account of anti–Semitism, lack of work (their shops were destroyed, etc.) and they are between the devil and the deep sea."[27] His intervention brought the Slovakians necessary funds. The following year, a Slovakian Rabbi wrote the JDC saying that Alsberg appeared in the "guise of a good angel."

Occupy Prague: Political Maneuvers

Alsberg, sent by the JDC solely to organize humanitarian efforts, couldn't stop himself from getting involved in political matters. He stepped outside his authority more than once but perceived these actions to be as necessary as providing food, shelter, and clothing.

In one instance, he organized a group of Slovakian Jewish delegates to meet with the Slovakian governor, who subsequently agreed to appoint a Jewish representative as official intermediary between the Jews and the government. "At least now the Jews who are persecuted by local officials have some court of appeal," Alsberg wrote.[28]

In another case, he arranged for a delegation of Prague Jews to visit President Tomas Masaryk, whom he considered enlightened. Alsberg prepped them to emphasize "the danger of the new republic being discredited in the outside world by its anti–Semitism. Masaryk, thereupon, behaved splendidly and gave them a letter assuring them of his Judo-Phillity. So things are better, but not cured. The word in Paris is still needed, and badly needed, as the rest of the government does not seem to agree on the Jewish point with Mr. Masaryk."[29]

Alsberg urged Strauss to press the Czech government at the Peace Conference. "For heaven's sake, don't let the Czechs get any concessions in Paris until they amend their rotten proceedings toward the Jews. An example should be made of every Jew-baiting mid European country," he wrote, adding that "if the government backs this policy of making life for Jews impossible, then $100,000 [of JDC's money] is like pouring money down a bottomless pit."[30] He also advocated pushing the American press to write about the atrocities. His friends in Paris heeded his call. Soon, articles appeared in the *New York Tribune* and the *New York Times*, where one of Alsberg's reports was quoted almost in its entirety.[31] By early April, Alsberg had established a JDC branch office in Prague with locally staffed committees to handle the needs of refugees, orphans, students, sick children, and the unemployed.

Journalistic Diversions

While most of his travel in the late winter and spring of 1919 was on behalf of the JDC, Alsberg could not neglect his correspondent responsibilities. As he mentioned to Strauss at one point, he owed *Nation* publisher Villard frequent articles, especially considering that the magazine paid his way to Europe.

While still managing JDC matters, he took brief sojourns to various European cities. Essentially, because he was still working as a reporter for *The Nation*, as well as the *London Herald* and the *New York World*, he was leading, if not a double life—for he did not hide his activities—at least two parallel lives, each one feeding the other. While drawing an ethical line between his work as a journalist and his responsibilities as an aid worker, he used each activity to motivate and inform the other. Alsberg's reportage, copious through 1919, painted expressive and intricate pictures for *Nation* readers, describing a Europe "laboring in the throes of recovery from war."

From Vienna he wrote that the streets were "empty and disconsolate" with the only crowds lined up to get their food rations. "As yet the Viennese go just as if they were always going to live together by taking in each other's washing. They are starving and despondent. But they do not think of going elsewhere, except the Jews, who all think of emigrating."[32] He lived among the people he reported on, eating only "half cooked cabbage three times a day" in Vienna and drinking "chicory and burnt malt" instead of coffee in Prague.[33]

His article on Czechoslovakia cast the new nation as "gradually taking shape." He described shortages of clothing and food, with the "poor Czechs" being near starvation. As he often did, he incorporated his own personal story to illustrate a point. "I tried to buy a hat yesterday; not wanting to look like a German tourist invading the Tyrol, I refrained from taking the only hat that fitted me. Tomorrow I shall regret my fastidiousness." In addition to covering the economic and political news of the nation, he highlighted the Jewish situation, writing ruefully, "President Masaryk no longer appears to be the chief controller of government policy. If he were, this anti–Semitism would have been impossible."[34]

In a similar vein, during the ongoing Paris Peace Conference, he wrote articles about the perpetrators of the Armenian Genocide given safe haven and living comfortably in Germany, at least partially off the proceeds of money stolen from murdered Armenians. Suggestive now of Nazi war criminals who lived out their years in South America after World War II, Alsberg pointed out that "these modern Caligulas of a whole nation still remain at large."

Alsberg, also becoming increasingly politicized about the situation of Jews worldwide, condemned one of those Turkish leaders for his mistreatment of Jews in Palestine. "He once said in Jerusalem, to a representative of the United States, so it is rumored, that he did not fear a land so far away as America, and would do unto the Jews and Arabs of Syria what he wished, which turned out to be plenty." (Likely he referred to Djemal Pasha, the military commander in Palestine.) "In short," Alsberg wrote, "Germany offers its hospitality to this whole gang of murderers and allows them to live quietly upon the proceeds of murder and graft." Alsberg took both the Germans and Allied countries to task for not bringing the war criminals to justice. "Five minutes of your precious time, Gentleman of the Peace Conference."[35]

Some of his articles, clearly sympathetic to revolutionary ideas promulgated by Bolsheviks, anarchists, and other radical groups, caught the attention of American authorities. His movements through Europe, along with his interviews and meetings with labor leaders and politicians of various political parties, aroused the suspicions of Allied military intelligence (a term he'd surely deride). They'd curiously followed his activities and whereabouts in 1919. One report charged that "under cover of his position with the American Food Commission" in Prague, Alsberg obtained military information "of interest to the Bolshevists" and assisted Bolshevik agents. These reports were unsubstantiated and short lived, quashed perhaps by evidence that his activities during this period related to his journalism and JDC work, not espionage.[36] Looking at his articles of the period, it's a wonder that he did not come under watchful eyes sooner.

As the first correspondent to enter Hungary after a communist government was proclaimed there, his subsequent *Nation* article, widely discussed and reprinted in U.S. newspapers, offered enthusiasm for what he saw as progressive and positive changes. Alsberg abandoned journalist objectivity and glamorized the new regime. After living and working in Czechoslovakia, where "race hatreds and passionate chauvinism" reigned, he extolled Hungary's "atmosphere of peace and goodwill among men."

Leftist readers no doubt appreciated reading about the "spirit of proletarian revolution." He spelled out reformist policies, including the rights of working women to vote and the prohibition on hoarding goods. Starvation remained a concern in all of the war-torn countries. For the first time since the war began, Alsberg wrote, "the rich and the poor eat much the same food." While admitting that food was scarce, he proclaimed it seasoned with "justice and democracy." He called Vladimir Lenin, who was pulling revolutionary strings a thousand miles away, the period's "greatest figure." Those on the other side of the political spectrum read his dispatches with alarm.

Believing that "the communist programme has been carried out without bitterness or violence," Alsberg cut the regime slack, whitewashing the reality of curtailed free speech and civil liberties and ubiquitous press censorship. For someone who would spend years fighting for these very ideals, he certainly had to cringe at his words later. But for now he believed—as he would later when defending the Russian Bolsheviks for similar transgressions—that these liberties would emerge once the government stabilized and after Western countries had withdrawn their economic blockades and provided support. Taking the Western allied powers to task for aiding Austria, but not Hungary, he wrote:

> We hurry to feed the dying population of Vienna, because we are suddenly panic-stricken at the idea that a starving Vienna may mean Bolshevism. We feed nobody without ulterior motives of profit to ourselves. We do not think of the Viennese as starving men and women and children, but as our pawns. And so we now do not think of the Hungarians as human beings, but as the opponents of our very doubtful political system. Where is there real charity among us?[37]

Alsberg's articles, subjective as they might have been, abounded with supporting statistics. And if he leaned in one direction, he was not alone. *New York Times* correspondent Harold Williams fervently supported the White Army forces in Russia. In a front-page article on White Army commander Anton Denikin, Williams characterized the general as a "great and noble man." Alsberg didn't agree, knowing that Denikin's forces bore responsibility for deadly pogroms and mass executions.[38]

Continuing JDC Work: War Orphans and "Fugitives"

Although the easily bored Alsberg lobbied Strauss to "find me some tougher job in some wilder place,"[39] he was actually hesitant about moving on and leaving unfinished his JDC job in Czechoslovakia. Particularly troubling to him was the suffering of two constituencies: children and refugees.

Some two thousand war orphans and other sick, hungry children in or near Prague needed help. Although he saw the pace of his endeavors as agonizingly slow, there were accomplishments. A children's clinic had been established and some orphans placed with families. A sort of Fresh Air fund was arranged so that hundreds of children could recuperate in safe areas of the countryside come summer. He arranged with the ARA to provide milk, rice, and other foods to JDC children's institutions.

The refugee situation proved more desperate. From the day he arrived in Prague, Alsberg took it as his personal mission to help the thousands of "fugitives," a term he used interchangeably with "refugees." In this work, he was an advocate, diplomat, and organizer. Although chiefly concerned with refugees in Czechoslovakia, his visits to Budapest, Vienna, Pressbourg, and other cities allowed him to assess the situation in the rest of the former Austro-Hungarian Empire. The various governments all planned to begin deportations in May, even though the refugees, for the most part, came from still volatile war-torn areas of Galicia and Bukovina, on the empire's eastern borders.

His missives to Strauss told the story. A mid–April letter tallied about 40,000 refugees, including 3000 in Vienna who had escaped recent pogroms. (The actual numbers of refugees varied constantly.) Although the Polish and Ukrainian governments provided minimal support, the majority of this exiled population remained destitute, with no means of living where they were and no means of returning to their former homes. The JDC over the course of the year sent at least $70,000 for refugees in Czechoslovakia alone. But attempts at repatriation came with nearly incomprehensible predicaments. "Bukovina fugitives can't travel back," Alsberg wrote. "This is for two reasons, partly because a portion of Bukovina is in the war zone, but largely because the Roumanian government refuses to give any permission for these people to return home."[40]

Refugees from eastern Galicia (now part of the Ukraine) faced even more serious circumstances. They were not allowed to pass through Poland on their way home because the two countries were at war. Consecutive waves of invasions had transformed their towns into rubble. Alsberg, horrified at the thought of the refugees' deportation into a war zone, said the Russians "conducted the war in a particularly barbaric manner, with the Jews as the chief object of their ruthlessness. The Jews were maltreated with a thorough and unrelenting fury, probably only comparable with the cruelties practiced by the Turks on the Armenians."[41]

After the Purim arrests and a pogrom in Lemberg (now Lviv) the previous year, he wrote that for the governments "to deport these people now, without any arrangements for their traveling, without permission of other governments for their departure, to deport them to places like Lemberg where there are pogroms and battles going on, is outrageous."[42]

Alsberg and other JDC officials tried to ease the way for the deportees by delaying transports. "My chief work in the last few days has been running around to ministries trying to get them to prevent local authorities from deporting fugitives ... the Hungarian borders are now shut so that it is impossible to send any of our fugitives out that way." He continued to push for food and funds for areas most severely affected.

Along with monetary requests, he passed on his hope to receive official help from the U.S. government, beyond the ARA's food mission. He even requested the company of a soldier for an assistant. "A uniform in this part of the world has everyone buffaloed," he wrote.[43]

There were smaller groups, too, for which Alsberg sought help. He petitioned Strauss, the British government, and Zionist organizations for assistance in transporting Jewish Palestinian refugees back to their homes. One telegram read, "200 fugitives in Bohemia mostly at Nikolsburg [refugee camp]. Natives of Palestine exiled two years ago by Djemal Pasha. Now wish to return home ... ask Zionist organization to use influence to get permission for them to go to Palestine."[44]

Travel arrangements for all the exiled Jews seemed insurmountable. They needed food and other commodities, permission to travel past various borders, and even protection against the local populations they would encounter during their travels.

A New Billet

An unexpected telegram from JDC headquarters arrived at Alsberg's office while he was in the midst of resolving the refugee situation. He was being transferred to Poland immediately. The vague wording of the telegram perturbed him. Despite his accomplishments (and the fact that he originally wanted to work with the JDC in Poland), he thought perhaps he'd done something to irritate JDC officials and wrote, somewhat petulantly: "If it is due to any kick on the part of anybody, why I will be glad and even anxious to quit. I have been neglecting my work horribly lately, I mean my newspaper work." He added that he would go "because I assume I am needed there very urgently to help" but also adamantly stated that he didn't want to remain in Poland any longer than necessary. And because he was raised by Bertha and Meinhard to be gracious and well mannered, he thanked Strauss for the opportunity of serving: "I appreciate your kindness very much and have had an interesting time."[45]

In actuality, Strauss thought Alsberg had gotten things well in hand. But the situation in Poland was desperate and the JDC's very able Boris David

Bogen needed help; Strauss thought Alsberg the best equipped to act as his "lieutenant."[46]

Alsberg found it difficult to leave Prague without completing his refugee work. The aftermath of the tragedy stayed with him. Years later, writing the history of the JDC, he described the refugees as people "who merely sought safety in flight from the war or anti–Semitic zones, but who neither knew or cared where they went."[47] By the end of April 1919, Alsberg heeded the JDC's second call to action. Earlier, he'd requested a transfer to a wilder place. That wilder place turned out to be Poland.

Destitution and Desolation

The trip from Prague to Warsaw was 500 kilometers to the northeast and eons back in time to an almost medieval Europe. The JDC's Warsaw office was already in place under the compassionate leadership of Bogen, who was one of JDC's early directors.

Alsberg was none too happy to be billeted in Warsaw. Despite his complaints, he hit it off with Bogen almost immediately. Bogen, in turn, was thankful for his arrival. "Alsberg has arrived the day before yesterday," he wrote to Strauss, "and he is a bully [fine] fellow."[48] Their friendship would last until Bogen's death in 1929.

Alsberg's transfer was part of the JDC's move to augment its presence in Poland following the recent massacre of Jews in Pinsk, then under Polish occupation. Approximately seventy-five Jewish leaders had gathered there to discuss the distribution of JDC funds; soldiers had entered the meeting hall, arrested the group, and later executed thirty-five people.[49] Strauss described conditions bad enough that he contemplated going there himself to help out. But he considered Alsberg, after even just a few months in Czechoslovakia, an experienced aid worker. "The only way I could get my conscience at rest over the matter was to feel that you were there to help, and that you knew more about such work in a minute than I did in a year." In that same letter, he promised to send uniformed army assistants.[50]

If Czechoslovakia was a bad dream, Poland was an unrelenting nightmare. Bogen described a scene with children sitting in a Warsaw gutter, begging for a piece of bread "in a pitiful sing-song Yiddish," dressed in rags that couldn't begin to keep the cold away from their skeletal bodies. Typhus and tuberculosis were rampant. He described the eyes of these children as "misery personified."[51]

Massacres. Pogroms. Starvation. Mutilations. Disease. Reports and letters from Alsberg, Bogen, and others were peppered with unimaginable descriptions of suffering. Alsberg, never at a loss for words, fell to using the word "indescribable" more than once, lamenting that he'd already used whatever words he could conjure up. How many ways can one convey misery?

It wasn't merely the typical war repercussions of hunger, unemployment, separated families, and destroyed homes. All of those conditions existed throughout the country, and not just for Jews. Yet thanks to endemic anti–Semitism, these conditions magnified exponentially for the Jewish population. The Polish government and military often sanctioned the violence against them and were not keen on sharing food and commodities donated for relief efforts.

By May, Alsberg was hard at work establishing milk stations and directing food distribution. When Bogen left to attend to matters in war-zone cities, Alsberg supervised the Warsaw JDC office. But he still fretted about his Prague relief programs and felt underused. "I don't know whether or how much Bogen thinks he needs me. As a matter of fact he doesn't need me at all. He is able to run the job here as [well as] anybody I know. He is such a kind-hearted chap that you would never know from what he says how useless the work [I am] doing is."[52] Nonetheless, Alsberg felt obligated, and promised to remain with Bogen at least through the end of May 1919.

Bogen hoped to keep him even longer. Writing to Strauss, he thanked him for sending Alsberg and hoped conditions would improve enough so that Alsberg would want to stay. "As it is, the situation is horrible and a person is liable to become pessimistic."[53] Alsberg, in the kind of gallows humor used by battle-front doctors and hardened soldiers, wrote, "After the first few days, when I had seen the poverty and hardship and misery, the novelty began to wear off."[54] Nonetheless, Bogen's remark was spot on: Alsberg had not yet become inured to the horrors around him.

Alsberg wasn't used to being so hands-on with the actual relief work and hands-*off* with political matters. He admitted in one letter that he was used to being in charge. He was also conflicted because as JDC chief in Prague, he'd been able to take off on quick journalistic trips to fulfill his obligations as a correspondent. His new JDC duties limited his news-writing opportunities and output.

"You may remember that relief work is only my avocation, that I really am journalist by profession," he wrote to Strauss. "Now in Warsaw for me as a journalist the situation differs somewhat from that in Prague. There, I could keep in very close touch with political conditions, and most of the people whom it was necessary for me to meet in order to keep up with the times." He felt "rather stuck in Warsaw, journalistically speaking, a regular Robinson Crusoe." Moreover, reporting from Poland would be irresponsible, he wrote. "The Jewish situation is so bad here that it would be very unwise to take any risks in having the JDC work connected with any newspaper."[55]

All of his entreaties did not procure him a requested transfer. Strauss wrote that they "could not withdraw you from Poland now, where you are so badly needed, and where Bogen writes that he now cannot get along without you."[56] That Alsberg was torn between his volunteer relief work and his writing—and that sometimes the relief work won out—is made evident by this account of his visit to Budapest the prior month. There, he resisted a journalistic scoop:

> Bela Kun, the Bolshevik Foreign Minister took a shine to me because I knew some of his American Bolshevik friends.... So Kun offered to send me to Russia and see Lenin's government myself and report impartially on it. They had airships running at that time from Buda[pest] to Russia every day. He offered to give me all sort of introductions and a free hand to write what I wanted if I'd go. I refused because of my [volunteer] work in Prague. I think that showed some self-control for a correspondent.[57]

"I Don't Know What You People Are Doing in Paris"

Living in Warsaw while historical changes transpired throughout Europe felt a little like lock-down to the journalist in Alsberg, but it's not as if he didn't write at all. The conditions he witnessed, coupled with his urge to put words to paper, resulted in a long report to his friend Felix Frankfurter, who was in Paris with the Zionist Commission at the Peace Conference.

Alsberg penned his treatise with a writer's instinct for veracity, a researcher's attention to details and statistics, a reporter's regard for reliable sources, and an editorialist's call for action. "In Warsaw there is filth and rags and disease and starvation." In the northeast countryside, he wrote, the poor Jews "who are not allowed to go out of the village's bounds to get food, have gotten down to eating grass, and what is worse, poison ivy soup.... Allow me to impress upon you, that if something is not done of a radical nature to relieve the situation, there will be no Jews left to go to Palestine."

Early in the letter he wrote, "I don't know what you people are doing in Paris, but I know what you ought to be doing." The concluding page, dense with proposals, verged on a tirade. Alsberg ended by saying, "Since I've been in Middle Europe, I quite understand the lure of Bolshevism."[58]

Interestingly, one of his proposals was to send a team of American investigators to Poland. Within six weeks of Alsberg's letter to Frankfurter, President Wilson appointed Henry Morgenthau to lead such a mission. Alsberg's letter did not necessarily set these events in motion. The condition of Polish Jews was well known in America. However, the idea for the mission likely came during a meeting in June with Frankfurter in Paris, after he received Alsberg's letter; perhaps the timing was not so coincidental.[59]

A trip outside Warsaw provided Alsberg with lasting impressions of further horror. Alsberg, Bogen, and a new JDC representative, Jacob Billikopf, wearing protective army uniforms provided by Lewis Strauss, traveled to Krakow, Lublin, and Lemberg, visiting small villages in the countryside along the way. (In an infrequent humorous aside, Bogen wrote to Strauss about Alsberg's affection for the uniform. Tall and strikingly handsome, with the family trait of full eyebrows, penetrating eyes, and a cleft chin, Alsberg cut an imposing figure in the official attire.)

The weather had warmed, and the first post-war crops tried to break through soil defiled by combat and ruined by neglect. Despite new vegetation promising to give life to the struggling nation, sadness imbued the trip. These were not picturesque excursions, but rather, *incursions* into dangerous territories. Bogen was concerned that their very presence would endanger the Jewish people they encountered on their journey. Of Alsberg and Billikopf, Bogen wrote: "They were desolated, seeing and hearing what I had heard and seen these many weeks."[60] Previously, of course, Alsberg's knowledge of areas outside Warsaw was limited to accounts gathered from others. When Bogen returned to Warsaw, Alsberg and Billikopf continued on to the eastern front city of Vilna (now Vilnius), recently captured from the Red Army by Polish forces and the scene of a recent pogrom.

Instructed to limit their activities to relief needs, the two were not there, officially, to investigate the April massacre and attacks. In fact, they were enjoined *not* to do that because it might spark "further suffering and trouble upon the Jewish population." Yet the Jewish residents of these towns saw the two uniformed Americans as their only source of help. Despite their efforts to "avoid suspicion that they were investigating the Vilna outrages, Mr. Alsberg and Mr. Billikopf could not in the last analysis shut their eyes and ears to the unsolicited information about the pogroms which poured in on them during their short stay in Vilna."

Their twelve-page report filed with the JDC included photographs detailing some of the horrors: the tortured body of an elderly man kidnapped to do forced labor, and whipped to death when he could dig no longer; the bodies of boys and men seized by soldiers and a town mob, marched to the cemetery, and shot; two children, starving and homeless found by Billikopf living on the street, orphaned by the pogroms.[61]

Back in Warsaw, Alsberg and Billikopf met with the American Ambassador to Poland, Hugh Gibson, but he was reputedly antagonistic toward the Jews.[62] All the while, Prague remained on Alsberg's mind. His concerns about the refugees did not abate, and judging from the mood of his letters, he practically wrung his hands with worry. In mid–June, Alsberg was relieved when a telegram arrived authorizing a brief return to Prague to assist Galician refugees. After a short time there, Alsberg was back in Paris by the time of the summer solstice.

Witness to a Treaty

In the City of Light, where the late June sun stretched the daylight hours to nearly 10:00 p.m., Alsberg, relieved to be away from the disorder and despair of the east, mixed socialization and work during this short time back in civilization. He animatedly recounted his experiences and offered his opinions to Lewis Strauss, Felix Frankfurter, and others. "Henry Alsberg blew in from Eastern Europe with shuddering tales of turmoil and starvation," said Ella Winter, Frankfurter's secretary and future wife of muckraker Lincoln Steffens.[63]

While minority rights for Jews and other groups were still being hammered out in preparation for the signing of the Peace Treaty, Alsberg and Billikopf reported on their trip to Vilna and other Polish cities to the Peace Conference's American Jewish Congress Delegation. Cyrus Adler, also in Paris, invited Alsberg on a two-day trip to view World War I battle sites in the Argonne Forest. They were accompanied by "the fighting Rabbi," Captain Elkan Voorsanger, who in 1917 left his American congregation and joined the American Expeditionary Forces, rising quickly through the ranks from private to captain. The group visited the deep forest, its dugout foxholes, and the many small cemeteries that held the war dead. They had to be cautious around unexploded bombs.[64] Alsberg returned to Paris before the end of the peace talks. On June 28, 1919, he witnessed the signing of the Treaty of Versailles. The war was officially over.

Morgenthau's Unofficial Advisor

Alsberg spent the summer of 1919 traveling Europe in service to both the JDC and journalism. Were a film depicting his travels to be made, animated trains would crisscross a map of the continent with stops in Paris, Vienna, Belgrade, and other cities. One place he had no desire to return to was Poland. In fact, he turned down an invitation to join the prestigious "Morgenthau Mission" sent to investigate the conditions of Jews in Poland.

He did, however, spend two days with the mission as an unofficial advisor. The diplomatic train carrying Henry Morgenthau, American Brigadier-General

Edgar Jadwin, and the other members of the mission left Paris after the treaty signing and headed for Warsaw. Alsberg traveled with them until Vienna. General Jadwin, in particular, sought out Alsberg for his analysis of the situation in Poland. Bogen, who was also on the train on his way to Warsaw, wrote that Alsberg "made quite an impression on the general."[65]

But the commission did not make a good impression on Alsberg. "I thank God every minute of my fortunate young life that I didn't fall for that Morgenthau job," Alsberg wrote to Strauss. "I had two days of him, and that was quite sufficient. He wanted me to go along awfully, and so did old General Jadwin. But nothing could have induced me to go, and spend two months keeping Morgenthau out of the Polish clutches. If I had more than one life I should be willing to devote one of said lives to the Jews. As it is they have had a number of perfectly good and irretrievable months."[66]

Alsberg needed a break from rescue work, which, as he continually tried to impress upon his JDC colleagues, and perhaps himself, was an avocation. He hopped off the train, both literally and figuratively, in Vienna, leaving Morgenthau and Bogen to continue on to Poland and focus on "Jewish matters," while he pulled away to concentrate on political reporting.

Throughout these travels, he kept in touch with Strauss, acting almost as his special emissary and providing him information throughout the summer on political issues in Europe. Alsberg and Strauss had mutual respect for one another and enjoyed an amiable, in the trenches together" friendship in those years. Their political paths couldn't be more disparate, however, with Alsberg about to enter radical anarchist circles and Strauss becoming an industrialist and, eventually, chair of the Atomic Energy Council and staunch advocate of building a hydrogen bomb. Their correspondence continued through the 1920s (there is no record of their friendship after 1927) and evolved to include not only JDC business, but politics, gossip, and, from Alsberg, playfulness.

Strauss had to chuckle at Alsberg's puns and mischievous digressions. ("Am going to Buda-Pesth tomorrow. I shall be awfully Hungary there, so they tell me." And, "give my love to Felix [Frankfurter] ... you must know that to have a name like Frankfurter ... would be a really dangerous thing in this neck of the woods just now. I swear the people would eat you up just because your name sounded edible.")

In a long aside, Alsberg also jested about how the Bolshevik government would treat him once he arrived in Hungary: "They strip you from head to foot, pry out the fillings of your teeth and the wax out of your ears, trying to find some reactionary documents. Then they put you in a cattle car, chain you to the floor and so you proceed in extreme discomfort, with all the wild Bolsheviks of the neighborhood taking pot shots at you ... in Buda, you are greeted at the station by a company of Red Guards and taken to the Revolutionary tribunal and searched once more. Then you have to prove that you believe in revolution ... and that you love sauer-kraut. For sauer-kraut is all they give you to eat, when they give you that. They feed it to you, however, quite plentifully, with a pitch-fork. I forgot to tell you that they accommodate visiting reactionary journalists in what was formerly the livery stable."[67]

Strauss, more serious and formal, did share some of his own secrets, including the job offer of business manager for the League of Nations. "Can you imagine me trying to business manage a bunch of prima donnas? Beeey-outiful mess I'd make of it."[68]

Journalistic Writings: Politics to Human Rights

Alsberg, free from JDC duties for a while, planned to wander the continent and beyond. He told Strauss he was off to Yugoslavia, then Constantinople, and then either to Bucharest, Odessa, or Palestine. "My plans are wide and elastic."[69] He met up with another relief worker and JDC leader, twenty-five-year-old Lieutenant James Becker. The two planned a sightseeing trip to Mediterranean coast, but this was not to be.

Through the fall of 1919, Alsberg reported on political happenings in Hungary, Yugoslavia, Bulgaria, Romania, and the Balkans. He remained particularly attentive to the overt prejudice between groups as well as to political machinations and their effects on the downtrodden. From Bucharest, his characteristic grim humor emerged in a *Nation* commentary about press censorship. "Formerly an offending column of material was simply wiped out by the censor. Now the offending editor is frequently wiped out by the police."[70]

Alsberg's writings often veered from politics into human rights. He wrote about Jewish inhabitants and their struggles in these articles, but he felt just as strongly about other subjugated minority populations and those who suffered due to ethnic conflicts. The Great War and its aftermath had stirred his pacifist tendencies. A few years later, his sympathies for all oppressed peoples were highlighted in an article about *The Dybbuk*, the mystical melodrama he translated, when he wrote "that what really counts is the universal brotherhood of all right-thinking and doing persons."[71]

Journeying from Serbia to Bulgaria, he struggled to understand how people on either side of the border, despite their similar clothes and language and landscape, were "brought up to hate each other unto death." Veering once more into themes of human rights and equality—or the lack thereof—he noted the poor peasant who "inherited the wrong dialect from his improvident parents...."

There are right nationalities and wrong nationalities. And the man whose nationality chose wrongly now has to suffer."

It didn't take long for Alsberg to move away from his enthusiasm for the Hungarian revolution, where along with granting new economic rights to the proletariat, the government also threatened the death penalty for looting and similar offenses. The pacifist in Alsberg denounced violence of any sort. Reporting from the Balkans, he said: "Since my stay in Europe I have become firmly of the opinion that force and violence, exercised ostensibly in whatsoever cause, cannot ever beget justice and peace and good will. But violence begets violence, and killing, even in a so-called righteous war, begets most hideous murder. This applies to the class war as well, and let my friends who are lovers of this last sort of warfare never forget that either."[72] Perhaps his hopes for a less corrupt Bolshevik system led to his new obsession: getting into the Ukraine and then Russia proper. The political intrigue of the Bolshevik revolution, the desperate and barbarous conditions—it's where any anarchist-leaning, humanitarian journalist worth his salt would head.

Late September 1919, just after his thirty-eighth birthday, found Alsberg writing *Nation* dispatches from the western Ukrainian city of Kamenets-Podolski. He arrived amid a bloody tug of war as the Bolsheviks, the White Army, and the Ukrainian Independence movement battled for control.[73]

Confusion reigned in late 1919. Alsberg made what had to be a perilous journey to Odessa before heading north to Kiev. Although it seems strange that he traveled in an armored train car with Allied military officers—considering that at least one British intelligence agent questioned his allegiance earlier that year—it was the safest way for him to make his way from Odessa to Kiev in December 1919.

But it wasn't *that* safe. Bandits derailed and looted trains on every route through southern Russia, requiring Alsberg and his traveling companions to wield guns "in expectation of a hold-up." In Kiev, Alsberg roomed with an American military attaché, near enough to the fighting to feel the booming cannon fire rattle his chest. Gunshots and explosions competed with the frigid weather to make life nearly unbearable. "In addition to the general misery there is the special misery produced by the almost absolute lack of fuel. In Kiev, during my stay, we had colder weather than any we ever have in New York. Yet nobody had any wood to heat with, not to mention coal. The only place one could exist in was one's bed."[74]

And yet he ventured out—lack of sleep, frozen toes, and all. Reporting on armies battling though the area—Bolsheviks, various anti–Bolshevik forces, and an anarchist army—Alsberg told of atrocities committed by both Red and White armies: the Bolsheviks who made a pyramid of 250 dead people in a courtyard in Kiev, the White Army's occupation and pogroms that left thousands of Jewish residents dead. He reported the terror of the Cossacks, especially against the Jews, to be greater than the Bolsheviks. His *Nation* article told of a young Jewish doctor who came to him in a state of terror, begging him to take her out of the city. He decried the Allied nations' hostility toward the Bolsheviks and its blockades of medical and humanitarian aid. Alsberg reserved some of his outrage for the American State Department, which he accused of doing nothing to help U.S. citizens living in Russia (of Russian birth) escape the war zone. "Our *Bolshephobia* drives us to condemn thousands to ruin and even death, and to forget our holiest traditions."[75]

Alsberg sent Strauss reports about the pogroms in Kiev and rumors of other massacres. In a fairly elaborate communiqué in December, Alsberg criticized the JDC for its initial inaction in southern Russia. He believed that thousands of Jews could have been saved from death by disease and starvation had help been sent earlier. He wrote to Strauss: "I can't understand the JDC at all. Denikin [leader of the White Volunteer Army] has been occupying one part of this territory and Petlura another part for months. During all this time the pogrom victims could have been aided and tided over. But it seems not a soul was sent from America to Southern Russia even to investigate. Now, when it is too late, and the Bolsheviks have come in, they want to do something. God Almighty, how tired they get me."[76]

The situation of the Jews in southern Russia, he wrote to Strauss, "beats anything for misery I've seen anywhere. And you know I have seen about every kind of misery to be seen in Europe and Eastern Asia." To another JDC associate, Harriet Lowenstein, he wrote: "I have seen the situation in Southern Russia from every side and I assure you that our people are suffering in a terrible way."

By New Year's Eve, Alsberg was in Bucharest. When he sat in his hotel to write his New Year's greetings, the exhaustion he felt from his year in Europe— beginning with the cold winter in January 1919 in London and ending in even colder Bucharest—emanated from the paper. He planned to leave for America in two months, telling Strauss, "When I finally get home I shall take a rest from fleas, lice, bedbugs, vermin, unheated houses and trains, human misery, and unhappiness." To Lowenstein he added that despite his desire and original plans, "I don't think I shall get to Palestine this time. I am too tired. America for the present looks pretty good to me."[77]

Russia Beckons

However good America might have looked, that's not where Alsberg headed. Despite his distaste for the cold, he gave himself the "gift" of an Eastern

European winter. Soviet Russia provided endless opportunities for foreign correspondents. Getting in was challenging, and it would take another few months for Alsberg to be successful. As the Bolshevik revolution began transforming political, social, and economic conditions, Alsberg, a believer in the utopia promised by a classless society, wanted to witness and write about those ideals made manifest.

In January 1920, he traveled north from Bucharest, with the intent of eventually going to Kiev and then Moscow. A stop in the town of Ataki in Romania, site of his punishing carriage ride, and then at Mohilev to deliver JDC funds to pogrom survivors, was a little more exciting than he'd expected, and included that trip across the icy, dangerous Dniester River under gunfire-lit skies. But his attempts to get further than Mohilev were unsuccessful. He'd been "circling around the idea of getting into Soviet Russia for a long time, like a hound dog about the heels of a dangerous tramp," he wrote.[78] "Then I went up further north to Poland, and I could not get a visa to go in there [Russia]. And then I went to Latvia and stayed there 6 weeks trying to get a visa to get in."[79]

While "circling like a hound dog," Alsberg continued his reporting through the bleak and icy winter, eventually moving north to the Estonian city of Revel, on the Baltic Sea across from Helsinki. Soon enough, however, his attention turned to a new political and military upheaval. Alsberg headed south, to his father's homeland.

The Ruhr Revolution

Just a few hours' west of his family origins in Germany lay the Ruhr Valley, an industrial center providing Germany with iron, steel, and coal. In March 1920, it was at the core of a short-lived workers' rebellion. Various left-wing and unionist factions (including 300,000 miners) declared a general strike and formed a "red army." The leftists captured some cities, but confronted both the regular German army and the Freikorps, the right-wing nationalist paramilitary. A truce was called, but soon broken.

Following the trajectory of the revolutionary wave as it popped up in short, staccato bursts across Europe, Alsberg arrived on the scene, attracted to radical stirrings. His intention may have been to cover the uprising as a journalist, but soon enough he was a participant, embroiled in the politics and even as a sort of diplomat to secure another peace agreement. He attended insurgent meetings, and then journeyed to Cologne, bringing with him two rebellion leaders to negotiate on behalf of the Reds with the occupying British commission.

It was an improbable scene. On arrival in Cologne, Alsberg and his companions, among them journalist William Ryall from the *Manchester Guardian*, visited the palace where the British Commissioner lived. A grand formal ball was under way, replete with ladies in evening gowns and men in dress uniforms drinking champagne and dancing the foxtrot. In the basement servants' hall, as music and laughter seeped in from upstairs rooms, Alsberg, Ryall, and the two Red leaders talked past midnight with the commissioner. Their appeals likely did not cause the new disarmament agreement that followed. In fact, the disarmament was preordained to doom. The German army and Freikorps battalions marched through the valley, the Freikorps especially brutal in quashing both the militants and the peaceful members of workmen's councils.[80]

Alsberg wrote about the failed rebellion for *New York Call's Sunday* magazine section.[81] He expressed particular ire against the German press, which, with the exception of a few leftist newspapers, "engaged in a conspiracy of lies and silence as to the real facts concerning the Ruhr revolution." He termed the article a "swan song" for the stillborn revolution.

His desire to see a living revolution was about to be realized in Russia.

CHAPTER 4

Tyranny by Prophets
May 1920–August 1921

[Henry Alsberg brought with him] the best that was in America—sincerity and easy joviality, directness and camaraderie.—Emma Goldman

The two men sprinted alongside the railroad tracks, desperate to catch up with the slow-moving military train heading out of the small Ukrainian village of Znamenka. Henry Alsberg—younger, taller, and more athletic—scrambled onto the car with less difficulty than his companion, Alexander Berkman. Earlier in the day, their own traveling party had inadvertently left them behind while the duo scoured the town for Alsberg's stolen money pouch. With no hotel and barely enough food for the peasants—let alone visitors—there were few worse places to be stranded. It would have been unthinkable to remain, penniless, in this war-weary town. They jumped aboard the military supply car with "the cost of a few scratches," and after convincing a Soviet Commissar to let them ride along, rejoined their companions a few hours later near Kiev.[1]

In August 1920, Alsberg had already been in Russia for three months. Now, traveling by train through the southern Ukraine, he was the only journalist accompanying an expedition to collect historic materials for the Museum of the Revolution. Emma Goldman and Alexander "Sasha" Berkman, the two anarchists famously deported from America to Russia in 1919, led the expedition. This venture would change the course of the next decade of Alsberg's life.

Alsberg's movement in through the 1920s was fourfold and rooted in both his idealism and his artistic urges. There was his work with the JDC in Europe and, to a lesser extent, back home in America; his launch into theatrical pursuits; and his journalistic endeavors. Perhaps it was inevitable that he'd also make room for political activism and that this activism would feed his writing—and vice versa.

His six weeks on the museum expedition with Emma Goldman and Sasha

Berkman heralded his entrance into the inner circle of these two societal out-casts. The story of Henry Alsberg's political activism links directly to his friend-ships with them. And if he was chasing after idealism, he couldn't do better than the larger-than-life Emma and the intellectually committed Sasha. His relationship with Goldman, twelve years older, strengthened into an almost mother-son bond. Alsberg often appeared boisterous and adventurous. But behind closed doors he was prone to periods of intense self-doubt. Throughout stretches of his adult life he would need at least one friend to help keep his internal conflicts and emotional demons at bay. During a long period Goldman became his confidante, offering him a soft shoulder to lean on.

A Look Back: Parallel Lives

In 1919, while Alsberg traveled in Europe writing about post-war politics and devoting his energies to his victimized coreligionists in Czechoslovakia and Poland, Emma Goldman and Alexander Berkman were serving federal prison sentences in America. Their anti-conscription and anti-war protests prompted their arrests in 1918 for conspiracy to violate the Draft Act. Up until this time, despite being hounded by police, government prosecutors, and the press, "Red" Emma Goldman steadfastly continued lecturing on women's rights, the Russian revolution, sexual liberation, freedom of speech, anarchism, and all manner of "radical" thought. As the country ramped up for war, the cli-mate became more dangerous for progressives, many of whom were jailed for offenses that ranged from distributing birth control information to not regis-tering for the draft. Shortly after their release from prison, Goldman and Berk-man were deported to Soviet Russia, part of the December 1919 expulsion of 249 undesirable "aliens" that garnered front-page headlines nationwide.

With the British Labour Delegation:
Meeting Emma and Sasha

After covering the failed Ruhr revolution in Germany, Alsberg traveled to Copenhagen, then ventured into the Ukraine again with a JDC delegation investigating conditions in the area.[2] During another attempt to obtain a visa into Russia, he met up with a left-wing British delegation on its way to Soviet Russia to make an "independent and impartial inquiry into conditions" there. He joined the delegation as a reporter and the group arrived in Petrograd in May 1920. He positioned himself to write not only for Jewish publications and the liberal *Nation*, but the leftist newspapers the *New York Call* and the *London Daily Herald*.

Some members of the delegation came predisposed in favor of the Bolsheviks, who spared little expense in treating the group to extravagant receptions and grand displays of life under the new order. The "Soviet authorities did not fail to make the most of propaganda possibilities," wrote one journalist.[3] In Petrograd, the delegation stayed at a nineteenth-century palace on the River Neva. The Soviets lavished their visitors with dinners served on fine china (spoils from the Tsarist royal family), colorful military reviews, and tours of model schools and factories.

Philosopher and political thinker Bertrand Russell, who accompanied the group as an independent observer, disliked the closely led tours and general surveillance. One day, slipping away from the Soviet chaperone, he brought Henry Alsberg to meet Emma Goldman and Alexander Berkman. The Soviets had provided Goldman and Berkman with lodging at the once (and future) luxurious Hotel

"Red Emma" Goldman, circa 1915–1919. During this period, she served time in prison for lecturing on birth control and protesting the Selective Service Act. Alsberg's friendship with her began in Russia in 1920, but he likely heard her speak during one of her many lecture tours through New York before she was deported from the U.S in 1919 (Library of Congress, Prints & Photographs Division).

Astoria, appropriated by the Communist Party for official housing.

For Alsberg, who had read about the two idealistic anarchists and likely attended their lectures and rallies in New York, it was akin to meeting celebrities. Carrying provisions that Goldman hadn't been able to secure herself, he was a welcome guest. Goldman was homesick for America and happy to have Western visitors; she was equally happy to cook for them, using the additional food to prepare a celebratory luncheon. Years later, Goldman wrote of that meeting in her autobiography: "We cherished every moment with our visitors and I liked Henry Alsberg in particular. He brought with him a whiff of the best that was in America—sincerity and easy joviality, directness and *camaraderie*."[4]

Russell, Goldman, and Berkman already suspected the "Bolshevik betrayal of the revolution."[5] Alsberg believed—naively, thought Goldman—that Soviet leaders would "relax the reign of repression" once civil war and invasions ceased and blockades were lifted. Nonetheless, the luncheon provided a respite for all four of them; they separated on friendly terms, with hopes to meet soon.

Alsberg and the British delegation traveled by train 250 miles through the countryside to the Volga River. The Soviets provided well-appointed sleeper cars—a far cry from the unheated freight cars and crowded, dirty passenger cars on which Alsberg had previously ridden. Journalist Marguerite Harrison described "spotless linen, and electric lights, a dining car where we had three good means a day, service and appointments being very nearly up to peace time standards."[6] At the riverfront, after a meal of smoked sausage, caviar, and radishes in sour cream, the group boarded a similarly luxurious steamer to sail down the Volga River.

Not all of the travelers were impressed. Bertrand Russell and Marguerite Harrison managed to leave the controlled tours to go off on their own. Alsberg, too, separated from the group, interviewing peasants and factory workers as he prepared a series on Russia for *The Nation*. All three noticed the disparity between their opulent travel conditions and the miserable circumstances of the general population.

International Carnival of Revolution

Alsberg returned to Moscow and met the cast of characters preparing for the Communist International Congress sponsored by the Soviet government. Alsberg roomed in the same hotel as the delegates, interviewing and dining with English shop stewards, Irish rebels, German sailors, "a vivacious black-eyed phalanx of delegates" from Italy, as well as representatives from Korea, Argentina, Sweden, Switzerland, and France. It was, at that moment, the biggest "show on earth." The vibrant and intriguing personalities, each bringing political mystique from all parts of the world, made for an invigorating mood. Adding to the pageantry was the hotel's ever-changing banners in different languages welcoming delegates: One day it was "Long live the Revolution; we started it; let us finish it together," aimed at the British; the next it was changed to "Il Trionfo della Dittatura del Proletariato" (the triumph of the dictatorship of the proletariat). Alsberg felt himself in a carnival atmosphere, writing, "Admission free, if you have your coupon from the Third Internationale!"[7]

Although Alsberg supported the revolution, his belief in utopian change was beginning to falter just a bit. If he wore his support as a coat of armor, there were, if not chinks, a few dents.

"I find my judgment quite fluid," he wrote, "varying from day to day with everything I see and hear." His indecision played out on the pages of *The Nation* as his writing veered from objectivity to its partisan opposite. On the one hand, he didn't trust the optimistic statistics readily provided by every commissar and government department. Conversely, he debated the utility of truthfully reporting the repression and censorship while Russia still reeled under the stress of war:

> Nobody any longer believes the lies that are told about Russia. When a man like [the British Reverend F.W.] North [who made headlines with his horror stories about Russia] goes back to London and states that the trolley-cars are not running, when as a matter of fact they are running day and night, such an obvious falsehood can be nailed easily enough by eye-witnesses. But when the Soviet Republic's well-wishers ladle out sweet syrup over the very human and very fallible revolutionary institutions, then, of course, the public begins to get suspicious.[8]

Inefficient transportation, Western blockades, and food scarcity nearly immobilized Russia's industries. It was a vicious circle: Farmers could not provide food because they could not obtain plows and shoes; factory workers could not provide the needed articles because they did not have enough to eat. Alsberg wondered in a *Nation* article how much was due to six years of war and the blockade, and how much to "the new system."

Hospitals, he wrote, had one thermometer for every hundred patients. Press repression and the Western blockades isolated engineers, researchers, academics, artists, and writers from all outside intellectual life. One scientist asked Alsberg for help getting up-to-date scientific journals. Russia existed "in the same stage of industrial development as the United States during the civil war," he wrote.[9]

Noting that private speculation still survived, Alsberg believed it necessary to temporarily encourage those middle-men in order to resuscitate the economy. In other words, capitalism, for a time, might be necessary or the "socialistic body will suffer materially and morally."[10] However, wanting to believe in the revolution, he continued to consider both sides through the summer months, still leaning toward the idea that war and barriers imposed by the Unites States, Britain, and other countries prevented the Soviet Russia from reaching its utopian vision more quickly. At one point he told *Nation* readers that the greater part of "the socialist program has been ... sketched in," adding, "a true democracy of material condition, even if it is one of poverty, has been enforced. There are no great differences in dress or standards of living. Everybody is always more or less shabby; everybody always more or less hungry." He praised the awakening of a cultural life, "theatres, music, education, and so forth. I have seen towns where they had put in electric light, where they had moving picture theatre, reading rooms, a library, adult schools." Additionally, he saw evidence that Jews were safer under the Bolshevik government.

Nonetheless, his journalistic creed of objectivity and truth pulled at him. "I feel very strongly that there should be a few sources from which truth-telling may always be expected and relied upon. Let there be a few voices crying in the wilderness. Let there be a few men willing to be cursed by friend and foe alike in the service of the goddess of candor,"[11] he wrote.

That he couldn't decipher this truth disturbed him.

By the end of July 1920 he moved half a step closer to Emma Goldman's camp, conceding, "Russia has not now a democratic form of government in any sense of the word" and had evolved into a dictatorship of the central party. Yet he still bought the party line about the "necessity of extreme measures in order to save the revolution" and compared Russia to the U.S. government during World War I, when it found "habeas corpus, free speech and such-like refinements ... superfluous."[12]

Meeting Kropotkin

Perhaps it was his search for the truth that brought him to the home of Peter Kropotkin. The foremost living anarchist, Kropotkin envisioned a free federation of communities in which each member would be rewarded according to need. Radicals of all stripes revered Kropotkin; even Lenin paid him a respectful visit. And while most food was rationed and agricultural provisions were requisitioned by the state for redistribution, Kropotkin received an extra food allowance and was famously allowed to keep his cow.

Alsberg and a member of the British Labour Delegation visited the elderly, ailing Kropotkin at his home outside Moscow. They accompanied him to a local council meeting as well. This short time with Kropotkin and his friendship with Goldman and Berkman sparked Alsberg's eventual evolution to his self-identity as a "philosophical anarchist."

Alsberg was coming to see that his own beliefs, centered on freedom and liberty, equality and justice, meshed with those of his anarchist friends. Kropotkin dreamed of a future "harmony in human relations which will be established freely when humanity ceases to be divided into two classes, of which one is sacrificed for the benefit of the other, the harmony which will emerge spontaneously from the unity of interests when all men belong to one and the same family, when each works for the good of all and all for the good of each .…"[13] Capitalism and bourgeois values would be eliminated in this society.

Alsberg's personal life played into his evolving political feelings. Anarchists (and, later, theater folks) could accept his sexual orientation; with some of them, at least, he could live more outwardly. If his inner psyche suffered from intolerance toward Jews and other minorities, it had to also ache, perhaps even more, to live in secret as a member of another oppressed and persecuted people. Even worse, there was no advocating against this oppression; as a homosexual, he was a member of a group that, for the most part, suffered individually and quietly.

The Museum Expedition

Emma Goldman and Sasha Berkman were desperate for work, but morally constrained against working for the repressive Soviet government. Their opportunity for what they considered ethical, nonpolitical work finally came with the offer to travel by train across the southern Russian countryside to gather material for the Petrograd Museum of the Revolution.

Their red-painted car, emblazoned with "Extraordinary Commission of the Museum of the Revolution," was attached to a train caravan that arrived in Moscow in July. Alsberg paid a visit to the Moscow train station, along with other journalists clamoring to join the expedition. Having already traversed some of the areas they'd be exploring and having witnessed the hunger, bloodshed, and abject poverty, it's surprising that he wanted to return. Luckily for him, Goldman liked him best, impressed by his open personality and intelligence on their first meeting a few months back. His experience also made him their best choice for this thousand-mile adventure.

Alsberg still needed permission from Soviet authorities. While Berkman spent days in Moscow collecting provisions for the trip, and Goldman hosted visiting reporters and friends, Alsberg scrambled through bureaucratic layers to gather authorizations. He finally secured written permission from a high-ranking Soviet official, as well as from the Foreign Office's Cheka (secret police). However, when Alsberg arrived at the Moscow station on the day the train was set to leave, a question arose as to whether or not he also needed to procure a special visa from the *local* Moscow Cheka. Goldman wrote in her memoir: "The Foreign Office 'guaranteed' that he would not be molested if he went on the expedition. Alsberg hesitated but we urged him to take a chance without the *proposk* of the Moscow Cheka. His American passport and the fact that he represented two pro–Soviet newspapers should save him from serious difficulties."

Alsberg was brash enough that he wouldn't let the issue of proper credentials keep him from the trip. He'd been filing his *Nation* series of news articles on Russia since March; the invitation to join the expedition was a journalistic coup. He'd also have the opportunity to investigate the condition of Jewish populations and report to the JDC. Thus, on July 15, 1920, Henry Alsberg became the seventh member of Emma Goldman's historical Museum Expedition.

They headed south from Moscow in a car fitted with a kitchen, office, dining area, and sleeping compartments. Their relative comfort embarrassed the group as they traveled through towns where crowds swarmed the train, desperate to escape their miserable lives. "Soldiers and workers, peasants, women and children," Berkman wrote, all tried to climb aboard, a "human, surging sea moved by the one passion of securing a foothold on the already moving train."[14] For families sleeping on top of the train, a bridge or trestle could sweep them to their deaths at night. The expedition team was torn, wanting to help these forlorn riders. But the fear of contracting typhus, rampant in the area, deterred them. They yielded their platform to women and children while other "rag-covered, bundle-loaded, exhausted people" managed to cling to other parts of the train.[15]

During the long hours moving south through the July heat Alsberg undoubtedly told his companions of his experiences in these areas just months before. Marauding bandits had already attacked him. Similar crowds of hungry, ragged peasants had swarmed him in railway stations and markets looking for food and money. He also knew every unfortunate aspect of the situation involving the Jewish population, which was quite large where they were traveling. Alsberg understood better than anyone aboard that they were heading into a danger zone.

Their first stop at Kharkov—capital of the Soviet Ukraine—offered a bit of a reprieve from the poverty and starving masses. A city of about half a million people, it was home to universities, cathedrals, and industries ranging from vodka distilling to locomotive manufacturing. They found a well-fed, if not well-dressed population. (A clothing scarcity led to some outlandish outfits, such as evening gowns and wooden shoes.[16])

The oppressive temperatures forced the group out of the sweltering train car parked at the depot and into the city for accommodations. Alsberg used his journalist's credentials to secure a room, which he shared with Berkman. Goldman and Berkman spent days meeting with Soviet officials, collecting documents about the revolution for the museum, and paying secret visits to anarchist friends and beleaguered intelligentsia in hiding. (The Communist State did not allow for anarchist or other counterrevolutionary allegiances.) Alsberg, as observer, accompanied them, absorbing the swirling passions of these insurgents.

While in Kharkov, the group persuaded a Soviet prison superintendent to let them tour a forced labor camp and a prison. The conditions they found could only be described as medieval. No doubt that Alsberg and Berkman talked late into the night in their shared room about these experiences. Considering his later work to save political prisoners, it seems strange that these prison visits did not totally erode Alsberg's support for the Soviets. Alsberg's own disenchantment slowed to a low simmer on the back burner.

In a *Nation* article from this period, Alsberg again blamed the lack of food and medicine on Western blockades, the long years of war, and the continuing battles between the Red Army and its enemies. He praised Soviets for their vaccination programs, which reduced cholera and smallpox outbreaks. He applauded their education system, which included free universal education from primary school to university, with provisions for adult education at university and technical schools as well. Alsberg saved his greatest acclamation for the arts programs. His description foreshadowed the Federal Arts projects that America would institute fifteen years hence with Roosevelt's New Deal Works Progress Administration, where Alsberg would make his greatest mark on American life and culture:

> You have only to see the audiences at places of public amusement to recognize that the proletariat has the orchestra stalls now. Moreover, and this is quite characteristic of the democracy prevailing in all departments of the Government, the Proletarian Culture Commissariat and that of Education are actually working to make the people take part in all these art enterprises, in workmen's and peasants' theaters, in choruses and orchestras and brass bands, in the painting of pictures and the making of literature. The participants in the drama not only act but also conduct the theater and do the stage carpentering and scene-painting and shifting themselves.[17]

As true as some of his points might have been, he was not yet ready to address the other facts that revealed the harsh dictatorship—a dictatorship that he admitted to but called "temporary."[18] Alsberg and Goldman discussed these matters frequently and sometimes heatedly.

They headed south for the next stop at Poltava. Stately chestnut trees shaded Alsberg on his walks to government offices to interview officials. Goldman went along as his interpreter. Later, the two found a taboo "radical intelligentsia" community. Included in this group was a woman who ran a children's welfare organization. There, Alsberg argued, "No matter what might be said against the Bolsheviki, they could not be charged with neglecting the children." He hadn't left his feelings for his coreligionists behind, and as a matter of fact, the idea that the Bolsheviks were less cruel to the Jews than were the Tsarists, or the White armies, may have swayed him toward supporting the Reds.

Anguish for the JDC

The expedition headed west through early August, stopping in a few towns along the way. In one, Alsberg and Berkman stole off in the night to secretly meet with the local Jewish contingent, whose members told Alsberg about a recent pogrom. Thus, while Goldman and Berkman gathered documents for the museum of the revolution throughout the trip, Alsberg collected evidence of pogroms for the JDC.

It's uncertain at that point whether Alsberg knew that just days before the expedition left Moscow, two of his American JDC co-workers met the same fate as many of those they were trying to save. On July 11, newspapers reported the murders of Professor Israel Friedlaender and Rabbi Bernard Cantor in the Ukraine. Less than a week prior, they had departed Kamenets-Podolski in the early morning. Their automobile was ambushed and they were dead by noon, killed by Bolshevik soldiers who mistook them for Polish army officers.[19]

That news could only have been met with worried anguish at the apartment on West 95th Street that Bertha Alsberg shared with her daughter, Elsa, and in the homes of Carl and Julius. Henry's mother and siblings all knew that Henry, intent on covering political and military uprisings, wandered across dangerous terrain, looking for action. Moreover, his constant travel impeded the efforts of both his JDC compatriots and his family to track him. *Nation* datelines and postmarks from letters forwarded by Lewis Strauss showed visits to Latvia, Estonia, Moscow, and, of course, the Ukraine. As Strauss told Bertha, Henry's address had been indefinite since he'd left Paris, and although he regularly and dutifully wrote to his mother, letters sometimes ran aground, taking months to reach their destination.

Finally, ten days after the news reports of the murdered JDC workers, a cable arrived informing Bertha that her son was safe. Strauss sent a separate, personal note to Carl the next day, reporting that Henry was "in fine health and spirits."[20]

And Then There Was Fastov

After Znamenka, where Alsberg's wallet was stolen and he and Berkman had to scramble to catch another train out of town, the expedition landed in the town of Fastov. By the time the group arrived in mid–August, almost a year had passed since a wave of Cossack-led pogroms had scourged the Jewish population. The horrors were still blatantly evident. The very presence of Alsberg and the other men traveling with Goldman panicked the women of the town. For in addition to bringing death and destruction, the Cossacks raped the female inhabitants, young girls included. Although Alsberg had seen tragedy close up before, Fastov particularly disturbed him. Being branded as a perpetrator, even momentarily, stunned him. But soon, the residents began to see Alsberg as a messenger from heaven and pleaded with him to let the world know the depths of misery inflicted on them. "They threw themselves upon him with avidity and would not let go," wrote Emma Goldman.[21] His deep feelings, if not evident before to his fellow travelers, were apparent now, his despair coloring his mood.

Emma Goldman wrote later that she'd never seen Alsberg "so affected as in Fastov. Not that he did not feel deeply in a universal sense. Henry was a bundle of emotions, though his male pride would have stoutly denied such an implication from a mere woman. Nevertheless it was true that his kind heart ached more when Jews were being persecuted…."[22] Before moving on to their next destination, the heartsick Alsberg dutifully interviewed witnesses. He then sent Strauss and *The Nation* the grisly details of yet another town's inhabitants suffering as various conquering armies stormed through.[23]

End of the Line: Kiev

Poor track conditions and "masses of desperate human beings" congesting railway stations slowed their travel so that the seventy-kilometer trip from Fastov to Kiev took an improbable six days. There, they expected to find treasure troves of documents for their museum. When local officials refused to grant Goldman and Berkman access, they resorted to their wild card, their "American sesame": Henry Alsberg. Apparently, officials would be impressed, even bamboozled a bit, by his prominence as "a native American son" and a "full-fledged correspondent." Goldman and Berkman did not have to work hard to convince Alsberg.

> Henry grinned assent. With a mischievous twinkle in his fine eyes he declared that as his interpreter, I had already induced people to say more than he had intended to ask them and that I had succeeded in making them think they would be serving posterity by helping the Museum of the Revolution. Between the two of us he was sure we should succeed in inducing the Ukrainians to co-operate with our mission. Henry's press card worked like a charm.[24]

They were given unparalleled access to high-ranking officials, food rations, and housing. (Their quarters weren't especially sumptuous; Alsberg and Berkman shared floor space with eight musicians for at least part of their time in Kiev.) On a visit to the Soviet Clinic, where many Fastov victims had been moved, Alsberg again confronted the consequences of the pogrom, meeting with women and girls who had been raped and children who had witnessed the murder of their parents.

The threesome of Alsberg, Goldman, and Berkman spent their last day in Kiev as tourists, with a walk along the riverfront and a visit to the Monastery of the Caves, with its eerie underground labyrinths. For Alsberg, it was a tranquil rest before the tempest that was the Soviet secret police descended on him.

Alsberg's Arrest

The Cheka was dreaded in every town, city, and village they'd traveled through, and for good reason. Without trial, without hearing, without evidence, the secret police would spirit people away for any suspected infraction, ranging from supposed counterrevolutionary activity to unauthorized food trading. Those arrested would be shot or, sometimes worse, left to die in an inhumane prison.

With official sanction from Soviet authorities in Moscow, the expedition group felt relatively safe from Cheka clutches. This all changed on the last day of August, after they left Kiev and began their swing south toward Odessa. Actually, only *Alsberg's* luck ran out.

Arriving in the railroad junction town of Zhmerinka, the group was unaware that Moscow Cheka officers had contacted local authorities, ordering them to arrest Alsberg and bring him back under armed guard to Moscow. Whatever permissions he'd secured at the beginning of the trip suddenly became worthless.

"All of our protests failed to save Henry," wrote Goldman. "We proposed that Sasha or I accompany him to Moscow. But Henry would not hear of it." He joked with his characteristic equanimity that his limited Russian vocabulary, along with a few impolite Russian expressions, could keep his captor entertained during the trip to Moscow. He assured his friends that "he had no fear and we need not be anxious about him.... Henry had endeared himself to us by his fine spirit, joviality, and ready wit. It was with a heavy heart that we saw him leave, led away by the chekists."[25] Goldman and Berkman did send an emergency plea to Lenin when they reached Odessa. "Dear Comrade, we are confident that the deplorable incident is due to some misunderstanding," they began in their four-page telegram. "We know Mr. Alsberg as a most worthy person, thoroughly reliable and fully in sympathy with the Russian Revolution."[26] Lenin never responded.

While his friends wrung their hands with worry, Alsberg worked his charm on his police escort. But confusion reigned on the long, circuitous trip back to the capital. Alsberg described in his diary an early morning stop at a station near the western border:

> Scene: Station of Winnitza in the western Ukraine. Time: End of August, 1920, six o'clock in the morning. I arrived at the station with my guide, protector, and guard, a revolutionary Lettish sailor from Kronstadt, who had been engaged in fighting bandits in southern Ukraine. At the station there is a terrible tumult and confusion. Men, mostly sailors, together with a few Red Guards, are running up and down the platform terribly excited, girding on their revolvers, getting together rifles. I ask a sailor to whom my guard introduces me, a sailor who could speak English, what was the trouble.
>
> "Why, [damn] it, a few days ago we sent a couple of our boys down to a village near here to collect the quota of grain due, and those [goddamn sons of bitches] bashed the heads of our men in."
>
> "And what are you going to do now?"
>
> "What? Why we're going down there and giving ____ what for. We'll burn down their village and shoot up the menfolks."[27]

The trip to Moscow took days, with the nonexistent train schedule making for an unpredictable journey. Alsberg made the most of it, introducing his guard to the joys of alcohol. Jerre Mangione later described the incident as it was told to him: "As the drinking became heavier, Alsberg found himself obliged to play the role of nursemaid, a role that became more pronounced when the agent, on the eve of their arrival in Moscow, collapsed with pneumonia." Alsberg brought the semi-conscious officer to the police station. "Here is the man you sent out to find me," he said.[28] Alsberg spent several weeks in jail, he testified years later.[29]

Goldman's version of the story, although secondhand, relates that he was held for a short time by the Soviet foreign office, and thankfully not in a Cheka prison, where he would have languished longer. Before leaving Russia, he met up with American friend Louise Bryant and entrusted her with the money Goldman and Berkman had given him when he was arrested (probably for bribery purposes and undoubtedly used to help procure food and the liquor for his guard), along with a note that he'd try to return by the spring.

Although their time together was cut short, the museum expedition cemented Alsberg's relationship with Goldman and Berkman, heralding long and close friendships. Berkman wrote of Alsberg as a loyal traveling companion, "whose cheerful spirit and ready helpfulness contributed so much toward

UNITED STATES PASSPORT BUREAU AT PARIS, FRANCE

Sworn to before me this _____ day of _____
(Month and year.)

[SEAL.]

_____
(Name.)

Vice-Consul of the United States of America.

WH

Identifying documents submitted as follows :　Records of this Bureau show that Dept.ppt.
No. 51643, issued Dec.1918,to Henry Garfield Alsberg, was sent to
the States Dept. on October 9,1920.(remained here until expiratio
　　　Ppt. No. 197, issued Feb. 11, 1920, by the U.S. Legation
at Warsaw, Poland, to Henry G. Alsberg, for countries within
requested.
　　　Special Passport No. 1500, issued Feb. 28th,1919, by the
American Embassy at Paris, France to Henry Garfield Alsberg.
Letter of reccomandation from Mr. Everett Somers,3, rue d'Anjou, Paris,
References in the United States/stating applicant is a journalist work
Abraham I. Elkus, Court of Appeals, N.Y. City.
Louis Strauss, 52 Williams St. N.Y. City.

Applicant exhibited letters and documents
concerning reasons for travel in within
requested countries.

Applicant states that he made a
Dept. ppt. application at the U.S.
legation at Warsaw on Feb.11,1920, at
the time of issuance of above Emer.ppt.
No. 197.

Alsberg submitted this application (November 1920) to the U.S. Passport Bureau in Paris for "journalistic work" in various European countries. He'd previously held two consecutive six-month "Emergency Special" passports, one for food relief work with the American Relief Administration and the JDC, and the other for journalism. Both expired by August 1920 and he didn't apply for another passport until November. With borders constantly changing, Henry Alsberg played fast and loose with travel, journeying, at times, into hostile Eastern European territory without proper documentation (U.S. Passport Applications, National Archives, Washington, D.C.).

making our journey more pleasant." Goldman particularly missed him: "I felt his involuntary departure most because he had been such a splendid companion and a most dependable help in our cuisine…. Henry was an expert in making flapjacks, in which he took great pride." When their train headed north again and passed through the town where he had been arrested, Goldman said she felt "doubly hard the loss of our good old Henry."[30]

"A clever and dangerous man"

Alsberg's new friendships left him vulnerable. In Moscow, Soviets interrogated him because they thought he was a British agent. The Russians apparently forgave him fairly quickly for his "indiscretions"; as Alsberg wrote later, he accompanied their delegation to the Russo-Polish peace talks in Riga the following year where he covered the signing of the armistice.

But he was again back on the U.S. State Department radar as a possible Soviet spy. Not only did he seem at home with the Bolshevik delegation—he called the head of the Russian delegation "a god of peace"[31]—but his time with Goldman and Berkman tarnished his reputation.

Alsberg's alleged espionage activities generated voluminous reports from October 1920 and onward for almost a year. One of the first reports transmitted to J. Edgar Hoover at the Department of Justice didn't even have his first name correct. The military intelligence director called *Charles* Alsberg a "clever and dangerous man" who was believed to be "paid by the Soviets." Another memorandum reported that Alsberg was born in Warsaw of Jewish parents.[32] In fact, Alsberg was also under surveillance because he was a Jew. To many in the military and State Department establishment, Bolsheviks and Jews were one and the same. A military attaché's dispatch to Washington stated that a number of Jewish correspondents were subsidized by the Russians, including Alsberg. "All are Jews and their reports from Riga were rather favorable to the Bolsheviks."[33]

The flurry of official letters and telegrams—taking on the air of a Keystone Cops routine—had Alsberg heading to either Berlin, Paris, or London after he left Russia. By then they had his first name correct, calling him "one Charles Alsberg, whose real name, the department has every reason to believe, is Henry Alsberg." Investigators cabled embassies and consulates in European cities to keep an eye out for him.

Despite at least two departments of the government investigating him for Bolshevik activities, when Alsberg visited Paris in November 1920, he was still able to secure a new passport, with the help of a recommendation letter from a JDC official to the vice-consul. His application indicated that he'd engaged in "general European travel" for the past two years. No mention of Russia appeared anywhere on the application, including the section where he listed the countries he planned on visiting as a journalist with this new passport.[34]

Autumn 1920: Return to the JDC

Alsberg continued his foreign correspondence work before rejoining his friends James Becker and Boris Bogen in Vienna. The occasion was the first-ever JDC conference of commissioners, a four-day summit in November to discuss how to continue aid in the face of JDC's dwindling treasury. Becker, now JDC acting European Director General, asked Alsberg to chair the budget committee—quite a feat, with delegates representing twelve countries vying for the shrinking pie. Alsberg continued to advocate for the Jews of the Ukraine:

> It's been one series of incursions and excursions, and burnings, and murder unbelievable ... there have been Jewish towns robbed and burned and pillaged twenty times, until there is nothing left. I HAVE seen these places. The only thing that is comparable to it is the Armenian massacres in Turkey. I believe that is the only thing in history in the last two thousand years that is comparable to it.[35]

The group, forced into an unfortunate argument of where to put their money, knew that in most cases, it would be barely palliative, let alone constructive. Alsberg despaired over the situation in Russia, which he likened to a doctor treating a dying patient with no hope of recovery.

With his journalism experience, Alsberg also presided over a session on how to develop publicity efforts in America and Europe to raise money. The JDC would follow through on his suggestions that he would be intensely involved with later, both in New York and from Russia. Becker ended the conference with public thanks to Alsberg for his contributions. The group's cables to New York led the JDC to launch a new ten-million-dollar fundraising campaign.[36]

Italy in December 1920

The pre-war tourists had not quite returned to Italy, but multitudes of Jewish refugees, seeking safer havens through emigration, journeyed to Italian port cities with hopes of emigrating to Palestine or countries in North and South America. The cosmopolitan city of Trieste, a geographic and cultural crossroads, lay where the Italian peninsula met the Balkans on the northeastern Adriatic Sea. Alsberg based himself here for two weeks to focus on matters where his concerns and diplomatic skills joined together: aiding refugees.[37] The polyglot that Alsberg heard in the piazzas and cafés reflected Italian, German, and Slavic cultures as well as the ethnic and religious minorities of Orthodox Greek, Ashkenazic and Sephardic Jews, and even West European Protestants who had settled in the city.

Again, following his pattern, he worked double time: Wearing his journalist hat, he interviewed the Italian fascist poet Gabriele D'Annunzio. For the JDC, he compiled an elaborate report on how to improve the lot of refugees seeking safer havens via Italy. Thousands of Jews made their way, mostly from

Romania, and headed to Trieste, Naples, and Genoa, looking for any way and almost any*where* to emigrate.

The Jewish communities of Italy, smaller, more assimilated, and richer than those of Central and Eastern Europe, were not the targets of murderous anti–Semitic impulses. For Alsberg, it was a relief to be in a place where he did not have to fret about keeping residents alive. Yet there were a number of problems Alsberg and his Italian associates needed to solve, with fifteen thousand people having passed through Italy over the past seven months and the number growing daily. Among the Jewish aristocracy who happily received Alsberg as the emissary of American money was Angelo Sacerdoti, a decorated Italian war veteran and Chief Rabbi of Rome. Jewish committees in Italian cities were already helping refugees navigate the emigration process prior to Alsberg's arrival; this included feeding and housing the scared and hopeful émigrés. Trieste, with its grand neoclassical synagogue, was at the center of Italian Jewish refugee work, and local Jewish groups provided well-stocked houses for refugees passing through.

Alsberg found an entirely different situation in Naples. Although this southernmost trip to the Mediterranean coast provided a respite from the brutal winters of the northern climes, Alsberg had no opportunity to enjoy it. Horrified by the squalor refugees endured as they awaited ship berths, he was too busy trying to overhaul procedures. During his short stay in Italy, he convinced the efficient Trieste committee to oversee operations in Naples and made arrangements for refugee housing there. While hundreds of refugees arrived daily—the influx in Naples numbered about a thousand a month by the end of 1920—he obtained permission for local Jewish delegates to board those ships to ease the refugees' transition. More importantly, Alsberg helped make arrangements so that those en route to North America could go directly to France, without stopping at Naples. He also needed to decipher complicated regulations involving passports and visas. Government directives gave Italians first crack at tickets to North America, and the imminent passage of an anti-immigration law in the United States caused significant scrambling for third-class berths. His actions and detailed recommendations helped the JDC improve conditions for the refugees and, more importantly, helped many reach their destinations. Millions of descendants in the Americas would never know that Henry Alsberg, Rabbi Angelo Sacerdoti and many unnamed Italians, and JDC benefactors set the stage for the successful exodus of thousands of displaced Jews in this period. In late December 1920, Alsberg departed the relative comfort of the Italian seaport cities and headed back north to Bucharest for another New Year's Eve.

Known as the "Paris of the East," Bucharest with its wide boulevards, museums, and nightlife suited Alsberg, physically and mentally, for a brief time-out during his last hectic months abroad. He was about to venture once again into the Soviet Union. But although he devoted most of his time remaining overseas to journalism, he also used his labyrinth network of friends and political notables to serve the JDC. He was happy to act as the organization's eyes and ears. As Bogen told him, "I know how near to heart you take the entire situation."[38]

Back in the USSR

Alsberg returned to Russia in February 1921. His journalistic output had slowed, so perhaps he wanted to revitalize his writing. The food situation had worsened and he entered during a brutal winter. Even his room at the former palace of a sugar mogul, luxurious on its face and with a grand view overlooking the Kremlin, hovered constantly just above freezing due to the lack of fuel. Notwithstanding the discomforts, being back with his friends in the maelstrom of Russian politics was invigorating.

Anarchist idol Peter Kropotkin, for whom Alsberg had smuggled out documents the previous year, died that February in his home north of Moscow.[39] Goldman and Berkman helped plan the funeral, as much an anarchist demonstration—the movement's last hurrah under the Soviets—as a memorial to their beloved leader. Newsreels and photographs captured the hundreds of townspeople and visiting mourners processing from Kropotkin's house to the train station. His body was brought to Moscow. There, larger throngs of the bereaved marched the snowy streets to the palatial Trade Union House, where his body would lie in state. Henry Alsberg, newly returned to the frigid city, paid his respects in the overflowing ballroom known as the Hall of Columns.

Alsberg stayed close to Goldman and Berkman as they helped lead thousands in the procession as it wound its way five miles to a monastery burial ground. A musical contingent played the melancholy minor notes of Chopin's *Funeral March* as Kropotkin's body passed the Tolstoy Museum.

While Kropotkin followers delivered speeches at the gravesite, the feeling of danger was palpable. For anarchists and counterrevolutionaries (many of whom were already imprisoned), for anyone in contradiction of the Soviets, they were balancing on a precipice that was about to give out and drop them into the tyrants' pit. The display of emotion seized Alsberg; while he was still not ready to totally repudiate the Soviets, he was in the first real throes of transformation that would lead to his eventual losing faith and his condemnation of their system.

The Kronstadt Rebellion

Momentous events the following month contributed to Alsberg's mindset. Striking workers in Petrograd, demanding winter clothing and better food rations, brought on the wrath of the government. Authorities declared martial law, arresting strikers and liquidating unions. The events caught the attention of sailors stationed on the island of Kronstadt, just offshore from the city. They joined the workers in solidarity with demands for freedom of the press and protests against harsh policies of the regime. It was met by an eleven-day assault from the Soviet military. The culmination: Hundreds died, thousands wounded, and countless numbers taken prisoner and later executed. Accounts of the carnage reached Alsberg in Moscow.

Throughout the coldest winter that anyone could remember, Alsberg continued his friendship with Goldman and Berkman. In fact, Goldman called him their closest friend. "He was always laden with gifts to replenish our larder, and his ready wit and fine human qualities helped dispel our gloom."[40] In the weeks and months following the Kronstadt uprising, Goldman noticed that Alsberg no longer defended the Soviets quite so much, as he puzzled out his own feelings toward the Bolshevik state. "He was intellectually too honest to deny that he was haunted by Kronstadt, as all of us were, and oppressed by the wholesale arrests of the politicals and their inhuman treatment."[41] Their intense conversations, with disagreements about the future of Communist Russia, were tempered by their fondness for one another.

He continued writing journalistic dispatches, but by May, Alsberg had suffered from food deprivation—perhaps not as much as the Russians—but enough that, he said, "I had to leave, because I had lost 25 pounds and there was not enough to eat."[42]

He paid a final visit to Goldman and Berkman before leaving the country, bringing them his extra winter clothes. The three friends joked that since Lenin ushered in a new economic policy allowing for some capitalistic ventures, Berkman could sell the extra clothing, most of which was too large for him. "If Lenin can become a shopkeeper, why not also Alexander Berkman?" wondered Alsberg.[43]

Visions of Utopia, Shattered

By the time Alsberg departed Russia for Germany, Goldman and Berkman were desperate to escape, but didn't know which country would admit them due to their anarchist beliefs and expulsion from the United States. In Germany,

Alsberg had the time and luxury of warm hotels and good food to deliberate on Goldman's forceful, compelling questions. With the end of fighting on the war fronts, what happened to the freedoms promised by the Soviets? Free speech, free press, amnesty for political prisoners—before Alsberg left Russia, Goldman had asked: "Where are they, Henry?"[44]

Fewer than two years prior, he condemned violence on all grounds because "it cannot ever beget justice and peace and good will." Just a year before, while still vacillating in his support for the new nation, despite his "own partiality for what has taken place here," he avowed the importance of accurate reporting.[45]

Mindful of his own deep beliefs, he could not very well continue to stand steadfastly by Soviet policies. And for whatever utopia he envisioned before, Kronstadt had finally pierced his armor of denial. It was the horror of the "sailors ... branded and shot, eight hundred of them," that finally brought him into Goldman's camp.

After long deliberation and soul searching, with Goldman's questions still ringing in his ears, he wrote "Russia: Smoked Glass vs. Rose-Tint," a blatant critique of the Soviet government. This *Nation* article became a sensation on both sides of the Atlantic, engaging readers from all sides of the political spectrum, as he blamed the Communists' "fall into this strange trance of belief in their own infallibility" at least partially on the "smoked-glass and rose-tinted" variety of journalistic coverage.[46]

The smoked-glass contingent, he contended, saw "everything Bolshevik in a darkened and distorted form," overindulging in sometimes comical lies. He pointed out one American newspaper's salacious story that "Trotsky had eloped with the premiere ballerina of the Moscow Opera and that Lenin had declared a love week."

On the other side of the chasm, he wrote, lay those who believed the Russian Revolution to be "the only true brand of revolution radical activity." They viewed Russia through rose-colored glasses, seeing "only sweetness and light, no matter how dark the night or how unpleasant the odors in certain obscure corners."

Despite his criticisms, he still managed to praise Lenin as "one of the greatest intelligences of our or any time" and the Communist Party for saving Russia from the Tsarists and the despotic menaces of the White armies and the Poles. But even his praise for Lenin did nothing to mitigate the anger of pro–Soviets, at home and abroad. "I know what I have written or may write will gain me the name of renegade." And as the only radical voice "crying in the wilderness" of protest against the Soviets, he was, as he predicted, cursed by friend and foe alike—but more by friend.

Max Eastman, don of the American radical press, skewered Alsberg on the front page of the socialist magazine *The Liberator*. Eastman characterized Alsberg's writing as "journalistic emotionalizing." Continuing his venomous attack for two pages, he ended by calling Alsberg "a petit-bourgeois liberal." The two men sparred again when Eastman himself broke with Soviet Union a few years later; Alsberg in turn critiqued him for this hypocrisy. He likely critiqued him later when, absurdly enough, Eastman eventually became a rabid anti–Communist, swinging so far to the right in his later years that he became a supporter of Joseph McCarthy.

The *New York Call* reprinted Alsberg's "Smoked Glass" article on its front page with an apologetic introduction. Ten days later a *Call* writer branded Alsberg "the latest addition to the band of radicals who are attempting to 'disillusion' the world about Russia." An article about Alsberg's change of heart even appeared on the front page of the moderate *New York Tribune*.

The commotion surrounding the publication of his article even reached Alsberg's JDC friends in Paris. Boris Bogen, in his usual wise and even-handed tone, provided words of support to Alsberg. "Bully from every standpoint!! I hate to tell you what I think of it really, because you might get a swelled head and that would spoil Alsberg…. I cannot see how anyone can think that this article has been written in any other spirit but that of helpfulness, I hope you are going to write again—the world wants it." It was one of the few buoying responses.[47]

Before leaving Europe, Alsberg advised JDC officials on the Soviet Union's political landscape and its potential effect on JDC operations. He was even brought to Hamburg, Germany, to meet with JDC Chairman Felix M. Warburg.[48] As if drained by his frenetic movements of the previous two years, his last few months in Europe were comparatively sedate. In June, Alsberg worked with the World Jewish Relief Conference to help send pogrom orphans to Palestine and South Africa.

As witness and worker, he had seen the transformation and transfiguration of Europe's geopolitical landscape, much of it through the lens of mass killings, famine, and oppression—all the worst humanity has to offer. Later in the summer he visited the Berlin home of banker Leopold Alsberg, likely a cousin.[49] Perhaps a rest at a quiet, stately banker's home in Berlin was necessary.

CHAPTER 5

At Sea, and at Sea Again
September 1921–September 1927

The French liner *S.S. Paris* pulled into New York in September 1921 with Henry Alsberg on board, traveling in a luxurious first-class cabin (so well appointed that it had a phone in the cabin to summon the porters). But he could not disembark and plant his feet on American soil just yet.

Agent Victor J. Valjavec, of the Justice Department's Bureau of Investigation, was waiting. In fact, Valjavec and his team boarded every vessel arriving at the Hudson River piers throughout that week, searching for him. Alsberg was interrogated and his luggage searched. All they found, reported Valjavec, were souvenirs and private letters, all "of no importance to this bureau." The aboard-ship inquiry closed out the investigation and was almost a formality. By then, the question of Alsberg's "Bolshevik" tendencies was actually, for the most part, resolved.

Agent Valjavec had already interviewed one of Alsberg's former colleagues at the *New York Evening Post*. He vouched for Alsberg, telling the agent that he was like others who "went to Russia as a Soviet sympathizer, and returned then to this country entirely cured of this utopia." The bureau also finally got Alsberg's biography right, noting that he'd worked for an Ambassador to Turkey and that his brother headed a large U.S. government agency.[1] But more than anything, it was Alsberg's *Nation* article, the one that so upset his radical friends, which stood him in good stead with the Bureau. Agent Valjavec's final report to J. Edgar Hoover noted Alsberg's "Smoked Glass" article.

Back at West 95th Street by his fortieth birthday, he savored his heated, well-lit home and his mother's roast duck and other entries from her "famous cuisine." Sound in body, but disturbed in soul, the shock of his peacetime home had to afflict all of his senses. After more than two years of ramshackle sleeping arrangements, he could now enjoy his own luxuriously clean-sheeted bed.

While New York City had its own cacophony of trolleys, elevated trains, street vendors, gasoline-powered vehicles, and newsboys calling out headlines, it was absent the clamor of carnage: deafening explosions, gunfire, and the unambiguous sounds of rioting soldiers and their dying victims.

Postwar America had no battle-scarred landscapes, but waves of social and cultural changes were rolling onto the shores. The 19th Amendment giving women the right to vote had passed the previous August. The Volstead Act ushered in Prohibition and the speakeasy culture, with hundreds, if not thousands of illegal drinking establishments "hiding" in plain sight in Manhattan alone. Liberals and radicals were gearing up their protests against the convictions of Bartolomeo Vanzetti and Nicola Sacco. Certainly, while overseas, Alsberg had taken respites to absorb the cultural scene in Paris, Vienna, and even Moscow. But only back home could he experience Eugene O'Neill's distinctly American *Anna Christie,* and the first World Series broadcast on radio that fall as Babe Ruth and the Yankees faced the New York Giants at the Polo Grounds, just uptown from his home.

Alsberg may have been back home, but he continued the activities he'd begun in Europe: working with the JDC and political reporting.

He wasn't done helping his coreligionists just yet. But for now, he changed his venue from soup kitchens and *shtetls* to office meetings and conferences, and soon enough he lit out for Chicago where the first conference of the American Jewish Relief committee convened. There, Alsberg was enlisted to prepare publicity for newspapers.[2] With the JDC transitioning from relief to reconstruction work, Alsberg's childhood friend James Rosenberg prepared to sail for Paris to oversee its work. Alsberg supplied him with a lengthy memorandum; if the dispatch wasn't top secret, it probably should have been. The in-depth analysis delivered a who's who of government officials, Jewish leaders, journalists, and philanthropists, across Europe and extending to Constantinople. He listed the names of people Rosenberg could trust, and those he should avoid. Thus, when Rosenberg arrived in Paris, he carried with him an intelligence report worthy of the highest placed spy.[3]

Alsberg had become a valuable member of the JDC's New York office, and his experiences made him a perfect fit for the Committee on Refugees. Thousands continued to sail from Europe searching for safe havens, and this committee helped transport those who, blocked by American quotas, landed in Cuba instead. Alsberg hit the lecture circuit, helping the JDC raise money by speaking to Jewish groups with his eyewitness accounts of European atrocities. Speechmaking, tedious office meetings, committee work—as important as it all was—lacked the fire of adventure. Alsberg had recouped his energy and was not content remaining bound to either desk or lectern for long.

JDC work occupied some of his time, but Alsberg also kept up with the large anarchist community in New York. As a friend of Emma Goldman, he now belonged to a circle that included writers, theater producers, and political activists. Greenwich Village, with its experimental theaters, hangouts like the Green Witch Restaurant ("where Bohemian and Cosmopolitan meet"), and an open homosexual subculture, became his second home. Openly gay writers, actors, artists, musicians, and others were drawn to the tolerant streets of "the Village." During these years he likely met gay African American writers Claude McKay and Richard Bruce Nugent, both of whom he later hired for the Federal Writers' Project.

Apparently his anti–Bolshevik article left no hard feelings between Alsberg and the editors of *The Liberator* and the *New York Call*, and he began writing for their pages. (Max Eastman left *The Liberator*; McKay became editor.) Alsberg, after all, remained a radical, even if he was less dogmatic about Soviet Russia than others. Intense debate was de rigueur among leftists anyway.

Impassioned articles on pacifism, equality for "negroes," justice for the jailed anarchists Sacco and Vanzetti, violence against labor unions, and rights for women shared space with Alsberg's *Liberator* pieces in early 1922.

The utopian castle in the sky hadn't completely crashed around his feet yet, and Alsberg accommodated some of the magazine's pro–Soviet stances. He hadn't totally disavowed the Soviets. He would never stop blaming the White Russian armies for so many Jewish deaths. His "A Polish Countess" recounted an interview with an aristocrat whose own star was about to fall as Bolshevik troops made their way to Kiev. Dressed in luxurious sables, the Countess sipped tea and vodka in her extravagant rooms high above the city while complaining about the Jewish Bolshevik conspiracy. Alsberg juxtaposed this with the scene outside the city, where during a lull in the pogroms there "lay a pall of snow as if to cover the stains of murder and silence the wails of the sorrowing and terror-stricken." The Countess explained to Alsberg's translator, a baron, that

> "The Jews must be taught a lesson ... the judgment must be carried out against them calmly, inexorably. I think that one male person should be selected from every Jewish household (they have awfully large families, you know) and taken out and shot. Then the Jews would remember never again to mix in politics. Will you have a bit more tea and vodka, baron?" As she bent over to fill the baron's glass her sables slipped down over her shoulders and revealed the divine whiteness' and perfect contours of her bust. And 'Boom, boom, boom,' went the Bolshevik guns not two miles away.[4]

His "I Own a Slave" was a mea culpa to wage earners of the servant class. He told of an Italian immigrant—dubbed "George"—who earned a pittance shoveling snow, taking care of the coal furnaces, and emptying garbage and ashes from private homes, including the one Alsberg shared with his mother and sister on West 95th Street. In mock superiority, he wrote, "George, therefore, I was pleased to learn, is my serf, in everything but the legal sense. He is chained to my house; he dare not leave for fear of starvation of self and family. He must stagger along from house to house doing serf labor until he drops. And by that time, I hope, there will be a little George to inherit his father's obligations toward our landed property."[5]

Still perhaps haunted by his "serf," and possibly trying to hone his creative writing skills, he wrote an allegory for the *New York Call* of capitalist society, telling of a tribe of monkeys newly discovered by a French explorer. One portion of this monkey civilization, which prized empire building and domination over others, represented the corporate and political power mongers, the ruling class of America and Europe. Another group represented the proletariat. Alsberg's strange "history" of this race folded the history of World War I, the Bolshevik Revolution, and the Paris Peace Conference into a tale that was quite a departure from his *Nation* journalism. Perhaps it represented his interpretation of what he had witnessed while covering the Peace Conference a few years prior. In his mind's eye, he saw world leaders as chimps, fighting each other over baubles amid "a kaleidoscope of flying, hairy arms and legs and a chattering pandemonium."[6]

"Carlos Marx in the Yucatan"

If Russia was Henry Alsberg's love affair, then sultry Mexico was about to give it a run for its money. His own restlessness—after all, he'd been home all of five months—coupled with political upheaval across America's southern border and the establishment of a socialist government in the state of Yucatan provided him another chance to uncap his foreign correspondent's pen and search for that elusive utopian dream. Alsberg spent eight weeks in Mexico.

While in the capital city interviewing officials of President Álvaro Obregon's administration, Alsberg didn't miss the parallels with Russia. The new Mexican government essentially faced an economic blockage—for without recognition from the United States, the country couldn't secure loans. In his *Nation* article, he accused the State Department of blackmail: The United States, he contended, would recognize Mexico only if it met the demands set forth by President Harding's administration, which included bowing to American capitalist concerns and excluding radicals from running for office. In a piece of reporting that presaged events later in the century, Alsberg accused the State Department of "putting into effect a private and unofficial imperialism of its own in Latin America."[7]

Reaction was swift. Although he had provoked debate before with his "Smoked Glass" article, this one hit a more mainstream nerve. Within a few days the State Department's anger was apparent as it vehemently denied Alsberg's claims. The nationwide stir hit big city newspapers such as the *New York Times* and *Chicago Tribune* as well as smaller papers like the *Grand Rapids Press*, which headlined "Alsberg's Bombshell" (and called him a troublemaker).[8] *The Nation* editors supported Alsberg's claims.[9]

Traveling to the Yucatan on this trip, Alsberg, of course, couldn't miss the other parallels to Russia. The rich *haciendados* (landowners), descended from Spaniards, controlled the wealth, while the indigenous Mayans provided what amounted to slave labor in the cultivation of the wealth-producing henequen, a plant fiber used to make rope. It was the bourgeoisie versus the workers all over again. A socialist administration brought land and educational reform, as well as more liberties to the Mayans—all without the repressive measures instituted by the Soviets.

Alsberg did not spend his entire trip on hard-nosed reporting. The port city of Campeche, with its mix of Mayan and Spanish culture and the picturesque land and seascape, enthralled him: "Night and the tropic stars burning,/ Fountains of green fires boiling in the waters,/ Myriad darts of phosphorescent fish shot hither and thither at random through the sea…. Church-bells incessantly jangled, out o' tune, wounded by stray revolutionary bullets."[10]

Merida, the Yucatan Peninsula's capital city, similarly captivated him. The wide Paseo de Montejo, the city's main boulevard, reminded him of Paris. Mayan caves and archeological sites ringed the city, and later writings showed his familiarity with them on his many return trips. The "Indios" in this city of five hills (named after the pyramids built by the Mayans) fascinated Alsberg.

Where his writing for *The Nation* was unsentimental editorializing, he took an opposite tack for the *New York Call*, submitting what was more like a free-verse love poem to the ways of the "Indio" and the new socialist policies that helped unshackle them from the *haciendados*. As an ode to "Carlos Marx," he wrote from his terrace of the neoclassical Gran Hotel in "the pleasant little Sodom and Gomorrah of Merida." All at once he showed his admiration for the indigenous people while criticizing the Russian collectivism that led to repressive measures and the proletariat working under the shackles of industrialization. Here in the Yucatan, he thought, may lie the true birth of an anarchist society.

> Paradise without the serpent—No temptations, but only indulgences—No distinction
> between sensual and sensuous—normal or decadent—Paradise without the serpent, unless

thou, far-fluttering Carlos, the Savior, shouldst ape that other Saviour, Turn doctrinaire, oppressor—serpent—Shouldst insist on a proletariat, factories, industries, Oil-wells, cooperative hennequen plantations, rope-factories, Sugar plantations, refineries, palm-nut oil, marmalade canneries, proletarian arts, crafts, pageants, drammer, aesthetic dancing, organized village festivals, meetings innumerable, parades.... Oh, Carlos I ask a tiny favor. Leave them their idyl.[11]

Alsberg came out of Mexico smitten. He would return for yearlong stays later in his life, after he'd given up on Europe.

He spent early summer 1922 dealing with fallout from the Mexico "Recognition" article, speaking to groups at anarchist summer gatherings in the Poconos, and reconnecting with his family. Despite his frequent travels, Alsberg remained devoted to his mother and spent time with her whenever he could to offset being away so much. But although he had been home for less than a year, he was not quite done with Russia.

A Second Tour of Duty

I feel very strongly that much of relief work is purely evanescent and often wasted, so that when the opportunity presents itself to do something concrete, I believe personal preferences or technical difficulties ... ought not to stand in the way of the work's being done and done as quickly as possible.—Henry Alsberg[12]

Meanwhile, on the other side of the world, the famine of 1921 had taken its toll on Soviet citizenry. The JDC once again teamed up with the American Relief Administration (ARA), providing Hoover's group with eight million dollars, the largest amount from a single group and much of it headed for nonsectarian relief.[13] The JDC was gearing up for its own innovative project: to aid Jewish families in the form of trade schools and the establishment of agricultural colonies in southern Russia. The efforts expended by the JDC, led by agronomist Joseph Rosen, were herculean.

The JDC sought Alsberg's help once again. His first response was an emphatic "No." Perhaps channeling his father he told Strauss, "I went to Mexico [to write], where there are no Jews at all."[14] He still didn't see relief work as being "his field." He had also chafed at the bureaucracy inherent in any large institution, and certainly felt more comfortable working independently, as he did as a freelance reporter. But by June he'd experienced a change of heart and Russia was back on his horizon. This was set in motion by the actual *constructive* plans to bring thousands of Jews to the land where they could support themselves through agriculture. This, he told Strauss, "would be worth six months or even a year of my life to see that the job is done."[15] Bogen cabled that he anxiously awaited Alsberg's help in Russia. Even JDC Chairman Felix Warburg pushed for him to go into Russia, although Alsberg pointed out that this could be problematic. "Mr. Warburg probably does not realize that our State Department may not love me very much."[16] (His travels with Emma Goldman and attendant run-ins with U.S. officials did not endear him to the State Department.)

Ironically enough, the city-bred Alsberg's first assignment would be in Berlin to purchase seeds and farm implements for the agricultural project. Bureaucratic visa technicalities delayed his departure, but he finally left America on the luxury liner *Olympic*, surviving sister to the *Titanic*.

As a volunteer, he had a fair amount of leeway, which he likely demanded, not to mention a good deal of responsibility. A JDC memorandum outlined his credentials, which included authorization to call on U.S. Embassy and Consulate officials for assistance. As much as he longed for important work and a modicum of adventure, he had enough experience that he did not travel naively. In a letter written aboard ship to a colleague, he jested that it was actually his last will and testament.

Alsberg's hopes for involvement in the constructive work were somewhat dashed, at least for a time, on arrival in Berlin in 1922. Miscommunications, more visa delays, and administrative tie-ups postponed his entrance into Russia. He was impatient with the bureaucracy and insecure with his own place in the project. The famine had spread, and he didn't want to waste any time "sitting around" in Germany or any other country while Russia and the Ukraine beckoned.

Writing to Lewis Strauss, Alsberg bluntly expressed his frustrations, stressing that with awful conditions still prevailing, he wanted to be of service. "But I want something quite definite and useful, where the results would be visible to my naked eye." He again emphasized his need to work independently "without being mixed up with complicated machinery."[17] He practically begged Strauss for an immediate reply, and for a real assignment. "If I don't hear from you.... I shall assume that the whole business is off, and that the JDC has blown in a lot of money on a joy ride for me to Europe, a joy ride in which I didn't really want to take. I shall then go off on my own somewhere, and take a *Kur* [treatment in curative baths] to recover."

Alsberg was a valuable asset and Warburg was none too happy to hear that he might lose him. "I do not like to have a man of his type say, 'I am wiring again today; if I receive no answer, I shall consider my offer to devote six months of my life, without compensation, where there is typhus, cholera and typhoid ... as refused, and I shall feel free to go about my own business.'"[18]

After a bit of sulking, Alsberg cooled down and helped purchase farm machinery in Berlin to be sent to Russia. He wrote, more reasonably and calmly, that he did not want to go home without performing "useful work" in Russia, appealing once again—now with the backing of Warburg and Rosen—to go into Russia and take over JDC work in one of the Ukraine districts.[19] (By then, Soviets had conquered most of the Ukraine.)

Waiting for a Visa

In the meantime, while visa arrangements were being untangled, Alsberg visited Goldman and Berkman, who had by then found temporary haven in Berlin. It was here that the quixotic Alsberg, undaunted by adding another cause to his plate, began his newest quest: to help free political prisoners rotting away in Russian jails. Alsberg worked with Berkman to compile lists of imprisoned radicals. He helped Berkman raise funds and contributed his own money to this cause, which he considered "his personal mission."[20]

Alsberg also spent time with his aunt in his father's hometown. He didn't appear to harbor any sentimental connections to Arolsen, despite its picturesque deer park and magnificent hundred-year-old oak trees. He complained in a letter to Louise Bryant about its conservative overtones and described prudish townsfolk "who object to ladies smoking, and would object to modern dancing had they ever seen it."[21]

Meanwhile, the visa delay gave Strauss the chance to plan a new assignment for Alsberg once he could gain entrance into Russia: providing press and public relations material to support JDC's mission.

From childcare programs run by the JDC and ARA, to tractors getting cranked up, there were human-interest stories aplenty. Alsberg had the necessary connections with correspondents from various newspapers and wire services in Russia. Strauss was adamant that Alsberg handle this. "You have simply got to look after it in addition to whatever else you happen to do if you care about whether we love you at all."[22]

Alsberg *did* care. And when he finally got word that he could enter Russia, he cabled Strauss, nearly delirious with excitement: "I have almost died of delay…. I shall try and [do] my best for the JDC."[23]

Getting In

Ironically, when Alsberg crossed the border into Russia in October 1922, he did so with the support—through the American Relief Administration

(ARA)—of the U.S. government. This association afforded him more freedom than his prior trips and a measure of protection that alleviated fear of arrest. He immediately went to Moscow to join the JDC's Russian unit. Within a few days, with Bogen and Rosen away, he held down the fort as acting director of the newly established Moscow office. Although he hadn't yet gotten the lay of the land in terms of how to actually run the office ("Whenever anything happens that I don't understand I look wise and say, 'I will see about it.'"[24]), he was in unusually good cheer while biding his time for work that he considered creative and constructive.

A year had passed since he had last been in Moscow, and its rebirth fascinated him. He may have spent as much time roaming the city streets as taking care of office matters. The enlightened cultural scene, with its Yiddish and Hebrew theaters, opera houses, restaurants, and art museums, was in sharp juxtaposition to the dilapidated buildings and bad plumbing. Arc lights kept the streets well-lit at night; cheerful Muscovites, shabbily but warmly clothed, crowded the streetcars and sidewalks. But not far into the shadows impoverished masses still suffered from high unemployment and, when they could find work, difficult conditions. This was true for old men and children as well as the able bodied. Alsberg described "a ride in a dirty old droshky [horse-drawn carriage] with a wheezy old nag and hairy isvostchik [driver] with a greasy wadded coat" and children "lugging heavy bundles on the streets, sweeping, driving droshkies."[25] Alsberg thought that Strauss, as a young captain of industry, would be interested in the state of Soviet manufacturing and commerce, so he gave reports of that as well. One wonders how the more formal Strauss took to his friend's teasing commentary: "This is a long letter. You will have to read it in sections between reorganizing railways and consolidating steel corporations etc .... If you weren't busy in America already, I should advise you to come over here and grab off a few of the industries that are being denationalized."[26]

As for providing publicity to JDC's New York office, Alsberg turned fickle. Just a few months prior he heartily agreed that good press was vital to support the JDC's fundraising efforts in America. By the end of November, he balked at the job. It's difficult to say if it was out of boredom or because he thought it not sufficiently creative. It may have been only a journalist's natural distaste for publicity work. Although he thought it necessary to have someone take up of these tasks, he said, "To be quite frank, I don't want to be this someone." It was not the first time he would complain before proceeding with a task anyway. So nearly in the same breath as his grumbling, he told about his arrangement to take correspondents from the *Chicago Tribune*, the *New York World*, and other papers on a driving tour of JDC-supported facilities.[27]

"Children at Play at a JDC Summer Camp." In 1922, war orphans, mostly refugees from pogroms, enjoy a respite at a colony operated and supported by the Jewish Joint Distribution Committee in Malakhovka, near Moscow. Dressed in ragged clothes, with bandages covering their wounds, some of the children appear haunted by the tyrannies they survived. Alsberg visited local orphanages while volunteering with the Moscow unit in 1922. He wrote to Lewis Strauss that the JDC provided blankets, clothes, and other necessities. He and another colleague chipped in to purchase drinking cups for the children in one such institution (NY 000745, American Jewish Joint Distribution Committee Archives).

Tales of His Tour

Henry Alsberg needed to be kept busy, and Bogen and Rosen obliged him, sending him on visits to hospitals, orphanages, and schools sponsored by the JDC and ARA in Moscow. There, he happily reported, the children were well fed and warm, "hopping around and cutting up just like normal American kids."[28] One orphanage, well supplied by the JDC, was missing only drinking cups. Alsberg donated those. Alsberg noted that in at least some institutions, the children's indoctrination by Communists led to some interesting conversations:

"The food and the clothing and the rest of the help we are getting from America, is all sent by the Jewish workers of America, is it not?" one older boy asked.

"No," Alsberg replied, "[it] comes from all classes, from the workers, the middle classes, and even the big capitalists."[29]

Within a short time, he was sent to Kiev and Kharkov to collect newsworthy information and photographs for distribution to American newspapers. For a time Alsberg cabled weekly news bulletins. From Kiev, he described hungry university students and provided photographs of a student kitchen. Visiting the "famous pogrom towns" of Trostianetz and Obodovks, he gave accounts of murder and destruction and the resultant JDC rescue work.

From Odessa he produced publicity materials sure to convince Americans that their money was being used fruitfully: a letter of thanks from a school for blind children, photographs of clinics and soup kitchens, and, from a Ukrainian Jewish newspaper, an article praising the JDC's work. He forwarded a press release he thought especially interesting to "the goyish press," focusing on the only vocational school in Russia to train Jewish railroad workers.[30]

In some cases, Alsberg penned the articles himself. At least two American Jewish newspapers published his "Close Ups of New Life and New Hope," emphasizing the JDC's good works.[31] Turning once again to the plight of children, he told of the home established for refugee children stranded on the border at Mohilev, the site of his own escape from bandits three years earlier. The word from New York that his reports, photographs, and cables gained wide coverage gave him the approbation he needed.[32]

Alsberg maintained his pace through the dead of winter and toured the Crimea and the Caucuses in January 1923.[33] The famine and economic situation left most of the population dependent on the JDC and other Western relief organizations. Here, Alsberg had the opportunity to become more deeply involved in caring for the large number of abandoned children as well as the impoverished, hungry adults who subsisted on "half a pint of bread and soup and kasha" per day. He carried large sums of money to distribute—in itself, very dangerous—so that local groups taking over "dachas" (former tsarist summer palaces) could settle children into new institutions. His diplomatic skills were often put to use. Once, when the ARA and another aid group were at odds, he arranged for the distribution of 100 food packages that had languished in a warehouse.[34] In the Crimea, a Communist official did not want to distribute food to a formerly "bourgeois" (i.e., non–Communist) Jewish community school. "My arrival in a sixty-horse power *Amerikansky automobile*, with an interpreter and all sorts of showy documents with prominent seals all over them, proved a great boon." This local politician did not understand, said Alsberg, the "international Jewish conspiracy of *stick-up-for-each-other* against the *goyim*."[35]

In another case, Alsberg found opportunity to criticize Jewish communist leaders. "To the Jewish communist, all people over sixty would naturally be social incurables. It would serve no useful purpose to describe here the misery, the toothless, palsied, starving misery, that inhabited those filthy, noisome, dank, unheated, overcrowded rookeries, before the non-communists and the foreign relief organizations got interested in them."[36]

His experiences with the elderly led to an amusing incident. When the residents of a JDC/ARA-sponsored old age home were forbidden to go into the city and beg, "a committee of outraged octogenarians laid their case before me. They would rather not be helped at all if they could no longer beg; to go out into the town and beg meant to have a steady occupation, and to see life, to hear the news and to gossip." They told him that if they couldn't beg, they would go on strike, leave the institution, and even take their crippled room-mates with them. "I am no trained social worker, and so naturally did the unscientific and cowardly thing, surrendered!"

Back in Moscow, he wrote accounts of the how the JDC "came in the nick of time" to rescue famine districts with coal for their soup kitchens and funds to outfit a children's colony, not just for Jewish children but for "Tartar, Greek, Armenian and Russian children."[37] He continued sending articles to the New York office, and when Bogen and Rosen traveled, he resumed the role as acting director of the Russian unit—certainly with more confidence than when he first arrived eight months back. But by late spring, he felt as if he had fulfilled his duties. He left Moscow for good in June 1923, never to return to the Soviet Union.

But he must have felt pleased that his work was not in vain. Later, when Bogen visited the Crimea and Ukraine, he told Alsberg that "in these places, many people were asking about you and I also had a chance to see the good work you had done there."[38] The recognition he craved also came to him from James Rosenberg. Falling back easily to their childhood nicknames in this correspondence, Hank told Jimmie, "I don't want anything from the JDC but the knowledge that you people have good will, etc. to me and feel as you do. I really appreciate very deeply what you told me about that."[39]

Rosenberg responded that he admired Alsberg "for being a really splendid Don Quixote," playfully adding that he'd forgive him for kicking him during a hiking trip in the Adirondacks back in their college days.[40]

In late June 1923, Alsberg returned to Germany where he reunited with Emma Goldman in time for her surprise fifty-fourth birthday party. There, with Goldman's friends and relatives, he didn't feel stifled by any conservative tendencies as he did in Arolsen. He spent the summer in Europe with "Queen E.G. and her court," as Alsberg playfully called them.[41]

He wanted to reengage with writing, and there is evidence that he began work on a book about his experiences in Russia. But he was caught in what seemed to be a recurring web that threaded through his life: starting to write a book but putting it aside for other activities. By late summer 1923 Alsberg had immersed himself in the movement to free political prisoners, a cause he would continue after returning to America.

Regaining His Land Legs: September 1923

Alsberg sailed from Rotterdam a few days after his forty-second birthday—his fourth transatlantic ocean voyage in five years. He disembarked from the *Rijndam* at Hoboken, New Jersey's Fifth Street pier in early October, walking the six cobblestoned blocks to the Lackawanna Terminal before taking the Hudson & Manhattan Railroad's subway "tube" to Manhattan.

Back home, he caught up with his family. Elsa, the one sibling involved in Jewish causes, may have been the only one who could truly value what he had been through. (She was secretary to the National Council of Jewish Women's department of immigrant aid.) Carl had recently left the Bureau of Chemistry to co-found Stanford University's Food Research Institute. At his friend James Rosenberg's request, Carl offered to host Chaim Weizmann, president of the World Zionist Organization (and future first president of Israel) on his speaking tour of the West Coast. Surprisingly, considering Henry's own involvement in the Zionist movement, Carl said he knew only of Weizmann's scientific work and not much about his labors toward creating a Jewish state.[42]

As the JDC's famine rescue work came to a close, much still lay ahead to restore economic life for the Jews of Eastern Europe. Alsberg saw two opportunities for American participation: ORT, a Russian labor and agricultural organization that operated trade schools and supported artisans, agricultural settlements, and consumer cooperatives; and Rosen's agricultural endeavors.

In 1924, the American ORT Reconstruction Fund aimed to raise $1,000,000. Alsberg, working again with fellow "soldiers" Billikopf, Strauss, Becker, and Bogen, used his pen to advocate for the group, seeing it as one of the few that could help the Eastern Jews become self-sufficient. "We have cut the Jewish masses off from the possibility of finding a better existence in this country [due to new restrictive immigration policies]. Neither Palestine, Canada nor South America, or Mexico, can within the proximate future serve as a sufficient outlet. The Jews must find their salvation in their present homes," he wrote to Billikopf.[43] Although historians view Rosen's continuing agricultural work in the Soviet Union—later called the Agro-Joint—as a fait accompli, it looked for a time as if it might not happen. Rosen laid the groundwork in 1923, with Bogen, Alsberg, and others deeply involved. But in 1924, according to several records, some at the JDC balked at committing more funds to the venture.

Alsberg saw these reconstruction activities as crucial; again wielding his pen, he entered crusade mode.

Alsberg worriedly wrote to Becker that the JDC seemed not ready to provide more funding to the agricultural settlements beyond its initial appropriations. "The Jews of Russia will never get such an opportunity again to migrate to the land, and the Jews of America will never again get such another opportunity to help the Russian Jews out of their economic dilemma." He went on to say that "there is no one here [in America] to take up the fight to get this project through. I think there is universal sentiment among the leading Jews in New York, but no one to push it."[44] Alsberg's intervention certainly did not cause the JDC to fund Agro-Joint, but he contributed words to agitate them in that direction. Within a few years, the Agro-Joint was in full swing, with Rosenberg as chair. The project remained in existence through the 1930s, spending sixteen million dollars and helping more than 150,000 Jews resettle land.[45]

Although he continued advocating for the welfare of Jews overseas, Alsberg's attentions were drawn in other directions as well. His feet remained on American soil, but the impetus for his expanding new interests was born in Russia. The persecution of political prisoners in Soviet Russia, which he witnessed firsthand, troubled him deeply. His artistic impulses were never far from the surface, and the Moscow theater scene led him directly to the downtown theater movement in New York. Alsberg would spend the next few years dividing his time between his humanitarian, political and artistic pursuits. (See Chapter 6 regarding his efforts on behalf of Russian political prisoners, and Chapter 7 on his work in theater.) These interests brought him great satisfaction but left him in mild financial straits.

Writing the History: The Book of Tragedy

Shortly after his return to America, he signed on for his first paid project with the JDC: writing the organization's history. Originally, he requested a budget covering nine months, "since it is apparently going to take as long to produce this book as to produce a child."[46] He could not have underestimated it more. In fact, even though he threw himself wholeheartedly into the project, collecting reports, and documents and correspondence; renting an office; and hiring an assistant, it was more akin to *raising* a child. JDC leadership considered it a matter of great importance and approved his initial request of $4000.

The nine months passed quickly, with no birth in sight.

Health issues (a throat operation), his fixation on the plight of political prisoners, his growing involvement with the theater scene, and the gargantuan amount of necessary research slowed his progress. From Palestine to Poland, he had to consult at least a hundred people and dozens of overseas organizations. He'd have to piece together fragments and puzzle pieces from these sources into a coherent whole, while struggling with how much context to include for readers. Within a framework of death and destruction, what should be included, what should be left out?

Shortly after Bogen returned from Russia to his California home, Alsberg headed west; the JDC's New York office forwarded boxes of files for them to peruse and the two men spent a good part of the spring discussing the Russian chapters. Later in the summer, Alsberg visited brother Carl in Palo Alto and worked on the book there through July. That happened to coincide with the nine-month mark, and he confessed to Strauss that he wasn't close to finishing. "I have a terribly guilty feeling about this whole job. It is the first paid job I ever had in connection with the JDC. I want to turn out a really good piece of work, and that takes time," he told Strauss. But as he pointed out, the JDC had been at work over ten years, in Europe, Asia, North Africa, and even Cuba. "The subject merits a good piece of work, which in turn, cannot be done on schedule."[47]

In the autumn of 1924 he sent a draft of the first two chapters to Warburg, apologizing for long introductory sections he thought essential to uninitiated readers. "These facts are no doubt an old story to you and the other members of the Committee, but to the innocent outsider, are less well known."[48]

Alsberg had good intentions. Although on one level he saw the book as his mission, his mood vacillated and he sometimes considered it more like a work-for-hire job. As he told friend Louise Bryant, widow of the American Communist journalist John Reed (author of *Ten Days That Shook the World*), he would be paid "quite a lot for it when it's done, if ever." He added, "God give me the patience to go through with that job."[49]

With each passing month, Alsberg realized the scope of the work was greater than he anticipated. "The book has occupied about five times as much time and energy as I had ever dreamed could be possible,"[50] he told Rosenberg. He continued to collect documentation and to write. By 1926, he was so troubled by the unfinished manuscript hanging over his head that he hired writer friend Isaac Don Levine to help wrangle the book into shape. JDC officials, getting more impatient, convened an editorial team to reel in what was turning into a massive manuscript.

Alsberg wrote to Rosenberg telling him he needed a few more months and asking for more compensation. It was approved; both Alsberg and Levine received an additional $2500 to complete the work, with Alsberg getting the

$700 advance he'd requested. (In today's money, that would be more than $7000—certainly enough to tide him over during another trip overseas.)

Finally by late summer 1927, Alsberg delivered a draft. Even brother Carl seemed surprised by this accomplishment.[51] Any doubts that he had been working hard on it were dispelled by the very heft of the manuscript—an encyclopedic thousand pages or so. No mere history of the organization, the added context and explication made for an exhaustive history of anti–Semitism in Central and Eastern Europe.

The tome's length and breadth stunned the editorial committee.

Rosenberg's assessment was both complimentary and critical. Despite saying that "ploughing through it" was a "superhuman undertaking," Rosenberg thought a fair amount of editing, along with a good preface and introduction, would bring it "near to being a magnum opus, qualitatively as well as in quantity." Alsberg, he said, created a "picture of tragedy, of the untold sufferings of untold human beings as to be overwhelming. Such a picture of the tragedy of being a Jew, of the plight, the suffering, the mental horror of these millions has never before been painted ... such a picture should be spread before the world."[52] JDC executive board member Cyrus Adler was more critical, apprehensive that the length of the book would scare away potential readers.[53]

Alsberg, along with Levine, continued to work on the final Russian section but was plagued, as in other times of his life, by intestinal problems. Within a few months, the JDC arranged for the history to be rewritten by journalist Herman Bernstein, in order to create a "brief, readable, interesting story." Alsberg would remain as the author of the Russian chapter of this new version.[54] The JDC expended thousands of dollars, and Alsberg, four years of his life, on this unpublished book. It still remains as perhaps the most exhaustive account of pre–World War II Central and Eastern European Jewry ever written.

A Gradual Transition

Alsberg's public-speaking abilities offered another way for him to support himself during this period, and he had what amounted to a thriving side business, speaking at temples, B'nai B'rith chapters, and similar venues on the East Coast and as far as the Midwest. At least one engagement at a Reform Temple rankled him. He gave what he called "a very interesting address on European Jewish conditions," but told Bogen "it was about the most unresponsive audience I ever talked to." Alsberg, perturbed by the congregation's attitude, described them as "assimilatos, very reformed, have services on Sunday and pretend not to speak Yiddish, and do most of their welfare work, except for an orphan asylum, on a non-sectarian basis with the Gentile organizations. I felt like organizing a pogrom right then and there."[55] Of course he could use this gallows humor only with someone who had spent so many dark days in the trenches of Eastern Europe with him. However, Alsberg's indignation against the "assimilatos" seems ironic. Perhaps he was disturbed because their assimilated ways reminded him of his own upbringing?

While his JDC colleagues continued their associations with Jewish groups, Alsberg gradually moved toward more secular—albeit humanitarian—undertakings. Most had the same idealistic underpinnings and quixotic impulses.

His longest lasting identification with Jewish life would be through *The Dybbuk*, the S. Ansky play that he adapted and translated (with Winifred Katzin) for the English-speaking stage (see Chapter 7). Relatedly, he promoted the work of Chaim Zhitlovsky, a writer who advocated Yiddish as the official Jewish language. Alsberg called him the founder of "a new Jewish literature" that encompassed novels, poetry, and drama.[56]

Alsberg's devotion to Jewish causes, however sincere and fervent, was often at odds with his writing aspirations, political interests, and own restless nature. His active participation, at least as documented, leveled off as he neared his fiftieth year. Throughout his life, he was often gung-ho about one set of causes or interests before moving on to other, seemingly more pressing missions.

In the mid-to-late 1920s, Henry Alsberg's political activism and theater interests escalated. He wasn't so much abandoning one cause as broadening his interests to include others, and it certainly did not mean that he deserted, as he put it, "the racial ship." His sense of social justice, his concerns for the persecuted and exploited of all races and creeds, and his need to attend to his own artistic impulses demanded a change of course. His chaotic temperament also left him no choice.

CHAPTER 6

"The best souls and brains of Russia are being exterminated"
1924–1929

You remember what Thoreau said to Emerson ... urging him to get out of jail by paying his poll-tax to a slave-holding-condoning state of Massachusetts? It is we, who should suffer these wrongs without spending ourselves to the last shred, who should be uneasy, ill-at-ease.—Henry Alsberg to Roger Baldwin, September 24, 1924, writing about Russian political prisoners who "Despite their suffering" enjoyed a "serenity of soul that only the just man can enjoy."

If the duo of Emma Goldman and Alexander Berkman inhabited the center of Western Europe's radical left universe, Henry Alsberg represented one of their more significant orbiting satellites. His presence in America did not make him any less a member of their tribe.

Strong political ties, as well as emotional ones, bonded Alsberg to them. The parallels began in their inner worlds. The two anarchists—outcasts from both the United States and Russia—tried with great difficulty to find a nation that would give them legal refuge. Alsberg's exile was of a different sort. While he had passport and, for the most part, the ability to obtain travel visas, he could feel at home only with those who accepted and loved him for himself. Anyone who'd been deported—figuratively or literally—or felt separate from conventional, bourgeois society would understand the disconnectedness he felt. Questions about his sexuality caused further separation. Shared beliefs in human rights and individual liberties united them, and his pivotal friendships with Goldman and Berkman changed the path of Alsberg's life over the decade and even impacted him later when conservative congressional committees hounded him.

After a few years of altruistic and adventurous wanderings, Alsberg didn't seem particularly pleased to be back in America. To ease his transition, he spent time in a French café where he wrote letters to friends still in Europe. In one, he told Louise Bryant that he "would not be able to stand it so long in these dear USA's of ours" and hoped to return soon to Europe.[1] Although he complained to her that New York was "hellishly expensive," his earning habits were as peripatetic as his travels. He derived his income from a number of different sources, including speaking engagements and theatrical work.

His newspaper writing output in this period was mainly limited to book reviews. Most of these covered Soviet Russia and appeared in the *New York Herald Tribune*. Journalistic ethics aside, the most significant were his reviews of books written by Goldman, Berkman, and Max Eastman.

Tempest in a Samovar

Emma Goldman's *My Disillusionment in Russia* appeared in print in late 1923 (sans the concluding twelve chapters, which the publisher cut without her permission); it was widely reviewed, but Goldman thought "of all the alleged 'reviews' only two deserve consideration as written by earnest and able men: those of Henry Alsberg and H. L. Mencken."[2]

Alsberg's appraisal in the literary review pages of the *New York Evening Post* continued his earlier arguments with Goldman. "All through her book Miss Goldman tries to escape the conclusion … that a revolution cannot be accomplished without terror, disorganization, and even wanton destruction, any more than an omelet can be made without breaking eggs." While not condoning the harsh methods employed by the Bolsheviks, he suggested her disappointment in the revolution was misguided. "Miss Goldman, unfortunately for her as a revolutionist, arrived in Russia after the honeymoon of the social revolution was over, after the first delirium, the ecstasy of the early episodes, the enthusiasm and rapture which spur all to brotherhood and sacrifice had largely evaporated." He knew from the time they spent together that Goldman's idealist expectations of revolution led to her great disappointment. Although he never used the word "naive" (probably because she wouldn't have stood for it), he explained that the reality was "so different from what she expected, one feels that Miss Goldman was trying to save her own revolutionary soul by proving that this revolution was a particular instance and not a generalized example."[3]

Alsberg's review of Berkman's *The Bolshevik Myth* brought into play the same considerations of preconceived romanticism. For Alsberg, the crux of the matter was that international radicals and revolutionaries had expected better from the Russian Revolution, the bold experiment for which they had waited so long. He firmly believed that anyone writing about Soviet Russia based his or her judgments on his or her own set of psychological and philosophical notions about revolution. "What you write about the Bolsheviks depends, very largely on what you, yourself, take with you to Moscow when you go there." He saw Berkman, "an old revolutionist," falling into that camp. Despite Berkman's "longing to identify himself with the revolution, [he] found himself very soon drifting into revolt against the Bolshevik regime."[4] (Alsberg's review left out any mention of his own appearance in Berkman's book, their close working and personal relationship, and the help he gave Berkman in finding a publisher.)

His review of Eastman's book came later but seemed to be payback for what Eastman, the once steadfast Communist, had written about Alsberg just a few years earlier in the *Liberator*. Eastman's *Since Lenin Died* critiqued the Soviet power structure, leaving him persona non grata in that nation. His book, as Alsberg backhandedly complimented him, created "a very interesting story out of a tempest in a samovar." Alsberg remembered their discussions on a cold Moscow street corner in the winter of 1923. He thought it odd that, considering Eastman's acceptance of earlier persecutions of political renegades in Russia, he now complained about the "lack of democracy within the Russian Communist party." Alsberg confronted him using the very words Eastman used to criticize Alsberg for the "Smoked Glass" article. "Comrade Eastman," Alsberg warned, "will shortly find himself on the outside of the fence looking wistfully in, surrounded by a lot of people whom only a short time ago he would have characterized as 'bourgeois-minded, pseudo-revolutionists.'" Alsberg turned the tables on Eastman and seemed almost gleeful about it.[5]

Aiding the Russian "Politicals"

When Alsberg was last in Europe with Goldman and Berkman, he became involved with their work to halt the persecution of political prisoners in the Soviet Union. They compiled a list of 800 detainees in Soviet jails, with a plan to mobilize an international committee of radical political luminaries. Alsberg believed that this committee could informally approach the Soviet government. Essentially, before going public with the list of prisoners and their particular circumstances, Alsberg naively thought the Soviets could be quietly persuaded.

The first person Alsberg convinced to join the committee was Bertrand Russell. "Had you visited Russian prisons as I have, and seen the miseries beyond belief that they contain, the filth, disease, starvation, and degradation, you would probably feel as keenly as I do," he wrote him.[6]

Russell agreed to help, and their correspondence discussed the various

European leftist leaders they could call on to sign the letter that Alsberg drafted and Russell modified—"a sort of appeal to the Soviet government to mend its ways."[7]

Although he would have to subsidize some of it himself, he had promised Goldman and Berkman that he would engage the radicals and progressives on this side of the Atlantic. For that, his best bet was to enlist a group already organized and doing similar work: the American Civil Liberties Union.

Although just a few years old, the ACLU's institutional structure was already in place. Roger Baldwin, co-founder and executive director, had previously skirmished with the U.S. government in support of political deportees, draft resisters, and anti-war activists like Goldman and Berkman. As a conscientious objector himself, he spent time in prison for violating the Draft Act during World War I.

Alsberg met with Baldwin in early 1924 and laid out the Russian prisoner situation. On top of Berkman's continued pleas for help, Alsberg's own inner moralities tugged at him. "I have had this whole business on my conscience and felt at any rate that I owed it to myself to exhaust every possibility for the amelioration of the condition of the Russian politicals," he told Baldwin.[8]

Alsberg then clarified his intentions, asking Baldwin to join him in the cause and proposing "the formation of an international committee, which should in a spirit of conciliation approach the Soviet government on behalf of these prisoners."[9]

New lists of prisoners sent by Berkman continued to arrive in his mailbox at West 95th Street. Alsberg, Italian anarchist Carlo Tresca, and others spoke at a protest held at New York's Webster Hall, but Alsberg no doubt realized that any American movement to save international political prisoners needed a bold leader like Roger Baldwin.

After a month passed with no reply from Baldwin, Alsberg sent him a rather petulant and sanctimonious letter, all but accusing Baldwin of cowardice for not taking a stance against Soviet Russia. "I imagine when you took up the matter you had no conception of the solid phalanx of opposition you were up against from the radicals on this side of the water," he told Baldwin. "The Civil Liberties' Union evidently can't take up this kind of unpopular issue.... There are very few people that can muster up the nerve to tell their own gang that they are wrong and narrow and prejudiced. Christ being crucified by the Romans was one thing, but Christ being crucified by his own disciples would have been quite another." Alsberg displayed his impatience, adding, "Meanwhile, unfortunately, the best souls and brains of Russia are being exterminated in Russian prison camps and jails, or in Siberian exile."[10]

In fact, Baldwin was ready to jump aboard, ignited by Alsberg's enthusiasm.

His stature among his liberal peers, coupled with his intelligence, forceful beliefs, and drive, made him the perfect partner. However, because the ACLU's charter limited it to fighting for liberties on the domestic front, another group would have to be formed.

And so, on November 25, 1924, the International Committee for Political Prisoners (ICPP), with Baldwin as chairman and Alsberg on the executive committee, held its first meeting. In tandem, Alsberg and Baldwin were a driving force, and with Baldwin's imprimatur, the ICPP recruited political powerhouses and intellectuals such as Felix Frankfurter, Elizabeth Gurley Flynn, and W.E.B. Dubois to the cause. Also involved were Alsberg's friends Carlo Tresca and Stella Bloch Hanau. "Operating much as Amnesty International does today,"[11] according to a description later provided by Baldwin, the group quickly widened its scope. Its mission to aid political prisoners and advocate for "Freedom of Opinion Throughout the World" sought to include not just Russia, but also Italy, Poland, Spain, Egypt, and India.[12] (Numerous accounts of the group's early years give Alsberg little or no credit for the ICPP's formation and activities. In fact, ICPP documents clearly show that it was his call to action that led directly to the group's creation and mission.)[13]

Alsberg and Baldwin didn't see eye to eye on all fronts. When Baldwin wanted to send the Reverend Harry Ward (ACLU chairman) to investigate Russian prison conditions and deliver the petition signed by Americans to the Soviet government, Alsberg protested, bluntly calling it "a half-baked plan." American voices alone would not move the Soviets to action, he said. Additionally, he thought Ward not up to the task. "Is he the caliber of man they will respect and be afraid of and will he see the business through and not allow them to bamboozle him, show him a few nice cells in a few nice jails, etc? ... He has as much chance of getting action in Russia, coming as he will, with his little list, as a snowball in hell." Saying Ward's visit would "lead to nothing," Alsberg impetuously threatened to drop out of the ICPP.[14] As far as Alsberg was concerned, his circle (Goldman, Berkman, and others) supplied more than enough evidence. Alsberg provided documents and a recitation of his own experiences while in Russia, which included smuggling eight hundred dollars to an anarchist group in Russia to help support the prisoners. He offered to sign affidavits attesting to what he had witnessed: persecutions, suppression of free speech, prison hunger strikes, lack of trials.[15] Alsberg was, by his own account, deeply and obsessively emotionally invested. "I think in order really to help those Russian politicals, we must first of all feel with them and for them, burn with the fire of indignation for their sufferings and martyrdoms, *believe in them....* You see, I have become something of a Russian myself, in so far as the spiritual side of this problem goes."[16]

Yet despite their occasional disagreements, the two men worked well together through 1924 and 1925, the whole time facing backlash from American Communists. The two even stood united when Emma Goldman called their efforts "weak kneed, naïve dabbling."[17]

It's important to note that neither Baldwin nor Alsberg called for the dissolution of the Bolshevik government. Their fight specifically lobbied for the welfare and freedom of political prisoners. Alsberg still harbored hopes that the Soviets would become less repressive while retaining what he saw as positive revolutionary changes. The two men struggled with a diplomatic balancing act, one in which they would pressure the Soviets into changing their ways while at the same time not feeding America's anti–Communist hysteria.

Alsberg constantly fretted that many of their American radical comrades wouldn't join their fight. Too many liberals were unwilling, he said, to believe anything negative about Russia.[18] They hoped a free-speech rally at Carnegie Hall would galvanize liberals because it called for relief for political prisoners in Italy, Spain, Hungary, Poland, and other countries, not just Russia. Nonetheless, Alsberg was worried. His fears, it turned out, were justified. Soviet and Communist supporters disrupted the rally. "The result was that our meeting, which until then had been worth only four lines of obscurity in the press, became a feature of next day's news and editorials," he wrote to a friend. Thus, paradoxically, the Communists' uproar at the meeting brought Alsberg's group needed publicity and even new supporters.[19]

Deep into the Cause of Political Prisoners

To ameliorate the "burning fires of indignation" Alsberg felt on behalf of oppressed political prisoners and suppressed free speech, he summoned his powers of persuasion, learned perhaps in debate sessions at Columbia and definitely honed in (mostly) friendly quarrels with Emma Goldman, one of the century's greatest orators. As he collected signatures for the American petition to be delivered to the Soviets, he continued his crusade through letters and lectures. Emma Goldman, doing the same work in London, praised Alsberg for awakening "the American labor and radical elements to the crimes that are daily occurrences in Russia."[20]

Getting involved in more local matters as well, he didn't hesitate to use his connections to heavyweights in the judicial world. Alsberg called on Judge Joseph Proskauer (brother Carl's close friend since college days) to intercede in the case of newspaper manager Benjamin Gitlow, who'd been convicted under New York's Criminal Anarchy law for publishing the Leftist Manifesto.[21]

He also corresponded with the liberal Republican U.S. Attorney General Harlan Stone to help a Russian cultural attaché, Roman Veller, whom he'd known through the ARA famine relief effort, gain entry into the United States.[22] He followed this up with a letter calling Stone's attention to the case of anarchist Carlo Tresca, sentenced to a federal penitentiary in Atlanta on obscenity charges for sending birth control publications through the mail. Ever the diplomat, the well-mannered Alsberg was unerringly polite in all of these exchanges, leaving his bad-boy persona of *The Masses* and *The Liberator* and *The Nation* behind.

He continued lecturing in New York, Baltimore, and Washington, D.C., on behalf of international political prisoners, attracting mainstream news outlets. The *Washington Post* reported his speech with the headline, "Alsberg to Describe Misrule of Soviets."[23] These activities helped him to collect $1600, which he sent to help support poverty-stricken Russian exiles in Berlin. As he wrote to Boris Bogen in December 1924, "I have been very much swallowed up by this business of the "Russian Politicals…. I wish I were a rich man so that I could devote all my time in straightening out this one little thing in the right way."[24]

The whole subject of the Russian politicals exploded in the pages of *The Nation* in 1925 when the editors decided to devote a good portion of the March 4 issue to the topic. Two main articles downplayed the severity of the prisoners' conditions. As a counterbalance, the magazine printed excerpts from two Russian political prisoners' letters provided by Alsberg, a summary of a Russian government report on conditions at one of the concentration camps, and an editorial calling for liberals to focus their attack on the abuses while not being carried away "into general denunciation of the Russian government and its leaders."

Reaction was swift from all sides. This issue of *The Nation* ignited the passions of various radical factions, from staunch Communists to their less-defined liberal counterparts. Seething disputes, waged in letters to the editor, raged for the next month and a half.

Alsberg's letter to the editor, published in the following issue, charged two of the writers with a "tendency to extenuate the Soviet government for its political persecutions." He called *The Nation's* editors to task, saying that they didn't go far enough in giving voice to victims of political persecution.[25] (*The Nation* used only a tiny fraction of the dozens of documents provided to them by the ICPP.)

Public outrage aside, in a personal note to Goldman, Alsberg conceded that the articles and subsequent letters helped their cause, if only to put it on the table for discussion. When Goldman complained that it was a mistake for

The Nation to be involved, he answered bluntly: "You don't know what you're talking about."[26]

Alsberg believed the continued persecution in Russia to be at least partially a result of complacency. As he wrote to Bertrand Russell, "the machinery has been built up and has acquired momentum. It needs somebody to throw a monkey-wrench, as we say in America, into the works."[27]

He and Baldwin realized that their actions had to be more forceful than petitions and rallies. Their "monkey wrench" would come in the form of a book. This, Alsberg thought, would prove to the world at large that the conditions he railed against exceeded the mere rantings of a few disaffected anarchists.

Alsberg and Berkman had already collected most of the documents that would comprise the book, eventually titled *Letters from Russian Prisons*. But the disparate parts had to be put together into a cohesive package by someone. That someone turned out to be Henry Alsberg. Just as his contributions to the formation of the ICPP were lost or ignored, so too was the case with the resulting book; there are conflicting reports regarding the book's contributors, but evidence is clear that Alsberg supplied many of the documents and served as the main editor. In a letter to Berkman, American anarchist Pauline Turkel was clear regarding Alsberg's role: "He really has given all his time to the organization of the committee … and now has worked for several weeks on the editing and getting ready of the material for the printer."[28]

Voices from the Wilderness

Prison walls covered in excrement. Meals consisting of half rotted fish or thin, greasy gruel. Cells packed with sick and dying prisoners. Caravans of people, including children and the elderly, forced to trudge through mud and snow. Alsberg spent the summer and fall of 1925 wading through documents of despondency. Fortunately, tedious editorial tasks kept him from dwelling too much on the sad facts. As he wrote to Goldman, "the editorial work, the business of my committee raising the money, the entire correspondence etc. has been on my hands. Even the proofreading and routine corrections."[29] (The fact that ten years hence he'd be called disorganized in his work on the Writers' Project seems almost laughable on viewing his detailed notes to Baldwin as he prepared the book for press. This ranged from contemplation of possible titles to budget difficulties and the arrangement of documents within the book.)

While Alsberg accepted responsibility for the editorial work, he also suggested that there be no names on the title page except for the list of the committee members.[30] So, despite his painstaking work on the publication, that is the only place Alsberg's name appears.

When published, the 300-page book opened with Baldwin's balanced and thoughtful introduction. Attempting to dispel the idea that it was a partisan book, he acknowledged that many members of the committee saw the "Russian Revolution as the greatest and most daring experiment yet undertaken to recreate society," and for that reason "they are concerned that this working class government should not perpetuate the evil practices of reactionary governments the world over."[31] Letters from intellectual celebrities (e.g., H.G. Wells, Bertrand Russell, and Albert Einstein), exiles, and prisoners followed the introduction. Maps showing locations of prisons and concentration camps, photographs, and documents on civil liberties, prison justice, and other material filled the book.

Alsberg's old college friend Simeon Strunsky wrote a full-page review of the book in the *New York Times* and called Baldwin's introduction "courageous and outspoken."[32] Another Alsberg friend, Roderick Seidenberg, covered the book for the *Saturday Review of Literature*, taking a philosophical, contemplative turn that likely meshed with Alsberg's own views. "It appears that Soviet Russia, like other governments, including our own, runs true to form in the manner of political prisoners. If one may judge a government by the prisoners it keeps, Russia has precious little to offer the suppressed and persecuted of other nations ... inquiring minds will ask of a revolutionary as well as of a bourgeoisie government whether the suppression of ideas is worth the preservation of any government," he wrote.[33]

A review by Louis Lorwin in the *New York Herald Tribune* (March 28, 1926) broached the biggest controversy surrounding the publication: that the book, hardly nonpartisan, opened a chasm between communists and other liberals. The committee, he said, "placed itself, consciously or unconsciously, in the midst of the partisan fight between socialists and communists."

Indeed, the book did polarize many within the liberal community. Even some members of the ICPP resigned from the committee because they believed the book too anti–Soviet. If the book didn't change the way the Soviets treated their prisoners, it certainly served as the inaugural American effort to recognize the plight of international political prisoners.

Run-Ins with Fellow Travelers

Alsberg's relationships with fellow American radicals suffered during the time he worked on *Letters*. "Everyone seems to have reason to be sore at me," he wrote to Goldman.[34] Except for Baldwin, others on their committee, and a few of his closer compatriots, he bemoaned later, "I lost most of my friends at the time, because I was considered the arch anti–Communist in America ... a lot of the liberals felt there should be nothing said about Russia that was not completely favorable.... I suffered; I was blacklisted; I could not get my articles printed ... for quite a while."[35] Although he didn't know it, his reputation suffered in Russia as well. The KGB noted in a report that Alsberg was part of the active nucleus of the ICPP and described him as having "animosity toward any organized government and toward the Soviet one in particular."[36]

On the other hand, his relationship with Berkman and Goldman continued, although it paralleled the two exiled anarchists' own unsettled lives: a rollercoaster of loyalty, misgivings, intensive bonds, and wounded egos, along with deep and abiding love and respect for one another. Indeed, the political prisoner work strained their relations. From his perch in Germany, Berkman complained at least once that Alsberg took too long getting the movement going in the United States. Mutual friend Turkel again defended Alsberg, noting his hard work and calling Berkman "unkind and thoughtless" in his criticism.[37] The only other near squabble the two men experienced came after the book's publication. Berkman was miffed that he was not given credit for his enormous contributions. (Baldwin later told Berkman that his name was omitted because "it would inevitably arouse widespread criticism at once as a source of partisan propaganda."[38]) The dispute smoothed over quickly and Berkman expressed his thanks to Alsberg for getting the book out in the first place. "I have always considered you as my friend.... I hope you did the same. Since you left, there have been some minor points of misunderstanding between us, but I do not think that these can affect our friendship."[39] Thus, with the book's publication, the dynamics of Alsberg's relationship with Goldman and Berkman strengthened. Goldman and Berkman accepted and encouraged Alsberg in his personal and professional life. Alsberg, enjoying more financial stability, often contributed to their upkeep.

As far as his work with the ICPP, Alsberg continued with the group for a few years, gathering material and editing *Political Persecution Today* and *The Fascist Dictatorship*, books focusing on Poland and Italy, respectively.[40] But his complaint—that other American radicals did not sufficiently support the political prisoner cause—eventually signaled his characteristic next move. After being chest-deep in the quagmire of the Russian political prisoner situation, he was preparing to emerge, shake the muck off, and, as he'd done so many times before, walk away. By 1928, Alsberg was no longer a member of the committee. Baldwin, more focused and persistent, chaired the group until 1942.

By then, it had agitated for the freedom of political prisoners in more than forty nations.[41]

Despite his withdrawal from the ICPP, Alsberg's political journey along the left side of the road—Roger Baldwin described him as being "somewhere between liberal and anarchism"[42]—did not abate.

He stayed in close touch with Alexander Berkman and Emma Goldman overseas. His writing was sparse, consisting mostly of letters to the editor. Notable was a long missive in the *Nation* after a Jewish anarchist assassinated Simon Petlura, the White army leader and pogromist. Petlura's death at the hand of an avenger, Alsberg said, added to the number of dead mass murderers—including the Ottoman leaders "who jointly ordered the wholesale Armenian massacres and deportations." Although Alsberg would have preferred the men be brought to justice through government trial, he seemed satisfied enough that they were dead.[43]

At this point in 1926, Alsberg was in the midst of theatrical success (see Chapter 7). Despite this, he found himself riding an emotional rollercoaster, which soon hit a dark turn. He felt alienated from his friends but had enough self-awareness to know his own black moods were likely responsible. Throughout the period of preparing the political prisoners book, Alsberg's letters to Goldman evolved to include communication of a more personal nature. The expressions of tenderness that would mark their many years of correspondence began to emerge. "I am getting terribly hypersensitive," he confided to her,

> and seem to see some unwelcome motive behind everything my friends do or don't do. I am afraid it is becoming a monomania with me.... I cannot work with other people. I have become too crabbed and high strung. I am too used to giving rein to my passing feelings and emotions, too sensitive to what appears to me at the time the callousness and obtuseness of people around me. Of course both the callousness and obtuseness are probably my own. But I find that I am becoming more like a man who has been flayed, and all of whose nerves and senses have been laid open so that every stirring of a breath of air or the slightest change of temperature causes his tortures. You can imagine then such a man's feelings if somebody carelessly flicks him with a whip.[44]

Alsberg also shared his political and personal philosophies with Goldman. He did not want to see the Soviets overthrown, and envisioned the country evolving into a "bourgeois farmers" republic. "The dreams will all be gone, and the fight for a new order will have to proceed there, as elsewhere, slowly." Of his personal ideals, he told Goldman, "I am passionately interested in freedom as an abstract proposition, and I am devoting my life to helping the acquirement of it along wherever I can.... I am hopelessly mugwump [neutral]. But I am as *Gawd* made, I fear hopelessly christian in sentiment, although hopelessly skeptical. I am bound to be stoned to death or crucified or both. And then, in addition, I am indolent in a sort of Buddhist manner."[45]

In this unsettled and disordered mood, he yearned to return to Europe. Paris and Berlin and their environs were not only home to his anarchist friends; the two cities were also home to a thriving Bohemian and, in some quarters, open homosexual subculture.[46] The works of Magnus Hirschfeld and Edward Carpenter, pioneering advocates of homosexual rights who even broached the ideas of gender fluidity discussed today, were read and talked about in this circle.

Perhaps he needed to reconnect with his anarchist friends and enjoy the opportunity to live more openly. He may have missed the intrigue of foreign correspondent work. Or maybe he hoped to find enough light to infiltrate the darkness enveloping his psyche. Whatever the reason, in the summer of 1927, bolstered financially by $700 (payment for the JDC book) burning the proverbial hole in his pocket, he once again crossed the Atlantic.

Although Alsberg had previously spent time in Paris and could handily make his way around the city and its environs, it is likely that he carried with him the Baedeker pocket guidebook. Travelers found it indispensable with its railway fares, colorful foldout maps, and listings of everything from annual art exhibits and telegraph office locations to the cost of a telephone call (25 centimes for three minutes) that one could make from the *cabines* situated in nearly all of the post offices. As much as the Baedeker guidebook might have served Alsberg in his travels, it was also noteworthy that it would become a model— in less than ten years' time—for the *American Guide* books, the centerpiece of his Federal Writers' Project.

Alsberg stayed at Hôtel des Ambassadeurs, on the Left Bank, and couldn't have felt more at home. Lost Generation writers and artists filled the streets and noisy cafés; fluent in French and German, he could keep up with any and all literary and political deliberations. Alsberg and other American expatriates, along with European anarchists, radicals, and progressives, went into emergency mode at the imminent execution of Nicola Sacco and Bartolomeo Vanzetti, convicted of murder in Massachusetts seven years before. Before long, Alsberg presided over a mass rally in Paris to show sympathy for Sacco and Vanzetti. The rally featured speeches by Alsberg and Luigia Vanzetti (Bartolomeo's sister) and a dance presentation by Isadora Duncan.[47]

He connected with Berkman in France, rekindling a friendship unhindered by the drama surrounding the political prisoners book. Like many of Berkman's friends, Alsberg did what he could to help the strapped Berkman deal with ongoing poverty. Alsberg succeeded in getting him translation work, which included a play later produced at the Provincetown Playhouse.[48]

When Sacco and Vanzetti were executed on August 23, Alsberg was wandering through Spain. He kept in contact with Berkman, telling him about a bullfight ("bloody but interesting") and his upcoming visit to Granada, where he said he planned to "buckle down" to writing. The return to their warm relationship is evidenced by Berkman's remarks to Alsberg, who failed to pay him a visit while passing through France before heading home to America in late 1927. Berkman teased Alsberg, promising to "give you hell when you return here, which I hope will be soon."[49]

And it was soon. His taste for Europe seemed almost insatiable; almost a year to the day after he returned to New York, he was back in Paris. He journeyed to the French Riviera to stay with Emma Goldman at her cottage in St. Tropez, a sleepy, out of the way fishing village. While Goldman struggled to finish her autobiography, *Living My Life*, he relished the chance to write and laze about the cozy house Berkman nicknamed Bon Esprit. Alsberg also spent time researching psychoanalysis and sought out Freud's lectures on sexuality.[50] Alsberg was pressed into service as Goldman's assistant and companion when her live-in secretary left. The two were amiable roommates; perhaps hinting at her own tendency to get involved with younger men and Alsberg's sexual leanings, she told Berkman, "He knows I have no designs on his maidenhead."[51] The two enjoyed cooking for one another, discussing her book, and living domestically until her travel bug matched his.

Just after Christmas, Alsberg happily brought along—and paid for— Goldman and a young male acquaintance of hers on a tour through Spain. "It is not often that a lady of questionable age is offered the chaperonship of two gentlemen friends—one very young [psychologist Otto Klineberg], the other very handsome [Alsberg]." Despite dismal weather, the threesome enjoyed a "mad rush" through the country lasting nineteen days, visiting the Great Mosque of Cordova, Moorish palaces in Seville, grand synagogues in Toledo (vacated by Jews by when they were expelled by the Spanish inquisition), and the Prado in Madrid. They even managed to fit in a thirty-six-hour jaunt to Tangier.[52] With the country living under a dictatorship, Alsberg and Goldman took particular interest in the political situation. Alsberg interviewed factions from a number of different parties and planned to write a book on political oppression in Europe since World War I.[53] (He never completed the book.)

When the travelers returned to France at the end of 1928, Alsberg moved in with Goldman's nephew Saxe Commins and his wife in Paris.[54] He enjoyed their company enough to help with the household and particularly enjoyed cooking. He suggested to Goldman—perhaps only half-jokingly—that they had both missed their real vocations. "We should never either of us have meddled into anything else ... after all, the world cannot be saved unless the arts are saved with it, and cookery is a part of that. A good omelet soufflé will make the most terrible revolutions palatable. And a good dish of gefilte fish makes all classes, exploiters and exploited, kin." The Commins' apartment at 11 rue Schelcher actually belonged to a successful commercial artist—proceeds from Maxwell House Coffee's "Good to the Last Drop" campaign apparently afforded one a luxurious duplex in Central Paris—and was the gathering place of literary, artistic, and political visitors, including poet Hart Crane, James Joyce, Berkman, and Margaret Anderson, publisher of the influential *Little Review*.[55] (The progressive magazine serialized the unpublished *Ulysses*, which earned her an obscenity conviction. Living openly as a lesbian, Anderson also used the publication to advocate for homosexual rights.) Alsberg and Goldman continued their close relationship. He also put on his lawyer hat when she entered into a contract to buy her St. Tropez cottage, helping her negotiate better terms for the purchase.

Through the early months of 1929, Alsberg continued his exploration into psychology and sexuality. Remembering that Goldman had once written an article for a publication put out by Dr. Magnus Hirshfeld's Wissenschaftlich-Humanitäre Komitee (Scientific Humanitarian Committee, which worked to promote homosexual rights), he wrote asking her for the group's address.[56] It's impossible to ascertain how open Alsberg was with Goldman and Berkman regarding his sexual orientation. But there are indications, at least from Goldman, that she was aware: his open interest in books and publications about homosexuality, her remarks about his "maidenhead," and a line she wrote to Berkman about her secretary being interested in Henry: "Nothing on his side though."[57]

The literary discussions Alsberg and Goldman had enjoyed during his stay in St. Tropez impressed her enough that she asked him to critique the manuscript of her autobiography. He begged off at first, saying he wanted to keep his summer plans flexible. For once, he felt tranquil enough to be unworried about the near future. "Instinct is a very poor guide, yet I have a deep-set rebellion against making up my mind at present about anything whatsoever. Not a very good condition for the vigorous task of biting into your book and delivering vigorous critical advice." Besides, he said, "I'd feel very much scared of advising you ... the responsibility is too big."[58]

Two months later, the eye trouble he'd suffered in the past returned with a severe bout of the flu. But it wasn't just his vision that was cloudy; the gray and overcast mood that he'd kept at bay was returning. Word from home related his mother's increasing problems with diabetes. Additionally, he told Goldman, "I think she misses me very much. And it is cruel for me to stay away when I suppose I could do the work I am doing or not doing just as well over there." He wrestled with a dilemma. Knowing he had to go home and help care for Bertha, he pondered: Should he spend his remaining time in Europe on a writing project or take a "last wild fling" for a month?[59]

It apparently did not present too much of a dilemma, for although he ostensibly extended his stay in Europe to consult with a famous eye doctor in Berlin, he did soon go on a bit of a jaunt with a friend visiting from America. Writing to friend Stella Bloch Hanau, he told about taking one of their mutual friends on an "American rush through the lowest life of Paris." He wrote that he would tell her more when he returned home about "what was in those 36 hours that the U.S. Postal department wouldn't let through."[60]

The melancholy that began in Europe returned with a fierce grip when he arrived home in May 1929. Luckily for Alsberg, his ship landed in the bloom of spring and not during the throes of a cold, dim winter certain to worsen his depression. By Decoration Day (now Memorial Day), he'd taken refuge in a shack that he built on his brother's land a few hours' north of New York City in the picturesque hills of the Hudson Highlands east of the Hudson River. The little house in Putnam Valley had running water, a cellar, and an outside toilet hidden behind a rock outcropping. A coal stove warmed two rooms on chilly nights. But even this scenic, tranquil backdrop—"so beautiful that it made me ache"—did not quell his ruminations: guilt at leaving his mother for so long and the yearning to be back in Paris and St. Tropez, his own uncertain future, life itself. Goethe's *Wanderer's Night Songs* haunted him: "Over every crest is rest/in all the trees/the breeze scarce touches you./Hushed is the wood-bird's song./Wait: before long,/you will rest too."[61]

But he did not expect rest; rather, he felt as if he were about to descend into a deserved hell for the "irresponsible and amusing and adventurous years" he experienced since 1919. Abandoning his usual—or, as Goldman said, "rotten habits as a correspondent"—he indulged in a flurry of dispatches to Goldman through June, expressing the depths of his psychological misery.

With his mother seeming to age rapidly, Alsberg realized he needed to devote more time to her. "I think I have a severe case of the Oedipus complex; at any rate I am certainly fonder of my mother than of anyone else in the world. No matter how far away I've been, she was always comfortably in the background." Guilt and worry, coupled with his wanderlust and subterranean mood, all fused together to the point where "the whole world, of my world, seems to be coming down about my ears. Well, well, in a year or two it will be time enough to join a suicide club, one that admits Jews."[62]

When not staying at his Putnam Valley shack, he lived at the family home on the Upper West Side. The face of the city had changed during his time away and continued to transform. The Manhattan of Henry Alsberg's youth was getting taller. The Chrysler Building and 40 Wall Street competed for "tallest building" status during construction in 1929; both, of course, would shortly be surpassed by the Empire State Building. The city was growing in other ways, too. Forty blocks away, the Museum of Modern Art opened its galleries. The 8th Avenue subway, which would run from Chambers Street in lower Manhattan to the island's northern tip, was under construction. Herbert Hoover, his old "boss" from the American Relief Association, sat in the White House; his future boss, Franklin D. Roosevelt, was Governor of New York State.

His stays in the countryside did temper his blue mood, as did visits from friends like Saxe Commins (also back in America). Alsberg especially enjoyed the company of his sister-in-law, Elsie, as they relaxed together on the little terrace he added on to his shack. Alsberg was fortunate that a utopian colony was growing in the nearby town of Mohegan, where he could spend time with radical friends.

Meanwhile, Goldman still hounded him about editing her book. While he wasn't quite ready to help, he was grateful for her friendship and told her so. When Emma Goldman turned sixty, he wrote a congratulatory, testimonial letter to her. "You have protected so many of the naked and helpless (physical and spiritual), been a mother to so many and a staunch friend without asking questions or demanding account, that even though some of them may have forgotten, the great Brahma, or whatever the eternal consciousness is in which we don't believe, but which inspires us to do noble deeds … will remember…. Meanwhile there are some of us who do not forget your great qualities."[63]

Alsberg's words lifted Goldman's own tender spirit, and she even scribbled, "Beautiful from Henry" on the letter. During her struggle to finish her autobiography, Alsberg and her nephew Saxe visited her publisher, Knopf, on her behalf to go over provisions for advertising her book.

Alsberg tentatively planned another trip overseas, but by the autumn of 1929 he informed Goldman that he wouldn't make it because his mother was ill and she needed him to remain nearby. Desperate for him to read her manuscript before its next revision, Goldman was none too pleased. She didn't quite buy his excuse, telling her secretary, "Henry's mother I am told really does not cling so much to him as he does to her."

Over these last few years, Alsberg had developed a parallel career in theater, and was on the verge of what appeared to be a major theatrical success. If it came to fruition, it would lift not only his professional standing but likely his emotional health as well. For now, it was time to stay home.

CHAPTER 7

The Interlude of
New York Theater
A "Portentous Possibility"
1924–1929

Describing the act of crossing from the physical world into the spiritual, as depicted in his adaptation and the first English translation of the play, *The Dybbuk*, Henry Alsberg called it a "curious transcendental union" between the "real and the 'other' world."[1]

Conceivably, this could describe Alsberg's own sojourn into the realm of New York theater as well. Overlapping with his years of travel, reporting, aiding Jewish relief efforts, and working for release of political prisoners, his time-outs in New York offered new artistic possibilities and a respite from the grief witnessed and adversities endured overseas. In between and paralleling these activities was the call of the stage. The downtown theater's social and political scene fit his sensibilities. If New York was home, Greenwich Village provided a kind of refuge within. The circle of bohemians residing there included old friends, writer associates, and newer friends who were mutual acquaintances of Emma Goldman and Alexander Berkman. It formed a network that intersected with the downtown New York art theaters of the Provincetown Playhouse and the Neighborhood Playhouse. Alsberg found a home and success in both companies. Although his time with them was relatively short, his impact was great, and he became more of a guiding force in their evolution than he has ever been given credit for.

As a producer, he shepherded major, historical plays through productions at Provincetown. During the same period, his monumentally successful translation and adaptation of *The Dybbuk* for the Neighborhood Playhouse made headlines by bringing the hitherto unknown—and now-renowned—Yiddish play to the attention of English-speaking audiences, first in New York, then worldwide. This success and fame, it can be argued, popularized it enough to help *The Dybbuk*—English, Yiddish, and Hebrew versions—find its way back to Europe and then Israel after World War II and the near-obliteration of Jews and Jewish culture.

His circle of friends and associates included Eugene O'Neill, director James Light, and Stella Bloch Hanau. (It's notable that both theater companies featured women, Hanau included, in prominent leadership roles[2]; Alsberg's time in this milieu offers another example of his ease in working with women, both in partnership and under their authority. This is significant, given the time period. He was already an advocate for women's rights, as demonstrated in his articles supporting birth control, another radical idea in that era.)

Of course, it wasn't just the setting and the lifestyles—alternative, leftward political, creative—that lured him to the theater. Alsberg's new venture led him down a fresh literary path, one that allowed him to use his contacts and experiences in Europe, as well as his various writing talents.

Looking back ten years, his fiction writing had shown a theatrical flair, employing two fundamental mechanisms of dramatic writing: the ability to paint vivid scenes and a facility for writing smart, stylish dialogue. His short story, "Soiree Kokomo," could have easily been transformed into a one-act play. This first-person tale of a visit to what seems like a modern-day performance art event—apparently enhanced by an unknown psychedelic substance—featured a nameless character's opening monologue, with dialogue and conflict provided by a small supporting "cast."

His inclination toward the theatrical, his need for diversion after the suffering he witnessed in Russia, and his untapped talents in dramatic writing all came together in the theater world to give him a place to focus his undaunted, frenetic energy. And with his finely honed progressive leanings, the theater would also enable him to convey, dramatically, the principles and convictions derived from witnessing the myriad injustices of the world, from Turkey to Russia.

Human misery, fortunately, wasn't the only experience he had in Russia. In between the political machinations and the wretched gloom he wrote about in *The Nation* and *London Daily Herald*, Alsberg did find time to take in the thriving and experimental Moscow theater scene. This would bear on his ventures at both the Provincetown and the Neighborhood playhouses. Alsberg's entrance into the downtown theater world of New York City coincided with the flourishing experimental "little" theater movement in the Bohemian dreamland of Greenwich Village.

A few years had passed since the Provincetown Playhouse moved from its original home on a wharf in Massachusetts to settle in Greenwich Village. By the time Alsberg arrived, the revolutionary theater company created by George ("Jig") Cram Cook, John Reed, Eugene O'Neill, Susan Glaspell, and others in the summer of 1915 was an established presence on Macdougal Street. It had already brought fame to O'Neill and changed the landscape of off-Broadway theater. Not too far away from Provincetown's home base near Washington Square Park was the Neighborhood Playhouse, founded by Lewisohn sisters Alice and Irene.

Just a few months after his forty-second birthday and his return from one of his many European trips, Alsberg jumped headfirst into this still-blooming, avant-garde haven. From 1924, when he acquired the English translation rights to *The Dybbuk*, through the latter years of the decade, when he was a director of the Provincetown Players' offshoot, the Experimental Theater, he immersed himself in the hectic, passionate life of show business. Fortunately, Provincetown's Macdougal Street theater, less than two miles from the Neighborhood Playhouse's digs at 466 Grand Street, was no more than a twenty-minute walk for the long-legged, energetic Alsberg, who shuttled between the two stages.

Provincetown Playhouse

Although Provincetown was, for the most part, a wholly American enterprise dedicated to producing American playwrights, and known particularly for introducing Eugene O'Neill, Alsberg contributed an international sensibility sharpened by his years abroad. That's not to say that all earlier productions were home-grown: numerous imported works included Sholem Asch's *God of Vengeance*, notable for featuring lesbian characters.[3]

Alsberg's arrival coincided with the theater's upheaval following the departure of its original, legendary leaders. Alsberg already had friends within the company, most importantly Hanau, a key figure in the theater's history.

Alsberg joined the group during this major reorganization. Eugene O'Neill, Kenneth Macgowan, and Robert Edmond Jones comprised the triumvirate running the operation, renamed the Experimental Theatre.[4] (The playhouse itself kept "Provincetown" as its name, even though the company had been officially dissolved. This name change contributed to confusion among audiences then and historians now.)

Like the other downtown art theaters, Provincetown had a social conscience, expressed in plays chosen for production. Alsberg became part of the new leadership, credited variously as a director and an associate director of the company through 1928. However, he was always more than those titles imply.

The combined forces of his enthusiasms and interests contributed to the production of shows that intersected with his progressive causes and his alertness to international socio-political movements. The functions and responsibilities of members of the production teams often overlapped in this small company setting. Within these blurry lines of operation, Alsberg's many tasks during his tenure there included unearthing scripts to produce, publicizing plays, handling actors' salaries, and writing adaptations.

He was in the thick of it when Eugene O'Neill's *S.S. Glencairn* opened November 3, 1924, at the Provincetown Playhouse for a short run due to poor attendance. Alsberg, along with director Light and others, moved the production uptown to the Punch and Judy and the Princess theaters, hoping for better results.[5] Without identifying himself as one of the producers, he promoted the play—and chastised audiences—in a letter to the *New York Times* (December 21, 1924). "Let us hope that now a wider public, too indolent to thread the mazes of Greenwich Village, will find easy access to what in my opinion is one of the most artistic and deeply theatrical entertainments of the season."

Perhaps it was the competition of the thriving theater season, but the "indolent" masses still did not rush the ticket booths. The play closed after a one-month run. To be fair, audiences had much to choose from: the Marx Brothers in the "laugh-a-minute" musical comedy *Cocoanuts*; the famous Ziegfeld Follies; and another O'Neill play, *Desire Under the Elms*, with Walter Huston. That doesn't even include the competition from motion pictures.

The group's next reorganization brought Alsberg the chance to become even more deeply involved. By the 1925–26 season, Alsberg was a director of the company, part of an elite group that included Light, M. Eleanor Fitzgerald, Harold McGee, and Cleon Throckmorton.[6] During his first full season as director, the company struggled both financially and creatively. Described as a season that began "not too propitiously,"[7] it finally picked up with the offering of Gluck's opera, *Orpheus*, hailed by drama critics.

By then, Alsberg was established enough to influence the company's offerings. Social justice issues were important to him, but international and classical themes also attracted him. In a true gesture of internationalism, he brought *Princess Turandot*—a fable about a Chinese princess written by the Venetian Carlo Gozzi—to the group in 1926. Alsberg had seen a Russian version in 1922 at the Moscow Art Theatre and, collaborating with Isaac Don Levine, translated it and adapted it for Provincetown's 1926 season opener.[8]

Despite its new offerings, the theater company's financial situation continued to decline. With each new production, however, there came the hope that its fortunes would turn. They worked hard to present artistic fare, a task made more difficult by the theater's small, dismal, downtown space. The group, trying to recreate the innovative aura of the Provincetown's early years, lacked the financial backing and, perhaps more importantly, the fresh patina that their forebears enjoyed as pioneers of a new kind of theater.

All of this *almost* changed with the production of *Abraham's Bosom* (1926). Subtitled, "A Biography of a Negro in Seven Scenes," it dealt with bigotry and racial injustices faced by the biracial son of a slave, set twenty years following emancipation. Countless producers turned young playwright Paul Green away. His play featured a nontraditional structure and an all-black cast. It would take a nontraditional theater company, one with a sense of adventure and a willingness to explore uncomfortable, unpopular topics. It would take a theater company staffed with progressive idealists.

Throughout the decade Alsberg had witnessed countless violent acts of bigotry and tyranny on foreign soil and certainly faced (comparably) more subtle forms of anti–Semitism himself at home in America. *Abraham's Bosom* offered a dose of home-grown American oppression, and its production fulfilled his desire to present issues revolving around social justice to audiences. With playwright Paul Green's new dramatic voice, James Light directing, Alsberg and Eugene O'Neill as associate directors, opera singer Jules Bledsoe (who would soon create the role of Joe in *Showboat* and sing "Ol' Man River") as Abraham, not to mention the controversy of presenting a play with an "all-Negro cast," the troupe looked with optimism toward the end-of-the year opening in 1926. It played for six weeks on Macdougal Street, then moved uptown to the Garrick Theatre where it was seen by *New York Times* theater critic J. Brooks Atkinson. He effusively called it "the most penetrating, unswerving tragedy in town, and surely one of the most pungent folk dramas of the American stage."[9]

Despite Atkinson's high praise, the play lasted only three additional weeks. Later, after playwright Paul Green won the Pulitzer Prize for this groundbreaking work, the company restaged it and even sent it on a road tour, hoping to profit from its newfound recognition. Going into public relations mode, Alsberg penned a letter to the *New York Herald Tribune* (May 8, 1927), boasting—and perhaps overstating—the Provincetown's role in Green's accomplishment. By taking on Green's work when other theater companies turned it away, he contended, the Provincetown "saved" him for American drama. He wondered if Green had "kept knocking at the unopened door, whether he might have abandoned the drama." Besides giving the Provincetown some credit for Green's Pulitzer honor, Alsberg, of course, was trying to sell tickets. But despite packed houses and public discussion fueled by issues depicted in the play, the Playhouse remained mired in a financial hole.[10]

Although the play did not provide the treasure chest the theater company hoped for, it *did* offer theatergoers a sensitive portrayal of a raw subject, which, considering the times, was itself notable. Lynching still made the news with alarming regularity, and millions of Americans belonged to the Ku Klux Klan. In any case, *Abraham's Bosom* was part of a pre–civil rights exploration of black literature and performing arts happening outside the geographic lines of the Harlem Renaissance.[11] For Alsberg, this production and its subject matter presaged what he dealt with later as Federal Writers' Project director. In that role, he advocated for stories of the African American experience to be told to a wider audience.

The pride Alsberg felt about the downtown theaters' contributions manifested itself later in at least one Federal Writers' Project book, *New York Panorama*. Although Alsberg was not officially involved in the nitty-gritty writing of the book (he worked out of Washington, D.C.), he kept close tabs on the New York City publications and influenced their content. *New York Panorama* described the New York legitimate theater scene in the 1930s as dependent for its survival on the work of groups such as the Provincetown and the Neighborhood playhouses. "These groups have done more to invigorate the theater, both legitimate and otherwise, than any other force." The book described the Provincetown Playhouse as "perhaps the most important," adding that "a notable accomplishment of this group was its work in bringing the Negro actor to the legitimate stage. Paul Robeson, Charles Gilpin, Frank Wilson, Jules Bledsoe, and Rose McClendon were made known to the public largely by way of MacDougal Street. No more brilliant array of literary and theatrical talent has enriched the American stage than that assembled by the Provincetown Players."[12]

No surprise, then, that during the 1930s, Paul Green's *Abraham's Bosom* would be presented by the Federal Theatre Project, the entity run by Alsberg's colleague, Hallie Flanagan. Alsberg's and Green's paths crossed again during this period when Green, back in his native North Carolina, came on as an advisor to the state's first oral history program for the Writers' Project.

The 1927 Provincetown production of *Abraham's Bosom* was notable not just for presenting an African American topic. Although the theater company had yet to produce a black playwright, the fact that it produced a play *about* African Americans and *starring* African Americans, and produced it with a sensitivity not seen in other entertainment venues, was indeed significant. According to scholar Thomas N. Walters: "Presented in an era which strove in large measure to nurture the extreme, the silly, the profligate, this play's stage was filled with realistically portrayed black people who were to be taken seriously. By way of contrast, anyone who sees motion pictures of the period cannot avoid the Negro stereotypes, the subtle and not-so-subtle debasing of a race through the 'Stepin Fetchit,' 'Little Buckwheat,' and 'Aunt Jemima' caricatures depicted on the silver screen."[13]

After *Abraham's Bosom* and its critical, if not financial success, the company sought a play that would fit the bill of being progressive, controversial, and experimentally creative.

After one of his trips abroad to arrange for financial support of the Soviet political prisoners, Alsberg returned with a souvenir: the script of *The Prisoner*. Translated by his anarchist friend Alexander Berkman from the Emil Bernhard script, *Das Reizende Lamm*, and set in a Siberian prison before the 1917 revolution, it would unite Alsberg's deeply felt cause working on behalf of freeing political prisoners with his current occupation.

It wouldn't have been difficult to convince the rest of the leadership to produce Berkman's play. Eleanor Fitzgerald ("Fitzi"), who had been a driving force in the company since its early days, had once been Berkman's lover. In fact, both Alsberg and Fitzgerald were close to Berkman and Emma Goldman, even working together on Berkman's behalf to get his memoirs published. Alsberg and Fitzi's relationship may have been prickly at some points, likely based on disagreements in the Playhouse operations. Shortly after Hanau and Helen Deutsch wrote and published a history of the theater, Hanau sent Alsberg a copy of the book. Although Fitzi was known as a nurturing, driving force, there is evidence, conversely, that she caused dissension in the ranks and was unhappy with the book.[14]

In his letter to Hanau after reading the book in 1931, Alsberg wrote: "Don't fuss about Fitzi. She is beyond good and evil. However, if you'd let me read the mms. beforehand, maybe I could have helped you to steer clear of some troubles. You know I told you I didn't give a d—n what you said about me (as long as you didn't tell the truth about my personal life)." He added, seemingly sardonically, "If you could set up a good controversy maybe it will sell the book better and better."[15] Talking about his "personal life" leads one to wonder if he meant his sexuality, of which Hanau was aware.[16]

It's possible that the controversy referred to was another Provincetown Playhouse production, that of E.E. Cummings' highly experimental three-act play, *Him*, in 1928. Hanau and Deutsch's book recognized Alsberg for bringing the play to the attention of the group and convincing his colleagues to produce it. Fitzi may have taken umbrage at this account. In fact, Alsberg and Fitzgerald both took credit for bringing the production to Provincetown, and various reports support each of their claims.[17] It is clear that Alsberg and Fitzi were at the very least *allies* in advocating for the play. (His feelings turned more nostalgic on hearing of her death in 1955. "The spirit de corps of the Provincetown

Playhouse in my day centered in Fitzi's heart and radiated from there with warmth and gaiety into the hearts of the whole outfit,"[18] he wrote in a memorial letter.)

It might have been a tough sell, because, as Alsberg later said, "Few of them could discover what the play was about."[19] Alsberg not only "got it" but also appreciated E.E. Cummings himself, praising the playwright as the only one he ever dealt with "who was reasonable, decent, intelligent, etc."[20]

Producing the experimental work of an established poet was just one motive for taking on *Him*. The producers' recent approach to bringing in bigger audiences—by mounting plays at uptown, more physically comfortable venues—had not been successful. Alsberg suggested they abandon that approach and go back to their roots. Instead of opening plays in Greenwich Village with an "eye to moving them uptown, why not make Macdougal Street a place where theatergoers would find what they could not find elsewhere"—artistic and daring plays that hearkened back to the heyday of the Provincetown Playhouse? Alsberg viewed *Him* as the vehicle to do just that.[21]

Alsberg threw himself into the difficult production of *Him*, becoming involved in the day-to-day rehearsals and technical activities. (At least one of those problems made the papers when an apartment over the theater caught fire, sending the costumed cast into the street and damaging scenery. Perhaps this was an omen.) Challenges included twenty-one scene changes and a shockingly large character list of 105 roles played by thirty actors. Scene changes were made all the more difficult because the small theater's stage lacked wings; actors had to help stagehands move scenery through a trapdoor on the stage that led to a basement. "The actors rehearsed scene changing like a military drill ... the self-sacrifice of the kids in the cast was something to remember. Some of them were married, most of them were broke; yet no one withdrew, even after salaries were pared down to keep the production going," Alsberg told an interviewer.[22]

Most critics slammed the play: "The most incoherent play ever mounted," according to *Variety*.[23] Provincetown slammed back, printing a brochure containing reviews, both pro (there were some) and con, in hopes of enticing a more sophisticated, artistic, bohemian audience—the type of audience that would bestow on them the cachet once enjoyed by the earlier incarnation of the Provincetown Playhouse.

It worked. According to Deutsch and Hanau, "Audiences of a new kind were filling the theater, made up no longer of old ladies who thought the playhouse quaint, or of sightseers and pilgrims to an historic landmark ... students and professors of psychology, esthetics and drama came to see the play not once but three or four times."[24] *Him* ran for six weeks. But these new, sophisticated audiences did not fill the coffers. Said Alsberg, "When the play closed because of budget difficulties, it closed to full houses."[25]

Him has since gone on to numerous productions. In a late-life postscript, Alsberg received an enthusiastic letter from Stuart Chenoweth, a professor at San Francisco State College. Chenoweth, directing *Him* for the college in 1968, was excited to learn that Alsberg, the original producer, lived in nearby Palo Alto. So at the age of eighty-six, Alsberg was a special invited guest to this production.[26]

When in 1929 Provincetown producers attempted to transform the group once again by moving uptown to the Garrick Theatre, Alsberg did not go with them. By this time, he was deeply involved in another project that promised bigger returns.

Between Two Worlds: Bringing The Dybbuk to America

His work with the famous Provincetown Playhouse notwithstanding, it was at the slightly less legendary, but still prestigious Neighborhood Playhouse where Alsberg earned his title of "playwright."[27] It came with the success of *The Dybbuk*, his reworking and translation of the Chassidic and Kabbalah-inspired mystical play about a forlorn spirit that inhabits a human. His adaptation of the folktale play by S. Ansky was called "a triumph" by the *New York Times*[28] and named one of the ten best plays of the 1925–26 season.[29]

In fact, in his own multitasking manner, Alsberg began working on *The Dybbuk* at Neighborhood Playhouse while still involved with the Provincetown. It would turn out to be his most successful venture in theater, one that brought him a measure of recognition and the specter of fame.

On the long days aboard the *Rijnd* in 1923, with an ocean lying between his experiences in Europe and his future back at home in New York, Alsberg's mind surely swirled with Old World scenes of the poor inhabitants of the ghettos and *shtetls*, as well as their counterparts in cosmopolitan cities of Eastern and Central Europe. Quite possibly he wasn't ready to reenter American life without incorporating the experiences he'd left behind. It's easy to imagine that he passed the hours on the Atlantic crossing keeping a diary. In words now lost to time, he probably noted his fascination with S. Ansky's play, *The Dybbuk*, the Jewish folktale play he'd seen performed in Moscow. Perhaps Alsberg was also fascinated with Ansky, the man. Although twenty years his senior, born nearly 5000 miles away into an orthodox religious culture alien to Alsberg's New York German-Jewish milieu, and dead by 1920, Ansky was, in many ways, Alsberg's spiritual twin.

S. Ansky (also known as Solomon Rappoport; his given name was Shloyme-Zanvl Rappoport[30]) was born in a Russian *shtetl* into a poor, Yiddish-speaking family. The family soon moved to Vitebsk where he was raised, mostly by his mother, a tavern keeper. He left his family in 1881, the year Alsberg was born, and became, as would Alsberg, a writer, publisher, journalist, and political activist, as well as an "organizer of aid work" and "ethnographic quests."[31] Alsberg, as director of the Federal Writers' Project, would, of course, lead the largest American "ethnographic quest" of the twentieth century.

Whatever the impetus that motivated Alsberg to focus his literary energies on *The Dybbuk*—a play that would go on to become the most famous dramatic work in Yiddish and Hebrew theater—he would be the man to bring Ansky's work to American shores and the English-speaking world.

Whether Alsberg actually met Ansky—they both spent time aiding Jewish refugees after World War I and traveled in radical political circles in Europe—remains unknown, but securing rights to *The Dybbuk* proved to be a success on many fronts. With Ansky's childhood friend Chaim Zhitlovsky acting as estate executor, Alsberg signed a contract in 1924 granting him sole English-language rights to the play (for publication, stage, and motion pictures), with a percentage of the income derived from productions to be given to the Ansky estate.[32] Contact with Alice Lewisohn (founder of the Neighborhood Playhouse with her sister, Irene) came soon after, and within six months Alsberg signed a contract with the Neighborhood Playhouse granting it stage rights in the United States and Canada, with royalties to him. He received a $250 advance.

At that point, *The Dybbuk* was not entirely unknown in New York; a Yiddish art theater had produced it earlier. Similarly, the play had enjoyed a period of fame in Poland (in Yiddish, by the famed Vilna Troupe) and in Russia (in Hebrew, the version Alsberg had seen performed by the similarly celebrated Moscow Art Theater's troupe).

But it was Alsberg's translation from Yiddish into English and the resulting critically acclaimed productions in 1925 and 1926 that really fed the flame of popularization and brought widespread recognition to this work of art. The Neighborhood Playhouse's version opened it up to a wide audience and served as a springboard for other productions and adaptations that continue today in English-speaking countries. Alsberg's own version, performed hundreds of times during his lifetime and after, saw productions (stage, radio, and television) at home, in Canada, and overseas in the United Kingdom and South Africa.

The Neighborhood Playhouse, located "in the heart of the great isolated, self-contained, exotic and teeming East Side,"[33] proved the ideal place to give life to the drama. The theater itself (now a celebrated off-Broadway theater and drama school) was part of the Henry Street Settlement House, where poor

Although a sometime producer at the famed Provincetown Playhouse, Alsberg's greatest theatrical success came with his translation and adaptation of the *The Dybbuk*. The Yiddish folktale mixed mysticism with a love story and opened to accolades at the Neighborhood Playhouse in New York City in 1925. Here, opera star Mary Ellis (with the two long braids, wearing a wedding gown) portrays the doomed lover, Leah, circa 1926. George Gershwin wanted to make *The Dybbuk* into his first full-length opera, but a music copyright issue thwarted the plan (photograph by Francis Joseph Brugière @ Billy Rose Theatre Division, The New York Public Library for the Performing Arts).

immigrant families received aid through education, health care, and arts programs. It was two miles and a world away from the bohemian atmosphere of the Provincetown, so Alsberg, like Ansky before him, was between two worlds. (Ansky's original Yiddish title was *Der Dibek: Tsvishn Tsvey Veltn*—or, in English, *The Dybbuk: Between Two Worlds*.)

The *Dybbuk*, described by modern-day critics as a melding of *Fiddler on the Roof*, *The Exorcist*, and *Romeo and Juliet*, tells the story of a well-to-do patriarch, Sender, about to marry off his daughter Leah to a boy from a rich family. Channon, a poor Talmudic student in love with Leah, is thrown into despair by the news of her wedding. Rebelling against the conservative teachings of the Talmud, Channon uses Kabbalah mysticism to try and win her hand. This encounter with mystical forces causes his death and allows his soul to enter her body.

That the two are meant to be together even in death is the great love story; after Channon is exorcised from her body, they call to one another: Leah, earthbound in her wedding dress as she is about to marry her father's choice of groom, and Channon, from his place in some ethereal plane. She cannot live without him: "Come back to me my bridegroom, my husband. We shall be with each other, and in the night in our dreams we shall cling to one another … and we shall rock to sleep our unborn children, and sing them wondrous lullabies."[34] She dies in order to be with him; their joyous souls merge in the final moment before the curtain falls. The haunting story, woven together with equally haunting Chassidic melodies and creative staging, reportedly cast a spell over the cast and crew even before the show opened.[35]

Looking more deeply at the play's content and subtext, Alsberg's political leanings cannot be disregarded as a motivation to obtain the rights and adapt the play. Although it may be a bit of a simplification—a rich girl dies because her father doesn't want her to marry a poor student—an anticapitalist subtext underlies this otherworldly folktale. As someone with anarchist leanings, Alsberg could identify with Channon's rebellion against the hierarchal authority of Sender's world. Even women's rights, supported by Alsberg in his writings and in his dealings with women throughout his life, became part of the thematic mixture.

Alice Lewisohn described taking Alsberg's translation with her on a trip abroad. "The characters seemed to emerge from the pages," she wrote. "The quality of the *Dybbuk* came through in the translation, but could its atmosphere, so foreign, so strangely remote, be recaptured for the stage?"[36] Apparently she thought it could.

With Ansky as progenitor, and the Vilna and Habima troupes as his children, Alsberg could be considered the prescient American cousin who carried the mantle and acted as the midwife to bring the play into the English-speaking world.

Established Metropolitan Opera star and Broadway celebrity Mary Ellis, twenty-eight, was chosen to play Leah. Lending an air of authenticity, David Vardi, an actor from the Moscow Habima troupe, was brought in to direct, a task he would share with Alice Lewisohn. Aline Bernstein, who would become the first female member of the United Scenic Artists Union in New York, handled costumes and scene design.

During ten weeks of rehearsals—"a terrifyingly short time," according to Lewisohn—the translation was readapted, and Alsberg, along with Winifred Katzin, worked with Vardi to incorporate portions of Habima's Hebrew version. Alsberg adapted on the fly, and the actors had to keep up. "It never ceased to be a miracle that the manuscript, molded from Hebrew and Yiddish and then pruned down to English, still held its natural flow and character,"[37] said Lewisohn.

All of this did add up to foreignness for American audiences and necessitated an extensive program note, written by Alsberg as a sort of explication and a way for "gentiles" as well as secular Jews like himself to understand the play. Alsberg wrote of Ansky's desire to "bring his audience back to the old conception of Judaism as a general system of morality, applicable to all mankind, something more than queer and strange local religious beliefs and ceremonies." Alsberg's program note closed by emphasizing what he saw as Ansky's universal message: "that what really counts is the universal brotherhood of all right-thinking and doing persons, and that this vast brotherhood will be only an expansion of the original conception of 'the chosen people.'"[38]

The show opened on December 15, 1925. The reviews were numerous and positive. Wrote *New York Times* theater critic Brooks Atkinson the following day: "Three acts of this strange, haunting play come off in a muted performance, though [sic] colorful scenes set in a synagogue, a courtyard and a prayer room, with chants and incantations, with processions of Jews of all degrees—as deep in tone as a Rembrandt canvas."

The shows sold out, the run extended. The attendant fame for Alsberg helped his general standing in the downtown theater world. David Vardi's direction received high praise, as did Mary Ellis' acting and the general production values.

Alsberg's translation, though not always noted in the newspaper articles, received attention from some reviewers. When the play was published in book form that year, theater critic Gilbert W. Gabriel wrote in the introduction that the production owed "much to the work of Mr. Alsberg, who so successfully translated and adapted it for the Neighborhood production." Gabriel made clear that the difficulties inherent in Alsberg's efforts were great. "A stilted word, an exaggerated wrench away from the softly clanking honesty of the Yiddish original, might have degraded the whole magnificence of its brooding mood."[39]

The show's popularity and positive reviews soon brought offers to move it to an uptown Broadway theater for an indefinite run. Alsberg and director David Vardi lobbied for this move. But in what would be his first disappointment of many, the producers decided against it.

When the Moscow Art Theatre's Habima version—staged in Hebrew—came to New York late in 1926, the Neighborhood Playhouse capitalized on the renewed publicity and staged a revival. That the two ran simultaneously did not present a problem and even offered a certain synchronicity that allowed each to feed off the other. In fact, some of the attention to the Habima version was due to the previous year's Neighborhood Playhouse production; English-speaking reviewers needed Alsberg's translated version in order to understand the Habima version.

Some reviewers were not kind to Habima, drawing ire from Alsberg, who was supportive of their U.S. tour and generous in his praise. Perhaps he saw them as partisans spreading the word about what would become—thanks to all of them—Ansky's folk classic. Alsberg's words of support were published in Gilbert Gabriel's *New York Sun* theater column (December 18, 1926): "I have just come burning," he reported, "from the Habima's performance of *The Dybbuk*, burning with a renewal of the old thrill I got from their performance in Moscow some years ago, and also, I must confess, burning with indignation at our New York critics for their very restrained and almost damning-with-faint-praise notices…. Had I been a dramatic critic, I should have exhausted Webster's dictionary for words with which to do justice to the Habima. In its presentation of Ansky's play, this company scales the dramatic heights with a combination of realism, the grotesque, the tragic and the sublime." Critic Gabriel ended the column: "Which the Habima, I am sure, may take to be praise from Sir Henry."

This flurry of *Dybbuk* activity caused a domino effect. In February, while the Neighborhood Playhouse and Habima productions were still running, the Yiddish Art Theater Players performed the play, in English, as a radio presentation on a local New York station. Alsberg's close ties with Habima were evident: In 1927, he served as secretary to the group's fundraising effort to reestablish the troupe in Palestine; the following year, Nahum Zemach, founder of Habima, chose to stage Alsberg's English version in San Francisco.

Gershwin Comes Calling

Soon after came the opportunity that would put Alsberg on the brink of making an even bigger splash uptown and giving him solid standing in commercial theater. George Gershwin, enamored with *The Dybbuk* after seeing it at the Neighborhood Playhouse, signed a contract with the Metropolitan Opera to adapt the play with Alsberg as the librettist.[40] Gershwin wasn't the only one interested in it. The *New Times* reported on March 25, 1926, that Arthur Hammerstein also wanted to produce an operatic version as a vehicle for the talented Mary Ellis. However, Hammerstein canceled his plans, according to the newspaper, after discovering that "another producer intends to produce the play in English on Broadway." He likely referred to Gershwin's proposed Met production.

Alsberg, according to his own earlier missives, showed more concern about adding to the artistic and political achievements of his generation than in achieving fame and fortune. The mainstream and commercial success that seemed imminent was not something he would have sought out in his younger years. Nevertheless, the opportunity to work with someone as notable as Gershwin, along with the added cachet of his work being staged at the Metropolitan Opera, had to be enticing. He also was not an artist out of touch with financial considerations. Closing in on fifty years old, the itinerant life of a journalist, freelance writer, political rabble-rouser, and sometime playwright and translator was wearying.

The times were precarious. The day before Gershwin signed the Met contract, the stock market crashed. But plans for the show persisted. Alsberg's passionate work on behalf of political prisoners had not ebbed, and he continued to contribute personal funds to that cause. Consequently, the $500 guaranteed after four performances at the Met would have been very welcome. Additionally, the contract spelled out plans for mounting the production not just in New York, but in Philadelphia, Baltimore, Atlanta, Washington, and Cleveland as well, so even more royalties would have been expected.[41]

Gershwin, eager to begin his first opera, met with Alsberg for "a few chats."[42] According to biographer Isaac Goldberg, Gershwin had planned a trip to Europe "for a month or so, to make a special study of Jewish music" and had begun to create melodic phrases. "He glanced at the notes and was soon constructing not only music but a scene. This slow lilt gradually assumed a hieratic character, swinging in drowsy dignity above a drone."[43]

This opportunity—for Gershwin, Alsberg, and the play itself—was stymied by a glitch in the copyright. Soon after the contract was signed, it was found that the musical rights (acquired separately from Alsberg's translation rights) belonged to the Italian composer Lodovico Rocca. Gershwin's first full-length opera was not to be *The Dybbuk*.

The outcome had to beg a lifelong question for Alsberg: Would it have reached the legendary fame achieved by *Porgy and Bess*, Gershwin's first full-length opera? Although Alsberg's *Dybbuk* did indeed play around the nation and internationally at venues ranging from small synagogues to large repertory theaters, and on television and radio, he would never see the commercial success that had appeared so close.

If all had gone according to plan, the Gershwin–Alsberg production of *The Dybbuk* would have opened at the Metropolitan Opera on April 1, 1931. The letter that Alsberg sent to friend Louise Bryant (after she had written him asking for a money loan) made clear his circumstances. He'd been financially generous with his friends and accommodated their requests when he could, but in a letter dated shortly before the operatic Dybbuk *would* have opened, he commiserated with her, saying he was "terribly sorry you are in such a fix. But I'm in very much of the same condition, or worse myself. I'm completely broke and jobless. I'm afraid I can't help you."[44]

Artistic Descendants

Throughout the years, and until the present day, Alsberg's adaption has continued to play. It also has inspired many other versions. Aaron Copland wrote the piano trio *Vitebsk* (1929) after seeing the Neighborhood Playhouse production and being inspired by the Chassidic folk song that functioned as the play's musical motif.[45] The musical notation of this haunting melody is included in *The Dybbuk* book by Alsberg and Winifred Katzin with the note "Jewish Melody sung in Vitebsk (Birthplace of Ansky)."

In his later years, Alsberg wrote about Ansky and may have offered a flash of insight about himself as well when talking about crossing the barriers between the real world and the "other" world. For Alsberg, this "other" world—far away from the hard facts of journalistic and political life—was the theater. The dybbuk, as he said, was not just a legend or myth to the Chassidim of Eastern Europe but "a fact, a portentous possibility."[46]

CHAPTER 8

"To the daring belongs the world"
1929–1934

The loss of the Gershwin production of *The Dybbuk* following on the heels of the stock market crash of October 1929 may have contributed to Alsberg's own, personal depression. His letters to Emma Goldman confirm his melancholy, but he wrote more vaguely and did not include such explicit complaints as before. (Strangely, he did not even mention his theatrical misfortunes.) He asked her to continue writing—even if he couldn't gather the energy to keep up his end of the correspondence—"As I need some words of cheer now and then from your kindly soul (when I can't get your gefilte fisch)."[1]

Despite Henry Alsberg's initial refusal to help with Goldman's autobiography, her insistence—"Be daring, old dear, for to the daring belongs the world"—had its desired effect and she eventually got her way. She even planned to name him "executor" of the manuscript, along with Sasha Berkman.[2] Perhaps the admiration she expressed for his literary judgment won him over. Indeed, it was high praise from someone so critical and demanding. She truly believed him to be the right person to advise her on the manuscript. "You happen to be in the fortunate position of understanding my part in the various social issues in the United States and also having sufficient feeling for the personal life I led."[3] Alsberg wasn't yet ready to return to Europe to work with her in person. Goldman had no choice but to grudgingly accept this. Her backup plan, to send him drafts so that he could make suggestions and critiques, would have to do.

The two had grown closer during their time together in France, with Alsberg signing off on his letter with "Love, Henry," and Goldman affectionately calling him by nicknames, such as "dear Lobster." Emma Goldman's family became part of Alsberg's extended family, at least for a short time, with her niece, Stella Ballantine, and Stella's two children, Ian and David, spending a few Christmas holidays with Alsberg and his family. (Ian, like his uncle Saxe, became a titan of publishing, founding Ballantine books.)

The work on Goldman's book buoyed Alsberg at least partially during this dark period. In January 1930, Goldman sent two copies of the first installment of her autobiography to the United States: one to her lawyer, who would deliver it to Knopf, and the other to Henry Alsberg. "I depend on you, Henry dear please don't fail me…. And don't for the love of Moses feel nervous about giving me a frank opinion…. I feel that of all of the people I know in America you are the guy to tell me exactly how the work impresses you … where can I find another being who has both the literary qualities for the criticisms I need?"[4]

Over a five-month period, Goldman continued to mail Alsberg installments of her book, and he reciprocated with suggestions and impressions. She was heartened by his first letter, which came almost immediately after she sent him the first 288 pages: "I know you haven't taken nourishment for days because you've been waiting to get my opinion. Eat, drink and be merry. This Sir Oracle thinks your book is swell!"[5] His next letter contained suggestions for specific changes, including a passage about a lesbian prison matron Goldman encountered at New York's infamous Blackwell's Island jail. Alsberg thought it wouldn't get past the censor.

By March 1930, with her manuscript running too long, she asked him to go over it page by page to look for material that could be cut. He did his best to keep up with her demands, but he was again dealing with his own troubles. Between his "personal insanities," which he did not elucidate, and hers (French authorities threatened to expel her), "one feels like an inhabitant of an insane planet," he wrote.[6] Alsberg was slightly more forthcoming with Sasha Berkman: "It is not loneliness exactly that I suffer from but the feeling of futility, plus personal worries, chiefly my mother."[7]

"My dear boy, I know you have something of a complex in that way," Berkman replied almost immediately, "but you have now spent a lot of time at home, and I think it is sure to do you good to come over here for a while … and for all I know, it may also do your mother good." Knowing Alsberg's love of the countryside, Berkman tried to persuade him to join himself and Goldman for what would be a reunion of sorts in St. Tropez. While Berkman wanted Alsberg to help with the book—Goldman trusted Alsberg's literary judgment more than Berkman's, it seemed, and she would fight him less about trimming passages—he also thought working in the garden and helping with minor bricklaying projects would ease his depression.[8]

"Just come," Berkman wrote.

"I'm very fond of gardening and pretty good at it. Everybody's garden but my own," answered Alsberg.

But even the offer of good company amid the peaceful village life and the opportunity to putter around in a garden couldn't convince him. Whether he referred to the garden metaphorically—he could easily have been referring to the help he gave others with their books and his inability to complete his own— is impossible to say.

Financial responsibilities may have also played into his emotional turmoil. While family resources likely still supplemented his finances, the country— much like him—was in the throes of a depression. So, he turned once again to what had always been a sure thing: freelance writing. It couldn't have been particularly lucrative; his writing during this period consisted mainly of book reviews for *The Nation* and other liberal publications.[9] (The family still employed a cleaning woman, so they were far from destitute.)

It helped that he knew the various players sitting in the editorial chairs. Childhood friend Stella Bloch Hanau edited *Birth Control Review*, founded by Margaret Sanger. Alsberg showed his old, indignant self in an article repudiating an economist who argued that if unskilled laborers and farmers had smaller families, it would relieve unemployment. "The problem of the poor settles itself. They die off when there are too many of them. Or, if they drag on in suffering and in want, Congress can always draw a red herring of an investigation of communist propaganda across the path of our [human] feelings."[10]

But what Henry Alsberg really needed was another cause.

Prison Reform in America

A series of prison revolts that rocked the nation brought prison reform into the public eye and caught Alsberg's attention. His emotions were likely already primed, having spent hours reading drafts of Emma Goldman's book, which included horrific accounts of her time in prison. He also had more than a passing familiarity with Berkman's *Prison Memoirs of on Anarchist* and, of course, the conditions faced by political prisoners worldwide.

It had all the right ingredients: a suffering population, indifferent government leaders, a desperate need for a change within the established system. And with his connections and knowledge about international prisoners, he could have been a frontrunner in giving voice to this liberal cause. He wrote Emma Goldman that he'd convinced the *New York World* to run seven articles he'd collected from expert penologists on the horrors of New York prisons.[11] In a nod to Mahatma Gandhi's *Hindu Swaraj*, which called for Indian home rule,

Alsberg wrote the article "Prisoners' Swaraj." It appeared in the *New Freeman* and called for nonviolent political action on the part of the incarcerated.[12] Later he wrote to Goldman about his fascination with Gandhi's nonviolent independence movement: "We must not use the implements of the exploiters in the fight against them … non resistance and non cooperation are weapons that terrify them and are to them incomprehensible." Besides, pacifism appealed to him because, he wrote, "it suits my indolent nature wonderfully."[13]

He also dusted off his notes for a book he had begun a few years before on the topic of political prisoners and told Sasha Berkman that Viking Press had agreed to publish it. The book was never published, but Alsberg continued working on it intermittently for a few years and sent Berkman a copy of the manuscript for his input. Berkman especially liked Alsberg's idea for "radicals of bourgeois stock" to go into jails to help prisoners organize for better treatment.[14]

Alsberg's only other public words on the topic during this period came in the form of a letter to the editor published in *The Nation*. In it, he agitated for inmates to develop a class-consciousness and organize a nonviolent, passive resistance movement modeled on conscientious objectors and European politicals. "Convicts must not engage in bloody aggressive prison rebellions. The blood must be shed by his jailers," he wrote. "The criminal … must develop an active conviction that poverty and lack of opportunity are his greatest crimes, and that therefore he is entitled to treatment better, not worse, than that accorded wild animals in captivity."[15] This 500-word, essentially inconsequential letter, would return to haunt him.

Emma Goldman's seemingly never-ending writing of her autobiography and struggles with her publisher continued to absorb much of Alsberg's time. When she asked if he'd be willing to become the book's associate editor—formally, not just an unofficial advisor—he agreed. All they had to do was get Knopf's blessing.

Perhaps mixing in Goldman and Berkman's affairs (Berkman faced a never-ending fight to legally stay in France) distracted Alsberg from his own emotional demons. "Have been by turns very depressed and the reverse. It will seem comical to you with your bigger *zorus* [troubles] that I should be depressed. But I suppose I haven't your infinite vitality and grit."[16] He was near "self-destruction," he told Goldman, and any gaiety in his letters was hollow. "My love-life, like that of an elephant is all wrong." He found some solace in the countryside on his brother's land; describing an early morning scenic view, he told of "swelling ranges of mountains, thickly wooded, soft and cushiony as expensive, green pan-velvet overstuffed love couches. Over all, '*der resige schein*' [translucent light] of a sun and sky that always makes me think of very young babies, just bathed and breast-fed. The sky was young, almost infantile and tender, somehow mother's breast and child in one."

Knopf turned down Goldman's request to assign Alsberg as associate editor. If it bothered him, he didn't let on his in letters to Goldman, but she knew him well enough to advise him to keep up with his writing, despite his *"selch ein faulenzer"* (laziness).[17]

Alsberg overcame his laziness, and perhaps his disordered moods, to pursue a few writing projects. His slow but steady output, seen over a five-year period, consisted chiefly of feature articles for the *New York Times* and book reviews for the *New Republic* and *Birth Control Review.* Topics ranged from the conventional (the bridges of New York City) to the political (dictatorships in Europe).[18] He also worked on a play but seemed insecure about it and, indeed, had trouble garnering interest.[19]

In late fall, Alsberg gathered with other American supporters of Goldman and Berkman for a testimonial dinner to celebrate Alexander Berkman's sixtieth birthday. Four hundred people filled the Central Opera House on East 67th Street for the two-dollar-a-plate dinner. Alsberg, among the speakers, wrote the biographical sketch included in the booklet published for the testimonial. Calling Berkman intelligent and courageous, he hailed his older friend's struggle against "industrial masters" and refusal to accept the "suppression of the voice of the masses." He praised Berkman unconditionally:

> The greatest tribute we must pay to Berkman is the tribute that more timid people, if they are quite honest, always must pay to undaunted courage facing all odds and all penalties on behalf of a good cause. He has spent his whole life lavishly in active rebellion to help the submerged and oppressed masses, without ever counting the cost to himself and the comparative hopelessness of succeeding.[20]

The celebration raised money and morale for Berkman, impoverished on both counts.

In Opposition to the Majority

New York and Paris were not the only strongholds for bohemian lifestyles. Improbably, 1930 Santa Fe offered artists, writers, and nonconformists a safe haven, with Mabel Dodge Luhan and D.H. Lawrence among its denizens. A young poet, twenty-five-year-old Clifford McCarthy, had landed in Santa Fe via Kansas City, Missouri, and New York, and soon, according to gossip of the time, the handsome McCarthy had taken up with U.S. Senator Bronson Cutting from New York. Although a small circle of people might have known of their relationship, it was in their best interests—particularly the senator's—to keep it hidden. Alsberg and McCarthy knew each other from New York, and when the senator paid for McCarthy's travel through Europe, Alsberg helped arrange for him to meet Goldman and Berkman in France. Surely McCarthy was not Alsberg's only gay friend, but this trip and subsequent letters are the only lasting testament to any such relationships.

Whatever their connection—lovers, for which there is no evidence, or friends—it had to be a great boon for Alsberg to have someone who could understand his own, mostly closeted existence. Alsberg's romantic loneliness had to make his depressive bouts that much harder to face—and perhaps even caused his torturous stretches of self-doubt, anxiety, and dis-ease with the world.

Goldman and Berkman, like nearly everyone who met Cliff McCarthy, were charmed by him but disturbed by his heavy drinking. Cliff, Berkman told Alsberg, "needs a strong though loving hand near him all the time. Too bad you're not with him here."[21] Alsberg, at times put off by McCarthy's unpredictable behavior and self-indulgent boozing, mostly considered him a sweet, incorrigible "kid." Those qualities, not to mention McCarthy's relationship with Cutting (which ended tragically in 1935 when the senator perished in a plane crash) may have kept their relationship platonic. Nonetheless, the two shared a fondness for one another. After the death of his father, McCarthy spent a day in New York with Alsberg, whose tender treatment of the young man led McCarthy to tell Emma Goldman that a day spent in New York with Henry "was as peaceful as a day with you."[22]

Approaching fifty years old during the "hellishly hot summer" of 1931, Alsberg wrote Berkman, describing the U.S. economic situation as desperate, with "absolute control by the owners and terrible wage reductions and unemployment. The textile industries are even worse off. Strikes etc. and no work. The winter is going to be awful for the poor."

He kept busy working on his shack on his "heaven-scraping hill" in the country—now more of a cottage, since he added a second room. "Would that these rooms were male and female and could give birth to a progeny of rooms," he joked. He also gave a speech on international civil liberties at the nearby Mohegan Colony. He playfully mocked his audience, "our well-fed comrades [who] sat about on a well-fed lawn, in the gloaming," enjoying "stuffed juicy sandwiches, cake and orangeade ... no rags or shabby clothes, no odor of perspiration. Most of them have several bathrooms in their houses,—and even use them. But I must say, in spite of an air of prosperity among them, they are swell people, kindly, gentle and rather idealistic. They will not fight," he said, but he commended them for donating money to be sent to impoverished and exiled Russian anarchists in Europe.[23]

Alsberg was growing more pensive about aging and death and love. Even before Emma Goldman's autobiography, *Living My Life*, finally came out in October (and continuing afterwards), his exchanges with Goldman moved beyond the book and editorial discussions to more philosophical musings. "The more people I see and have about, the more lonesome I am. Life closes in on us." And: "As we grow older, folly grows on us apace. When I was young and twenty I was the most sensible, restrained and decorous person in the world. As one goes downhill the pace gets swifter and more hysterical." On the suicide of his best college friend: "Life repeats, especially in pain giving." On his thoughts about personal and political pacifism: "Passive or active, I shall always be in opposition to the majority."[24]

Goldman tried to reassure him. "You do have depth and intensity even if you pretend to be amused by the devil don't care attitude to life ... you are a Yid my dear, you'll never free yourself from the woe of the world." And as if to punctuate that, she added to their running joke: "Come when you can, '*die*' gefilte fisch will be waiting for you."[25]

By Christmas 1931, he was ready for a change of scenery. Alsberg longed for Europe and prepared to make what would be his final trip to the continent.

While the political machinations leading to the tragedies of World War II were unfolding, the hoped-for post-war peace was also dissolving into militaristic fascism. In Switzerland, the League of Nations met for what would turn out to be futile disarmament talks. In Germany, Hitler had lost the presidential election in March 1932 but was steadily gaining power anyway and laying the groundwork to secure his Nazi Party's future. The Depression, of course, wrought its own unrest as well.

It was under this backdrop that Alsberg, looking for inspiration and escape, arrived somewhat unexpectedly in Europe in the spring of 1932. He was admittedly not the most dependable correspondent, which led Goldman and Berkman to complain that they never knew when he would show up for a visit. Nevertheless, Berkman once quipped, "What is ever definite with that Lovable Vagabond? But he is a good fellow for his lack of organization."[26]

Details of this trip are scant, merely outlined in letters of the period. He visited Emma Goldman in St. Tropez and Alexander Berkman and his companion, Emmy Eckstein, in Nice. He rambled through France for at least part of the time with Jimmie McGraw, who in a few years would become one of his trusted Federal Writers' Project assistants.

This was at least partially a working trip. Still "monkeying around" with his political prisoner book, he journeyed to Spain and remained for six weeks. (His first trip to the country was five years earlier, with Emma Goldman.) In Seville he had to chase members of the political prisoners committee "all over town for three days until we could meet somewhere the police were not likely to show up." He submitted articles to *The Nation* on political conditions in Spain but admitted they weren't "awfully well-written." (They were not published.)

In August, Alsberg attended the World Congress Against War in Amsterdam, where he interviewed refugee radicals for his book; although he was listed as an American delegate and worked alongside Americans Theodore Dreiser, Sherwood Anderson, John Dos Passos, and Upton Sinclair, Alsberg quickly grew disenchanted. Thousands of people attended the congress, held in an armory. With sunlight pouring through the skylights and raising the temperature on the already emotionally heated scene, he watched as the communist factions took control of the meeting. Alsberg and other pacifists wanted to pass a resolution against all war and in favor of peace. The communists who dominated the meeting "wanted a resolution passed against all imperialistic wars and to protect Russia." He did not sign their resolutions and left the Congress, returning to France.[27] He again visited Goldman in St. Tropez for five days, and Berkman in Nice, and even took time out for a pleasure trip to Monte Carlo with Jimmie McGraw, Sasha Berkman, and Emmy Eckstein.

After a short stop in Germany, Alsberg boarded the steamship *Bremen*. His last transatlantic journey came to an end as the ship passed through a winter coastal storm that hit the Eastern Seaboard. Despite the high seas and heavy winds, the *Bremen* arrived on schedule on November 28 at Brooklyn's 58th Street pier.

Aimless in the Metropolis

His letters during his European tour contained no mention of mental anguish or mood swings. Rather, the travel and writing and social visits seemed to energize him. However, his first letter to Goldman after his return to the United States signaled the reappearance of the doldrums. Although he didn't get specific, he told how her how he was "plunged at once" into sentimental troubles. He found conditions in America discouraging and railed at the inequities faced by the poor as the country sank lower into the depths of the Depression. "Many people who still have a pretty good income act as if they were on the bread line. And there is the same disgusting twaddle all over urging people to do their share in helping allay suffering, while the rich bankers etc. don't do anything.... I wish you and S. [Sasha] were here to rouse the sluggish souls of the hoi polloi." He added sarcastically, "It is wonderful what people will stand for in this country without a murmur. The propaganda is, of course, in the press, marvelous, so that even the hungry are persuaded that they are not hungry but merely have indigestion."

Alsberg had told Berkman that he would get to work on the political prisoner book once he was back home. He once jokingly said, "Don't encourage me, because encouragement always discourages me. It is contrary to my nature." Berkman cheered him on from afar anyway. "I know you can write, and write well, so go to it, old fellow." But Berkman understood Alsberg well enough to know he'd need a push, and appealed to Jimmie McGraw. "I don't know if you are familiar with Henry's writings .... Henry can write; and more than that he has ideas and he is not afraid to express them. And that is enough to produce a good work."[28]

Alsberg never published this book on political prisoners. Instead, looking back on his life over the last fifteen years, he decided to try his hand at an autobiographical novel, and began working on that. By the end of the year, as the nation sank more deeply into its economic and spiritual quagmire, so did he. He could well have been talking about himself when he said, "Nobody knows which way he is coming or going. But we are all hoping that a mysterious providence which takes care of drunken sailors and Americans will do something about something." He was aimless, without a compass in "this garbage-strewn strand that calls itself a metropolis." Once a respected foreign correspondent, he now labored on projects that he couldn't finish and that no one ever saw. "I have fallen from even the modest imminence I may once have occupied. I am less than nothing ... nobody pays any attention to me anymore, and I don't pay attention to anybody. I am in complete retirement, mentally, physically ... and morally. A complete debacle intellectual liberal."[29]

Feeling at the end of his rope and with no job in sight, he even toyed with the idea of joining a cooperative farm that friends had started near Detroit. He felt he could offer something—teaching and cultural work, as well as the physical labor of carpentry and farming. ("I can tell a cucumber from a strawberry, and lettuce from cabbage.") He also thought he'd be able to write at the farm "better there than here" because of fewer distractions. His insecurity fed his indecisiveness, and he turned to Goldman for advice. "I have doubts insofar as I fear mental isolation, and petty bickerings about plumbing, toilets and drainage disposal. Also sentimentally, I don't want to be entirely stranded. On the other hand, to be in something productive and real and profitless is a great temptation."[30]

1934: Henry Alsberg's New Deal

While he considered joining the farm cooperative and worked on his autobiographical novel, Alsberg reconnected with his American network of writers, artists, and even government and civic officials. Franklin Delano Roosevelt had taken office, giving liberals new hope and reviving the germ of idealism lying somewhat dormant in Alsberg. "Without being naive," he told Goldman, "I do think there are forces at work to overcome the old reactionary spirit."[31]

Brother Carl had been appointed to a commission convened to study international economic conditions and advise President Roosevelt. Cliff McCarthy worked in Washington with Senator Cutting. Henry Morgenthau, Jr.—son of the former U.S. Ambassador to Turkey, and with whom Henry had traveled as part of the Jewish Joint Distribution Committee—was Secretary of the Treasury. Soon-to-be Supreme Court Justice Felix Frankfurter was a close advisor to Roosevelt. Even more significantly, an acquaintance from New York, Jacob Baker, had secured a high position in the New Deal's Federal Emergency Relief Administration (FERA). Alsberg must have wondered: Would there be a place for him?

Henry Alsberg looked forward to conferring with Emma Goldman in person, on American soil. In early 1934, government officials granted her a three-month visa for a lecture tour of America. She arrived with great fanfare; viewed through the lens of newpaper accounts, she was by this time perceived by some as more of a cuddly, benign grandmother, not the dangerous radical deported years earlier. Alsberg and Cliff McCarthy paid her a visit in New York, bringing a bottle of champagne to celebrate. The next day, Alsberg spoke at a dinner in her honor at the Town Hall Club; he met her for a more intimate lunch a few days later.[32]

By March, as Goldman's tour moved to the Midwest, Alsberg turned south. Jacob Baker, had, in fact, tapped Alsberg to join the publications division of FERA. This new agency, one of Roosevelt's New Deal initiatives put into place to bring the country out of the Depression, distributed relief funds to states and employed millions of people. Its activities would need to be publicized.

Washington, D.C., then, as now, was a three- to five-hour train ride from New York City, shorter by far than the days' long trips Alsberg had made so many times across the Atlantic. But in some ways, his home capital was more foreign to Alsberg than Paris, Berlin, and Vienna. Ironically, he was also moving away from the anarchists, who believed in the absence of government, to the U.S. government's seat of power.

Goldman may have sensed that gradually Alsberg was taking leave of her flock. She knew him well enough to understand that once he was pulled into Franklin Roosevelt's administration, he might be lost to her. Throughout Goldman's time lecturing in America, she tried to secure a visa extension, asking friends, including Alsberg and Cliff McCarthy in Washington, to intercede with government officials. They in turn attempted to contact friends in the administration, but neither really had sufficient influence. Goldman never received the extension and left the United States at the end of April 1934.

In her desperation to remain in the United States, she wrote snappish letters admonishing Alsberg for his lack of interest in her tour and his lack of help with her visa. Despite what she felt, he hadn't abandoned her, and both he and McCarthy continued to raise money to donate toward Goldman's and Berkman's living expenses. Like an errant son, Alsberg promised to do better but said his work consumed him.

Alsberg's FERA assignment, to edit a book about the agency's accomplishments, drew him in. If he couldn't complete a book of his own, he could do it for some other entity while on assignment and with external deadline pressures. Published in September, *America Fights the Depression*, a sturdy, 160-page large-format book, promoted the accomplishments of the Civil Works Administration, a component of FERA.[33] Containing well over 200 photographs with accompanying commentary, the enthusiasm of the editor—Alsberg—shone through. As a matter of fact, whether by assignment or his own design, it reflected his ideological leanings. Women, minorities, and other ignored segments of the population appeared throughout the book. In a section lauding the Civil Works Administration's support for musicians, a photograph of an African American choir appeared right next to a white symphony orchestra from San Francisco. Both black and white children were shown frolicking in CWA built playgrounds and schools. And in a nod to open-mindedness not usually found in government-sponsored publications, men and women in a sculpture class observed a nearly nude male model as they worked on their sculptures. As if ensuring that every multicultural and sexist barrier was, if not broken, then at least cracked, another photograph showed an Asian woman archeologist appraising a museum piece. In a section on healthcare, a photograph of a dental clinic operated by African Americans shared a page with a similar photograph of a white clinic. The book celebrated women's accomplishments in fields ranging from laundrywomen to lawyers. Cooperatives of craftsmen, farmers, coalminers, and bakers illustrated the administration's support of this veritable socialistic economic system. A section on Native Americans revealed not only those working at stereotypical "Indian" crafts but also artists involved in public works art projects.

Working on the book seemed to help Alsberg get through a personal crisis. On a trip to New York, he suffered a profound loss when mother Bertha died in August 1934. The family held the funeral at their West 95th Street home. News of Bertha's death filtered to Goldman. She eased her criticism of his lax correspondence in her condolence note, offering, "It is not often that sons are so attached to their mother as you had been, hence you must feel her passing away much deeper than the other children."[34]

However his mother's death affected him, he blamed his "lousy moods" for not responding to Goldman until the following April. With the FERA book completed and in bookstores by September, he now worked on the more lack-luster job of writing publicity for the agency. He pronounced himself already tired of it, but couldn't give it up because he had little cushion by then to fall back on. Although Alsberg didn't have the courage to give up a good job, he expected it would be "remedied soon when they fire me." This minor adjourn-ment in his dedication to the New Deal led Alsberg to once more express the desire to return to France and live with Goldman in her St. Tropez cottage. "I am homesick as h-l for Europe; Europe with all her faults, still retains the better part of my affections."[35] Goldman knew better. "Europe is not so pleasant now," she replied.

The two friends' correspondence fell to a trickle—mostly due to Alsberg's negligence—but Goldman had softened. "You are a hopeless correspondent but a damned good friend. And that's the rarest thing of all in this horrible world of ours," she wrote him. To their mutual friend Emily Coleman, she wist-fully wrote, "My esteem and affection will never be affected by his long silences."[36]

Despite Alsberg's fears, Baker didn't fire him. In fact, the administration's plans to extend the white-collar works projects to employ musicians, artists, and writers intrigued Alsberg. Perhaps he could find a home in Washington.

His entanglement with the pessimistic and gloomy lives of outcast anar-chists slowly gave way to the enthusiasm inherent in the propaganda he once criticized, a segue aided and abetted by the New Deal's hopeful vision to remake the country economically and socially. In the midst of reevaluating his life, he needed to find yet another track to follow, another channel for his idealism.

Emma Goldman once called Alsberg "the best that was in America." His big toe still remained in the Old World, but that world was on its way to anni-hilation. If he could loosen his emotional grip on Europe and regain the youth-ful energy that made him so productive in the 1920s, he could, even at fifty-three years old, take root and re-embrace America. The ideological principles, the art, the culture that he chased across Europe, even amid war and terror, could be excavated right in his own backyard.

"Something New or Strange"

Perhaps Alsberg's note to Goldman a few years before presaged the new life about to engulf him, to which he would devote himself more fully than he had to anything previously. "I have such a tentative feeling about myself and my immediate career, as if I were winding up things and getting ready for something else new or strange, a sensation about absence of alarm about my future, when, from every point of view I should be worrying about it like everything."[37]

In the recent past, he had suffered great literary and theatrical setbacks. He had labored, and ultimately failed, to complete two books (his autobiographical novel and one on political prisoners). His theatrical career had basically ended (although it would have a brief resurgence in his later years). He couldn't have known he was about to embark on a venture that would overshadow his former endeavors, even the most successful ones. If Gershwin's musical *Dybbuk* had escaped the copyright snafu and seen the fame achieved by *Porgy and Bess*, Alsberg may never have heeded the *first* call from Franklin Delano Roosevelt's administration that brought him to FERA. And he certainly would not have then become part of an enterprise that allowed him to shape the American literary landscape in entirely different and profound ways. It took a few failures to get him there, but Alsberg was about to take the helm of the Federal Writers' Project (FWP), one of the greatest national artistic achievements of the twentieth century.

Without Henry Garfield Alsberg—energetic and adaptable, alternately melancholic and boundlessly enthusiastic—the FWP may have turned into just another long-forgotten, worthless government experiment. Assessing his own past few years, he never could have imagined how many books would eventually carry his byline. Forget two books, his name would appear on hundreds.

As director of the Federal Writers' Project, he would steer a course into literary history. Roosevelt's New Deal and Alsberg's personal new deal, packaged together, primed him for this "something else new or strange." Henry Alsberg was about to fall in love with America.

CHAPTER 9

The Man Who Wrote America
The Federal Writers' Project
1935–1938

Circus people is like other human bein's. How I started was when I met my husband in Buffalo. He was doing a wire act and we was married six months after.... We was with the Circus 12 years until 1926. That's when we had our accident.—Maude Cromwell, Circus Performer, Life History interview from Federal Writers' Project, 1939[1]

The bark was as cranky as a racing shell and the river as full of ice as the Delaware when Washington crossed it a number of decades ago ... ice floes kept booming up against the sides of the little shallop, spinning it around like a top and turning it up on edge. I, at the bow, and the boatman at the stern, pushed, coaxed, and bullied our way through as best we could.—Henry Alsberg, crossing the River Dniester, war-torn Russia, 1920

My most immediate concern is in carrying out the purposes of the great work program just enacted by the Congress. Its first objective is to put men and women now on the relief rolls to work and, incidentally, to assist materially in our already unmistakable march toward recovery.—Franklin Delano Roosevelt, Fireside Chat, April 28, 1935

The thrill of a high wire act, the perils of navigating a bureaucracy almost as dangerous as the icy Dniester River, the political ideology meant to heal a nation. Henry Alsberg was about to encounter it all.

In April 1935, Alsberg, not so happily, still toiled away writing copy for the Federal Emergency Relief Administration (FERA), a job, he wrote to Emma Goldman, that was "of doubtful utility and just now of uncertain tenure."[2] That same month, President Roosevelt introduced to the nation his "great work program," known as the Works Progress Administration (WPA).[3]

The world teetered on a precipice. In Germany, deadly restrictions against

Jews were already in place. Persecution of other groups, including homosexuals, increased, too; students and storm troopers destroyed Magnus Hirschfeld's library at the Institute for Sexual Science in Berlin, burning some of the same books Alsberg had read while visiting the continent.

In contrast, threads of optimism ran through Roosevelt's audacious plans to move the country out of the Great Depression. The Executive Order creating the WPA in May 1935 promised to move the unemployed from relief rolls to jobs. Alsberg, like so many others, wanted to believe.

Historically, the New Deal projects that still catch our eye are those of the public works variety. Proud, poverty-stricken masses built bridges, schools, and hospitals, along with airports and thousands of miles of roads, thanks to government jobs. An "alphabet soup" of public works programs, before and during WPA's life span, also provided employment.[4] But there was more to relief than construction projects. The WPA also funded education, vocational training, healthcare, and housing for the poor. The government hired seamstresses to provide clothing for those down to their last, tattered outfits; nurses to care for the indigent sick; librarians to deliver books (sometimes traveling by mule) to rural households; and teachers for the new schools. Artist Conrad A. Albrizio's mural, *The New Deal*, is illustrative of the period, lionizing a tall and muscular Franklin Roosevelt. In this idolized manifestation he wears a work smock, his hands resting kindly on the shoulders of a tired wage earner. Surrounding them are industrious men and women at various occupations.

As FERA's supervisor of reports and records, Henry Alsberg watched as the government offered an outstretched hand. He could almost believe he'd been transported to a model Bolshevik society. Meanwhile, as jobs programs got under way across the country, writers who had been agitating for relief all along took to the picket lines. On a cold February day, a photographer from New York's *Daily Mirror* captured an image of protesters, with one carrying a sign reading "Children Need Books, Writers Need a Break, We Demand Projects."[5] Writers' unions petitioned the government with proposals for assorted projects to aid desperate writers. Thus, as New Deal architects developed blueprints for WPA operations, writers got onto on the radar. Luckily, Harry Hopkins, supervisor of FERA, and later the WPA, believed in a relief program that would also employ white-collar professionals, writers, and artists in useful and creative enterprises. ("Hell! They've got to eat just like other people."[6]) Alsberg saw a glimmer of light, a nascent hope that perhaps he could escape the drudgery of writing unemployment reports and promotional materials.

Alsberg moved to an apartment in a brick house on the shady, tree-lined Lamont Street, a few miles north of the White House, and spent time with Jacob Baker (his FERA boss) and others in the left-leaning community. He

and other officials batted around ideas for hiring professionals and artists—
teachers, librarians, writers, artists, musicians, actors—through the early part
of 1935.

In this Federal Writers' Project publicity shot
(circa 1936, Washington, D.C.), Henry Alsberg appears optimistic that he will be able to
fulfill his mission—to help Americans redis-
cover America—by producing high-quality
guidebooks, providing jobs for unemployed
writers, and completing the ex-slave, folklore
and "social-ethnic" studies and their accompanying publications (Library of Congress,
Prints & Photographs Division).

Federal One

Federal Project Number One,
the WPA program that would
encompass the Theatre, Art, Music, and Writers' Projects, would
not officially commence until
August 1935, but its creation took
shape throughout the spring and
summer, culminating in an off-the-
record meeting at Alsberg's home
on a steamy summer's night. WPA
Director Harry Hopkins and Jacob
Baker led the unconventional summit, inviting Hallie Flanagan,
director of experimental theater at
Vassar College; Holger Cahill,
from New York's Museum of Modern Art; and noted conductor
Nikolai Sokoloff. Henry Alsberg
and FERA associate Clair Laning
discussed the Writers' Project plans.
"It was one of those evenings in
which everything seemed possible," said Flanagan.[7]

Alsberg, who searched the
world—most notably, Russia—for
collectivist enterprises, found it
instead in the most unlikeliest of
places: his own nation's humid capital. He was like someone who, in
an attempt to view the aurora borealis, traveled to faraway spots in the
northernmost parts of the hemi-
sphere, only to be disappointed by

its absence, yet on returning home and looking up one night, witnessed the brilliant greens and reds and blues—the northern dawn appearing in his own backyard after all.

Less than three months after the executive order creating the WPA, Hopkins announced the plans for employing out-of-work creative artists, naming his four directors: Flanagan, Cahill, and Sokoloff for the theater, art, and music programs, respectively, and Henry Alsberg as director of the Federal Writers' Project (FWP).[8] The four programs and their directors fell under the umbrella dubbed "Federal One."

Right Man for the Job?

The choice of Henry Alsberg surprised some and did not meet universal praise. No one contested his creative gifts, his intellectual aptitude, or his boundless energy. His compassion toward the hungry and the poor went unquestioned. Some criticized his management abilities, and one WPA official called him an "odd duck," saying quite erroneously, "He isn't a writer."[9]

Jerre Mangione's memoir of his time on the Writers' Project as national coordinating editor and Monty Noam Penkower's account of the FWP both celebrated the creative impulses Alsberg brought to the project. Both also reported on the complaints about his administrative style. He refused to keep carbon copies of letters; he didn't like to fire people; he was indecisive. Critics grumbled that his relaxed personality led to administrative confusion that damaged the Project. (Those who questioned his ability to finish projects had legitimate reason to worry.) In his exhaustive portrait of the arts projects, William McDonald painted a contrasting picture of Alsberg. On one hand, his praise flowed: "Henry G. Alsberg combined in a remarkable degree a genuine sympathy for the plight of writers in need of relief with a lofty conceit of writing as an art and as a vehicle for the expression of the national character. For that reason, the [American] Guides are, and always will remain, a monument to his magnamity and professional integrity." McDonald also noted supervisory deficiencies, saying, "His natural tendency was to act as editor rather than administrator."[10] However, evidence against this viewpoint comes from Jacob Baker. "Alsberg was the shrewdest and slickest at getting his people approved," according to Baker, and hit the ground running even before the official start of the FWP, ready with names of potential administrators who could pass political and artistic muster as regional directors.[11] (A quintuplet of books, including those written by the above-mentioned authors, report on nearly every aspect of the FWP, save for Alsberg's life story. It would be unproductive to duplicate in detail what these authors so ably covered. Thus, readers who want a more in-depth look are directed to these studies.)[12]

Criticisms published in the earliest FWP histories were perpetuated in subsequent writings. Whether they represented myth, truth, or fell somewhere in between may not matter; Alsberg was the right man for the job *because* of his casual, creative style.

The project that began with the intent to write an official "guide" to the United States might have turned out merely *that* under the leadership of a crackerjack administrator, but without a visionary leader, it certainly wouldn't have produced the sheer volume of books that it did, certainly not books praised for their literary quality nor the classic *American Guide* book series. This series that began as a tour guide turned into an act of preservation, with descriptions of now-vanished towns and forests and railways and charming country lanes—portrayals that would have been lost to history. And the FWP surely would not have evolved to produce thousands of publications and documents that provide other timeless examinations of the past: memories from elderly ex-slaves; folklore of the nineteenth and twentieth centuries; books on typically ignored segments of American society, namely immigrant groups and African-Americans. That Alsberg also pushed for the Project to support the creative work of young writers like Richard Wright was a then-unimagined windfall.

Any expectation that a multimillion-dollar enterprise with thousands of employees could be flawlessly administered is naive. The administrator who could wrangle together the many parts of that gargantuan project, with its tentacles reaching from Puerto Rico to Alaska, probably did not exist. This publishing venture was larger in scope than anything ever attempted by any government institution. Alsberg, along with his fellow Federal One arts administrators, entered virgin territory, with no map to follow. For Alsberg, this was ironic, considering that he would be responsible for creating one of the most renowned tour guides in U.S. history, the eminent *American Guide* series. Alsberg and his colleagues leading the music, art, and theater programs had to make it up as they went along—all under the public's watchful and critical eye.

Alsberg admitted early on that he never expected that volume of organizational work. Maybe he shared some characteristics with older brother Carl, who, like Henry, was described as inspiring loyalty and devotion from friends and co-workers, but could also be "forgetful of appointments" and overcommitted. Some have attributed Alsberg's success to his smart and capable assistants, and while it's true that skilled assistants strengthen and support a visionary leader, without that leader's farsighted and prophetic imaginings, what would there be to support?

John Edgerton, a scholar with a sympathetic view toward Alsberg, described him as having "just the right mix of political savvy and artistic sensitivity. In the constant tension between creative expression and government propaganda—and between the idealism of a nation trying to rise to its promise and the reality of a nation beset by gangsterism in the North, racism in the South, and poverty everywhere—Alsberg somehow managed to steer a steady course."[13]

The experiences Alsberg brought with him—from diplomatic service, relief work, and reporting in the hostile lands of Eastern Europe to the New York theater world and Emma Goldman's anarchist dreams—made him singularly prepared to navigate between the bohemian world of writers, the bureaucracy of Washington insiders, the jumble and jungle of state political machines, and the dignified societal airs of the White House.

His FERA job begun the previous year marked the first time that Alsberg earned a regular salary in at least a decade. There is something ironic in the fact that he continued on the payroll of the U.S. government (with a starting salary of $6200), administering a program that would allow destitute, unemployed workers to engage in the types of labor for which they were best suited. American masses likely never noticed its similarity to radical political ideas, particularly the Marxist maxim, "from each according to his abilities, to each according to his needs." It wouldn't have been lost on Alsberg and other social reformers. Besides, Alsberg needed a place to vent his pent-up ideology; he was a rebel who needed another cause. In 1935, all his paths converged in glorious synthesis, merging his obsessions with social justice, writing, and politics under the FWP canopy. He devoted himself like never before, immersing body and soul into this adventure. He did not flounder. For a brief, glorious time, at age fifty-four, his skills and experiences found a suitable American home.

An American Baedeker

When the Writers' Project opened for business in August 1935, it had a bank account of $6.2 million and plans to hire 10,000 writers and ancillary workers (i.e., clerical staff, researchers, photographers) from the relief rolls.[14] The initial plans called for the agency to publish a five- volume *American Guide*, divided into regional sections. Other early proposals might have appeared overly ambitious, and included journalism instruction; translation work for historians; studies of racial groups; compiling American folklore, archeological, and "Indian" material; and writing local travel guides.[15] These pie-in-the-sky dreams were mostly realized. Besides jobs, the FWP would provide something useful and tangible for communities and, indeed, the nation. It's easy to imagine Alsberg excitedly brainstorming with his staff. A newspaper photograph shows him, in a cool, white summer suit, confidently signing papers to get the project under way. His more realistic "lieutenants," George Cronyn and Reed Harris, had to think that just getting out the *American Guide* would be enough.

The Baedeker guidebooks Alsberg used in his European travels were held up by some as the model for this new venture, thus the nickname, "an American Baedeker." The timetable called for written materials from regional and state offices to be sent to Alsberg's central staff in Washington by May 1936—less than a year away.

But what shape could such a guidebook take? Would the FWP turn out easily obsolete, "dry-as-dust" recitations of lodging, landmarks, automobile routes, and tourist attractions? Would such a book be, essentially, a government-sponsored promotional compendium? FWP editor Katharine Kellock successfully called for—and dedicated herself to—the inclusion of tour routes. From the beginning, however, Alsberg harbored loftier ambitions, and he adamantly insisted on the inclusion of essays exploring the cultural landscape of the regions, essays that would "attract attention to the whole of American civilization and its development."[16] He wanted to examine the history, the anthropology, the artistry of America. And what of the influences beyond white, Anglo-Saxon stock? How would indigenous peoples, African-Americans, and immigrants fare in these essays? Alsberg sought to elevate the *American Guide* to something higher than a chamber of commerce tome. *This* book would not, in a few seasons, lie fallow—its pages creased, sun-damaged, and sticky with picnic foods—in the rumble seat of a Chevy Mercury or Buick Roadmaster. Left to bureaucrats, the *American Guide* might have turned out that way.

Editors, writers, and researchers (along with teachers, librarians, and some with less "writerly" credentials) came from the relief rolls around the nation: established authors, promising young writers, newspaper reporters, and even, as the picket signs in New York called for, children's book writers. "I've been planning for more than a year ways and means of giving work to authors which will at the same time take them off relief rolls and result in a work which will be of help to the Government and the American people as a whole," Alsberg told the Washington, D.C.'s *Evening Star*.[17] Early on, Alsberg had the idea that some writers could even be paid to work on their own creative pieces, including novels.[18]

The announcement of the FWP was greeted with interest in some quarters and scorn in others. From the beginning, Roosevelt's foes labeled the relief programs as "boondoggling" (wasteful) enterprises. In July, before the project even had a chance to get its sea legs, the *Washington Post* satirized both the

With a massive statue of Neptune watching over them, Writers' Project employees in Washington, D.C., work in makeshift headquarters in the ballroom of a mansion taken over by the government. To their great delight, writers discovered leftover cases of champagne in the basement from the mansion's gaudier days (RG 69-N, National Archives at College Park).

project and Alsberg's desire for high literary quality, calling the proposed guide-book a "Boondoggling Baedeker."

The first few months were a blur of exploration, planning, proposing, toss-ing ideas into proverbial wastebaskets, and planning again. Working out of an old converted theater in Washington with the other Federal One agencies (art, music, and theater programs), Alsberg's office was in a former backstage dress-ing room, quite fitting for someone preparing a major production for the largest audience of his career. One of the FWP's earliest fans was Eleanor Roosevelt, who invited Alsberg and his staff to visit her at the White House to discuss their plans for writers.[19] The First Lady gave her blessing and remained sup-portive throughout the FWP's existence.

Soon, Federal One personnel were relocated into a similarly improbable and unsuitable building, the abandoned, once luxurious McLean Mansion. The mansion's ballroom was transformed into the Writers' Project headquar-ters. Interior photographs show a massive statue of Neptune, trident in hand, presiding over the 100 or so desks, each covered by piles of paperwork, with only a few small fans providing ventilation. Add to this the cacophonic sound-scape—ballroom acoustics were unsuited to office conversations, typewriters, phones, and "occasional shouts of the office drunk."[20] (Perhaps the discovery of a case of champagne hidden away in the basement, left over from the man-sion's glory days, helped this along.)[21] Alsberg's staff worked through the sum-mer and fall, alongside Neptune and other statuary gods (excellent hat-holders, as it turned out), amid huge hanging tapestries and lavish woodcarvings, ornate candelabras, and chandeliers. Except for these adornments and surroundings, it had the feel of an old-time city newsroom. This, indeed, would be the hub, where copy from around the nation was sent for editing and approval. Alsberg himself took refuge in one of the few enclosed offices behind the ballroom. This room, with its multiple, constantly ringing phones, acrid cigarette smoke from his chain smoking, and his unending bottles of pink bismuth for his chronic dyspepsia, does not bring to mind a "refuge." It was an unlikely place to write the people's story of America.

In the midst of giving interviews and speeches, and working with his able assistants to set up the Washington office, Alsberg also had to recruit regional and state directors. In some cases this was straightforward, with Alsberg finding novelists or other well-known writers ready to take on the task. (Certain admin-istrative jobs did not require workers to be on relief rolls.) On other occasions, it proved more complicated. WPA state administrators, who worked separately from Federal One, often obstructed Alsberg's choices. On top of that, he had to juggle requests for jobs from politicians and friends of friends.

In an almost comical conversation, Alsberg and assistant George Cronyn weighed the merits of a request from Senator Thomas Gore of Oklahoma, a WPA critic who earlier that year voted against the agency's funding.[22] Gore wanted a man named A.E. Emory appointed as his state's FWP director. Although Alsberg did not take this recommendation, the abridged discussion below is illustrative.[23]

> CRONYN: We just got this wire from Senator Gore.
> ALSBERG: Who is Gore?
> CRONYN: He is that famous blind senator.
> ALSBERG: I think the blind senator is dead.
> CRONYN: I'll look it up. (A moment passes as he checks. Gore is alive and well.)
> ALSBERG: I do not think we ought to allow any senator to tell us what to do.

Some friends successfully lobbied Alsberg to hire the Harvard-educated son of a prominent author. The young man, though qualified, had more finan-cial resources than most, and his appointment represented a less principled decision. Alsberg was pragmatic when the First Lady called him in December 1935 to request a position for one of her husband's oldest friends who'd squandered his money. She feared the president's childhood pal would "do something desperate. He has no income whatever." Mrs. Roosevelt made clear that the friend should not be given *too* important a job. Alsberg went right to it, calling the state director in Virginia later that day. "His great drawback," Alsberg said, "is that he imbibes every once in a while, and she was worried for fear we would give him a supervisory job."[24]

Alsberg worked day and night through the fall months. Word of his appoint-

Henry Alsberg in his FWP office with devoted secretary, Dora Thea Hettwer, circa 1937. She later worked as an editor with him when Hastings House Publishers reproduced the *American Guide* series in the 1940s. They remained friendly throughout their lives, with Hettwer pronouncing Alsberg "the Guiding Star" of the FWP (Katharine Amend Kellock Papers/Library of Congress, Prints & Photographs Division).

ment reached Emma Goldman in France. After congratulating him for "helping starving people get back on their feet," even she lobbied him for jobs on behalf of two poor writer friends in the states.

"I am laboring as but I can to cut the mass of red tape entangling us to get 5000 intelligentsia to work on our writing projects. The job has me working day and night," he told Goldman when he finally wrote back on Halloween. "You'd laugh at the busy executive I've become. I try to stay human however." He praised the New Deal, calling Roosevelt's administration "pretty decent.... I know of no cases of discrimination against destitute people because of their political or religious beliefs or because of race." (WPA policy forbade discrimination on account of race, religion, political affiliation, or union activities.) In his last known letter to Emma Goldman, Alsberg enclosed a $100 check written out to her. He made no mention of wanting to return to Europe.[25]

Their worlds, once so entwined, were now forever separated by geography, by personal and professional pursuits, by the times in which they lived. Goldman wrote him a few more times. In October 1935 she expressed surprise ("I never would have believed that you would display such sticktoitivness") and admiration. "I take off my hat to you, old dear. That you will find the bureaucracy limiting and hard to break through was to be expected. Just the same I am delighted that it is YOU, and not some corrupt person.... I feel certain that you are doing your damndest to enable a few at least to ply their profession." Her last letters to Alsberg in 1936 recounted Sasha Berkman's painful illness, and subsequent death. Perhaps she knew they'd not be in touch again. "Goodbye dear old lazy Hank," she wrote. While Henry Alsberg allowed the Writers' Project to swallow him up, Emma Goldman continued her quest for a better world, working with the Spanish anarchist revolution. (After Franco's ascension, she moved to Toronto, where she died in 1940.)[26]

As in the past, Alsberg needed a coterie sympathetic to his causes, personality, and maybe even lifestyle. To this end, Alsberg brought on writers not only from the relief rolls but also from his own address book. (Some qualified for WPA relief jobs; all needed the work.) His helping hand mirrored past times when he readily and generously gave ten or twenty or hundred dollars to a needy friend when he had the cash. (And it was a reciprocal arrangement. For instance, when Alsberg had needed work, Stella Bloch Hanau gave him freelance assignments for the magazine she edited.) Alsberg also knew that the people he hired possessed something many patronage beneficiaries do not: talent, if not actual genius. Throughout his life he had been fortunate, or made it his business, to surround himself with the intellectually gifted and progressive. Thus did he tap Hanau, Roderick Seidenberg, James McGraw, Philip Coan,

Clair Laning, Mary Lloyd, and Greenwich Village anarchists Leonard Abbott and Harry Kelly, among others.

Talent and freethinking ways were not the only characteristics he considered. Although working in Washington as a government employee could have been a stultifying experience by itself, another, more personal reason, may have triggered his decision to surround himself with friends. As a homosexual in 1930s America, danger loomed constantly. Homophobia and persecution were the norm. After all, "fairies" and "inverts" were all thought to be depraved perverts with no place in "normal" society. The repercussions Alsberg faced if exposed ranged from losing his job to losing his life. Between those two extremes lay myriad other horrific possibilities. The law of the land supported this: Same-sex sexual activity constituted a criminal act. Although Alsberg documented no personal recollections of troubles he may have faced, the published diary of Jeb Alexander, a pseudonym for a government employee who worked in Washington during the same era, paints a grim picture of living as a closeted homosexual in Washington. Alexander describes an office Christmas gift that he found "insinuating" and insulting: The gift, a pack of chocolate cigarettes, contained a note reading, "You'll find these a very particular fag."[27] Although an underground homosexual culture existed, it might have been difficult for Alsberg to find his way into it. He would have had to be especially heedful in a city that was relatively unfamiliar to him.

It's impossible to ascertain to what extent Alsberg concealed his underground lifestyle from friends and colleagues. With Hanau, for instance, he could be open about his sexuality. Many anarchists supported equal sexual rights, even homosexual rights, so he may have been able to be less guarded with those associates as well. Close friendships with James McGraw and his wife lasted their lifetimes and reflected a familiarity and understanding that could come only through such trust. Dora Thea Hettwer, his faithful secretary, likely fell into that category as well. Later correspondence between New York City FWP editor Vincent McHugh and Jerre Mangione indicate their awareness of Alsberg's sexuality. But there also could have been a range of disclosures, including a "don't ask, don't tell" attitude. In books about the FWP, Alsberg is consistently described as a "bachelor," often used as code for "homosexual." One account published two years after Alsberg's death discussed his homosexuality. The author claimed Alsberg was blackmailed, but this assertion was in the context of otherwise inflammatory falsehoods.[28]

In a painful paradox, Alsberg, while striving to *uncover* America, had to remain hidden. While struggling to foster equal rights for women, African-Americans, immigrants, and other groups, he could not even hope to enjoy them himself or to give voice to his own struggles. He depended on his friends' loyalty and discretion.

Community Service at Its Core

If Harry Hopkins could have traversed ten years into the future, he would have been astonished by the WPA's accomplishments. The public works projects built 8,000 bridges, 24,300 miles of sewage facilities, 57,000 miles of new roads, and 35,000 new public buildings. Federal One's Music and Art projects brought concerts to people who had never heard live orchestras, and art to public buildings. They offered classes to rural as well as cosmopolitan residents, children and adults, nationwide. Hallie Flanagan's Federal Theatre Project introduced hundreds of dramatic productions to Americans in every state and employed thousands of actors, stage managers, and directors (including twenty-year-old Orson Welles).

The FWP employed both established writers and newcomers. Among the thousands on the roster were Richard Wright, Zora Neale Hurston, John Cheever, Margaret Walker, Studs Terkel, Saul Bellow, Ralph Ellison, Anzia Yezierska, and May Swenson. Charles Seeger, father of folksinger Pete and deputy director of the Federal Music Project, contributed music essays to Project books.

The *American Guide*, first envisioned as a five-volume work, moved away from this model to evolve into a series comprised of state and city guides. The *American Guide* series became the centerpiece of the FWP. Eventually, guidebooks for all forty-eight states, along with Alaska, Washington, D.C., and Puerto Rico, as well as city and regional guides, were published. (A set of *American Guide* books sells for as much as $5,000 in the current market. Reissues of guides with updated prologues continue to be published.) Other multibook series, children's books, and countless regional and local books were issued as well. With books underwritten by sponsors (i.e., nonprofit organizations, historical societies, nonfederal government agencies), no federal funds were expended for publishing, easing the way past WPA critics and anti–New Deal politicians. This complicated formula devised by Alsberg is described in detail by McDonald, as well as by Mangione,[29] whose post as national coordinating editor involved arranging for sponsors to contract with large, commercial publishers. Those publishers printed the books and marketed them at their own expense, selling them below market price, as dictated by the WPA. Sponsors received royalties to defray any costs incurred, with any leftover funds transferred to WPA coffers. This scheme, besides being financially advantageous to both publishers and the government, ensured quality printing—something the Government Printing Office could not provide.

Each book in the *American Guide* series contained illustrations, photographs, descriptions of natural resources and geography, suggested tour routes, maps, and similar, typical travel-guide fare. Alsberg successfully pushed to include cultural and scientific essays. The overall results remained uneven; while some books were banal and included racist commentary (Alsberg would have been happy to leave these to molder in America's rumble seats), others, like the *Cape Cod Pilot*, garnered critical acclaim for their literary styles; still more became best-sellers.

As Jerrold Hirsch wrote in his cultural and intellectual study of the FWP, Alsberg wanted to make a "deeper examination of American Culture."[30] He and his liberal, intellectual staff pushed to imbue the writings with cultural diversity. Alsberg appointed Howard University English professor Sterling Brown as national head of Negro Affairs, with the intent to include essays describing African American communities in the state guidebooks. Out of these goals to celebrate cultural and ethnic diversity came ancillary projects, in the form of the ex-slave narratives, and the folklore and "social-ethnic" studies projects. The massive amounts of research collected for these included interviews with former slaves, immigrants, Western pioneer settlers, Native Americans, factory workers, unionist activists, farmers, ranchers, and street cleaners, among others. First-person narratives—ten thousand, by some estimates—were collected and transcribed. Taken together, the *American Guide* books and cultural studies projects proved to be historical treasures.

In 1935 it was all a quixotic dream. But everything began with the *American Guide.*

The American Guides: A Self Portrait

By the fall 1935, three thousand writers and support staff worked in offices across the nation. Field workers roamed and combed city streets and country towns, looking not only for tour guide material, but also for people's life stories. Alsberg's staff had already prepared and sent out a fifty-five-page *American Guide* manual with instructions for writers and editors. Like people battening down for a storm, Alsberg and his team prepared for the onslaught of words. Alsberg likened it to an author whose publisher has paid a large advance but had yet to produce anything. Alsberg was savvy and pragmatic enough to know that it was imperative to sell the *idea* of the guide, well before any physical volumes existed, to commercial interests and the American public.

He loved to lecture, and it paid off handily in the interviews he gave to the press.

"People do not need to motor long distances, buy steamship tickets, or expend large sums in railroad fares to enjoy new and interesting sights, but they do need to know what to look for and where to go," he said. "Right in your own backyard, relatively speaking, may be the beginning of the trail which ends on a mountaintop; or just across the road may meander a small stream which will carry your canoe through canals and rivers to some inland sea or to the very ocean itself." Alsberg also extolled the value of such a guide for foreigners. "Although the foreign visitor has heard of New York, Washington, D.C., the Chicago stockyard and Niagara Falls, there remains a lurking impression Indians still rove the primeval forest."[31]

As a seasoned European traveler he considered the tour and travel sections of the guidebooks important in their own right. He also believed they should go beyond merely utilitarian writing, an important nod to those writers pushing for more creative work. "Even within the framework of the tours I insist that interest and vividness be preserved. The tour form is a difficult form; it is like a sonnet."[32] He predicted students would find special uses for the guidebooks as they used the anthropological and historical essays to learn about their own local areas, as well as far-off regions.

And the words poured in. With manuscripts covering his desk and the telephone receiver seemingly permanently attached to his ear, he was as industrious as a cub reporter trying to impress a stern editor-in-chief. Alsberg's indefatigable energy did not fail him. His team caught his fervent optimism. Mangione said Alsberg possessed a "a relentless optimism streaked with naiveté ... to work with him was to come under the spell of his faith in the future, a kind of dogged if somewhat doleful conviction that somehow complex problems could be solved, virtue could triumph."[33]

What happened to that tortured soul who'd written of his depressive bouts just a few years before? At least through the eyes of his co-workers, he was not that person; in fact, another being—maybe a *dybbuk* of his own?—seemed to inhabit the rumpled, hyperactive administrator. Perhaps the impossible-dream quality of the Project motivated him. Whatever private torments he might have confronted, Alsberg put on a good public face. Saxe Commins, Emma Goldman's nephew, related that Alsberg almost lost his directorship in 1936, a circumstance not alluded to in any other writings about his time on the FWP. Whether this was accurate information or derived from a conversation with Alsberg during one of his bouts with insecurity is not known.[34]

But there were struggles, and they extended beyond merely getting the books written and published. Alsberg, so politically astute in the European sphere, may not have foreseen brutal political battles, bureaucratic troubles, ongoing and erratic budget cuts, incompetence among some state directors and their staffs, unionized opposition, and worker strikes. He faced the added pressure of dealing with racist leaders who fought his insistence on African American inclusion in guidebook passages and hiring. Not just a ceremonial head who gave speeches and wrote reports, he dealt hands-on with these situations. He felt continually frustrated with bureaucratic rules that left destitute writers in dozens of states and cities out in the cold because they missed relief roll sign-up deadlines. He might have been a whimsical visionary, but he also handled mundane tasks such as placing requisitions for personnel and equipment.

In more than one instance Alsberg had to dispatch someone from the Washington office to handle protesting writers, ill-chosen directors, and similar disputes that today would be handled by an entire human resources department. He traveled often to Philadelphia, New York, and Boston for one-on-one talks with his assistants there. He helped ease books past local non–WPA government officials.

As early as 1936, the Project's machinery began to fall into place. With thousands of words of copy coming in from states and cities, Alsberg joined his assistants in tackling editing responsibilities. (One example of a "Daily Report of Material Received" showed incoming copy of over 55,000 words.) His love of travel, interest in eccentric (and accurate) details, and, as it turned out, an almost encyclopedic knowledge of American history made him an exceptional editor. He went over books page by page, line by line. One example shows Alsberg questioning a paragraph about a monument to Mary Washington, mother of George, which had been funded and built by women. Which women? Alsberg wanted to know.[35]

Even when Alsberg nitpicked, he remained innately courteous. When pointing out a case of plagiarism to the head of the Virginia project, he politely suggested that the material should "not follow too closely the wording used in copyrighted books." Not all of his Washington colleagues followed suit, and he tried to reign in their sharper editorial comments. He admonished them not to sound "as if we were posing as little tin gods. There has been a definite school-teacherish method of expression used ... this sort of phraseology is very poor. It immediately antagonizes the reader," making editorial comments "sound like a slap. There are very few times when it is necessary to use this type of language in dealing with state directors. It must be assumed that they are intelligent human beings."[36] Alsberg could also dole out praise and seemed pleasantly surprised when reviewing copy from Vardis Fisher, the passionate novelist who'd taken on the state directorship in Idaho. Soon, however, he wouldn't feel too congenial toward Fisher.

Idaho vs. Washington

[The cave's chamber was] a spangled fairyland of ice crystals, as if a glass blower had been busy here exhaling millions of frozen petals and tiny spires.[37]—from *Idaho, a Guide in Word and Picture*, 1937

Alsberg's report in the summer of 1936 to Ellen Woodward, WPA administrator in charge of Federal One, showed the FWP's progress.[38] It had been barely a year since his appointment. Of the ten publications described in the report, two were already printed and the others neared publication. Although they represented "lesser books"—pamphlets and booklets about towns and cities—he could also boast about the imminent printing of the District of Columbia *American Guide* book. It would be the first hardcover comprehensive book in the series, replete with photographs, maps, essays, and tour routes. That the capital city's guide would be the first was a politically significant and planned move, and Alsberg and staff looked forward to finally having something to show for their work. But 2,000 miles away, Idaho state director Vardis Fisher—the same state editor Alsberg praised nine months prior—thwarted their plans. Racing to an imaginary finish line, Fisher informed them that he was going to press with *his* state book. With the ice caves of Idaho trumping the Washington Monument, it represented a lapse in Washington's control—Alsberg's control, really. It was a kick to his ego. Despite his anger, appeals, and reportedly underhanded tactics to delay it, *Idaho, a Guide in Word and Picture*, came off the presses in January 1937, the first state book in the *American Guide* series. Thus did Idaho steal Alsberg's political thunder.

Alsberg felt undermined at first, but quickly regained his equanimity. When he sent the book to WPA Director Harry Hopkins in late January, it was with a mixture of apology and pride: "Compensation for sins of omission and commission in the text is to be found in the vivid style in which the book is written."[39]

They were boondogglers no longer. Alsberg pointed with pride to the first *American Guide* and set off to promote it as if it were the first Bible off the Gutenberg press; it didn't hurt that much of the writing was of high quality, mostly written by Fisher himself. Reviews in prominent magazines and newspapers praised the book and the Federal Writers' Project. The *Saturday Review of Literature* pronounced the book "an almost unalloyed triumph. Fifty-odd volumes of the national guide, if they are up to this standard, will not only vindicate the Writers' Project but will heighten our national self-consciousness, preserve invaluable antiquarian material that might have perished, and facilitate our knowledge of ourselves."[40]

Alsberg did get his way at least a little bit. A month before *Idaho* rolled off the presses, Alsberg supplied the *New York Times* with a preview of the manuscript dummy for *Washington: City and Capital*. The resulting article, complete with photographs from the upcoming book, appeared as a three-page spread in the Sunday magazine section, labeling it as the "first" of the *American Guide* books. Noting that it was a "wide departure from the worn formula of guidebooks," the article extolled its virtues, one of them that writers did not shy away from the city's faults. "Perhaps these guides, taken together will enable us for the first time to hold the mirror up to all America."[41]

The actual arrival of the Washington guide (three months after Idaho) gave Alsberg another reason to celebrate. Numerous small publications and two major books in the *American Guide* series were out, with others on their way. By the fall, Massachusetts, Connecticut, New Hampshire, and Vermont added their states' books to the *American Guide* series. Alsberg could feel useful at his newest chosen profession as publisher.

Sacco-Vanzetti, 41; Boston Tea Party, 9

Those good feelings lasted until August 18, 1937. The previous day, Alsberg and Woodward were in Boston to publicly present a leather-bound copy of *Massachusetts: A Guide to Its Places and People* to Governor Charles Hurley. The governor had written the preface and signed off on it, so his comments to the press offered no surprises. "I shall be delighted to recommend that the book be included in every library in the state and in every school."[42]

However, furor erupted the following day when conservatives attacked the book for its essays on the 1912 Lawrence textile strikes and other labor issues. Even more sacrilegious to these critics was the coverage of the Sacco and Vanzetti affair. The statistic spread across front pages nationwide reported that the book gave the Sacco and Vanzetti case 41 lines of type, compared with nine for the Boston Tea Party. (That someone actually counted is itself remarkable.) Although noted scholars proclaimed the "questionable" passages fair accounts, a former governor and others called for book burnings. The publicity certainly didn't hurt; a first printing of 10,000 copies sold out in short order. WPA chief Harry Hopkins defended the book and even made light of the controversy: "If we turned handsprings every time somebody complained, we would be spending all our day doing it."[43]

Alsberg, however, suddenly disappeared from the radar and was not heard from publicly during this tempest. News reports said he couldn't be reached because he was on vacation. With temperatures topping over 90 degrees in the Northeast, it wouldn't have been unusual for him to stop at his summer cottage for a cool respite. Was he angry, surprised, dismissive, complacent? Considering his strong feelings regarding censorship and the executions of Sacco and Vanzetti, along with his past depressive episodes, this situation might possibly have caused a mental slump. If anyone had gone into the Boston Public Library and scoured newspapers from 1927, they would have known that Alsberg presided over an expatriate demonstration in Paris protesting the executions. Perhaps he worried that his past activism would lead to his ouster. It's also likely that because he was so obsessively driven to keep the flow of books and other projects moving forward, he decided that a "disappear and keep mum" tactic would be the most politic. Or perhaps he was just tired of defending himself.

This "Teapot Tempest of the First Order"[44] wasn't the first time, nor would it be the last, when accusations spread that "Reds" were taking over the Project. The previous month, Alsberg responded to charges that the Project was rife with radicalism and incompetence. He ignored the radicalism charge and instead boasted about the FWP's productivity. He cited bestsellers, favorable reviews from newspapers and scholars, and book-of-the month club listings. He even noted the popularity of a children's book, *Who's Who in the Zoo*, put out by the New York City unit.[45]

The previous year, Alsberg *did* respond to Republican charges that he was a communist who had appointed other communists to high positions. (Right-wing ideologues painted anarchists, socialists, Trotskyites, and generic liberals with the same broad "Red" stroke, labeling them all communists.) He defended his writers and editors and, knowing the difference, called one of his anarchist writers a "bitter anti–Red." Alsberg explained (somewhat paradoxically) that the Soviets banned him from their nation because he attacked "communistic suppression of freedom of speech." Less forthcoming about two other staffers, he told the press he knew nothing of their politics, when, in fact, he knew the men personally and would have known their allegiances.[46]

Henry Alsberg: Reluctant Member of the Establishment

If attacks from the outside weren't enough, Alsberg faced internal conflicts that were, in some ways, more dangerous to the Project. Although Katharine Kellock's work on the sightseeing tour portions of the guidebooks remained essential, her presence brought early indications of anti–Red shadows hanging over the Project. "Pro-Russian and Pro-Communist!" shouted Republican critics about Kellock and her husband, Harold (Alsberg's friend from college). A

Eleanor Roosevelt supported the FWP's mission from its inception. In January 1938, she joined Alsberg to help promote a WPA Exhibit in Washington, D.C. (RG 69-N, National Archives at College Park).

Republican trade group branded the *American Guide* books "a Red Baedeker" and said that putting the tour route sections "into the hands" of such a woman was "indisputable evidence of the COMMUNIST CHISELING that is being winked at in high quarters."[47] She was recalled from fieldwork and brought to work in Washington. The national office tended to be understaffed, so perhaps this proved a blessing. She played an indispensable role there. The move also quieted critics who worried that she would see too much of "navy yards, military airports and coast fortifications." (Notable for the time, women represented 40 percent of FWP employees, with fourteen women appointed by Alsberg as state directors.)

But that wasn't the only shadow hanging over the Project. Alongside the literary stars and hard-working writers on the FWP were those who were more interested in composing radical manifestos. This was particularly true on the New York City project, the largest unit in the country. There were enough communists there to start a small Soviet *kolkhoze* (collective farm); their walkouts and hunger strikes were legendary. Various leftist factions unionized and warred with one another, with project administrators, and against the New Deal itself, which they believed did not go far enough in its initiatives. Alsberg's own workers were revolting, and against *him*! Unfortunately, this provided fuel for the soon-to-come congressional investigations. Thirty years later, FWP editor Jay Du Von gave context to the incidents, saying, "Naturally, I think the arts project attracted more than its share of people who were liberals and leftists of one kind or another. I think it was inevitable.... Some of them were very short-sighted in their tactics, and it hurt the project."[48] Alsberg was criticized for letting the situation devolve, for being too tolerant. While he sympathized with labor issues such as increased pay and more lenient hiring regulations, he didn't agree with protestors' tactics, which threatened the entire Writers' Project. Alsberg regained control after he made administrative changes and put McHugh, McGraw, and Donald Thompson in charge. The New York City unit turned out to be one of the most prolific of the Project.[49]

Alsberg never did regain the upper hand during a situation in Missouri, which began when the state Democratic Party machine overturned his choice for state director. The patronage appointee, racist and insensitive to the spirit of the *American Guide* books, ruffled the liberal writers on staff, and when she fired one of them, the other writers went on strike. The commotion led to charges, not altogether far-fetched, that Alsberg did not support his writers over an incompetent director. But although he ordered an investigation and arranged for the eventual removal of the state director, accusations against Alsberg ricocheted from Missouri to Washington and then New York. The *New Masses* published an incendiary article asking if the intent of the Writers' Project was to support writers or to "stifle and emasculate them, close their mouths, keep them in intellectual bondage and submission twenty-four hours a day."[50]

To Alsberg, it had to be strange to be viewed as part of the "establishment." Did his own long-standing radical credentials *not* impress his fellow liberals? There is ample evidence that Alsberg and his close associates pressed states to incorporate reformist attitudes and socially progressive activities in their books. For example, the Arizona guide told of unions springing out of the "dangerous and semi-feudal conditions" of mining camps and included the story of the Bisbee Deportation, during which townspeople-turned-armed-vigilantes arrested over a thousand striking miners, locked them in boxcars, transported them to the desert, and abandoned them.

Perhaps the editors at the *New Masses* overlooked the fact that Alsberg's hands were tied by political realities such as Roosevelt's upcoming election, not to mention miles of red tape.

Fellow Travelers, Divided

Arturo Toscanini, Count Basie, Benny Goodman. The usual denizens of Carnegie Hall in New York City made way for three days in 1937 to Ernest Hemingway, Richard Wright, and hundreds of other writers gathering for the League of American Writers' Second National Congress. The meeting was a call to action to fight fascism at home and abroad. Hemingway spoke on the opening night, and Alsberg, introduced by Wright, closed out the congress on Sunday. His talk offered another call to action and represented one of the few times he publicly aired his grievances. After discussing the function and purpose of the FWP, he professed his frustration that writers' organizations (the Author's League, for example) provided little support to the FWP and, in fact, that their neglect hurt the Project and writers as a whole. One can imagine Alsberg, leaning intently over the podium, his dark, penetrating eyes fixed on the audience, striving to keep his frustration in check.

> I get very little help. We invite criticism.... We have a body of over 4,000 people, pretty well-organized, willing to back you, willing to help you, but wanting also help and support from you.... I do not think that most of you know what we are doing, and I feel most of the time that nobody cares. And yet these are your comrades. These are the young people who are going to do something in the near future, the people who are carrying the torch on, in the next generation.[51]

Alsberg, nearing his sixth decade of life, was looking for a legacy, and in that off-the-cuff speech, he articulated that it wouldn't be just books. It would be writers.

The congress approved a resolution after his speech that urged members to cooperate with the FWP. But much like the Bisbee miners left in the desert, Alsberg may have felt abandoned by his compatriots. Less than a year later, when he asked the League of American Writers to support the FWP's creative writing magazine, he was turned down. It was a case of another left-wing partisan dispute: The league official didn't approve of the political stance of Alsberg's choice of editor. Henry Alsberg, who once proposed a World War I peace plan and a ceasefire in Germany during a workers' uprising—and was taken seriously by the American Secretary of State and an official with the British occupied forces—couldn't now broker a deal with his own comrades.

Alsberg was smart enough, at least on some level, to know that the threats and accusations, emanating from all sides, were a harbinger. Waiting in the wings, the House Committee on Un-American Activities prepared to take center stage in these attacks. Press criticism, though tempered by positive reviews, continued. A Hearst newspaper columnist lashed out and called Project writers "pompous fakes, conceited smarties, brazen parasites and lazy young squirts without a smitch [*sic*] of talent."[52] (Although a gross exaggeration and generalization, there were certainly cases of drunkenness and loafing for critics to unearth.) Within this atmosphere, Alsberg obsessed over the FWP's survival. There were dozens of "big book" *American Guide* manuscripts headed for print, along with countless smaller publications. Perhaps he feared them sharing a fate with his own personal, unfinished manuscripts moldering away in storage. If only he could stave off the attacks and keep the Project afloat long enough to shepherd its books to fruition.

Meanwhile, now more than ever, he was still a man who needed approbation. Thankfully, along with attacks, accolades also flowed in to give him solace and assuage his spirit. *The Nation*, his old journalistic stomping ground, named him to their 1937 Honor Roll. Among the roster of Americans who "deserve the applause of their countrymen," he was celebrated "for translating the talents of the WPA writers into the splendid American Guide Series."[53] But it wasn't just the liberal press. *Time* magazine, with a photograph of Alsberg in the center of its spread, acknowledged the Project's immense scope and successful literary undertakings, which by then included creative writing and ethnic heritage books.[54]

Literary critic Lewis Mumford, an early supporter, offered unassailable praise, calling the guidebook series "the finest contribution to American patriotism that has been made in our generation: let that be the answer to the weaklings who are afraid to admit that American justice may miscarry or that the slums of Boston may be somewhat this side of Utopia. Let it also silence those who talk with vindictive hooded nods about the subversive elements that are supposed to lurk in the WPA."[55] The literary journal *Prairie Schooner*, even while commenting on the varying quality of books, supported the Project's significance.

One can only hope that, two decades later, Alsberg read John Steinbeck's *Travels with Charley*. Steinbeck, driving his lumbering camper (named the *Rocinante*, after Don Quixote's horse) on a 1960 cross-country trip with his dog, Charley, lamented leaving behind his *American Guide* collection:

> If there had been room in Rocinante I would have packed the W.P.A. Guides to the States, all forty-eight volumes of them.... The complete set comprises the most comprehensive account of the United States ever got together, and nothing since has approached it.... If I had carried my guides along, for example, I would have looked up Detroit Lakes, Minnesota, where I stopped, and would have known why it is called Detroit Lakes, who named it, when, and why. I stopped near there late at night and so did Charley, and I don't know any more about it than he does.[56]

CHAPTER 10

Cultural and Creative Expressions
The FWP's American Mosaic
1936–1938

> *Little racial groups have within our own time awakened to the preciousness of their own individuality, of being themselves, of singing their own songs, writing poetry in their own tongues ... no amount of ridicule or oppression will wean them from their goal.* —Henry Alsberg

Writing in 1917, Henry Alsberg observed Czechs, Ukrainians, and Hungarians as they strived to stand proud and separate amid myriad Eastern European cultures.[1] He already appreciated "cultural pluralism," an idea popularized by Horace Kallen and others that supported the retention, celebration, and coexistence of varying ethnic, regional, racial, and cultural identities within American society. Alsberg brought that sensibility to the FWP as he worked to expand the scope of the Project, planning from the very beginning to incorporate folklore, ethnic, and cultural studies into the guidebooks.

While "ethnography" might have been relegated to university academics in the 1930s, Henry Alsberg meant to incorporate it into popular culture through the FWP. Writers and researchers in the field might have felt as if they were completing a sociology assignment when reading some of the directives from the *American Guide* manual, calling for states to address "ethnography": "Give brief explanation of the effect of different racial groups on the history of your district, on its architecture, on its social customs." And "Trace causes of large immigrations of foreign populations into your district."[2] Alsberg included Native Americans, and in early 1936, asked noted anthropologist Franz Boas for help in finding a writer, editor, anthropologist—or all three rolled into one, if possible—to supervise editorial matter relating to American Indians.[3]

The quality of reportage varied and results were mixed. The Arizona book, while on one hand celebrating Mexican culture, changed tack at one point to assert that the Mexican's "economic status is such that he has little opportunity to adopt the modes of life followed by the lighter skinned people who employ him, but it is also true that he has slight inclination to change his ways."[4]

The California book did not shy away from bigotry in its history. Perhaps Alsberg's old friend Alfred Kroeber, one of the advisors to the book, had a hand in the guide's recounting the massacres of Native Americans and the destruction of their cultures. On the other hand, although the book did acknowledge violence against Chinese immigrants during the late 1800s and anti–Japanese legislation after the turn of the century, only one paragraph dealt with "ethnography." In this, the Chinatowns of various cities were depicted as "dark and grotesque alleyways." African Americans hardly rated mention.[5]

In some cases, Alsberg or his staff had to remind state directors of the assignment to include ethnic groups in their state essays. However, despite the varied success of the experiment, it had worth. The New York guidebook recounted the history of immigrants, from early Dutch and English settlers to the more recent influx of Italian, Irish, German, Jewish, French Canadians, and other groups in the twentieth century. From Basques in Idaho to the Welsh of Maine, from the Cajuns of Louisiana to the Greeks of Florida, immigrant and ethnic groups for the first time found inclusion in these histories of America. Alsberg often personally interceded when he came upon mischaracterizations in copy. In a letter to a Midwestern state director, he expressed what was probably an outlandish view at the time, that the "Indian outbreak of 1864 was not accidental" but due to encroaching white settlers. "It looked like a good time for the original owners of the land to reclaim it."[6]

Alsberg seemed just as focused, if not more so, on African American representation, both in the essays as well as in the writers hired to write the pieces. He was sensitive to race issues, as expressed through his writing and the production of plays on African American topics during his Provincetown days. His friendships with African American writer Claude McKay and NAACP leaders Walter White and Joel and Arthur Springarn also would have sensitized him. Spurred on by prominent African Americans, Alsberg and associate director George Cronyn attended a dinner at Howard University in November 1935 to discuss the matter. By the end of the month, Cronyn drew up a plan to include a "Negro Culture in America" section in every state guide. In early 1936, Alsberg, concerned that the American Guides "do justice to Negroes," appointed Howard University Professor of English Sterling Brown as national head of Negro Affairs.[7] But that path to attempted inclusion wouldn't be easy.

Their objectives for the "Negro Culture" essays were to provide an honest history as well as to show African Americans as participants in American life.

This frequently brought Brown, Alsberg, and Cronyn at odds with editors, particularly in Southern states. Alsberg was forced to send a field representative to Georgia to ensure the hiring of African Americans there. Sterling Brown had to push for an unsegregated water fountain for the one African American worker in Oklahoma.[8] While putting together the tour sections, the men wrestled with issues of where "colored people" could find lodging. Alsberg had to send reminders to state directors when they submitted drafts that neglected mention of Negroes.

Another startling example of bigotry, and a resulting ruckus, came with the submission of a draft history essay from Alabama, which left out any mention of Booker T. Washington, founder of Tuskegee Institute. George Cronyn sent a piercing letter to the state director, Myrtle Miles, telling her "a history of Alabama that makes no mention of Booker T. Washington has no right to be considered comprehensive."[9] Disputes over prejudicial attitudes in Alabama and other Southern states continued, with Alsberg, Cronyn, and Brown constantly stepping in, attempting to foster more enlightened mindsets. Whatever compromises either side made, in many cases it was impossible to entirely edit out Jim Crow attitudes. In a section on "Negro Folkways," the Mississippi guidebook points to the "Mississippi folk Negro today" as "carefree and shrewd and does not bother himself with the problems the white man has to solve."[10] Passages that infiltrated some books remain a sad testament to the biases of the day, biases that cause today's readers to cringe, just as surely as Alsberg and his compatriots did. These faults were not lost on some reviewers of the time, either. A *Nation* article praised most of the state, city, regional, and local guides that had been published by the end of 1938. The praise ended with the Mississippi guide and its "three highly objectionable anti–Negro passages.... If many such passages of arrant nonsense creep into the copy, the usefulness and prestige of the guide series will be seriously impaired."[11] But even some Northern states ignored their African American populations.

Alsberg supported Sterling Brown's forthright portrayal of African Americans in *Washington: City and Capital*. Brown's essay extolled the contributions of African Americans and the socially progressive whites who worked with them. But he did not hold back on a matter-of-fact rendering of African Americans' struggles to build schools, careers, and lives amid appalling conditions. Describing the slum alleys built by real estate investors: "Shacks costing as little as $10 proved highly profitable investments. Here, in these disease-infested sties, ex-slaves got their first taste of freedom. And it is here that, in too large numbers, their children's children still drag out their lives." The essay ended with a commentary: "In this border city, southern in so many respects, there is a denial of democracy, at times hypocritical and at times flagrant. Social compulsion forces many who would naturally be on the side of civic fairness into hopelessness and indifference. Washington has made steps in the direction of justice, but many steps remain to be taken for the sake of the underprivileged and for the sake of a greater Washington."[12] Conservative congressmen attacked Brown's essay for stating that George Washington's adopted son fathered a daughter with a black woman. Brown later said, "What they didn't like was my attack on the real estate interests, but what they got me for was saying that George Washington Parke Custis had a colored daughter."[13]

Just a few years later—with Alsberg no longer on the FWP—new editors revised the essay for an updated edition of the book. Brown's once forceful treatise lost its astute, analytical, and, most of all, honest essence. The editors omitted his last paragraph and replaced it with one praising "contemporary Negro writers." Perhaps by way of apology, they included Brown among the acclaimed writers in this final note.[14]

Cultural Pluralism Beyond the Guides

> *I've had eight years of the yards. It's a lot different now, with the union and all. We used to have to buy the foremen presents, you know. On all the holidays, Xmas, Easter, Holy Week, Good Friday, you'd see the men coming to work with hip pockets bulging and take the foremen off in corners, handing over their half pints…. Your job wasn't worth much if you didn't observe the holiday "customs." The women had to bring 'em bottles, just the same as the men. You could get along swell if you let the boss slap you on the behind and feel you up.*—Anna Novak, Chicago stockyard worker, 1939.[15]

From Alsberg's vantage point, the guidebooks alone, as if they weren't ambitious enough, could not tell the full story of America. This growing self-portrait would need close-ups of factory workers, granite cutters, trapeze artists, butchers, seamstresses, farmers. It would need the stories of immigrants from south of the border, north of the border, and all points in Europe; Native Americans; covered-wagon pioneers; and former slaves—everything and anyone not a part of the Anglo-Saxon American establishment. How they spoke, how they lived, what cultural customs they held dear, what stories they told their children at night—what, as Alsberg asked in his *Nation* article of 1917, was the "preciousness of their own individuality?"

Alsberg's knowledge, background, personal interests, and friendships placed him at an intersection where he could tap the best and brightest, the academic experts who shared his goals of celebrating cultural and ethnic diversity and promoting tolerance. He recruited sociologist Morton Royse and folklorist/writer Benjamin Botkin (on his way to a storied career) to join Sterling

Brown; they guided these ancillary endeavors that fell broadly under the headings of social-ethnic, folklore, and ex-slave projects. Lead by Alsberg's intellectual team, FWP troops moved beyond libraries and typewriters, venturing out to Chicago stockyards, Harlem street corners, rural circuses, and city union offices to collect oral histories—or "life history narratives," as they are described—to gather the stories that no one else bothered about. They collected folklore in a new way, learning about and recording urban and occupational folklore, ethnic customs and traditions, songs and games. They talked to children in the streets and beggars in the parks. Workers of nearly every ethnic vintage became part of the mural. The sights, sounds, and smells, transmuted onto countless pages, meant to create a lasting snapshot of American history for future generations.

It could be likened to the Georges Seurat paintings that Henry Alsberg almost certainly viewed during his travels to museums in various European cultural centers or in New York. One can imagine him stepping back, finding the right vantage point, and seeing the points and luminous colors come together to form one impressionistic representation. Perhaps some unconscious memory of those moments guided him to see individual life stories as tiles in an American mosaic.

While most of the ten thousand (by some accounts) life history narratives did not find their way into the books that Alsberg and his FWP associates loftily envisioned for publication during the life of the Project, many were resurrected over the ensuing decades. They appear in books and online; others are barely preserved on microfilm; and some remain in their original form: typewritten reports in varying states of preservation in repositories. Their content is unpolished, filled with the faults and prejudices of real people, with history as remembered and misremembered. Urged on by the FWP's "living lore" and "life history" units, many of those ten thousand spoke not just of their everyday Depression-era lives. They also recounted memories from their childhoods, thus providing an everyman's history stretching back to the mid–1800s.

Ten Thousand Stories

> We had lots of Indian scares and I never knew what them wild Apaches were goin' to do next. I hated the old squaws. Sometimes they'd knock at my door, and when I'd open it, there they'd be, all wrapped up in blankets. They always traveled in pairs. They wanted water but they couldn't understand me, and I couldn't understand them. So they'd grunt away down in their throats, open their mouths and point at the hole in their faces.—Western pioneer, describing the homestead she moved to at the turn of the twentieth century, 1937.[16]

Ahm in New York, but New York aint in me. You understand? Ahm in New York, but New York aint in me. What do I mean? Listen. I'm from Jacksonville Florida. Been in New York twenty-five years. I'm a New Yorker! But I'm in New York an New York aint in me.... Ah come here twenty-five years ago. Bright lights, Pretty women. More space to move around. Son, if Ah had-a got New York in me Ahd a-been dead a long time ago.—Anonymous interview conducted by Ralph Ellison, 1939.[17]

In 1938, the publication of the guidebooks came with relative regularity and provided a framework that would support the newer components. Royse, Botkin, and Brown, sometimes in tandem and often with their work overlapping, each had the passion and boldness to dive into the unknown. Throughout 1937 and 1938, Alsberg wrestled with the myriad problems of essentially running a publishing company—albeit one where his efforts were stymied by regulations, prejudices, and politics. Nevertheless, he was excited about the newest ventures.

"In developing our theme song, 'How America Lives,' we have begun a series of ethnic studies in many parts of the country," he told one audience. "We are studying the ethnic groups from the human angle, and much of the field work will be done by those of our workers who belong to the respective groups that are being studied, who know the language and the traditions." He was "immodest enough to imagine," he said, that the resulting publications would "affect the conception of America by Americans."[18]

And although sometimes whites interviewed blacks, or city dwellers interviewed farmers, other times it was more consequential and the cultural stars aligned, so that twenty-four-year-old Ralph Ellison interviewed a Harlem bar philosopher, or poet and novelist Mari Tomasi (the thirty-year-old daughter of Italian immigrants) helped tell the story of Italian granite workers.

Older writers participated as well. Zora Neale Hurston, well into her forties, interviewed turpentine workers in the Florida pine forest. Hilda Polacheck, a Jewish immigrant from Poland and only a year younger than her boss, Henry Alsberg, shared much of his sensibilities. As a writer active in both peace and women's rights movements, she contributed folklore from Chicago's immigrant neighborhoods.

Parallel to these efforts was *These Are Our Lives*,[19] edited by Alsberg's Southern regional director appointee, William Couch. This book offered a broad selection of Southern life histories, both black and white. Alsberg and Couch stayed in close touch about the aims of the book, one of which was to convince critics of the importance of such studies. Couch later lamented that after Alsberg's ouster, the series was cancelled due to a lack of support from new administrators.[20]

Zora Neale Hurston at the 1937 *New York Times* book fair, holding *American Stuff*, the book which gave FWP writers an outlet for their off-time work. Hurston, already an established folklorist, anthropologist and novelist before joining the FWP, contributed to Florida's guidebooks and folklore units. Unfortunately, despite Alsberg's push with state officials, she was denied a supervisory position due to racial discrimination (Library of Congress, Prints & Photographs Division).

"Negro" writers' units were formed in some areas, including Chicago, New York, and Virginia, with the intent of moving beyond the guidebooks to tell about the African American experience. Ralph Ellison, Arna Bontemps, Richard Wright, Margaret Walker, and Claude McKay illuminated the list of writers. According to Maryemma Graham, the FWP made "the largest single impact on black writing before the civil rights movement," even more than the Harlem Renaissance.[21]

Results included *Cavalcade of the American Negro* (from the Chicago unit) and *The Negro in Virginia*, with the latter notable for including photographs by Robert McNeill, then a twenty-one-year-old novice and now remembered as a groundbreaking African American photographer. Florida's rich history benefited from Zora Neale Hurston's presence and her contributions to the guidebook. Despite her experience and literary background—and Alsberg's lobbying Florida WPA officials to appoint her editor of *The Florida Negro*—she was denied a supervisory position. She performed unofficially in that capacity, but without commensurate compensation.[22]

The idealism inherent in FWP's department of Negro Affairs paralleled that of the New Deal as a whole. Nevertheless, Alsberg, Brown, and their staff faced almost insurmountable levels of bureaucracy and bigotry. Despite this, at least according to press releases put out by the FWP, enthusiasms did not wane. In addition to the *American Guide* series, the FWP had "in process twelve books which give an excellent account of the Negro in the American scene," touted one press release.[23] It noted that the number of African American writers, editors, researchers, consultants, and typists reached 180 nationwide, though this number fluctuated.

With the social-ethnic, folklore, and Africa-American programs as a base, Alsberg and his team looked forward to three major publications: *Portrait of the Negro as American, Guide to Composite America,* and the *American Folklore Guide.* The writers' productivity outpaced the Project's publishing capacity; enough material arrived to compile those books and more. Alsberg knew enough to worry whether the Project would live long enough to see the planned landmark texts published. He wondered if the "American public thought the product valuable enough so that the work can be organized on a more or less permanent basis."[24]

Former Slaves Remember

> When I was six years old, all of us children were taken from my parents, because my master died and his estate had to be settled.... I can't describe the heartbreak and horror of that separation. I was only six years old and it was the last time I ever saw my mother for longer than one night.—John W. Fields, eighty-nine-years-old, 1937.[25]

Perhaps the most ambitious and, ultimately, culturally valuable work of the "ancillary" projects was the collection of oral histories from former slaves. Smaller programs at two Southern black universities and an earlier attempted project by the Federal Emergency Relief Administration preceded the FWP. With the intent to record the memories of elderly African Americans before they died, FWP officials knew they worked under an unusual deadline.

Carita Doggett Corse, the Florida director, and Carolyn Dillard, the Georgia director, had already begun collecting former slave narratives, and they, along with John Lomax (who preceded Benjamin Botkin as folklore editor) pressed Alsberg to formalize the program. Alsberg gave his blessing and in June 1937 sent a memo to state directors requesting their participation.[26]

After Lomax's departure, Botkin joined Brown in shaping the program. Over a two-year period, more than 2,300 people—most over eighty years old—were interviewed in seventeen states.[27] Like every other aspect of the FWP, it was an imperfect system. Evidence shows that some narratives were edited by white state officials to ameliorate criticism of slavery.[28] Representation of former slaves' speech varied significantly, due to confusion regarding central office instructions, white interviewers' biases, and the writers' unskilled interviewing techniques.

The slave narratives gained wide public attention in 1945 with the publication of Botkin's *Lay My Burden Down*, comprised of excerpts from the slave narrative collection, and, again in 1970, the year of Alsberg's death, with Norman R. Yetman's *Voices from Slavery*. Both works heralded a growing interest, with myriad books and media giving attention to this historic collection.

Nurturing the Creative Impulse

> It is easy for the accountant to frown on W.P.A. for its inefficiency and for the artists to sneer at it for its bureaucracy, but the fact remains that, thanks to it, a number of young artists of talent were enabled, at a very critical time in their lives, to get started on their creative careers. As for the rest, the executive [Alsberg] might just as well—and I dare say would have been glad to—have been honest, given them their weekly checks and sent them home, but the legislature which could endure such honesty could only exist in heaven.—W.H. Auden[29]

Henry Alsberg could not forget that underneath the facade of a bureaucratic administrator (criticized as he was in that position), he was also, first, a writer. Despite his statements that the guidebooks could remain utilitarian yet provide an outlet for writers to exercise their creativity, one wonders if this was part of a campaign designed to retain support from conservative elements while also placating writers who hoped to work on more than "mere" guidebook copy. Although his own creative impulses never found a home with the FWP, Alsberg recognized the talents of others; he wouldn't be the one to let them squander those talents during the lean years of the Depression. If he couldn't be that writer, he could foster others' creative urges by acting as patron.

From the very beginning, writers harangued Alsberg about the drudgery of guidebook writing. Many hoped, as Katharine Kellock put it, that the government relief jobs would give them the opportunity to produce "masterpieces—dramas, pictures, novels, operas, epic poems."[30] And although Alsberg was practical enough *not* to envision such grand patronage, even in the early days of the Project he believed that some could be paid to work on their own creative pieces. "If a writer with a recognized name should be found on relief rolls in these days of thin sales and invisible advances it is possible," he told a *New York Times* reporter, "that he will be paid to work on a novel."[31]

Of course he knew enough to bide his time. He'd have to be diplomatically expedient and as patient as a schoolyard monitor in a playground of overgrown children. The established WPA organization and conservatives rested heavily on one end of a figurative seesaw; facing them on the opposite side sat the wild-eyed poets. Like children, both sides competed to see who could push off with enough force to cause those opposite them to crash to the ground. Alsberg straddled the middle space, his long legs wobbling to keep the teeter-totter balanced. And as impractical as creative artists could be, Alsberg felt pulled toward them. And because so many were his friends, he didn't want to let them down.

With no provisions under WPA policy for subsidizing creative writers, but nothing disallowing it, either, Alsberg pointed out more than once that with a regular paycheck and a relatively short workweek of thirty hours (in line with union agreements), writers could have the financial security and enough free time to commit to their creative projects.[32] He was right. In California and Nebraska, writers put together mimeographed creative anthologies. Josef Berger wrote the novel *Bowleg Bill: The Seagoing Cowboy*, as well as the nonfiction *Cape Cod Pilot*, which later was absorbed into the *American Guide* series.[33]

Even as the bureaucracy threatened to swallow him up, Alsberg kept an eye out for exceptional WPA writers. Perhaps tired of the criticism that his writers lacked creative outlets, he decided to meet this issue head on. The first unconsummated attempt came in October 1936 with plans for a small creative writing branch to produce a national prose and poetry magazine. Some state unit directors allowed select writers to focus on creative works. Alsberg retained right of approval and insisted on limiting it to writers who'd already proven their mettle. "Creative writing, as a proposal of work, should not, for reasons of office routine, be advertised among workers, lest too many ask to be thus employed," said Alsberg.[34] In other words, circumspection was key.

With the hope that a national magazine could still come to fruition, Alsberg solicited writers for their "off-time" work. In 1937, arrangements were made with Viking Press to publish *American Stuff: An Anthology of Prose and Verse by Members of the Federal Writers' Project*. The book, illustrated with prints from the Federal Art Project, compiled work by fifty WPA writers (chosen from hundreds of submissions) during their off-time—those weekend or late evening hours when, as Richard Wright said, the nights were "long enough."[35] Some works came from editors on the project, including Sterling Brown, Vincent McHugh, and Jerre Mangione. Others came from well-known WPA writers such as Kenneth Rexroth, Nathan Asch, and Jim Thompson. (Although women were well represented for that era, they represented only eleven of the forty-eight writers.) One of the manuscripts came from Richard Wright, not yet thirty years old.

In early June, two months before *American Stuff* came out, Alsberg, introduced by Wright, addressed a crowd of 500 writers in New York. Perhaps because he was speaking extemporaneously, Alsberg gave voice to both sides of that tottering seesaw in his mind. "I think writers should get subsidies … there are a good many writers, and some of the best, especially the poets, who never do earn a living and never did earn a living." He hoped the upcoming book would force the WPA and other government officials "to let us bring out a regular magazine of creative writing. This is the only way we can give the younger people, who cannot get published elsewhere, a chance."

In counter point, he asked, "If I had everybody working on their own manuscripts, I would be asked inside of one month, what are they producing? Where is it going? What use is it to anybody? They may be writing the great American novel at home and it will not be doing the Project any good. We have to show some production in order to justify the project at all."[36]

By August 1937, the creative writing experiment arrived in bookstores with Alsberg's foreword: "This is the American scene to the very life, very often as it appears from the roadside ditch, the poverty-stricken tenement or shack, the relief station. The style is sometimes crude, the technique often perhaps inexpert or diffuse; but there is sincerity in it, a solid passionate feeling for the life of the less prosperous millions."

The book was widely reviewed, with most commentators supporting the notion of WPA writers showing off their more imaginative "stuff." All applauded the inclusion of African American writers. Wright's autobiographical essay, *The Ethics of Jim Crow*, received the most attention. From the African American journal, *Opportunity*: "In nine sketches covering fourteen pages Mr. Wright succeeds in very effectively portraying the more savage side of jim crow life in a stark and unforgettable manner. It is haunting stuff."[37] Wright's piece similarly affected a *New York Times* critic, who said the writing "hit me squarely between the eyes" with its "shocking accounts of a youngster learning to be a Negro in the South."[38]

Alsberg's ability to recognize writing talent and good storytelling first surfaced when he edited his college literary journal and continued through the 1920s both at the Provincetown Playhouse and with his transporting of *The Dybbuk* to America. Now he had the chance to escape from the utilitarian job of putting out guidebooks and act as literary scout and publisher. After deciding to include Wright's piece in the book, Alsberg approved the developing writer's requested transfer to New York City from Chicago, where he worked both in the vibrant FWP unit as a supervisor, then in the city's Federal Theatre Project. Alsberg's friend James McGraw of the New York City unit helped select pieces for *American Stuff*. He recalled the thrill of coming across Wright's submission after wading through "some pretty heavy epic poems and I suppose I'm allergic to epic poems … the *Ethics of Living Jim Crow* did change things."[39] Wright's literary life after *American Stuff* became deeply entwined with the FWP. His contributions to guidebooks and "Negro" studies books, and his own creative works written during his time on the Project, proved a boon to the FWP legacy.

Not surprisingly, *American Stuff* struck a negative chord with conservative readers. The Constitutional Educational League condemned the material as being communist propaganda and accused Alsberg of allowing it to be done on government time.[40] Disregarding rising conservative threats, Alsberg strove to build on the anthology's critical and commercial success. (A letter from the printing contractor telling him how grateful they were for "gainful employment of hundreds of workers" raised his spirits.[41]) The second edition of "off-time" writing was under way almost immediately and came out in spring 1938 within a special issue of *Direction* magazine. It also brought additional political turmoil. When Alsberg chose Harold Rosenberg as editor for this second creative FWP venture, influential writers' groups led by pro–Stalinists withdrew support because they considered Rosenberg to be a Trotskyite—not the right kind of radical, in their view.[42] At the same time, conservative Hearst columnist Elsie Robinson took Alsberg to task, accusing the FWP of spending government money on these literary endeavors, when, in fact, Viking Press and *Direction* financed the publications.

Alsberg kept Rosenberg. He himself was on the advisory board for the special issue, along with close associates Vincent McHugh, James McGraw, Jerre Mangione, and others. With both creative writing publications, the FWP achieved commercial success and satisfied at least some writers. Nonetheless, Alsberg, who would never consider himself a political centrist, once again found himself straddling a seesaw, with the far right on one side, the far left on the other. He managed to enrage two extremist ideological blocs, both of which blocked his hope of continuing *American Stuff* magazine on a regular basis. As he should have learned during his time advocating for political prisoners, he could make no one happy.

Taking another tack, Alsberg urged other magazines to provide his writers with creative outlets. An exhilarated Alsberg commended the editor of *Poetry Magazine* after it gave over its July 1938 issue to FWP poets. Others that followed suit included the *New Republic* and the *New Masses*.

Some writers flexed their creative muscles for the *American Guide* books. Poet and novelist Vincent McHugh, appointed by Alsberg as co-director of the

Along with posters for Lifesavers and a funeral service company, an advertisement for the FWP's guidebook, *New York Panorama*, also tempted straphangers (circa 1938) on New York City's 8th Avenue subway (photograph by Eiseman, Federal Art Project, WPA; Library of Congress, Prints & Photographs Division).

New York City project, wrote the lauded introduction to *New York Panorama*: "The rumor of a great city goes out beyond its borders, to all the latitudes of the known earth. The city becomes an emblem in remote minds ... the stencil marks on a packing case dumped on the wharf at Beira or Reykjavik, a flurry of dark-goggled globe-trotters from a cruise ship ... or a Harlem band playing Young Woman's Blues from a phonograph as the safari breaks camp in Tanganyika under a tile-blue morning sky as intensely lighted as the panorama closed by mountains in the ceiling dome of the African section at the American Museum of Natural History."[43] Of the book itself, gushed one reviewer, "There is nothing like it in our literature."[44]

Writers' Underground

It's been referred to as "the secret creative writing unit," but the covert nature of its existence is disputable. Alsberg's desire to be benefactor and patron led him to sanction about a dozen people to work at home on their personal writing during WPA hours. Most were from New York City and included Richard Wright, Charlotte Wilder, Helen Neville, Anzia Yezierska, and Harry Roskolenko.[45] A few other writers scattered around the country received similar treatment, but the operation was cut short in spring 1938 when Alsberg felt the pressure to complete the guidebooks. However, even for those not chosen for this special group, the FWP experience offered a sort of ongoing salon as writers met after work for hours of camaraderie and literary and political discussions—similar to what Alsberg experienced while living in Paris—and a chance to draw on their experiences in later writings. Roskolenko and Yezierska recounted spending time with Richard Wright and John Cheever in Manhattan cafeterias and bars.[46] Mari Tomasi's *Like Lesser Gods* and Zora Neale Hurston's *Seraph on the Suwanee* drew from their FWP fieldwork experiences. Ralph Ellison used a lyrical piece of an interview conducted in Harlem—"I'm in New York, but New York ain't in me"—in *Invisible Man*.

The person regarded as gaining the most from the FWP was Richard Wright. During the "secret" writing unit phase, Wright began work on *Native Son*. In 1938, Alsberg urged *Story Magazine* to sponsor a writing contest for WPA writers. Wright entered and won the $500 first prize for his entry, "Fire and Cloud," a novella from his book *Uncle Tom's Children*. As part of the prize, Harper and Brothers published the book in March that year. The story also won Wright a $200 second prize in the prestigious O. Henry Memorial Award contest in November.[47]

While it's true the FWP helped advance Wright's career, his success also buoyed the FWP and Alsberg, personally, in almost equal measure. The fact that Wright was an avowed Communist for most of the time that the two knew one another—Alsberg certainly was a maligned and less-than-beloved figure in that group—did not affect the mutual respect they had for one another. McHugh called Alsberg the "father bear" of the Project,[48] and it was in this manner that Alsberg took pride in Wright's achievements. After Wright sent him a signed copy of *Uncle Tom's Children* in April 1938, Alsberg (still, essentially, his boss) wrote him a gracious thank you letter. He also asked that Wright send a copy to WPA Administrator Harry Hopkins. "I know that he is always very pleased when one of our writers produces a creative work of such a high order."[49] When Wright applied for a Guggenheim Fellowship later that year, Alsberg provided a recommendation. Wright won the Fellowship and left the FWP in May 1939.

Monomania Redux

The various Writers' *projects* consumed Alsberg. That's not surprising, considering his equally compulsive efforts on behalf of Jews in Eastern Europe and political prisoners in Russia.

For although his coworkers were certainly dedicated—Mangione called the Writers' Project "a cause I believed in, a mistress I cherished"[50]—none could come close to Alsberg's fervor. The FWP was his child, lover, and the great American nonfiction masterpiece rolled into one. It's not surprising that the monomaniacal Alsberg worked "morning to night" and "took the project home in his briefcase" most evenings.[51] A character based on Alsberg in WPA writer Jack Balch's novel *Lamps at High Noon* depicts him at Washington headquarters as "insatiably" tearing "at the stacks of letters, communications, and telegrams before him."[52]

By 1937, Alsberg had moved into a large house on Wisconsin Avenue. Sharing the space (a former brothel) with colleagues Mangione, Clair Laning, and two others, Alsberg held court over dinner parties, his inherent enthusiasm creating a salon-like atmosphere focused almost entirely on the Writers' Project. Visitors such as Mary Heaton Vorse, Mary Maverick Lloyd (also on the Project), and Josephine Herbst, then well-known radical writers and friends of Alsberg's, complemented the atmosphere.[53]

Even as things were about to fall apart with the advent of congressional investigations, the mood carried over to camaraderie of a more raucous order. At one Wisconsin Avenue party described by Mangione, invited guests, who included the Washington office staff and Alsberg's New York friends Vincent McHugh and James McGraw, enjoyed libations plentiful enough to leave one FWP writer laid out in a drunken daze on the front lawn talking to the moon. Alsberg's boss, Ellen S. Woodward—a genteel Southerner from a prominent Mississippi family who'd recently been put in charge of Federal One—also attended. The party made news not because of boisterous goings-on or drunken federal workers. Rather, newspapers picked up on a rant from Senator Theodore Bilbo of Woodward's home state. Bilbo accused Alsberg of inviting "the flower of Mississippi womanhood" to a party also attended by African-Americans. "If this had happened in Mississippi, long before the sounds of revelry had died, the perpetrator of this crime would be hanging from the highest magnolia tree."[54] The Baltimore newspaper *Afro American* reported the event in a more progressive light. "Mississippi-born Mrs. Ellen S. Woodward, white WPA assistant administrator, knows how to mingle socially with colored people despite traditions of her Southland. Mrs. Woodward went to a party at the home of Henry Alsberg, white, chief of the WPA writers' project, and had her round of introduction to colored guests. The Southern-bred official appeared gracious and happy."[55] It wouldn't have occurred to Alsberg to hold a whites-only party or to keep white and African American guests apart.

Jerre Mangione's memoir painted a picture of a man prone to soliloquies; he described Alsberg at work as he juggled phone call after phone call, whose "outlandish" driving habits caused staffers to avoid getting in any car driven by him, as a kind philosopher who could offer sage discourses, and also coarse adulterated Shakespearean passages ("Ah, farting is such sweet sorrow").[56]

Alsberg's younger colleagues viewed him as cautious and, except for a few, did not know about his daring exploits in Europe. Balch's novel portrays him as both a weak leader bending to the will of the Missouri state political machine during labor troubles and an erudite world traveler conversant in seven languages. The complicated labor issues notwithstanding—and viewing FWP documents, clearly exaggerated—Balch also saw him the way friends and colleagues had for decades: "The man's charm was infectious."[57]

However, his charisma didn't always help. Both allies and foes noticed his propensity to make himself look good. Even friend Vincent McHugh, the young editor Alsberg appointed to help wrangle the New York City project books into shape, complained about his chief's habits. When Alsberg showed up at the New York headquarters, as he frequently did, the staff would grumble as he assigned them extra work—perhaps touching up a speech he had to give to publishers or making additional changes to copy. A disagreement led to McHugh's sudden departure from the Project after Alsberg interfered with the production of two New York City books.[58] McHugh, nevertheless, didn't hold it against him. McHugh, along with McGraw, Dora Thea Hettwer, and Stella Bloch Hanau, remained loyal friends until Alsberg's death, and defenders of his legacy afterward.

The Family Circle

After the sale of the home on 95th Street following the death of Alsberg's mother in 1934, family life was no longer centered in New York City. Brother Carl, after leaving the Bureau of Chemistry, had moved with wife Emma to the West Coast, where he worked as a chemistry professor and co-director of the Stanford University Food Institute. In 1937, he left for a similar post at the University of California at Berkeley. In the typical Alsberg fashion he volunteered for various groups and became active in the nongovernmental Institute of Pacific Relations, a group formed to improve relations with Asian nations.

Elsa, also on the move, had left her social work and education position with the National Council of Jewish Women's Department of Immigrant Aid. She co-wrote a book for educators of immigrant children and traveled the country to speak on the topic. She continued to pursue the cause of aiding immigrants, organizing the Citizens Committee for Adult Literacy in New York City and co-founding the Travelers Aid Society, formed to assist entering immigrants, particularly women.

Julius and his family still lived in Manhattan and bucolic Putnam Valley, New York. Henry's temperament, coupled with the demands of the job, necessitated more than ever that he spend time at the cottage he'd built on their land. Just fifty miles north of Manhattan, where Alsberg spent a considerable amount of time either "interfering" with his handpicked editors or trying to straighten out the strife brought on by Communist agitators, the trip to peaceful Putnam Valley was a relatively easy ride by either train or car.

Julius, a successful chemist and engineer with his own consulting firm (the only well-to-do sibling), also became politically active, albeit on a smaller scale, as chair of the local zoning commission. Nephew George started as a freshman at North Carolina's Black Mountain College, a progressive co-educational institute but, likely lured by his Uncle Carl, transferred to Stanford University. Cora was probably the closest to her dear "uncle Hen" with her free-spirited temperament. Raised to be an independent woman, she traveled alone by steamship from New York to Los Angeles in 1936 to begin her college life as a student at Pomona College, where she focused on philosophy, languages, and photography.

By contrast, the Alsberg relatives in Germany faced growing threats from the Nazis. Julius had taken his family on an expansive tour of Germany, Switzerland, and France just a few years before his children left for college. On arrival in France, fourteen-year-old Cora wrote to a friend in 1932 that the family had "quite enough" of Germany and had no intention of returning.[59] It's impossible to say whether this statement was motivated by the anti–Semitism that led up to Hitler's ascension in 1933, just a few months after the Alsbergs returned to America. On his European visits, Henry had spent considerable time with his aunt Frieda Alsberg in Arolsen, commenting on the town's stodgy, but placid atmosphere. When Hitler came to power, Frieda still lived in Arolsen and other relatives lived twelve miles away in Volkemarsen, where, according to distant cousin Elizabeth Alsberg Stoerk (who survived the Holocaust and emigrated to America after the war), the patriarchal family name originated in the 1700s.

Neighbors viewed Frieda, white-haired and seventy-eight years old, as an elegant, stately woman who sat by the front window of her sturdy, brick house and watched the neighborhood children play, sometimes giving them candy. Harassment of Arolsen's Jewish residents began in 1933, when Nazi officials demanded a list of the town's sixteen Jews. In November 1938, as Kristallnacht, the "night of broken glass," terrorized Jews across Germany, Frieda Alsberg faced the horror of *Hitlerjugend* (Hitler Youth) rioting in front of her own home. Perhaps the very same children who gleefully accepted her candy a few years earlier now terrorized her as she undoubtedly cowered in an upstairs room. Rioters plundered the apartment of the other remaining Jewish family in Arolsen. By 1939, Frieda was the only Alsberg—and for that matter, the last Jew—remaining in the town. The Nazis forced her to give up her house to the German Red Cross; specifics after that are scarce, but she moved to an old age home in Frankfurt and died in 1940. Witness testimony to Yad Vashem, an international commission that documents the Holocaust, led to the declaration that Nazis murdered her.

It's hard to imagine that the American Alsbergs did not attempt to extricate their relatives. Elsa reportedly helped a cousin, his wife, and two sons from Hamburg enter the United States during the war. Frieda's advanced age would have added to the complications of navigating the nearly impossible hurdles of obtaining emigration papers before communications were completely cut off. At least one Alsberg from Volkemarsen is listed as being murdered at Auschwitz; others, likely more distant relatives, died at Theresienstadt and Treblinka.[60] Documents also show that a few kin escaped to Palestine and South America. Max Alsberg, a Berlin friend of actor Peter Lorre who had achieved fame as a criminal attorney and playwright, fled Germany under Nazi persecution and committed suicide in Switzerland in 1933. However, for many of Alsberg's German relatives, their fates remain unknown. The town of Arolsen today hosts the offices of the International Tracing Service, which preserves records of Holocaust survivors and victims to help relatives trace their ancestors' fates. Its headquarters is a mere 160 meters, or a two-minute walk, from Frieda Alsberg's home, which still stands.

All of the siblings devoted much of their time to helping the downtrodden, and yet here they were powerless. How Henry Alsberg handled this emotionally can only be surmised. Knowing how he felt during his time working with the JDC, he must have felt especially traumatized. Many years later Alsberg told McHugh that he could not imagine that such horrors—concentration camps, particularly—could transpire. This, from someone who witnessed the terrible pogroms and other persecutions in Eastern Europe. Perhaps Jonas B. Colon, the fictional character based on Alsberg in Balch's book, can shed light on this. When Colon is first introduced, certain descriptions of Alsberg's traits and background ring true: his larger-than-life personality; his enchantment with European culture; his background as a foreign correspondent who wrote "witty, allusive articles" and hobnobbed with the statesmen of the day; his memories of long discussions in Swiss cafes regarding the merits of the peace talks. That Alsberg harbored a deep sadness for what was occurring in Europe would be expected. So perhaps it wasn't too much of a stretch to present the fictional Alsberg's thoughts as they might have been in 1935. Sitting in front of a gigantic

map of America marked with red and green pins to show FWP offices, Colon/
Alsberg ruminated:

> With all of the beauty and erudition, what had happened in Europe? How was it that he'd
> suspected nothing, trusted until the very end? Where were all the wise men, why were the
> shrugs and the subtle triple implications of no avail when the storm burst? From where the
> age old cry "Jew! Jew!" in pleasant Vienna as a mob pursued an old man and tore his
> beard?... And Hitler—where was Beethoven's spirit that day? The gentle German folk?
> Almost wistfully, he lifted his eyes to the great pin-pricked map of America.[61]

Staying the Course

Through 1938, Alsberg pushed on to extol the virtues of America through
the FWP. Perhaps being in a position where he could promote the most un–
Aryan of cultures—immigrants and African Americans—drove him. Of his
personal pursuits, Alsberg's ongoing theatrical interests brought him to the
Civic Theatre in Washington where he served on the board. He hadn't given
up on playwriting, and with Hallie Flanagan's endorsement, submitted one of
his plays to the Federal Theatre Project (FTP), the Writers' Project's sister
agency. It was never produced; he came closer with *The Dybbuk*, but as production arrangements got under way, the FTP was embroiled in a losing battle
for funding, so that did not come to fruition.

The world's turbulent orbit in 1938 found Europe descending into chaos;
the League of Nations grew more feeble by the day, like an elderly statesman
who lived beyond his mental capacity, if, indeed, he ever really possessed it in
the first place. In America, millions sat glued to their radios on a muggy June
night to listen to the heavyweight-boxing match from Yankee Stadium that pit-
ted African American Joe Louis against German Max Schmeling. (Louis beat
him in two minutes.) A few months later, Orson Welles—who'd recently moved
from his groundbreaking work with the Federal Theatre Project—produced
the *War of the Worlds* radio broadcast that had multitudes of Americans believing that Martians invaded the Earth. Amid these tumultuous times, New Yorker
and world traveler Henry Alsberg prepared to fight his own battle. He entered
the proverbial ring, up against a conservative political machine led by Texas
Congressman Martin Dies. The two men, from such disparate backgrounds,
might as well have been from different planets. Alsberg was in a fight not for
his life but for his heart and soul: the Federal Writers' Project.

CHAPTER 11

"Naked before his enemies"
1938–1939

You were the guiding star of our project. You inspired us to do our best, to do the almost impossible because you yourself showed us the way.—Dora Thea Hettwer to Henry Alsberg, August 15, 1939[1]

I remember one time when an FBI man came in to see me. He wanted to know about Henry Alsberg, and he said, what is his basic political philosophy? "Oh," I said, "He is a democrat, a new dealer, liberal. Basically, he is a philosophical anarchist." This FBI man got all bothered about this. I said "You know, like Thoreau." He says "Oh, this Thoreau, what's his first name?" We went through this business and I went along with it, just to humor myself. He asked, "Where does he live?" I said, "Walden Pond."—Jay Du Von, 1964, FWP editor.[2]

Henry Alsberg was miles away from Walden Pond in 1938.

Most people associate the House Committee on Un-American Activities (commonly known as HUAC) with Senator Joseph McCarthy and the Red purges and blacklists of the 1950s. But McCarthy was still a small-town lawyer in Wisconsin when the zealous Martin Dies, Jr., a thirty-eight-year-old Democratic congressman from Texas, founded HUAC in 1938. Known for spouting anti-immigrant and anti-labor rhetoric, Dies would have no inclination to support the liberal cultural goals of the FWP or, for that matter, any cause in which Henry Alsberg had ever believed.

In a long-winded article in the *Saturday Evening Post*, appearing April 20, 1935—about the same time Alsberg and others were formulating their plans to bring cultural pluralism into the FWP—Dies bemoaned the fact that immigrants from southern and Eastern Europe destroyed the "racial unity" of the country and blamed these "aliens" for the unemployment crisis.

Adept at using the media of the day to promote his ideology, Dies eagerly sought the spotlight, opportunistically dominating radio microphones and newspaper headlines. He and HUAC's other anti–New Dealers, made up mostly

The media savvy and sensationalist Texas congressman Martin Dies went after the Writers' and Theatre Projects—and their leaders, Alsberg and Hallie Flanagan—with a
vengeance. As chairman of the House Committee on Un-American Activities, his
unfounded accusations that the Projects promoted communism made headlines nationwide and helped lead to their eventual shut-down. Here, in early 1940, even after both
national projects no longer existed, Dies talks to reporters about ferreting out communists in the government (Library of Congress, Prints & Photographs Division).

of Republicans and Southern Democrats, operated under the pretext of comb-
ing America for Communists, Nazis, and fascists (including the Ku Klux Klan).
But their investigations into the latter groups were merely cursory.

Dies' real plan was to go after anyone who emitted even the faintest whiff
of Communism and to link him or her to FDR's administration. HUAC set its
sights on Federal One, zooming in on the Theatre and Writers' Projects. If
these two agencies symbolized a bright burning lantern in the wilderness, hoping to spread the light of culture throughout the land, the Dies-led committee
represented a wolf pack surrounding their cozy campsite, eyes glowing through
the dark woods as they studied their prey.

The inquisitorial scare tactics, innuendo, and unsupported accusations famously used by McCarthy in the 1950s first saw the light of day with this early HUAC. Those accused could not examine evidence against them, could not present their own witnesses, could not cross-examine accusers. The rules of such committees allowed for holding secret sessions and presenting findings in an edited form.[3] The scenario was right out of the Soviet courts that Alsberg had condemned in his 1920s writings, except this time, *he* was under attack and, paradoxically, accused of supporting and spreading Communism in the United States.

Henry Alsberg's first venture into a congressional hearing room in 1938 came under friendlier circumstances when Congressman William Sirovich, a New York Democrat, sponsored a bill to create a federal Department of Science, Art, and Literature. It would have essentially made the arts projects, or something like them, into a permanent department. The hearings in support of the bill gave Alsberg a chance to boast about the FWP's artistic successes and cultural importance.[4] Although the Sirovich proposal might have offered a fleeting hope to Alsberg and the other Federal One directors, House conservatives roundly ridiculed the bill before voting it down.

From the day Federal One was created, Henry Alsberg and Hallie Flanagan (Theatre Project director) had to defend their programs from the conservative elements in the government and the press. In 1937, the year before Dies' committee got under way, Ralph Easley, chairman of the conservative National Civic Association, wrote a series of letters to President Roosevelt, charging racketeering, incompetence, and overspending in the WPA as a whole. Even worse, due to the political climate revving up against Communists, he charged that officials in Washington promoted the formation of Communist-led labor unions that operated under orders from Moscow. Easley singled out Alsberg and the Federal Theatre Project (FTP)'s Hallie Flanagan as Communist sympathizers. His attack on Alsberg was misleading, although not totally off the mark:

> Leader of an anarchist club and close associate of the deported Alexander Berkman in the latter's anarchist-communist movement. Revolutionary and atheist writer, compared the advent of Lenin to the birth of Christ. Went to Soviet Russia and was employed there in making a historic survey of the Russian Communist Party. Never occupied an executive position in this country. On his return from Soviet Russia was appointed national director of the Federal Writers Project.[5]

Alsberg responded in a statement to the *New York Times*. He did not address *all* of the charges (just as well, because some were correct) and concentrated on the FWP's impressive list of achievements.[6]

The catch-22 for Alsberg was that although he was accused of hiring Communists, he also had no choice. WPA regulations did not allow agencies to discriminate against employing workers based on their political affiliations. "This was the first intent of Congress.... They were very worried that the WPA would be used as a political machine to perpetuate the Roosevelt regime. They wanted to be sure that it would be against the law to discriminate against anyone," said FWP editor Jay Du Von.[7]

All of the earlier accusations, as well as press attention to the hornets' nest of actual Communist activities and divisiveness plaguing the New York City unit, made the FWP a prime target for Dies. It also set the stage for disgruntled workers in New York and spies in Washington to use the congressional hearings as a platform to accuse the FWP as a whole, and Alsberg specifically, of promoting class hatred and Communist propaganda. In May 1938, the Dies Committee received appropriations to begin hearings to investigate "the extent, character, and objects of un–American propaganda activities in the United States."[8]

The Committee was "just bound and determined to prove that the Federal Arts Projects were communist ridden ... they didn't have much ability or desire, it seemed to me, to separate the truth from the fanciful," according to Du Von.[9]

Although full hearings did not commence until August 1938, the Committee began surveillance of New York Federal One operations that spring. Within a few months, J. Parnell Thomas, Dies' enthusiastic Republican HUAC colleague from New Jersey, held confidential hearings in New York City, interviewing members of the FTP and FWP. Afterward, he called the two projects "hotbeds of communism."[10] Among the initial charges: Soviets provided financial support to labor unions, which then took control of the projects, and applicants to the programs would be hired only if they were card-carrying Communists.

When the full hearings got under way in Washington, initial testimony focused on German-American Nazis on domestic soil, but the Committee quickly turned to Communism as the devil in the works. HUAC gave "friendly" witness Walter Steele, a conservative magazine editor, great leeway to express for the record what true patriots considered "six major Un-American menaces": communism, socialism, Nazism, anarchism, ultra-pacifism, and atheism. He later softened his statement about Nazis, adding that they did not present as grave a threat as the others.[11] Steele also named specific people and groups as having communistic tendencies; if Alsberg hadn't been so busy preparing for Dies' onslaught, he might have been amused to hear that his fellow radical travelers included child star Shirley Temple and the Camp Fire Girls.[12] (J. Parnell Thomas saw only four menaces: fascism, Bolshevism, Nazism, and "New Dealism."[13])

Great Storms of 1938

On the home front, Alsberg vacationed that summer at his cottage, doing carpentry and odd jobs and working on his own creative writing, a book whose title and content is lost to history.[14] Back in Washington, he moved into the Majestic, a new art deco apartment building. Some forces within the FWP steadied—enough that *American Guide* books and specialty publications flowed out on a regular basis (they would soon number 200). The office environment had all the distractions of any organization; a few of the men—Alsberg's room-mate Clair Laning included—vied for the romantic attentions of colleague Mary Maverick Lloyd. It could be likened to a domestic household, with yelling and crying, arguments and make-ups. One staffer's disagreement with Alsberg about an office matter escalated into a shouting match. When each realized they were wrong, "I thought we'd both cry on each other's shoulders."[15] Other internal strife developed while the Dies committee geared up; Alsberg's assis-tant, Reed Harris, quit the Project over what he saw as Alsberg's weakness in reigning in the New York City radicals.[16]

But outside forces, namely Dies and his band of conservatives, really gave Alsberg the greatest angst. Mother Nature, in the form of the Great Hurricane of 1938, provided a metaphor for Alsberg's own stormy season. He was in New York on business when the devastating hurricane hit on his birthday, September 21, killing hundreds, from Long Island to New England. If he could have known the future, he would have perceived it as an omen.

Six days earlier, an addled, possibly mentally unstable sixty-six-year-old New York City FWP employee precipitated Alsberg's devastation. Edwin Banta could easily have been an actor following a script written by Martin Dies and associates. Up until two weeks prior to testifying before HUAC in September 1938, he belonged to the Communist Party. He lied both to the committee and to the FWP (when he applied for relief work) about his journalism career; he was not, as he said, an investigative reporter for the *Evening World*, but worked in the classifieds department.[17] Banta testified that 40 percent of FWP workers were Communists and that they controlled the agency, while adding that the Workers' Alliance, a Communist labor group, had to approve employment applications to the FWP. All of his accusations were denied in a brief filed by Alsberg and the FWP. Banta's testimony was also notable for introducing Richard Wright's *Ethics of Jim Crow* into the hearings. Instigated by Represen-tative Joe Starnes, Banta contended that the pieces from *American Stuff* had been written on Project time. Banta also called Wright's essay "so vile that it is unfit for a youth to read."

Even with morale threatened by the hearings, the Project managed to keep putting out guidebooks. A remarkable example is the publication of *New England Hurricane: A Factual Pictorial Record*, which FWP workers researched, photographed, and wrote in record time. The storm hit in September and the book was in readers' hands by October. Sales led to three more printings by November.

Spy vs. Spy

Intrigue worthy of the FBI and CIA imbued the testimony of two FWP employees, Louise Lazelle and Florence Shreve. Working on Alsberg's staff and seen later as spies by their colleagues, they likely caused the most harm. Ellen Woodward hired Lazelle following the Sacco–Vanzetti debacle specifically to ensure that radical passages did not appear in the guidebooks. One Washington editor believed Lazelle also worked for Dies and called her a double agent out to undermine the Project and Woodward.[18] Laning and Alsberg later believed that Woodward used Lazelle against Alsberg. In any case, Lazelle's testimony was tailor-made to fulfill Dies' aspirations to indict the FWP and Henry Alsberg:

> THE CHAIRMAN: Have you found, or do you know as a fact, that Mr. Coy [a central office editor] and Mr. Alsberg, at their headquarters of the Federal Writers' Project, have shaped their material for propaganda purposes?
> MRS. LAZELLE: Yes, sir.
> THE CHAIRMAN: Against business and against industry as a class?
> MRS. LAZELLE: Yes sir, and against the Government.

When Lazelle's statements weren't strong enough, Dies helped clarify them, with the gist being that the *American Guides* were written to stir up class and race hatred and to promote communist propaganda. Florence Shreve, hired for typography and layout, took on editing duties at some point and began deleting words, phrases, and paragraphs from *American Guide* copy. As she told Dies, "I had been taking out the little subtle things."

> THE CHAIRMAN: What had you been taking out? Just characterize it?
> MRS. SHREVE: Oh, the struggle between capital and labor; that the Negro had been downtrodden; and always—there was a word that they used; I can't think of it at the moment—
> MRS. LAZELLE: Underprivileged.
> MRS. SHREVE: That is it—underprivileged; the underprivileged Negro.[19]

Shreve made unsubstantiated, easily disproven, and, in some cases, ridiculous charges, some of it based on office gossip: that Alsberg sent out memorandums promoting Communist magazines (the memorandums she produced as evidence said nothing of the sort); that millions of dollars were funneled to Viking Press and *Poetry* magazine; and, not knowing Alsberg and Communists had equal distaste for one another, that Alsberg was being recommended for "meritorious service" to the Communist Party.

The writing so roundly acknowledged by literary reviewers went unmentioned. The attempts made by Alsberg, Sterling Brown, and others to get Southern states to portray the African Americans in a fair manner was disparaged. Accolades from chamber of commerce offices, scholars, and publishers—none of this was deemed important enough to add to the record.

Both women's testimonies came during secret sessions, so Alsberg likely did not yet know the specific accusations when Dies announced to the press that he had evidence that "Communist phraseology had been inserted in guides from the states and in the office here in Washington."[20] When someone discovered that Shreve was "giving dope to the Dies Committee," Alsberg fired her.[21] He appeared unruffled in the press, but behind the scenes, the whole business rattled him. One friend told of a call from him one evening. "Henry … asked us to come over, he was feeling despondent, was his sweetest on the telephone and said 'I really need somebody'—so we naturally went, and I probed as usual for the cause of his unhappiness, he did his usual evasions, oh it was everything, he wasn't competent at his job…." Although he complained that his misery stemmed from the resignation of trusted assistant Mary Lloyd, still recuperating from tuberculosis, it was more likely that he fretted about the recent not-so-secret testimonies from his own staff.[22] Another friend reported that at a party a few days later, Alsberg appeared "sober and sad and looked a bit grey."[23]

Alsberg and his FTP counterpart, Hallie Flanagan, were desperately anxious to set the record straight in front of the committee. They were not called to testify. The two also wanted to make public statements to the media, but were not permitted by their supervisors to do so.

In September, a *Nation* reporter wrote prophetically that "Our first impulsive reaction to Martin Dies and his Congressional committee on 'un–American' activities is one of unbridled mirth. But then, on reflection, it becomes difficult to decide whether to laugh at the fatuousness of his charges and his 'evidence' or to feel rather somber about their potential and probable consequences."[24]

With great media fanfare in early December, Dies sent a federal marshal to subpoena galley proofs and manuscripts from Alsberg's office. The marshal appeared in the middle of "one of those nice family arguments" between Alsberg and Hettwer, his secretary. The bickering ended with the arrival of the marshal, and the entire staff spent the rest of the day preparing the necessary papers. Said Hettwer, "Mr. Alsberg was beautifully calm, as he always is, in a real crisis."[25] The upside was that, finally, Alsberg would have a chance to testify the following week.

On Sunday, December 4, the day before Alsberg and Flanagan were set to testify, Woodward called them to her office and told them she would represent them on the stand instead. Alsberg and Flanagan were stunned that they wouldn't get their day in court. "Henry Alsberg and I pointed out with a good deal of heat that we had been silenced for months, while our projects were being subjected to attack, always on the promise of a day in court," said Flanagan.[26]

Woodward appeared December 5, armed with Alsberg and Flanagan's briefs and her own statement. Journalists and cameraman filled the high-ceilinged room. Arrangements had been made for Theatre and Writers' Project publicity posters, as well as FWP books—152 of them—to be on hand for both formal court exhibit and as an informal reminder of the Projects' activities. From *Who's Who at the Zoo*, with its playful monkey on the cover, to the bright colors of California's *Guide to the Golden State*, these sea-to-shining-sea adornments did nothing to dispel the somber mood faced by Woodward in the stodgy chamber room. It was not a good day for the dignified "flower of womanhood" from Mississippi. She attempted to read a prepared statement, but her inquisitors interrupted her repeatedly.

Representative Joe Starnes again displayed his animosity toward Richard Wright's *The Ethics of Jim Crow*. As FWP scholar Jerrold Hirsch points out, the portion of the story read and emphasized at the hearing contained obscenities; with no discussion about Wright's protest against racial injustice,[27] the same piece that moved literary critics was depicted by Dies as "the most filthy thing I have ever seen."

Underneath Woodward's gentility lay a tough foundation. Throughout her three-plus hours on the stand, she answered impertinent, badgering questions. More than once, she reminded the HUAC members of the law *they'd* passed that prohibited making inquiries into WPA workers' political affiliations: "As members of Congress, whenever you get ready to change that law, we'll follow any law that you enact." By and large, though, her statements, insofar as she was allowed to complete a sentence, were ignored.

Following a short lunch recess, Woodward returned to the heavy wooden witness table, bruised but not broken. Alsberg and Flanagan attended this afternoon session; word circulated that they would be called soon.

The congressmen turned Woodward's attention to the FTP. And much like their obsession with the Writers' Project's *American Stuff*, they were similarly outraged by the FTP children's play, *Revolt of the Beavers*, which they branded "communistic." For nearly three hours, the congressmen nit-picked the play in which, as Flanagan described, "The beavers had a bad king whom they drove out so that all the beavers could eat ice cream, play, and be nine years old."[28] Citing the absurd nature of this line of questioning, Woodward quipped, "I feel like I have gotten into the kindergarten when I start to discuss the *Revolt of the Beavers*, because it is so childish." The hearings resumed the next day with a similar tone. Before the morning ended, Woodward gave up trying to finish her statement and submitted it into the record in writing.

Hallie Flanagan followed Woodward to the stand. The spirited theater director parried with Congressman Starnes in a now-legendary exchange. Starnes quoted to Flanagan an article she had written in 1931 about theatrical workers' unions in which she used the term "Marlowesque madness":

MR. STARNES: You are quoting from this Marlowe. Is he a Communist?

MRS. FLANAGAN: I am very sorry. I was quoting from Christopher Marlowe.

MR. STARNES: Tell us who Marlowe is, so we can get the proper reference, because that is all we want to do.

MRS. FLANAGAN: Put in the record that he was the greatest dramatist in the period of Shakespeare, immediately preceding Shakespeare.[29]

Approach to the "Inmost Cave"

Christopher Vogler's interpretation of Joseph Campbell's archetypal mythology describes a point in the hero's journey where he must enter a dark place, "often deep underground" or a "dangerous chamber." The hero must "descend into hell to retrieve a loved one, or into a cave to fight a dragon and gain a treasure."[30] For Henry Alsberg, the "inmost cave" described by Vogler was the HUAC hearing chamber; the loved one he was trying to save was the Federal Writers' Project; the fire-breathing dragon, Martin Dies, Jr. Perhaps after watching Hallie Flanagan and Ellen Woodward, he decided to take a different tack: He would charm the dragon.

Although the two women each performed admirably, the damage inflicted was obvious. Alsberg hoped for a better outcome. With dozens of books in various stages of publication, ranging from initial editing to galleys ready for the printing press, perhaps he felt that, like a dying man bargaining with God for just a few more months, he could find a way to stretch out that time and settle his FWP affairs. He knew that the public and the media were beginning to lean in favor of Dies' ideas. He also had to know that he wouldn't get out of that hearing room unscathed—but would he leave crippled or paralyzed?

Mangione recorded the moment Alsberg stepped up to the seat vacated just moments before by Flanagan, describing Alsberg as "nervous." A young staff member helped him wheel a library truck filled with FWP books, perhaps for Alsberg to use as a visual aide, lucky charm, or security blanket. By way of support, the staff member quietly reminded Alsberg that Hopkins gave permission for him to "spit in the faces of the Dies Committee."[31] Under the glare of lights and photographers' flashbulbs, Alsberg began answering questions in a voice so quiet that Dies had to ask him to speak up.[32] A few moments later, when Starnes asked about subversive activities in the New York City Writers' Project unit, Alsberg had his ace-in-the-hole answer, which was to tell of his own battles against Communists during the previous decade.

"I don't know whether the committee wants to know my attitude toward communism," he said in a louder and steadier voice. "I think I have a history on that—a personal history on that—which will make it quite clear that I am the very opposite of a Communist."

If the committee had been, indeed, a pack of wolves, their ears would have tilted forward, alert to this new frequency. All in the room paid close attention as Alsberg described writing articles and making speeches on the suppression of civil liberties in Soviet Russia, on the publication of the Political Prisoners book. Starnes was confused.

> MR. STARNES: Now, what Russian situation did you have reference to—under the Czarist regime?
> MR. ALSBERG: Oh no; under the Soviet regime.

The committee mentally regrouped—could Alsberg's anti–Communist credentials be better than theirs? He went on to tell them that he lost most of his friends at the time, "because I was considered the arch anti–Communist.... I suffered; I was blacklisted; I could not get my articles printed." Dies pounced on this:

> THE CHAIRMAN: I am very much interested in your statement that when you wrote this against Russia, many of your friends became incensed about it and many liberals were angered about it...
> MR. ALSBERG: ...I think a great many of these same people have changed their minds very much.
> THE CHAIRMAN: From some of the abuse and satire that has been heaped on this committee by certain people, I am very much in doubt as to whether they have changed their minds.
> MR. ALSBERG: Perhaps I should not have brought this up.[33]

Alsberg treaded a thin line; on one hand, his anti–Communist vehemence surprised the Committee and made them seemingly more sympathetic; on the other, some radical colleagues saw him as a traitor because the Committee treated him a bit more gently than they otherwise would have.

For ten minutes, he told of his reportorial and refugee volunteer exploits

Henry Alsberg testifies before the House Committee on Un-American Activities in December 1938. Despite the unprecedented number of publications and glowing reviews from book critics, he was ousted in 1939. Shortly thereafter, the Project converted into small, state-based programs before ending completely in 1943 (Library of Congress, Prints & Photographs Division).

in Russia, always emphasizing his stance against the Communists. He told about meeting Lenin for three minutes. He *didn't* tell them that at first he supported the revolution. When asked about his relationship with Emma Goldman, he acknowledged meeting her in Russia and told of "bitter quarrels" with her about her views on revolution. But he denied knowing anything about her American activities. It's impossible to believe that Alsberg didn't know about Goldman's and Berkman's radicalism that led to their deportations in 1919. Not only did it make front-page news in both mainstream and left-leaning newspapers, it became the talk of the radical world, of which he was very much a part. He was circumspect about what he told the committee and what he left out.

When it came to Emma Goldman, still seen as subversive, he downplayed his relationship with her and even lied. While he acknowledged seeing her and spending time with her in Spain, he did not say that they traveled there together, that he lived with her in France, or that he edited her book. He did not mention his continued friendship with Saxe Commins, her nephew.

Alsberg defended his writers and editors and expertly deflected interrogators when they tried to pin him down on the political affiliations of FWP writers and editors, with the hope of protecting his people from the wrath of the committee. When it came to the New York project, Alsberg acknowledged that the Communist factions, which recently had come under control, had been a headache for him. Alsberg, a little too forthcoming, told Committee members that when he was in New York the month before, he complained about the small Communist faction: "I said, 'For Christ's sake, cannot they peddle their [Communist] literature somewhere else except the entrance to the project door?'" He recounted sit-down strikes and the picketing that followed personnel cutbacks. But he also hastened to add that such problems occurred in New York City only, emphasizing that the unit there represented only about 500 people—and that just a fraction of them were involved—out of 4,500 employed nationwide.

During the remainder of the afternoon session, Dies focused on alleged leftist propaganda in the subpoenaed *American Guide* galleys. Alsberg admitted some of the labor essays had needed some "toning down" but again tried to deflect the discussion. He pointed to the library cart, extolled the guidebooks' virtues, and told the committee there had been no complaints about those books containing subversive material. (He likely left the Massachusetts book with its Sacco–Vanzetti controversy off the cart.) By the time Alsberg departed the witness seat, Dies not only commended him for his attitude (he called him "one of the frankest witnesses" to appear) but also shook his hand and asked him to autograph some of the guidebooks.

The perception of Alsberg's testimony—both at the time and in subsequent decades—depends on who was looking and what their expectations were. There is a notable similarity to Alsberg's 1924 review of Alexander Berkman's book, *Bolshevik Myth*. "What you write about the Bolsheviks depends, very largely on what you, yourself, take with you to Moscow when you go there." A parallel statement can be made about Alsberg's testimony: What his contemporaries said about it depended largely on what each individual believed about Alsberg, Dies, and Communism.

Mangione held that, except for Dies, "no one complimented him for his conduct on the witness stand." Mangione wrote that "initial reaction to his testimony was harsh," and liberals on his staff saw Alsberg as "too deferential."[34] But evidence contradicts this.

In fact, numerous co-workers, including the most liberal (which most of them were, anyway), immediately congratulated him for his "brilliant perform-ance" on the witness stand. "He did a very good job with the Dies Commit-tee—everybody was very pleased with him—from both sides—including himself, except that the *Daily Worker* said he proved he was a Red-baiter himself but the radicals here in town and government liked him very much," said Jacob Baker.[35] Alsberg's friend Roderick Seidenberg, who sometimes disagreed with Alsberg on personal and policy matters, said similarly, "Henry acquitted himself with much honor and glory before the Dies committee ... it was touching to see him so proud of himself, and I cannot help but like the old scoundrel for it!!"[36]

The emotional aftermath of testifying left Alsberg with a need to decom-press. He and Seidenberg took in a French film, then returned to Alsberg's apartment. There, the men talked about the philosophy of "outwitting the Dies Committee and the WPA and everyone else including his trembling advisors."[37]

Only a few people—Baker, Seidenberg, roommate Clair Laning, and Mary Lloyd—knew that Alsberg had seriously contemplated resigning after the com-mittee hearing. "Now that this is over, Henry wants to quit—because he doesn't like Mrs. Woodward or some of her folks, nor the limitations that hedge him and he has $10,000 and wants to go to Peekskill [his country cottage in Putnam Valley] and nest and write etc.," Baker wrote to Lloyd. "Roderick told him he had a duty to the project and that he had one to the folks around him. I didn't feel either was true and in any case I recognize it wouldn't matter if he were sufficiently fed up on it—oh yes, he also says the exchange rate makes Paris very nice indeed. I did advise him to have some fun in resigning, making it over some issue that makes sense or noise or something."[38]

Threatening to quit, wanting to retreat to his country sanctuary—this was typical of Alsberg, reminiscent of his moods that he described to Emma Goldman during the 1920s. He wasn't naive, telling Mary Lloyd, "I did well with the committee, but the reverberations will still be long and unpleasant." Despite his friends' positive attitudes about his testimony, Alsberg suffered a bout of insecurity. His words to Lloyd almost mirrored what he'd written to Emma Goldman during his *Federal Emergency Relief Administration* (FERA) days: "I'll probably be shortly out of a job."[39]

He did not resign, possibly due to Woodward's transfer to the Social Secu-rity Board. Alsberg's and Woodward's dislike for one another was well known among some of his contingent. (Laning once described Alsberg's loud reaction on returning from a meeting with Woodward: "Do you hear that scream? It's our Mr. A. back from Mrs. W's.")[40]

Meanwhile, Alsberg could take at least a little joy in the fact that the newspapers weren't filled with *only* Dies' attacks. *Pathfinder*, a large-circulation news magazine, gave the FWP positive coverage and called the Committee's tactics into question. It acknowledged that some WPA writers were left of center, but called the Project's "20-million word experiment in collective writing" one of unquestioned "historic importance."[41] A two-page spread in the *New York Times* magazine excerpting parts of the *Almanac for New Yorkers* read like a publicity man's dream. Even Dies would have had trouble labeling the *Almanac's* story about Charlie the talented sea lion as communistic propaganda. New York's *Daily News, The Post*, and, less comfortably for Alsberg, the communist *Daily Worker* also promoted the books. As part of publicity efforts, the FWP distributed posters promoting *New York Panorama* and *Birds of the World* for display in subway cars and schools; they arranged with the Banker's Club of America and the Merchants Association of New York to display the books and distribute them at conventions. Subways, schools, the Banker's Club, and the merchants' group—these were hardly dangerous liaisons for a "communistic propaganda machine" like the FWP.

After a trip to Chicago for a regional FWP conference ("most fruitful and made me for the first time feel I was doing my job instead of piddling"[42]) and a quiet Christmas with local Washington friends, Alsberg waited for the Dies Committee report.

1939: HUAC's Report

Alsberg, who'd managed to get in more complimentary statements about his project than either Woodward or Flanagan, might have left the hearings in December with the notion that he had helped extend the life of the FWP. But any reassurances he might have given himself were short lived.[43] His "monomania" about finishing something bigger than all the things that he had *never* been able to finish before—none of it mattered. When the Committee released its final report in January 1939, it concluded that "Communist activities were carried on openly in the FWP" and that the "Communists used the FWP as a splendid vehicle for the dissemination of class hatreds." Alsberg, they said, "did not deny that a substantial number of the total employees were admitted Communists, and that they had been very active on the project, but Mr. Alsberg said he did everything within his power to stop these activities." It was bad on all fronts for Alsberg. The report misconstrued evidence, lied about his testimony, and questioned his competence. Further, it included all of the testimony against both the Writers' and Theatre Projects but no supportive testimony from Alsberg or Flanagan. The report left out the legal briefs the two had submitted to answer charges against their programs.[44] Even worse was finding out about Lazelle's secret testimony when it was published in January 1939. According to Laning, Lazelle perjured herself under orders from Woodward. It was, Laning said, Woodward's "last parting shot at Henry."[45]

The stressors from within and without increased Alsberg's micromanaging tendencies, late-night work, and dependence on indigestion medications. Mangione described an "anti–Alsberg" sentiment popping up among some in the office, partially because he appointed Laning assistant director.[46] His colleagues couldn't know that insecurity and anxiety likely led to this move. Laning, his platonic roommate, proved himself to be a trustworthy friend, and Alsberg leaned on the younger man as tumultuous events gained momentum. Laning's letters to Mary Lloyd during this period offer one of the few real glimpses into Alsberg's emotional state and private life as he witnessed Alsberg's eccentric habits and impulsive moments. ("He was all occupied worrying about his car; it seems the transmission made a sound that the garage man said would cost forty dollars to fix. You know how Hank feels about repair bills—so after lunch we went out and bought a new Ford."[47])

Alsberg grew easily agitated and needed a tolerant, even-tempered friend. He wouldn't give his roommate privacy ("really, the guy is impossible," Laning said) while also complaining about his visitors. "Do you have to have women around all night?" Alsberg asked when a friend of Laning's came to the door. Laning quipped to Mary Lloyd: "It was 9:30." Maybe it was Alsberg's legendary charm, but these petty annoyances didn't drive Laning away: "so much for Hank, the duck, our faithful friend."[48]

Danger Ahead

Threats to the WPA and the Theatre and Writers' Projects appeared daily. A newly elected, more conservative Congress cut $150,000 million from the WPA budget in early 1939, while at the same time quadrupling HUAC funding to continue its investigations. Roosevelt's administration was slowly abandoning the arts projects. In January the WPA laid off 6,000 people from Federal One.[49] WPA architect Harry Hopkins had left his position for a post on Roosevelt's Cabinet at the end of 1938. Although his successor, Colonel Francis Harrington, initially supported Federal One's existence, that would not last.

Alsberg, under the gun to publish as many books as possible, went on the offensive and released a report in February pointing out the Project's accomplishments: more than 170 volumes in the *American Guide* series published, with 400 more in preparation. Polls showed that three-quarters of Americans favored the continuation of the Dies Committee; nevertheless, it didn't stop them from buying FWP's diverse offerings, which included *The Oregon Trail*, *Skiing in the East*, *Reptiles and Amphibians*, *The Albanian Struggle in the Old World and New*, *These Are Our Lives: 35 Histories of Southern Whites and Negroes*, and *Radio in Education*. The FWP added the *WPA Guide to Minnesota* and *New York City: A Guide to the Metropolis and the 1939 World's Fair* to its output. *New York Panorama* was even published in Great Britain.

Like a recurring nightmare, Congress haunted Alsberg. These new threats came from a House subcommittee on appropriations, steered by the anti–New Deal Virginia Democrat Clifton Woodrum, who had his sights set foremost on the FTP, with the Writers' Project close behind.

In March, the Woodrum committee called Colonel Harrington and Florence Kerr, who'd assumed leadership of Federal One, to testify. It didn't take long for Woodrum to turn to the tactics Martin Dies had used so well. In some ways, the new attack was even more threatening. Not only did Woodrum have the power to sway public opinion, his committee also held the purse strings. Federal One, with the one-two punch of the Dies and Woodrum committees, faced what amounted to the death penalty.

Like HUAC, this committee employed its own investigators. One of them planted incriminating Communist propaganda in the New York City Writers' Project office. James McGraw found a photographer taking pictures of the fake evidence and ordered him out. Another showed up at the Washington headquarters demanding Alsberg's files, but Alsberg had already taken them home for safekeeping, leaving only an extra pair of suspenders and his medication in his safe.[50] Still another investigator took less drastic action. He went to the library. There, he found a ten-year-old copy of *The Nation*, and in it, the editorial letter Alsberg had written in 1929. In that period, Henry Alsberg had spent years fighting for prisoners' rights abroad. When prison revolts occurred in the United States, he felt compelled to share his fury about their conditions and suggest solutions such as teaching criminals to develop "class-consciousness" and to organize, like a union. "They must slough off their own sense of guilt and must develop a conviction that they are victims of society, not culprits," he wrote.[51] Woodrum read the contents aloud at the appropriations hearing while questioning Florence Kerr. She, of course, knew nothing about that letter and stressed that it had nothing to do with Alsberg's present work. Although Colonel Harrington didn't register much alarm at the time, it sparked a slow burn that eventually would ignite into a full-fledged blaze. Alsberg prepared a statement explaining that the *Nation* letter was written "under the influence of the particular situation then existing and was intended to provoke a more serious and effective effort to do something for the inmates of our prisons." He pointed out that he had written nothing about the prison situation since then and that the letter represented a "fantastic scheme in a spirit of paradox, to draw public attention to a situation where reform was then, and still is badly needed."[52]

Alsberg neither sold himself out nor disavowed the need for prison reform. And although he truthfully added, "I have never had, of course, any intention of promoting any organization among prisoners," he was a bit disingenuous about the letter being written in the spirit of a paradox. The topic of prison reform deeply affected him, and he meant every word he wrote in 1929 and probably in 1939. One of the ironies is that Alsberg's article of the same period in the *New Freeman* presented an even more piercing indictment of the prison system. That no investigator discovered this less accessible article is not especially surprising, but the Dies and Woodrum committees displayed other ineptitudes as well in their attempts to oust Alsberg. The *Nation* letter was the least of it. In 1930, just a few years before Alsberg started working at FERA, he'd presided at a banquet honoring Alexander Berkman's sixtieth birthday, even writing the flattering biographical sketch included in the event's published pamphlet. Despite his own pacifist views, Alsberg admired Berkman and his philosophies, including Berkman's struggles against the "suppression of the voice of the masses." Alsberg's conservative foes would never have seen past the criminal who'd been imprisoned for stabbing industrialist Henry Frick.

The committee soon turned its focus away from the prison letter and, after queries about Alsberg's salary and age, moved on to other topics.[53] With the prison letter seemingly forgotten, Alsberg would nevertheless soon feel its reverberations. If the Dies committee had been a pack of slathering wolves, Woodrum and his associates—except for one liberal defender of the projects—were venomous serpents.

Through spring 1939, Woodrum expressed particular vitriol against the FTP and Hallie Flanagan. Appeals from public figures—Tallulah Bankhead, James Cagney, Orson Welles—fell on indifferent ears. When the committee turned again to the Writers' Project, it brought back Ralph De Sola, an FWP worker who had previously appeared before the Dies committee. As opposed to his earlier testimony, this time he proved anything but innocuous; he and others made damning, unsubstantiated charges against Alsberg and other staff members.

On May 1, Alsberg submitted a twenty-five-page brief, along with documents and records to refute each charge. Among the newer claims: that Alsberg instigated a sit-down strike in New York City and, in a racist harbinger of the "birther" movement that plagued President Barack Obama, that Richard Wright was an "alien," not born in the United States. Each charge was preposterous in its own way. The strike that Alsberg supposedly instigated was at least on some level a protest against him as director. Alsberg seemed to take particular offense about the claim that Wright, born in Mississippi, was not a citizen, calling it "the most fantastic of all charges." Alsberg called attention in his brief to the letter signed by nearly fifty book publishers—venerable publishing houses such as Viking Press, Random House, Oxford University Press, and Alfred Knopf—that declared the FWP books were not projects of propaganda but instead made a "genuine, valuable, and objective contribution to the understanding of American Life." He quoted letters from the Book of the Month Club (which recommended all *American Guides* to its subscribers) and the American Hotel Association, testifying to the importance of the books.[54]

Others tried to come to the rescue, too. Eleanor Roosevelt, a supporter of the FWP from inception, included kind words for the Writers' Project in her syndicated newspaper column. William Couch, director of the University of North Carolina Press, attempted to sway his fellow Southerners with forceful letters and positive reviews of *These Are Our Lives*.[55] The *New Republic* devoted three pages to the FWP, bemoaning the Project's possible demise. "Now that the Federal Writers' Project is in danger of being abandoned, the value of the work it has done stands out sharply: the least publicized of the three art projects, it may emerge as the most influential and valuable of them all."[56]

The 1939 World's Fair: A Surreal Facade

While congressional theatrics played out in Washington, the Writers' Project flaunted its stuff at the New York World's Fair, which opened in April 1939. During the same period that he worked to strategize a defense, run the Project, and lobby officials, publishers, and various organizations, Alsberg managed to stay involved with the FWP's contribution to the fair. Visitors to the gargantuan grounds certainly had flashier exhibits to visit: the Futurama model city of 1960, Elektro, the seven-foot-tall Westinghouse robot, and the futuristic technology of television. The FWP display located in the WPA building on the Avenue of Patriots consisted of a large, three-dimensional map of the continental United States complete with oversized *American Guide* books imbedded into it, a mural depicting a writer at work, and a counter to let visitors browse through the guidebooks. Certainly not as stimulating as other exhibits, it still brought in visitors.

Alsberg, in New York when the fair opened, likely visited that day or shortly thereafter. Back in Washington, he monitored the FWP exhibit, seeing it as another good public relations tool. By this time, Mangione noticed that

Alsberg was "tormented" by the possibility of both the Project and his direc-torship coming to an end.[57] Hence, every conceivable approach to promoting the FWP took on import. When he discovered the attendants couldn't answer questions about the guidebooks, for instance, he made arrangements for new attendants, people who "had thorough knowledge of Project," to take over. It was just as important, he said, that the new attendants "not enter into any sort of argument about the work of the Project."[58] His paranoia wasn't unreason-able.

Alsberg's tenacity, mixed with a good dose of anxiety and uncertainty, drove him through those months to expedite each new initiative. He encour-aged Morton Royse to continue gathering material for the ethnic studies pro-gram, sent out press releases promoting the FWP books on African-Americans, and wrote critiques for editors in states still working on various guidebooks, which by now included specialty titles like *The Oregon Trail: The Missouri River to the Pacific Ocean.*

The tenuous mood of the project left the staff feeling as if the WPA, the bigger organization of which they constituted a minuscule part, had betrayed them. In June, Laning took Alsberg and other staffers on a weekend ocean retreat. At one point, Alsberg tried to ease his belly pain with the warmth of the sun. After undressing under an umbrella, he settled down to read. "Then his *New Yorker* [magazine] blew away and H [ran] hard after it for a half mile down the beach, naked except for his panama hat and his glasses."[59]

On their return from this brief respite, neither James Cagney's telegrams nor Eleanor Roosevelt's quiet support mattered when it came to a congressional vote on the Emergency Relief Appropriation Act of 1939. The bill, which Pres-ident Roosevelt felt pressured to sign because it still provided some funding for work relief, eliminated the Theatre Project as of July 1, 1939. It made pro-visions for limited continuation of the other Federal One projects if they could secure partial state sponsorship. The Federal Writers' Project, to be renamed the Writers' Program, was not dead yet.

But for Henry Alsberg, the end drew near. Even before Roosevelt signed the new relief bill, Colonel Harrington asked for Alsberg's resignation. Alsberg defiantly demanded more time. He wanted to ensure that all of the *American Guide* books reached their publishing houses. "The thing that is haunting me," Laning commented at the time, "is what they have been trying to do to Henry. It's all beyond belief." Laning convinced Alsberg to take some sick leave to nurse his ailing digestive system; on his return, Laning reported, everyone in the office felt reassured by Alsberg's calm. As long as he remained there, no general firings could occur. This saga—Harrington demanding Alsberg's res-ignation and Alsberg ignoring him—continued through July and part of August.

"Henry, bless him, has turned into a stubborn bull who refuses to leave the pasture and get out on the lonely road. Occasionally someone shakes their apron at him, but our Hank pretends not to see and goes around smelling flowers or pushes his nose in their laps, which is terribly unethical and very embarrassing," Laning wrote.[60]

Alsberg offered to retire if they brought in his suggested successor with whom he could work until they sorted out the reorganization. Harrington, apparently with the full impact of Alsberg's infamous "prison" letter now lodged in his mind, denied the request and gave him a deadline to resign by August 1.

Alsberg was intent on staying longer and worked determinedly to obtain the state sponsorships necessary under the new law to keep the FWP afloat. A flurry of letters and memos during the last week of July kept his secretary occupied as she contemplated losing her beloved boss. In one letter, he outlined to a potential publisher a dozen books in progress: these included *Men Against Granite, The Negro in Virginia, America Eats, A Guide to Boston,* and others. *Negro in Virginia* came out under the Writers' Program. Like so many other "lost" WPA manuscripts, the Boston guide never saw publication. *America Eats* and *Men Against Granite* finally emerged via books published in the 21st century.[61]

Alsberg's last few office communiqués reflected the end of an epoch. By late July, he knew he couldn't really save himself but wanted to keep the program in motion. With his small, remaining staff, Alsberg wrote to regional administrators outlining the procedures on setting up the new statewide projects.

On August 1, the day he was supposed to resign, Alsberg did not. Instead, he went in to work and helped a New York supervisor fill out the requisite WPA form that would keep the program running there.[62] Where he once perceived the young writers of the Project as his legacy, perhaps now he now he viewed the Project in its entirety as his legacy. The deferential Alsberg seen at the HUAC hearings was gone, replaced with the true, rebellious, stubborn Henry Alsberg. Still referring to himself as "Director of the Federal Writers' Project" on August 4, he wrote to the Florida FWP director, with the all-caps type indicating crisis mode: "PLEASE MAKE ALL POSSIBLE HASTE IN FINAL CHECKING OF REMAINDER STATE GALLEYS."

When Alsberg continued work through another week (on August 8, he made final contractual arrangements with Hastings House to publish three guidebooks), a furious Colonel Harrington ordered Florence Kerr to fire Alsberg.[63]

The Snake Pounces

"You're to get rid of that man. I don't want to hear his name again," Harrington told Kerr in no uncertain terms. Years later, Kerr recollected, "I called

Henry in to see me .... Well, it was a very unhappy severance when Henry had to accept the fact. He was just heart-broken .... He loved the Project, and of course I think he felt I was a weakling and everybody else was a weakling and we never did have a director that amounted to a hill of beans after that."[64] Alsberg's "heartbroken" state wasn't necessarily about leaving but about being barred from managing the reorganization and completing production on remaining manuscripts. In fact, Alsberg, although proud of the FWP's many accomplishments and attached to it like a mother to a suckling child, was actually exhausted from the nonstop, four-year effort. He may have felt a sense of relief that this wild ride would soon come to an end. "H. is as cheerful as a panhandler in Battery Park suddenly,"[65] Laning remarked when they received initial inklings in June that the Project would end.

Harrington then appointed the relatively obscure John Newsom, Michigan State FWP director, to assume Alsberg's job on August 9. "In god's name, what happened?" asked Southern California editorial director Leon Dorais. "I've been sick at my stomach all afternoon after seeing the piece in the local papers here."[66] Before departing Washington, Alsberg attempted to secure the jobs of the national editing staff and wrote to Harrington requesting they be retained. He advised his secretary to ask for "assured status" so that she could remain employed. If Alsberg felt irate or hurt, he didn't reveal it publicly. "Henry said that getting out of the WPA gave him the same feeling he had when he got out of Russia," wrote Laning. But as Alsberg feared, his departure did leave left the Project in "complete and utter chaos."[67]

Alsberg sounded at ease when he explained to the press that he couldn't obey the directive to leave by August 1 because "[he] did not want to go on record as leaving the project while the process of reorganization was going on. As a result, [Harrington] terminated my services." Alsberg related that Harrington told him that he did not administer the project well. "I asked him to cite specific examples," Alsberg said. "Colonel Harrington did not do that. Maybe he wanted to spare my feelings." Laning wrote that "Harrington didn't like Henry because of his more or less radical notions."[68] This may have included rumors circulating about Alsberg's homosexuality.[69]

Less than a week after sending his last memo as FWP director, Henry Alsberg returned north to his countryside "shack." Letters of condolence came from various quarters. *Publishers Weekly* called Alsberg's dismissal a "further loss to the Writers' Projects, already badly crippled by the provisions of the new relief law."[70] Liberal publications such as *The Nation* and *The New Republic* denounced the action and listed the impressive achievements of the FWP under Alsberg's leadership.

Personal letters came in, too. The NAACP's Walter White told him, "You have made a very real contribution which petty minds do not have the capacity to understand or appreciate." The most touching note came from his secretary. Teary-eyed, she said, "You had the imagination and the courage to go on."[71]

Perhaps Alsberg and his fellow FWP stalwarts felt a sense of vindication as some of the men who helped bring down the FWP were shown to be scoundrels of one sort or another. In 1944, a jury convicted Edwin Banta of framing a man for rape. Representative J. Parnell Thomas, an instrumental member of the Dies Committee, began a prison sentence in 1949 after a fraud conviction. During the McCarthy HUAC era, Martin Dies, despite trying mightily, did not get a place on the committee.

Stella Bloch Hanau (circa 1938), a lifelong friend of Alsberg, was a strong and early advocate for the women's rights and birth control movements. A writer and editor, she worked with Alsberg at the Province-town Playhouse and helped him get free-lance writing work in the early years of the Depression. She became a staff editor with the FWP in 1938. As evidenced by their frequent cross-country correspon-dence, their friendship lasted through Alsberg's final years (courtesy Suzanne Stella Bloch Sodergren).

Lights Out

A reduced staff stayed on in Washington under the new director to oversee the publications already set in motion before Alsberg's departure. (Most states secured sponsorship for writers' programs.) Benjamin Botkin, Sterling Brown, and Morton Royse continued with their work until the summer of 1940.

During what essentially amounted to a plodding, years-long shutdown of the program, Botkin headed the Writ-ers' Program unit at the Library of Congress that catalogued and organ-ized the voluminous remaining mate-rials. He organized two thousand slave narratives, which were published in 1941.[72] The Writers' Program strug-gled on for a few more years; after the completion of all of the state guides in 1941, it changed direction to focus on the nation's war effort. A year later, subsumed into a War Services unit of the WPA, it produced Army training manuals and serviceman's recreational guides—a long way from the Project's cultural beginnings. In May 1942, a handful of Washington staffers closed down the office. Afterward, Katharine Kellock, Dora Thea Hettwer, Merle Colby, and Stella Bloch Hanau met at a cocktail bar. Whether or not they toasted the Project or each other, or just sat together quietly letting the finality of it all sink in, is anyone's guess.[73]

By the Numbers

It's impossible to view the success of the Writers' Project merely through the number of publications issued, if only because those numbers have never been fixed. In 1972, Mangione wrote, "To this day no one knows exactly how many published items it produced." That remains true now, with the qualification that, forty years later, even *more* books have seen publication using FWP materials—the documents transferred to the Library of Congress and cataloged by Botkin, and others from the National Archives and from smaller repositories nationwide.

When Alsberg left in 1939, the FWP counted 321 publications (about 100 of those full-sized books) and about 200 more nearly ready for the presses. There were hundreds of additional FWP writings in various stages of production, such as pamphlets, radio scripts, children's books, ethnic and immigrant histories, and accounts of African American life. While some were completed under Newsom's directorship, most of those were initiated under Alsberg. By 1942 the output numbered 1,200 items. In terms of writers, librarians, clerks, and others taken off the unemployment rolls, the number peaked in 1936 with 6,686 employees and an estimated total of 10,000 over seven years.[74] The folklore, social-ethnic studies, and the slave narratives projects continue to be mined, and *American Guide* books continue to be reprinted, with a count of over 1000 new or reissued books since 1980. Add to this more than 5,000 life histories and slave narratives on Library of Congress websites, and the FWP's accomplishments, while not entirely told by the numbers, are astounding.

A Personal Evolution

In 1934, during a fit of depression shortly before journeying to Washington, Henry Alsberg wrote to Emma Goldman of his desire to be useful. He felt adrift after losing even his "modest imminence" among the journalists of his time. Franklin Roosevelt offered a golden road of hope to millions of unemployed Americans, including Alsberg. But his path through the FWP years was anything but smooth. His goals from 1935 through 1939 were the same as they had been during his previous incarnations as a refugee worker, a journalist, and an advocate for political prisoners: to employ his ideals in service of a greater mission and, in the process, if at all possible, even make a name for himself. The Federal Writers' Project was not just a government agency. It was the embodiment of converging forces: politics, the arts, the growing importance of cultural pluralism, and personally, for Alsberg, an opportunity to re-engage with American life. Given his restless nature, the fact that he could sustain such focus for four years is almost astonishing.

The Federal Writers' Projects was once called a "20-million word experiment in collective writing." Those millions of words have increased exponentially since Henry Alsberg's arrival in Washington more than eighty years ago. His name now appears on the title page of hundreds of books, giving him perhaps the "modest imminence" that he desired. When Alsberg departed Washington for New York in 1939 as the deposed director, he couldn't know that what began as a job would eventually be seen as his life's work. Through his remaining years, he would never realize that his part of the story was not over.

CHAPTER 12

The Radical Lives
of Henry Alsberg
1939–1970

Little is known about Henry Alsberg's transition from director of the nation's largest creative enterprise to the world of the unemployed. For four years he'd spent nearly every waking hour consumed with creating and sustaining worthwhile jobs for unemployed writers. Now, he was chief among their rank. He spent the first six months laid up "with a very bad case of indigestion." The return to his old haunts—both his hangouts and his anxieties—might have seemed like a dream.

Like an astronaut returned from an alien planet, Alsberg slowly found his equilibrium. If Alsberg had shared his brothers' scientific outlook, he might have likened his time in Washington to being stranded on Jupiter, a gas giant with gravity more than twice as much as Earth's but no solid place to stand. While the Federal Writers' Project (FWP) books that he helped guide to fruition continued to roll off the presses, and while Martin Dies unrelentingly sought out Communist influence in government, Henry Alsberg, lighter and with less purpose, drifted back and forth between Greenwich Village and Putnam Valley. His internal landscape remains a mystery. Even if he felt relieved to escape the tribulations of the capital, a shroud of melancholy wouldn't be surprising, considering his past susceptibilities.

If not for the war raging in Europe, there's little doubt Alsberg would have jumped aboard a ship to the continent. His time in Washington was an aberration, albeit one that provided him with a regular, respectable salary. His adjustment and reentry into his old world in 1940 meant a return to a more capricious lifestyle. And much as he did when returning from his European excursions, he turned to public speaking and writing, the former to make a living, the latter to give an outlet to the overflowing verbiage in his head.

In the spring of 1940, he secured a speaking tour with the American Association of Colleges, traveling to institutions around the nation to talk about his "Adventures in Journalism and Literature." Part of his reengagement with *his* American society stemmed from relationships with friends both old and new. When Richard Wright's *Native Son* came out that March, Alsberg wrote sent him a congratulatory note. "I hope its sales will be commensurate with its quality," Alsberg said. "It is most gratifying that one of our people has come through with such a marvelous novel. Now to be more practical: do I rate a copy?" He certainly did, and Wright visited Alsberg's Greenwich Village apartment to discuss the recent publication and give him a personally inscribed book.[1]

Alsberg rejoined old anarchist friends to celebrate the twenty-fifth anniversary of the progressive Modern School and community of Stelton, New Jersey. The dinner memorialized Emma Goldman, who had died just a few days before in Toronto. Fortuitously, the Modern School's communal movement had established another leftist community in Mohegan, New York, a few miles from Putnam Valley, giving Alsberg potential social and political outlets when he stayed there. Friends Clair Laning and the McGraws visited him in Putnam Valley often. Laning's retreat to the cottage in June 1940 found "Hank" looking healthy and "doing a fine impression of The Man Completely Relaxed. He keeps speaking vaguely of work, but such thoughts only trouble him to the extent of occasionally fixing a screen or stealing an armful of wood from Julius' woodpile."[2]

For holidays, Alsberg enjoyed the company of his family. Brother Julius, sister-in-law Elsie, and nephew and niece George and Cora lived down the hill from his cottage in "the big house." Sister Elsa lived in New York City. Brother Carl and his wife, Emma, visited New York in the fall of 1940, and likely a family reunion took place in the big house. Sadly, it would be the last such reunion; Carl took sick on the train returning home to California, and by the time he reached the West Coast, the illness progressed to pneumonia. Despite being rushed to a hospital, he died on October 31 at the age of sixty-three.

Living on the Fringe

In 1920 Lewis Strauss had written to Alsberg's mother, Bertha, that her son seemed to have no fixed address. Now, although his wandering took place in a smaller geographic area, his frequent address changes still confounded his friends. In the summer of 1940 with only a small inheritance and no regular salary, he sublet his Greenwich Village apartment and—semi-permanently—moved to the cottage to focus on writing. During this on-again, off-again subletting, he'd stay with friends, rent a hotel room, or even rent a different apartment altogether when back in Manhattan. Like other times in his life, his psyche seemed just as unsettled as his physical whereabouts.

Early in 1941 he sold a piece of his inheritance, a building on the Lower East Side of Manhattan, for $7,000, a decision that allowed him the freedom to devote more time toward writing. He leaned, as always, toward the political. America had not yet entered World War II and debate raged across the political spectrum over how far America should go to support its European Allies against Germany.

Liberal, intellectual factions had their own arguments, many based on pacifist principles. Months before the Japanese attacked Pearl Harbor, Alsberg had dinner with a friend when the topic arose. The man, in favor of America's immediate entrance into the war, screamed at Henry for not taking a definitive stance then and there.[3] In an article for *Antioch Review*, Alsberg sidestepped the issue, probably infuriating his friend still further. Instead, he skipped ahead to advocate for post-war peace settlements that the (assumed) victorious allied countries should make. So, while others debated either the urgency or apprehension of entering the war, Alsberg pressed for an immediate declaration of "war aims," that is, "the outlining of a pretty detailed program for world settlement, after Hitler is defeated." His article represented an extension of his utopian vision, one that necessitated the formation of a society of nations meant to ensure universal disarmament and the pooling of all raw materials and food, making them "freely accessible to all nations." It also served as a history lesson, outlining the mistakes made after World War I that left Europe unstable. He pointed out his own government's "stimulus of official propaganda" before World War I, which brought American public opinion to "phenomenal heights of war hysteria," and predicted that the United States would soon create an official agency to "whip up popular sentiment and overcome opposition." "Undoubtedly," he wrote, "when we get further along, such an agency will be set up in order to stimulate American 'solidarity' in support of the all-out aid and defense program." (He was correct. The Office of War Information soon was established. He did not predict, however, that he'd work for this government agency.) Considering less than two years had passed since he faced Martin Dies, it's no surprise that he also pointed out the growing wave of hysteria against supposed un–Americans of all stripes propagated by the Dies committee.[4]

German refugee Klaus Mann, son of Nobel Prize winner Thomas Mann, landed in the United States during the 1930s, after escaping persecution stemming from both his criticism of the Nazi regime and his homosexuality. The short-lived magazine he founded in 1940, *Decision: A Review of Free Culture*, attracted contributors from a venerable list of intellectuals, poets, philosophers, artists, and journalists. Thus, when it accepted two of Alsberg's articles, he was in good company with the likes of William Carlos Williams, Rebecca Pitts, Dylan Thomas, Aldous Huxley, W.H. Auden, and Somerset Maugham.

In "Post War Apocalypse," he came out in support of "an all-out effort to defeat the Axis" powers. His conception of the post-war world, based on the horrors he witnessed throughout Europe after World War I, envisioned more of the same, including victims taking "revenge against the oppressors."[5] He did not know the mass of the victims would be six million Jews and the survivors too few and feeble to take revenge.

Speaking of revenge, his other article for *Decision* was more personal. In "What about the Federal Arts Projects?" Alsberg finally publicly aired his feelings about the smiting of the Federal Theatre and Writers' Projects. Enough time had passed by May 1941 to allow his thoughts to settle into a coherent discourse. Obviously, he hadn't stopped thinking about the consequences of Dies' attacks, nor about what he perceived as the Roosevelt administration's abandonment of the arts projects. Referring to himself in the third person, Alsberg stated, "The National Director of the Writers' Project, who refused to resign, was forced out." It galled him that John Newsom, new director of the Writers' Program, received credit for publications begun under Alsberg's leadership. It no doubt bothered him even more a few months later when the WPA championed the completed guidebook series during its American Guide Week, part of a "Take Pride in America" promotion.

Under the new regime, he wrote, "censorship has begun to rear its ugly head." He cited as example an essay on labor organizers that the new editors had deleted from the final manuscript. Even worse, he contended, were the many planned books on American culture, folklore, ethnic groups, and African Americans. That program, he noted ruefully, "has been almost entirely jettisoned."

He told of his and Flanagan's bitter conflicts with state WPA officials, who provided greater support to construction projects than to the arts programs. When upward trends in private employment allowed for curtailment of WPA construction jobs, federal arts jobs were also cut. But what worked for laborers did not work for artists, Alsberg pointed out: "You cannot drop an artist who is painting a mural without killing the mural."

That the remaining arts programs were about to transform their efforts to aid the defense effort might have irked him the most. Alsberg proposed a return to Federal One's original function as he, Flanagan, and others originally planned it in his Washington home during the summer of 1935: to employ needy, talented artists to produce art of the highest quality for the American public. Of course, he knew this proposal was in vain. But he needed to get it off his chest.[6]

What might have turned out to be the most interesting of his writings during this period remained unpublished. Laning described "a sort of Horatio Alger–Jules Verne version of the world when Hitler falls ... to my surprise it reads very well, even in rough draft ... if he can keep it up, I think he might have an exciting book." Laning pushed him to finish it but told Mary Lloyd, "I will believe it when I see it." It probably shocked Laning when Alsberg completed a draft by Columbus Day, 1941. Alsberg, however, must have felt insecure about the whole venture: He asked Laning to keep it a secret. The manuscript may ultimately have been stashed in a desk drawer or burned in Alsberg's wood stove. For reasons unknown, the book never saw publication.[7]

Another work provides some insight into his feelings of Jewish identity while Jews were being persecuted in Europe. In 1941, he wrote about the spreading tide of anti–Semitism in America. With the nation's entrance into World War II under debate, he saw his fellow American Jews faced with a dilemma: Those who supported the war would be perceived as doing it for "racial reasons," thus being part of a "great Jewish international plot"; those against U.S. entrance would be seen as opposing a government fighting the Nazis. Either way, American Jews, he said, were overly solicitous in not speaking up due to fear of an anti–Semitic backlash. That approach would not stem the tide of anti–Semitism, he said, because Jews would always be seen as outsiders. He exhorted Jews not to abandon the social and ethical underpinnings of Judaism and to express their political feelings. His appeal, however, also idealized suffering for a good cause, calling it "soul-satisfying to be persecuted for belonging to a group that believes in the ideals of justice." Notably, he wrote this before the existence of death camps became widely known in America.[8]

Away from the buttoned-down world of bureaucrats Alsberg could once again indulge in the eccentricities his friends usually found charming and his critics found annoying. Actually, his quirks could annoy even the closest of friends, such as Clair Laning, whose letters to Mary Lloyd elucidated Alsberg's peculiarities. As much as Laning liked Alsberg's "Horatio Alger" manuscript, he grew impatient with their discussions about the book. "[Henry], I don't need to say, is worse than a four year old child. If you don't like an idea of his, he thinks you are jealous of his wonderful thought, and if on the other hand you show that you like it, he thinks you are getting ready to steal it." On another occasion Laning found Alsberg at his apartment door in Manhattan "carrying a typewriter and what looked like an armful of straw, but turned out to be his book manuscript." Alsberg's own apartment was being painted and he needed a place to write. Laning was shocked by his friend's habits, which bore no resemblance to actual work. Soon after Alsberg had repaired to the bedroom to write, Laning heard "snickers and snorts." Alsberg had instead picked up Laning's copy of a humorous book on the joys of Spanish cooking. Alsberg sank into the bed and spent the afternoon reading, laughing, and commenting on the book. At the end of the day, Alsberg carried his armful of loose papers and typewriter out the door, saying, "Thanks very much for the use of your room." Laning recounted another time when Alsberg, who'd sublet his own apartment and needed a place to stay while visiting the city, moved into Laning's kitchen for a few days. Luckily, Laning enjoyed Alsberg's company. At least Alsberg shared the accoutrements of his new hobby: rare Americana books. An interest piqued by his exposure during the FWP days, Alsberg spent hours rummaging through used bookstores, paying pennies for old history books and novels.

Another anecdote is less amusing. Alsberg invited Laning, McGraw, and an editor of *PM Weekly* (for which Alsberg wrote book reviews) to dinner at a Chinese restaurant. When Laning arrived, "Henry was not to be seen. He finally rumbled in in his undershirt and a dark look," Laning wrote to Mary Lloyd.

"I don't want to go to dinner with these people. Why did they ask me?" Alsberg said to McGraw.

"They didn't ask you. You asked them," McGraw replied.

"Well I can't go anyway. I'm going to call them and tell them I can't go."

After he made the phone call, he invited his friends to a different restaurant. Laning opted to stay at the Chinese restaurant, commenting to Lloyd that "it was probably silly not to go along with him and humor him—but it was such a relief not to. When he gets in his petulant-old-man role, he can ruin an evening ... as for [Henry], he was probably feeling frustrated about something."

Laning's letters featured the recurrent theme of Alsberg's relocations between Manhattan and Putnam Valley. And moving meant tying mattresses and chairs and other furniture to his car for the drive along the curving, hilly roads to his home in the Hudson Highlands. "Those gypsies on the parkway will turn out to be Henry!" Laning exclaimed.

Alsberg's generosity complemented his quirks. Emma Goldman knew in the 1920s that although Alsberg couldn't seem to finish his own books, he had a great ability to help others write theirs. Laning similarly commented, "Alsberg's talent is knowing other people's talents." He continued to help writer friends in the 1940s, among them Mary Heaton Vorse. Unhappy with a draft of her latest book, she gave it to Alsberg. His suggestions buoyed her. "H. has pinned new wings on her and now she is speeding ahead again with the final work,"[9] wrote Laning.

While surviving correspondence tells of Alsberg's frequent moves, writings, gossip, and dinners with friends, remarks about his romantic life, if he had one, are absent. Friends were circumspect. A few comments about his sexuality came after his death—Vincent McHugh wrote of the vicious FWP rumor mill that churned unfounded tales of which men on staff were "fruit" with Alsberg—but nothing reflected the suffering such rumors might have caused. Interestingly, Alsberg rented an apartment in the early 1940s at 55 Christopher Street. At the time, the building next door housed Bonnie's Stonewall Inn, a restaurant that first opened as a tearoom catering to gay women. Its name eventually shortened to the Stonewall Inn, the establishment evolved into the bar that gained fame in 1969 (the year before Alsberg's death) as the birthplace of the gay rights movement. While Alsberg did not live long enough to see it designated in 1999 as a National Historic Landmark, he likely heard the news of the rebellion that took place in his old neighborhood. Full-sized bronze sculptures of two gay couples, male and female, now memorialize the Stonewall events. These monuments are located in only two places in the world: a park on Christopher Street directly across from where Alsberg lived in New York City, and 3000 miles away, in Palo Alto, California, where Henry Alsberg died.

1942: Washington, Yet Again

Book reviews, subletting arrangements, and proceeds from family inheritances did not provide Alsberg with sufficient income. After the Pearl Harbor attack, thousands of government workers transitioned from New Deal agencies to those supporting the industry of war. Using unimpeachable references such as Supreme Court Justice Felix Frankfurter, Alsberg joined many former FWP colleagues applying for jobs with the Office of War Information. His appointment came in early October. The District of Columbia that Alsberg returned to in 1942 did not resemble the city he departed in 1939. Escalating numbers of military officials swallowed the capital. Nearly half a million government workers also packed in, creating travel quagmires every morning and evening rush hour. A 1942 transit map advised housewives to do their shopping in the middle of the day in order to avoid getting in the way of those involved in the labors of war. Blackout drills, precipitated by piercing sirens and supervised by air raid wardens, kept residents on edge.

If Henry Alsberg hated working for the Federal Emergency Relief Administration prior to his FWP appointment, he probably detested his post at the Office of War Information (OWI) even more. His new job as a senior features editor paid less than the FWP directorship. Worse than the salary cut, he was now a mere cog in the bureaucratic wheel of a propaganda machine working to mobilize patriotism across the nation. Whereas just months before his writings focused on future peace plans, now he wrote whatever was assigned to him: articles on social welfare, conservation, education, and irrigation. For better or worse, thanks to the twin devils of homophobia and his old nemesis Martin Dies, Alsberg's delicate ego wouldn't have to take it for long. A month after he started at OWI, the Civil Service Commission opened an investigation into accusations that Alsberg was involved in an "immoral relationship," that is, a homosexual relationship, with a former colleague.[10] He denied the charge and continued working for the OWI through the New Year. Soon after, Martin Dies, who had been out of the news for a while, must have felt like it was time to get back into the game.

"Dies Denounces New List of Reds," proclaimed a headline February 2, 1943, in the *New York Times*. As if the government weren't busy enough with war preparations, Martin Dies demanded the purging of forty "subversive," communist-leaning employees—"crackpot and radical bureaucrats"—from the governmental payroll. Alsberg's name made the list.[11]

On the floor of the House of Representatives, Dies made a show of his indignation at Alsberg's return to the government. "I call your attention to the case of Henry G. Alsberg who is now Senior Feature Writer for the Office of War Information.... In the early life of our committee, back in 1938, we exposed ... some of the Communist filth which was put into the official publications of the Federal Writers Project. As a result of our exposure the Congress abolished the Federal Writers Project. Who was the head of the Federal Writers Project? None other than Henry G. Alsberg, who has crept back in the Government in the Office of War Information."[12]

Shortly after Dies' speech, Alsberg was called to a Civil Service Commission hearing. Subsequently, Alsberg resigned his OWI position. In April, back in New York City, a HUAC subcommittee called him to testify in the federal court building there. When his interrogators implied that his resignation stemmed from the recent civil service investigation (without saying what it concerned), Alsberg denied it at first, saying that he resigned so that he could spend time working on a book. Then, comparing the investigation to past inquiries he faced both in Soviet Russia and in front of U.S. congressional committees, he acknowledged, "I didn't want to go through it again."

Alsberg emerged from this short and unhappy stint in Washington with a new vitality. In fact, he was sincere in telling the congressional committee that the book he was working on—which evolved from his philosophical inclinations toward post-war peace—had piqued a publisher's interest.

From the time he began the book during the war until its publication after the war's end in 1945, his sphere of family and friends changed as much as the outside world. Sister Elsa retired to California, where she volunteered with the Palo Alto Fair Play Council, a group that helped Japanese Americans just released from internment camps. Eventually Elsa became executive director and the group expanded to fight for civil rights issues of all types. Brother Julius led a group of engineers on a months-long expedition to Africa to help Ethiopia develop its natural resources. George was in the army. Elsie and Cora, a professional photographer, remained in New York.

Let's Talk About the Peace

In October 1944 representatives from the United States, Great Britain, China, and the USSR met to lay down a blueprint for an international organization that would eventually evolve into the United Nations. Perhaps his strong feelings on their proposals compelled Alsberg to finally finish a book. "Will anyone be so naive as to imagine that this facade of a League of Nations can long be depended on to keep the peace?" he asked in the foreword to *Let's Talk About the Peace*, published by Hastings House in 1945. Alsberg employed the convention of two characters—an international affairs expert dubbed "the Lecturer" and an American soldier—examining strategies necessary to form lasting world peace. The Lecturer (presumably Alsberg) analyzed and criticized the "Big Four" plans, and then proposed solutions based on his own, more idealistic visions. His framework for a permanent peace included total disarmament by all nations; a world government consisting of a legislature, court, and board of executives; and self-government for colonized peoples. He tackled the ever-unpopular problems of overpopulation, birth control, and immigration policies. Like Alsberg himself, the book was ambitious and idealistic. He believed "the power to prevent wars must be taken away from the foreign offices which have never prevented any wars." While acknowledging his ideas as utopian, he insisted that it "should not discourage those of us who want wars stopped ... unless this Utopia is achieved, mankind faces eventual destruction."

The *Chicago Daily Tribune* called the book "the year's best on international relations." *The Nation*, not surprisingly, also commended it as "a first-class Primer of World Affairs." Less kind was the *Saturday Review*'s appraisal, commenting that the book "does not suffer from intellectual modesty or any moral humility."[13]

If reviewers had known about Alsberg's Jewish Joint Distribution Committee activities, they might have pointed out a bewildering aspect of the book. While Alsberg wrote that "Nazi leaders and perpetrators of atrocities must be tried and sentenced and the sentences must be carried out," he also suggested that some Nazis ("at most two-hundred thousand Nazi leaders and their families") should be deported from Germany and dispersed to countries around the world in a humane fashion. He gave short coverage to Hitler's annihilation of the Jews. For anyone else, this would have less bearing, but for someone who had put his life on the line to fight anti–Semitism and who had relatives and friends murdered by the Nazis, it's perplexing. A possible explanation was his belief that "violence begets more violence."

On the other hand, Alsberg did appeal to the British to lift their quotas for Jews wishing to emigrate to Palestine and worried that "the atrocities have been so unbelievably terrible and on such a tremendous scale, they are actually in danger of being understated." He proposed that Germans be forced to go on "gruesome sight-seeing tours ... the horrible truth must be brought home ... so that no future rabble-rouser can ever in later years denounce the record of atrocities."

Let's Talk About the Peace showed that Alsberg never believed Jews were the sole owners of human suffering. While writing that "the Germans have been guilty of the most frightful mass atrocities committed by any so-called nation in civilized times," his list of victims included Jews, Poles, Russians, and others. Alsberg also pointed out that the Germans were not the only nation "guilty of wholesale atrocities," noting the extermination of Armenians, mass executions carried out in Soviet Russia, and "the record of the white races in Africa" as "pretty unspeakable."

Déjà Vu All Over Again

In addition to a book promotion tour, Alsberg made yet another foray into New York theater, working with, among others, Eugene O'Neill, Jr., a Yale professor and son of the famous playwright. Newspaper drama columnists gave their newly formed "Readers Theater" group considerable support. As readings, no sets or costumes would be required. Actors would rehearse, but not have to memorize lines. The idea, or "pet scheme," as it was described by Wilella Waldorf in her New York Post column (November 14, 1945), would give New Yorkers an opportunity to see public readings "of great dramas now almost never produced on the stage." The first production, Oedipus Rex, opened at Broadway's Majestic Theatre. Alsberg and O'Neill wrote a narrator's part played by O'Neill. That and another show, the seventeenth-century Spanish drama The Mayor of Zalamea, garnered interest, but mixed reviews. This theatrical venture proved unsuccessful, never getting beyond a few performances.

Before the year's end, Alsberg got another opportunity to do something that meant even more to him than theatrical fame. The New York publishing firm Hastings House wanted him as editor-in-chief to bring back the *American Guide* as a one-volume book. This new post signified a financial and psychological bonanza for Alsberg, giving him the autonomy that he could not have dreamed of as a government bureaucrat. Other than the necessary word count limitation, Alsberg and his handpicked team worked free of administrative interference, red tape, and politics. They faced no months-long waits for typewriters or pencils, no attacks from newspapers on wasting taxpayers' money. No Martin Dies.

Alsberg chose some of his FWP compatriots as editors, among them Dora Thea Hettwer, his former secretary, who could now put her college degree to better use. The updated version favored Americana; the essays, although shorter than in the original guidebooks, appeared without the compromises forced on them under the FWP. Scholars in various fields wrote them, and Alsberg's liberal stamp appeared throughout. The labor essay did not shy away from union history and violence against workers; the New Deal was hailed as a champion of social justice; essays incorporated African Americans' contributions, as well as their travails as slaves and their continuing struggles in modern life. A section on the Southern states noted, "the southern bloc in Congress has consistently   prevented the passage of an anti lynching bill." Jim Crow bigotry was not welcome.

Over the four years putting the guide together, Alsberg encountered his usual doubts. Writing to childhood friend Alfred Kroeber, he said, "I shall shortly no doubt be out of a job. This thing I am laboring at … is dragging out too long … it would be a boon if it were wound up and I were fired. Maybe I could do something that would be more interesting to me."[14] He did not totally abandon other pursuits. He shopped around a play, a mystery novel, and a book on unconventional American women. He signed a contract for the latter with Hastings House, but never finished it. His play and mystery book never found a home. During this period, he limited his political activities to keeping up with current events. Roger Baldwin, with whom Alsberg worked in the 1920s on the political prisoner cause, kept in touch about free speech cases brought before the Supreme Court during the late 1940s and early 1950s redbaiting scares. Similarly, Alsberg and acquaintance Lewis Mumford, the social critic and historian, corresponded about the moral implications of the atomic bomb. "I am glad to find at least one other mortal in such close sympathy," Mumford wrote to Alsberg.[15] Alsberg's viewpoint on the build-up of nuclear weapons was evident in a letter to Kroeber. In a backhanded manner, he skewered Columbia University over its involvement in the Manhattan Project, which produced the first nuclear bomb. Sounding nothing like a pacifist, he wrote, "The first bomb should drop on Morningside Heights. Blessings on its little uranium soul."[16]

The encyclopedic 1400-page *American Guide* (and, shortly thereafter, a four-volume set) came out in August 1949. The publisher's publicity department touted both Alsberg's experience on the FWP and the book's attributes: "Over 100,000 points of interest; Your Best Traveling Companion to the United States; 40 pages of maps ... no unfolding necessary." *The American Guide* became a Book of the Month Club selection, ensuring a high readership, and on October 2, 1949, it hit the *New York Times* best-seller list.

An Innocent Bystander

> *In the Joe McCarthy period the FBI harried the life out of Henry ... at that time Henry was living in a walkup in the Village. Henry finally told one of the agents that if he didn't stop bothering him, he, Henry would throw him downstairs. "No you won't" the agent said.... But the mere picture of a man of seventy or so, in that hysterical time, offering to throw an FBI man downstairs... —Vincent McHugh*[17]

As it had for so many decades before, Greenwich Village in 1950 provided a haven for the unconventional: artists, writers, homosexuals, societal outcasts, political reformers. With the success of the *American Guide*, Alsberg impressed Hastings House publisher Walter Frese enough to be kept on as an editor through the next decade and a half. Now in his late sixties, Alsberg's political stance as a "philosophical anarchist" remained firm, but beyond letter writing and chat sessions, he removed himself from politics. That, however, did not stop the tendrils of postwar anti–Communist fervor from entering his haven and knocking on his door. Alsberg, along with so many others, was fair game.

In 1950, the actual target was Anna Rosenberg, President Harry S. Truman's nominee for Assistant Secretary of Defense. She possessed strong credentials, including the support of General Dwight Eisenhower. However, Senator Joseph McCarthy, who was even more zealous against supposed Communists than Martin Dies, moved to block her nomination. Her chief accuser: none other than Ralph De Sola, who seemed to make a career out of red-baiting. He testified that he had seen her at a Communist "John Reed" Club meeting in 1934.[18] This same De Sola, of course, had been at the center of the accusations against Alsberg and the FWP during Martin Dies' HUAC hearings. Although De Sola was soon discredited and the Senate confirmed Rosenberg, the affair spurred an FBI probe. Thus, Henry Alsberg was dragged back into the muck.

When an investigator showed up at his apartment on the morning of December 9, 1950, a contentious Alsberg told him that "he had thrown FBI agents out of his office on the last three or four times that they attempted to interview him." Under duress he consented to talk this time. The FBI's report portrayed an argumentative Alsberg responding to accusations, among them, that he was a communist sympathizer. The interview lasted less than half an hour. Alsberg told the agent that he barely knew Rosenberg; that he *did* know John Reed, the radical American journalist, but never was a member of any of the clubs that popped up in his memory after his death; that the FBI engaged in nothing but character assassinations.

"I'm glad I'm no longer in the government service. I'll never cooperate with this government again," he told the agent. "I believe in the case of Anna Rosenberg. She is strong, she'll fight back, and the FBI will not be able to get her."[19] Alsberg's name surfaced again during the McCarthy crusades when Reed Harris, his former FWP assistant, came under attack. Harris, who quit the FWP over Alsberg's handling of the New York City communist situation, still regarded Alsberg positively. The committee asked him about Alsberg's communist leanings. Harris denied them, calling Alsberg "a man of great kindness and a man who would give the shirt off his back to his fellow man."[20]

Hasting House's *American Procession* series, for the most part, remained politically nondescript, offering Alsberg, as chief editor, a kind of safe haven during the heated McCarthy era. Books on eighteenth- and nineteenth-century America—frontier exploration, the Great Plains, the unexplored American wilderness—wouldn't rouse the ire of congressmen ferreting out "un–American" activities. Even some exceptions—books on more rebellious movements such as the farmer revolts and communes—did not draw undue attention.

Alsberg still dreamed of writing his own books, including an autobiography. He considered leaving Hastings House and told his old colleague Katharine Kellock, "I may move to something else, or just retire for a year or go on unemployment and Old Age retirement." He wanted to concentrate on "a book or two that I have begun but never finished and that are dear to my heart." He told another friend that he was "sweating at an editorial desk at Hastings House" and "managing badly; the editorial job is not to my taste." Yet his missives also told of taking a certain pride in his work; he was deeply appreciative and even surprised when the authors acknowledged his editorial expertise in their books.[21] He stayed put for the time being. He unsuccessfully lobbied Hastings House to extend its reach into fiction. Again his eye for talent did not fail him. Although he had to turn down *Pocho*, a novel by Mexican-American writer José Antonio Villarreal, he wrote encouragingly to the young author. "I am writing to you merely as a personal expression of my individual judgment. I frankly want to encourage you to go on writing.... I have great confidence in my own judgment, although that may sound conceited." The book, published two years later by another company, is recognized as a landmark in Chicano literature.[22]

One book Alsberg brought to Hastings House in 1954, *Stefan and Friderike Zweig: Their Correspondence*, represented a departure from Americana. Austrian author Stefan Zweig, born two months after Henry Alsberg, enjoyed a prominence that extended beyond Europe and into the United States. His companions between the two world wars epitomized erudition and included Rainer Maria Rilke, Sigmund Freud, and H.G. Wells. Despite Nazi threats, Zweig, a secular Jew, collaborated with Richard Strauss as librettist for an opera performed in 1935. As Nazis burned his books and pursued him, Zweig fled, eventually landing in the United States before his final exile in Brazil. There, he committed suicide in 1942. Alsberg edited and translated the letters (with Erna MacArthur) between Zweig and his first wife, Friderike. Alsberg's translation was widely valued, both by Friderike herself, who expressed her thanks in the book's preface for "his sympathetic understanding," and by reviewers. "To say that the translation does not read like a translation is to accord it high praise," said Harry Zohn, in *The Jewish Advocate* (September 16, 1954). Alsberg became an important link to a lost European culture, returning attention to Zweig's work. Zweig came to the forefront more recently with the 2015 Golden Globe and Academy award-winning film, *The Grand Budapest Hotel*, based on his works.

Dybbuk *Rebirth*

In a display of his remarkable energy level, Alsberg returned yet again to the theater, even while working as a full-time editor. Alsberg's *Dybbuk* reanimated for another run, giving him one final journey with Ansky and his mystical world. The play premiered in 1954 at the Fourth Street Theatre, with David Ross at the director's helm. Alsberg had strong misgivings about Ross' handling of the production, and at one point didn't want to be associated with it. *New York Times* critic Brooks Atkinson at least partially agreed with Alsberg's assessment. Referring to the original Neighborhood Playhouse production, he wrote, "It is pleasant to be reminded of its dark grandeur again" but was critical of the new production.[23] Nonetheless, the play ran for ten weeks, affording Alsberg a modicum of financial consolation. And despite his wish to remain behind the scenes, he did acquiesce to Ross's request to write an article for the *New York Times* to promote the show.

Alsberg's thoughts on the meaning of Ansky's work had evolved significantly since the 1920s. Where once he concentrated on the mystical and the political, his *Times* article emphasized a more psychological approach. He noted Ansky's "flash of Freudian insight. Like Shakespeare, who clearly demonstrated the Oedipus complex in his Hamlet, Ansky clearly indicates the inextricable interrelation of the spirit and body."[24]

This latest *Dybbuk* provided the bookend to Alsberg's theatrical career. He earned a steady, if not plentiful income throughout his life from productions at synagogues, college theaters, and repertory groups, at home and internationally. A BBC televised version earned him $260. Alsberg almost realized a financial windfall in his later years, with a $10,000 figure bandied about, but negotiations with the likes of Paramount, the William Morris Agency, and others never came to fruition.[25] Nonetheless, decades after Alsberg's death, his translation of Ansky's story on the melding of life and afterlife continues to grace the English-speaking stage.

By 1956, at age seventy-five, editorial drudgeries took their toll; for most of the decade he stayed out of the way. Now, he needed to *get* away. Alsberg's sphere of travel once included Europe and later, the smaller geography of the Northeast, namely New York City and the Hudson Highlands. Now he looked westward. Perhaps he was drawn by his sister's offer to put him up in Palo Alto; he had read and edited widely about the westward expansion, so conceivably this played a role as well. But his real destination seemed to be Mexico where he had enjoyed a respite in the 1920s. After subletting his Greenwich Village apartment, he left New York and headed to Cuernavaca to rekindle his love affair with Mexico.

Alsberg spent most of 1956 in Mexico. Because Walter Frese wanted to keep him on as an editor, the two men arranged for Alsberg to work from Mexico and California during this period. Shuttling between Cuernavaca and Palo Alto, where he could use Stanford University's library, Alsberg edited three more *American Procession* books. When Elsa visited him, the siblings took time for a tourist venture, traveling the hills of western Mexico to see historical and archeological sites, including sixteenth-century monasteries and the Popocatépetl volcano, which had erupted only a few years before. He still yearned to work on his own fiction, and indeed composed around 100,000 words' worth of stories. Unfortunately, he told his old FWP friend Vincent McHugh, "[I] haven't even tried to market any of it. Subject matter not such as permits publication, I fear ... my heirs will be embarrassed by the accumulation of stuff I shall leave behind."[26]

He was referring to his "Mexican Stories," a set of tales he wrote in Cuernavaca that gave free rein to his reveries about romantic and sexual love between men and his longing for a social climate that accepted homosexuality. One story took place on a prison island where same-sex love was an accepted part of the culture. The protagonist, "an Americano del Norte," visited the island presumably as a journalist, attending a party that reminded him of similar fetes in Greenwich Village, complete with marijuana cigarettes passed around. "Only instead of a stuffy, candle-lighted room, and a feeling of furtive sinning, here the air was freighted with a delightful flower fragrance, and the guitars and marimbas were certainly more pleasant than a broken down ukelele badly strummed, and nobody seemed to feel the weight of guilt." Another depicted an Aztec warrior who wept at his inability to feel attracted to women and his subsequent loneliness because his heart's desires "could not be fulfilled without transgressing the laws of the Gods and Man." A more contemporary story told of a young anthropology professor forced to act in a conventional manner to keep his job. "For diversion he went to New York, had his usual luck—beatings up and a spot of blackmail now and then." Through this series, Alsberg bemoaned the plight of living in "contravention of the established and accepted norm of conduct." Society made his protagonists "feel that we were social pariahs." Alsberg knew enough that the stories would be considered obscene and illegal; it's telling that he signed them as "Henry Garfield."[27]

One of his short stints back to the states included a visit to McHugh, who lived in San Francisco. Mexico suited Alsberg, McHugh commented: "he looked like a Victorian adventurer, lean and black/brown."[28] Alsberg considered San Francisco, "after New York, the most alive town in the U.S." and enjoyed accompanying McHugh for jazz and bar hopping. He was there when the Republican Convention nominated the Eisenhower/Nixon ticket. "It was a veritable madhouse," he wrote to a friend subletting his New York apartment. "I hope you are going to vote for Adlai [Stevenson, the Democratic candidate] … I should hate to think that a Nixonite is plotting deviltry in 29 Jones Street."[29]

Alsberg visited Cuernavaca again, staying through the New Year, then returned to New York in 1957 where he resumed his life, "bogged down in editorial work, trying to keep my nose above quicksand."[30] Now in his late seventies, he cut his office schedule to a few days a week. Although he stayed active writing, editing, and keeping up with the theater and music scene—he often attended live jazz performances featuring his friend, the prominent drummer Zutty Singleton—the old ghosts of depression haunted him. Friends were getting sick and dying. His eyesight was beginning to fail, making his work that much more difficult. The changing world forced itself on him and he noticed. "The insanity called rock an' roll," as he described it to McHugh, invaded the airwaves. He listened enough to tolerate it. "Hillbilly and jazz overlaid with a syncopated beat. It's amusing though it gets monotonous." When Russia pulled ahead in the space race he commented that the United States produced fewer scientists because it lacked a free university education system. He worried that Russian and American imperialism would eventually lead to colonization of the solar system: "My Gawd, there may be oil, uranium, and what not valuable metals in them thar astral hills." McHugh, heavily involved in the Beat poetry scene in San Francisco, kept Alsberg up-to-date with literary happenings. Thus, when McHugh's friend Lawrence Ferlinghetti was arrested on obscenity charges for publishing Allen Ginsberg's *Howl and Other Poems*, Alsberg had a front-row seat—albeit 3,000 miles away. McHugh, a prominent poet in his own right, testified at the trial as a literary expert. When Alsberg sent McHugh $25, as he often did to help his broke poet friend, McHugh let him know that part of it went to help the cause against censorship.[31]

Meanwhile, Alsberg took over as author of a Hastings House manuscript, this one on the Louisiana Purchase. He was so determined to finish it that it was publicized as an upcoming book. "I've got to do it, or perish in the attempt. I hate to start something (except a fight) I can't finish." The massive research itself led him astray so that he felt the book "stretched out in a vista toward the never-ending horizon" with "the field widening out like the ripples following a stone thrown into a lake." He also began to feel the pressure of age. "If I do not get the bends before I reach the light, I may be alright. It is an awful thing to be working under the shadow of the GREAT UNDERTAKER."[32]

Alsberg perhaps unconsciously stumbled on the reason he had so much trouble completing writing projects. Discussing a friend's progress on her manuscript, he wrote that on completing a book "one has a bereft feeling, as though one has lost a child, or one's children have gone to college. That's the way I felt after *The American Guide* wound up. I wandered lonely as a lost lamb on the trackless prairies. One ought never to have to finish a writing job."[33] He worked on the Louisiana Purchase book for a few years and came close to finishing it. But it remains among his unpublished works.

Final Moves

"I am the last survivor of a shipwreck on a raft overloaded with skyscrapers."[34] Alsberg loved New York but complained about the high cost of living. The "big house" in Putnam Valley burned down years before, and Julius and his wife moved to Washington, D.C., leaving Alsberg without his country escape. He yearned for Cuernavaca, but discomfited by the language barrier and finding it "intellectually lonely," he knew it couldn't be a permanent residence. His sister Elsa tempted him again with an offer to share her home in

Palo Alto. He would be just south of San Francisco, a short bus hop, with jaunts to Cuernavaca just a few hours away by plane.

Alsberg's restlessness remained intact as he approached his eightieth year. When in New York, he wanted to be in Cuernavaca; when in Mexico, despite its semblance to paradise, he longed for the stimulation of a city. When he ultimately moved west, the transition to suburbia proved difficult, despite the fact that Elsa herself, a year older and still working as an advocate for integration and fair housing, enjoyed a circle of friends culturally and politically akin to Alsberg.

Through the early 1960s Alsberg undertook periodic editing chores for Hastings House, tooled around with the Louisiana manuscript, and made at least one trip to Mexico. Still, he remained morose and bored and suffered from an inability to settle down and write. He managed to start a story that featured a cannibalistic protagonist. Describing it to McHugh, he wrote, "I wish I were Shakespeare or Henry James (but who doesn't) so that I could squeeze every last drop of psychological horror out of the hero's innards. Well, I suppose I am a nut. But there you are, writing pleasant and normal things; and here I am, not writing at all, but imagining all sorts of bizarre writing projects which I shall likely never finish."[35] He also complained to McHugh of being "in a desperate frenzy of solitary confinement.... I don't seem to be able to buckle down ... it drives me nuts." Homesick for New York, he couldn't adjust to what he termed "the pleasantly padded cell" of his newly adopted hometown. "Je suis désespéré," he wrote. "I can never do anything except under pressure; and pressure doesn't exist here in

Photograph of bearer

Henry G. Alsberg

PHOTOGRAPH ATTACHED
DEPARTMENT OF STATE

Although he no longer journeyed to Europe, Alsberg still had the travel bug at age 78. He used this final passport (1959) throughout the 1950s and 1960s for his frequent visits to Mexico (Passport Photograph, Henry Alsberg Papers, AX597. Special Collections and University Archives, University of Oregon Libraries, Eugene, Oregon).

Palo Alto." He told him that "if my present state of mental (not moral, God knows I wish there were an opportunity for moral) desuetude continues, I shall shortly either be rattling the bars in an asylum, or commit a deed of violence, when I'll be rattling the bars of a jail cell." Most concerning was Alsberg's talk of committing "hari-kari," even though he admitted that he didn't have "the nerve or the sufficient impetus."[36]

McHugh wrote back almost immediately, imploring his friend to move to the North Beach area of San Francisco, center of the beatnik subculture and home of the City Lights bookstore. (Co-founded by Lawrence Ferlinghetti, the bookstore still endures as a mecca for intellectuals, writers, and bohemians.) McHugh told him that North Beach was "enough like the Village to make you feel at home … think about that, Henry, and see if we can't do something."[37]

Alsberg never made the move, but visited McHugh often, sometimes meeting him at City Lights. These outings perked him up, but he still missed New York. He wrote similarly despondent notes to old friend Stella Bloch Hanau. She alternately encouraged him, making arrangements for him to stay and write in New York, and chided him: "Pull yourself together young man!" She likely referred to either his autobiography or a history of the FWP—both of which he was rumored to have been working on—when she asked, "WHAT ABOUT THAT BOOK … you must, must finish it. Seriously, my hunch is that you've got a wundrous lot of good stuff."[38] He did not take her up on the offer to spend the summer in her apartment or country house to write.

Alsberg still had the will to travel, and even the financial resources. He earnestly asked McHugh for help in arranging a trip to the South Seas, on a ship sans passengers because he couldn't "endure the torments of passengers … when one leaves the U.S. one should also leave all the USSians behind. No doubt they are nice people, but I cannot endure them. But then that is no insult to USA, since I can't endure myself either."

Save for local trips, short visits back east to see family, and excursions to Mexico, physical limitations ended his roving ways. Alsberg's wanderings instead infiltrated his letter writing. His sentences veered off topic and literally, due to worsening eyesight and shaky handwriting, off the page. Typing helped only a bit, as his fingers, often as not, hit the wrong keys. His tendency to lapse into French and German and Latin and combinations thereof made for correspondence that appeared flippant.

One long, rambling letter to McHugh started off about poet Allen Ginsberg: "I am not derogating the poetic genius of our Ginsberg. Altho I am unfamiliar with his poetry, I will, without hesitation, decorate his brow with a crown of parsley, or more appropriately, with a wreathe of gefilte fisch." It then strayed into an absurd retelling of the beheading of Sir Thomas More in 1535.

Making reference to a royal English family, he signed it, "Henry Plantagenet. Rex." (His munificence of words matched his financial generosity: with his expenses low, $50 or $100 would occasionally show up in Vincent McHugh or Stella Bloch Hanau's mailbox.)

In between detours off the road of readability, he remained sharp enough to discuss world events. In 1966, Alsberg lamented the U.S. involvement in Vietnam and worried about the war's expansion. "Are we going to get more deeply involved in SE Asia?" he wrote to McHugh. "I should dislike very much having the U.S. fight another one of its futile wars." He commented on the Arab-Israeli Six-Day War in 1967, saying, "I admire the spunk of those co-religionists of mine defying the whole Arab world."[39]

By the late 1960s, loneliness and the recognition of his fading physical health fed Henry Alsberg's melancholic disposition. When a slightly younger colleague from his long-ago journalism days suffered a stroke, Alsberg felt desolate "to see younger chaps falling by the wayside while I linger endlessly on in the eroded hillside of Time." But that's not to say that only dark ruminations dominated Alsberg's life. With his sister, he shared a relaxed domesticity. Friend and writer Anne Nevins Loftis, the daughter of Alsberg's old *Evening Post* friend Allan Nevins, said Elsa walked home every day at lunchtime to put drops in his eyes. The octogenarian siblings "had an appreciation for each other and were a gallant pair. I remember going to the door of the apartment house and he would answer the door, have a cigarette hanging from his mouth and a great cloud of smoke coming up to his hair. I sort of got the impression that Elsa was the scolding older sister and Henry was the scamp. She was amused by him, but she felt she had to keep him in hand."

Writing to Stella Bloch Hanau in 1968, Alsberg offered a tongue-in-cheek description of a country fair organized by Elsa on behalf of her organization. "There were donkey rides, hoop tossing, poison ivy, and all the things that make nightmares of picnics. Basta for that."[40] Nevertheless, he enjoyed the placidity of Palo Alto enough that new construction in the town alarmed him, particularly when bulldozers uprooted his favorite fig tree to build a parking lot across the street from his home. By that time, Alsberg didn't have the energy to connect with people, which is unfortunate because the intellectual Stanford crowd would have appreciated his early life exploits. "He would have been very interesting to certain people. He was an historic figure," said Loftis. "I tried to get him to talk about Federal Writers' Project, but he didn't."

Return of the FWP

During his last years Alsberg remained close to FWP colleagues McHugh, Hettwer, Hanau, and McGraw. He lost touch with Clair Laning. Mary Lloyd lunched with Alsberg in San Francisco once but sensed that "Henry was tired and I was an echo of the past with quite a few painful overtones."[41] Other FWP alumni kept in touch with one another more frequently, sharing news of their lives and careers. This intensified in 1968 when Jerre Mangione reached out to former co-workers as he began writing his history of the FWP. He traveled from the East Coast to Palo Alto to interview Alsberg, who at that point was recovering from a bad bout of sciatica. Mangione didn't seem to come away with much. "I did get to see Henry," Mangione wrote to a former colleague. "He talked for two days. But he was as vague and garrulous as always and I wasn't able to get much specific information. However, I did recapture by means of his monologue, the flavor and atmosphere of those days in Washington."[42] Except for sciatica and eye surgery, Alsberg displayed remarkable health for an eighty-seven-year-old smoker and still met McHugh for occasional lunches, sometimes sporting a beard. McHugh, of course, remained closest to Alsberg, and kept Mangione apprised of Alsberg's status. "Henry's day to day memory's about gone. Not the long range one. He's amazing. He can tell you what Lenin said about John Reed in 1917."[43]

Poet and novelist Vincent McHugh helped lead the New York City unit and wrote the poetic introduction to *New York Panorama*. Even though he left the unit following a disagreement with Alsberg, he remained a steadfast friend. McHugh's unwavering dedication to his former chief may have facilitated a more positive portrayal in Jerre Mangione's book on the FWP. When Alsberg moved to Palo Alto in his eighties, McHugh already lived nearby in San Francisco. Their friendship deepened, with the younger man providing Alsberg a link to the world of literature and arts, as well as significant social and personal support (watercolor by Patricia Tool McHugh, 1963. Courtesy Patricia Tool McHugh).

In May 1969, still working on *Dream and the Deal*, Mangione wrote an article about the FWP for the *New York Times*. His depiction of Alsberg left the older man angry. He surely couldn't mind that Mangione described him as providing "the creative zeal and high standards" of the Project, but after that, the representation descended to questioning his administrative abilities. He was described as a "colossus of chaos," tangled in phone cords and surrounded by crumbled papers. For Alsberg, the article was ill timed. He had recently undergone surgery for a broken hip and was recovering in a nursing home, hobbling about with a cane, going stir crazy with no one to talk to, and hardly able to read because of his eyes. He was already beyond miserable. He may have lost most of his eyesight but mustered up enough ocular strength to read the article. He had not lost the ability to be indignant.

McHugh and McGraw became their former chief's greatest defenders, writing to Mangione with a zeal that likely served to transform the portrait of Alsberg that later appeared in the completed book. McGraw told Mangione that the "totally uncalled for" depiction made Alsberg out to be "a demented idiot." Mangione defended himself, saying that the newspaper deleted the paragraphs that would have balanced the portrayal. He insisted that his intentions toward Alsberg were honorable.[44]

Vincent McHugh took a lighter tack with Mangione. "Let this be a lesson to you. Don't write about people while they're alive. I talked to Henry the other day. He's pulling out of the hip fracture very well indeed—which is far from usual at his age. But he *is* pissed off about you, not least—I'd guess—because he always thought of you as a close friend.... I'm hoping to get Henry into town for dinner next week and I'll see what I can do in the way of mending fences." Mangione seemed genuinely upset that he'd hurt Alsberg's feelings. "I hope Henry gets to read the completed book, for then he'll realize, I think, that I'm no villain," he wrote to McHugh.[45]

(On the book's publication two years after Alsberg's death, McHugh told Mangione, "Even at the last, when he was pissed off at you, he was pissed off *as a friend.*"[46])

Alsberg's Last Writings

While Mangione worked on the East Coast to complete the FWP book, Alsberg, too, took a trip—back in time. Throughout the decade Alsberg allowed his pent-up frustrations and story ideas to emerge. Now, unable to physically ramble, Alsberg settled down at his typewriter. Stories, poems, and essays that had simmered over eight decades rose to the surface and onto the onionskin pages that spooled through the typewriter. The writings were marred by Alsberg's legendary long-windedness, failing eyesight (making the typewriter keys more elusive than ever), cigarette ashes that burned the page (and miraculously did not ignite the paper), and a rambling quality that reflected an old man's imaginative musings. Nonetheless, they gave voice to both humorous and solemn ponderings. He scribbled notes to himself—"nonsense should be thrown away"—on some pages, while political, religious, sexual, and pacifist themes played out. The writing quality fluctuated wildly, but an editor, such as he had been for others, could have shaped some of them into publishable pieces, especially in a more broadminded era.

"The Understanding Magistrate," while mostly lighthearted, portrays "Jabez," who is released from night court after soliciting an undercover policeman. Amid liaisons with the judge and other men, discussions about Emma Goldman, the Kinsey reports, and the "barbarous" laws against homosexuality, Jabez must juggle his ex-wives' alimony demands. In another nod to his whimsical side, Alsberg wrote "The Thirty Days' Ant War," based on his sister's battles to keep ants from invading their kitchen and his imagined peacekeeping talks with the leader of the local anthill, who called humans a "talented but slightly demented race."

His reimagined Bible stories included the playful "Eden," in which God second-guesses his creation and considers Satan's suggestion to wipe out Adam and Eve. "I'd send down a few very effective thunderbolts and wipe out this couple before they have time to breed a whole host of young who in turn will breed innumerable descendants to turn your pleasant little work of art into a sort of replica of my domain," says Satan. The discussions between God and Satan range from philosophy to labor unions (the heavenly choir is on strike) to future writings of Shakespeare, who is yet silent in the womb of time.

In "The Avengers," a more serious tone suffused a story about German vigilantes. Shamed by the atrocities committed by their countrymen, they plot revenge against Nazis and civilians who "remained criminally silent... [I]n many of our larger communities the stench of decaying corpses in the adjacent concentration camps was overwhelming. Yet where is the popular outcry among us for punishment of the perpetrators?" Their quest for vigilance is offset by a character who implores them to let an international court handle the perpetrators. This perhaps represented Alsberg's own leanings toward pacifism at odds with his desire for retribution.

An untitled play about American soldiers takes place in a frigid army barracks in Korea. The mix of characters includes a Jewish socialist, a gay soldier, an African American, and a Harvard preppy as they sort out how to help their court-martialed buddy who faces a firing squad for falling asleep on watch. Arthur Garfield Cohen, a character possessing Alsberg's middle name and politics, provides a discourse on capitalism: "We socialists don't believe in that kind of democracy. Equality—for what? So a shavetail [a newly commissioned officer] can piss on you. Freedom—for what? So the war profiteers can drive around in Cadillacs—Free enterprise—with all them blood suckin' capitalists pilin' up profits while we wallow in mud an' shit an' blood." If Alsberg based this character on himself, it might also yield some evidence about his religious beliefs. "Yuh know I'm an atheist—I eat ham and blintzes on Yom Kippur."

Death, God, and Armageddon all appear in this late-life collection of writings that now reside in Alsberg's papers at the University of Oregon. Peering through the thick lenses of his eyeglasses, Alsberg's fragile fingers laid out his beliefs and questions—and, perhaps, anger toward a God he wasn't even sure he believed in—as he approached his own departure from the world. "Man, tired of killing innocent and wild beasts, has now turned to hunt and kill his own kind. God, in his All-wisdom, has invented patriotism."

A Jewish Mosaic

In his final writings, he also returned to his Jewish roots. Yiddish words and commentary on Jewish topics were sprinkled through his long letters to friends. He still took umbrage when he felt the sting of anti–Semitism; writing to his childhood friend Stella Bloch Hanau, with whom his family shared secular Christmas celebrations, he posed the question: "Do Jews count as full-bred Caucs. [Caucasians]? Hitler didn't think so."[47] Another time he wrote to McHugh that he was thrilled to hear about the success of poet Allen Ginsberg. "When I was a kid, my father, like many Jewish intellectuals, was an impassioned anti–Semite, always maintained that there were no really first class Jewish achievers." He may have regretted never visiting Israel. In what could just have been an old man's musings, Alsberg asked his McHugh if he'd accompany him to Jerusalem. "The last time I went to shul, was when my grandmother took me there when I was 10, not for piety's sake, but because she knew it would infuriate my agnostic papa, which it did, and he gave my ma a hard time about it, too. He particularly loathed Rabbi Stephen Wise, to whose synagogue she took me. I was never circumcised and thus never Barmitzvaed. But I think I am just as Jewish as the Grand Rabbi of Turkey, nevertheless."[48]

A photographic montage illustrating Alsberg's Jewish life would begin with the sepia-toned image of a little boy walking to *shul* with his religious grandmother. The final series of shots, in the Kodachrome colors of the 1960s, would skip ahead to the elderly Alsberg at his writing desk in Palo Alto working on his last story, "Lazarus, Sojourn on the Syrian Desert." Alsberg indulged his own droll humor and employed a decidedly Jewish tone to continue the New Testament story of Lazarus after Jesus brought him back from the dead. In Alsberg's retelling, Lazarus returns home only to be banished to the desert because "a martyr is no martyr if he continues to circulate among ordinary, non-miraculous people," attending *shul* like any "non-saintly individual" and selling his "wife's fragrant knishes from door to door without any evidence of his harrowing experience." Alsberg's Lazarus went on to live a peaceful existence with animal-folk and the occasional delivery, from Sarah, of her famous knishes.

When the book of life closed on Henry Alsberg on November 1, 1970, it's unlikely anyone recited the *Mourner's Kaddish*, the Jewish funeral prayer. The memorial service was small and quiet. The Star of David does not adorn the humble plaque on the niche in the sunlit California cemetery where his ashes are interred.

Alsberg might have been surprised at the attention paid to his death through national newspapers' obituaries, although not particularly enthused about all of it. The *New York Times* and *Washington Post* both gave coverage, with the former concentrating on the communist controversy swirling around Alsberg and the Writers' Project, and the latter giving his FWP work a more positive spin.

Letters of condolence to Julius and Elsa conveyed more personal sorrows. Dora Thea Hettwer told Elsa that she would miss Henry's "guiding spirit, which, even during these last months when he could no longer write to me, always cheered me up and on." Old colleague Isaac Don Levine wrote, "Henry was such a *humane* being who belongs to a vanishing—if not vanished—race and age, and the few who knew him who are still around, will be lonelier than ever without him." The venerable publisher Alfred Knopf, a close friend of Julius, reflected on Henry's full and useful life. Hastings House publisher Walter Frese wrote that "[Henry's] spirit goes on in many ways, including the *American Guide* series, which was perhaps his greatest contribution to America."[49]

Henry Alsberg's steadfast friend Vincent McHugh wrote what could have been an epitaph—albeit too long for any gravestone—the year before Alsberg died. The eloquent poet wrote to Mangione about Henry's past, reminding him of the creative dynamo, the daring radical who still inhabited Alsberg's frail body. Hearkening back to Alsberg's younger days, McHugh called on Mangione to recognize Alsberg's courage:

> He doesn't make any show about it, but the man's a lion ... it's the picture of Henry wandering off by himself down through southern and eastern Russia—that really gets me. Riding boxcars, drinking with the people, sleeping in haystacks. And also, let us note, observing arson, pillage, killing, executions ... courage? I don't suppose he even thought of it. But there must have been people who would have been quite willing to knock off a wandering American for what his boots were worth.

McHugh added him into the pantheon of other lights of his generation, people like John Dos Passos and E.E. Cummings, men who had a "largeness of vision ... a large ironic grasp of human circumstance—and a public sense, if you like;

this feeling for broad human movements and how people are caught up in them."[50]

Again, one is reminded of the Federal Writers' Project's preservation of the life stories of thousands of people who otherwise would have faded into oblivion. This same transmigratory circle includes *Dybbuk* with its permeable wall allowing ethereal slippings from death to life and back again. In a foreword to a *Dybbuk* production in 1928, Henry Alsberg wrote about these tenuous connections: "the living are the unreal entities; the dead, hovering all about us, are the real beings."

Epilogue
Lost Treasures

Be of good cheer. The world rolls on anyway.—Henry Alsberg

A resurgent interest in the legacy of the Federal Writers' Project (FWP), overlooked for so many years, began in the 1960s, multiplied in the 1970s, and exploded exponentially through to the present day. Mangione's *Dream and the Deal* brought the FWP back into the public eye. Other books, most following Mangione's, contribute to the understanding of this complex national writing experiment. Museum and library exhibits, plays, DVDs, and websites also help tell the multifaceted stories of the FWP. With Project records dispersed across the nation, from the Library of Congress and the National Archives to town historical societies and municipal archives, they offer researchers a seemingly bottomless treasure chest. The unfinished business of the FWP goes on.

Except for his rambling interview with Mangione, Alsberg seems to have avoided involvement in this resurgence. A rumor existed that he kept his own set of Project records in Palo Alto. If he did, none of those documents made the trip to the University of Oregon, where his papers were donated after his death. It befitted Alsberg's life's wanderings that his letters, manuscripts, articles, telegrams, photographs, and more are scattered in archives around the globe, residing in Amsterdam, the United Kingdom, Israel, Russia, and dozens of U.S. universities, libraries, and depositories. But whether by chance or his own design, the one-box archive at the University of Oregon is the most personal. There are no rumored diaries or parts of an autobiography. It does contain letters to "Uncle Hank" from the children of a college friend, ever grateful for the help he had given their jobless grandfather during the Depression. Drafts of resumes hold only modest, three-line accounts of his work with the Jewish Joint Distribution Committee, and none includes his volunteer years dodging bullets and crossing dangerous rivers. His stories about the persecution of homosexuals are evocative of his own struggles and the sad realization that he lived long enough to see only a glimpse of the emancipation to come. The towering windows of the manuscript reading room at the University of Oregon afford a majestic view of the campus and its sequoias. Wood-carved relief murals created by WPA workers bookend the room, offering a quiet and coincidental reminder of the FWP years. The library itself, built as a WPA project, adds a touch of providence.

By September 21, 1972, on what would have been Henry Alsberg's ninety-first birthday, book reviewers had the *Dream and the Deal* in hand. Alsberg's remaining siblings, Elsa and Julius, along with Stella Bloch Hanau, died that year, before the book hit the market. Thirty-five years later, in 2007, I stumbled on a Library of Congress Federal Writers' Project website. To meet the Project is to fall in love with it, flaws and all. The same was true as I fell into the life of Henry Alsberg. Like all love stories, my early vision of him as some sort of hero gave way to a more realistic portrait, in which his tenacity and charisma, idealism and compassion, deeds and exploits balanced with his imperfections and failures. It is a wholly odd thing to peer so deeply into another's life, and frustrating when the countless dots don't all connect. If I could resuscitate Henry Alsberg for an hour and actually meet him in that Fifth Avenue coffee shop near Bryant Park, I would ask him to fill in those blank spaces. So many questions.

Because I felt I knew him so well—I could recognize his awful handwriting and the cadences of his sentences anywhere; I read enough to know of his dreams and fears—there were times when I felt certain of his motivations and actions without any attending evidence. My temptation to follow those routes faded as Henry Alsberg, my spectral partner, took me by the metaphorical hand out of the darkness, sometimes passing me off to Emma Goldman or Clair Laning or Stella Bloch Hanau or Vincent McHugh, so that their flashlights could illuminate his serpentine path.

Contact with the children and grandchildren of his friends led to the fond recollections of a man, "tall, straight, with a huge mustache—jovial and indulgent in company, with the proverbial twinkle in his eye." When I visited Palo Alto, I walked past the house he shared with his sister on Webster Street, where he once wrote to a friend, "The roses are blooming in my sister's garden, and the hyacinths are hyacinthing, and violets are being violated." I passed the parking garage that displaced his favorite fig tree. (I imagine the ants have relocated and found another household to make their battleground.)

Seeing the world through the lens of Henry Alsberg's life reminded me that there are people alive in every era who, even while struggling through their own life scrapes, seek utopia on our planet. "We made a fine glare and stink in the world," Vincent McHugh wrote of the Writers' Project in 1973. Referring to political and cultural activism of the 1960s and 1970s, he added, "We were one of the Berkeley's of the 1930s and for precisely the same reason: our collective business was to knock the middle class off its collective butt and make a new center. We lost, of course."

But attempts to fight injustice are never inconsequential. Understanding Alsberg's principled struggles for a more humanistic and pacifistic society and viewing his contributions—particularly the vast legacy left by the FWP—lead us to a deeper, more nuanced understanding of both his times and ours. Certainly, the tumultuous, historical events that marked Henry Garfield Alsberg's world in the first half of the twentieth century would have taken place regardless of his presence. But it would have been a different show.

Chapter Notes

Abbreviations in Notes and Bibliography

Alsberg Files, NARA
   Records of Henry Alsberg 1935–1939, Entry PI 57 2, Records of the Federal Writers' Project, General Records of the Works Projects Administration, Record Group 69. National Archives at College Park, MD.

Alsberg Papers
   Henry Alsberg Papers, AX597. Special Collections and University Archives, University of Oregon Libraries, Eugene, Oregon.

Anna Rosenberg FBI Files
   U.S. Department of Justice, Federal Bureau of Investigation, Anna Rosenberg File. Special Inquiry, New York, December 7 through December 9, 1950. "Allegation of Alleged Membership of Anna Rosenberg in the John Reed Club; re: Henry Garfield Alsberg." Bureau File 62-10641, sub A, serial 41, 56 and 67.

Berkman Papers, IISH
   Alexander Berkman Papers, International Institute of Social History (IISH), Amsterdam, The Netherlands. http://www.socialhistory.org.

Bertrand Russell Archives
   Bertrand Russell fonds, Bertrand Russell Archives, McMaster University, Hamilton, Ontario.

Bogen Papers, AJA
   Boris D. Bogen Papers, MS-3, American Jewish Archives, Cincinnati, Ohio.

Bryant Papers
   Louise Bryant Papers (MS 1840). Manuscripts and Archives, Yale University Library.

Cronyn Files, NARA
   Records of George Cronyn 1935–1939, Entry PI 57 3, Records of the Federal Writers' Project, General Records of the Work Projects Administration, Record Group 69. National Archives at College Park, MD.

Goldman Papers, IISH
   Emma Goldman Papers, International Institute of Social History (IISH), Amsterdam, The Netherlands. http://www.socialhistory.org.

Hanau Papers
   Stella Hanau Papers, Sophia Smith Collection, Smith College, Northampton, MA.

HUAC 1938
   U.S. House of Representatives, Special Committee on Un-American Activities, *Investigation of Un-American Propaganda Activities in the United States*; Hearings on House Resolution 282, 75th Congress, Third Session, volumes 1 and 4, 1938. (Washington, D.C.: U.S. Government Printing Office, 1939).

HUAC 1943
   U.S. House of Representatives, Special Committee on Un-American Activities, *Investigation of Un-*

American Propaganda Activities in the United States; Hearings on House Resolution 282, 78th Congress, First Session, volume 7, 1943. (Washington, D.C.: U.S. Government Printing Office, 1943).

ICPP, NYPL
  International Committee for Political Prisoner records. Manuscripts and Archives Division. The New York Public Library. Astor, Lenox, and Tilden Foundations.

JDC
  JDC Archives, Records of the New York Office of the American Jewish Joint Distribution Committee, New York, NY.

Kellock Papers, LOC
  Katharine Amend Kellock Papers, Manuscript Division, Library of Congress, Washington, D.C.

Kester Papers, NYPL
  Paul Kester Papers. Manuscripts and Archives Division. The New York Public Library. Astor, Lenox, and Tilden Foundations.

Life Histories, FWP/LOC
  American Life Histories: Manuscripts from the Federal Writers' Project, 1936–1940. WPA Federal Writers' Project Collection Library of Congress. Manuscript Division, http://www.loc.gov/collections/federal-writers-project/

Lloyd Papers, NYPL
  Mary Maverick Lloyd Papers. Manuscripts and Archives Division. The New York Public Library. Astor, Lenox, and Tilden Foundations.

Mangione Papers
  Jerre Mangione Papers, Rare Books Special Collections and Preservation Department, University of Rochester.

McHugh Papers
  Vincent McHugh Papers, Yale Collection of American Literature, Beinecke Rare Book and Manuscript Library.

Permanent Subcommittee on Investigations, 1953
  Executive Sessions of the Senate Permanent Subcommittee on Investigations of the Committee on Government Operations, 83rd Congress, First Session, Volume 1, 1953. Printed for the use of the Committee on Governmental Affairs, U.S. Government Printing Office, Washington: 2003.

Records Pertaining to Negro Studies, NARA
  Reports and Records Pertaining to Negro Studies 1935–1940, Entry PI 57 27, Records of the Federal Writers' Project, General Records of the Works Projects Administration, Record Group 69. National Archives at College Park, MD.

Smithsonian
  Oral Histories, Archives of American Art, Smithsonian Institution, Washington, D.C.

Strauss Papers, AJHS
  Admiral Lewis Lichtenstein Strauss Papers; P-632; American Jewish Historical Society, New York, NY, and Boston, MA.

Strauss Papers, Hoover Presidential Library
  Lewis L. Strauss Papers, Herbert Hoover Presidential Library and Museum, West Branch, IA.

Voice of America
  State Department Information Program—Voice of America, Hearing before the Senate Permanent Subcommittee on Investigations of the Committee on Government Operations, 83rd Congress, First Session, Pursuant to S. Res. 40, Part 5, March 3, 1953 (Washington, D.C.: U.S. Government Printing Office, 1953).

Woodrum Committee
  Further Additional Appropriation for Work Relief and Relief, Fiscal Year 1939, Hearings before the Subcommittee of the Committee on Appropriations, House of Representatives 76th Congress, First Session on H. J. Res. 209 and 246 (Washington, D.C.: U.S. Government Printing Office, 1939).

Wright Papers, Yale
  Richard Wright Papers. Yale Collection of American Literature, Beinecke Rare Book and Manuscript Library.

Preface

1. "Their Own Baedeker," *The New Yorker*, August 20, 1945; Sarah A. Stephens, personal email; Inez Robb, "American Guide," *Associated Press*, August 11, 1949.

Introduction

1. Dora Thea Hettwer to Henry Alsberg, August 15, 1939, box 14, folder 7, Jerre Mangione Papers, Rare Books Special Collections & Preservation Department, University of Rochester; Jerre Mangione, *The Dream and the Deal: The Federal Writers' Project, 1935–1943* (Boston: Little, Brown, 1972), 373.

Chapter 1

1. Henry G. Alsberg, "A Dip into Russia," *The Nation*, March 20, 1920, 20.
2. Landmarks Preservation Committee, "Upper East Side Historic District Designation Report," volume 1, City of New York, 1981. http://www.nyc.gov/html/lpc/downloads/pdf/reports/UpperEastSide_Vol1.pdf.
3. Temple S. Hoyne, *The Medical Visitor*, volume 8 (Chicago: W.A. Chatterton, 1892), 65.
4. Joseph Stancliffe Davis, ed., *Carl Alsberg, Scientist at Large* (Stanford: Stanford University Press, 1948), 5.
5. *Ibid.*, 4.
6. *Ibid.*,14.
7. *Ibid.*
8. W.L. Holland and Paul F. Hooper, *Remembering the Institute of Pacific Relations: The Memoirs of William L. Holland* (Tokyo: Ryukei Shyosha, 1995), 436.
9. Theodora Kroeber, *Alfred Kroeber: A Personal Configuration* (Berkeley: University of California Press, 1970), 17.
10. Henry Alsberg to Elsbeth Kroeber, March 17, 1961, Henry Alsberg Papers, AX597, box 1, correspondence folder, Special Collections and University Archives, University of Oregon Libraries, Eugene, Oregon.
11. Kroeber, *Personal Configuration*, 22.
12. *The Book of 1900, Columbia Arts and Mines*, volume 1 (New York: privately printed, 1926), 22.
13. Graduates wrote short autobiographical pieces for this class book. All but a few included their birth dates, showing that Alsberg was two or three years younger than most of his classmates, and very likely younger than all of them.
14. *The Naughty Naughtian, Columbia College, 1900* (New York: Cheltenham Press), 176.
15. Kroeber, *Personal Configuration*, 45.
16. John Erskine, *The Memory of Certain Persons* (Philadelphia: Lippincott, 1947), 97.
17. Its name was officially changed in 1932 to *The Columbia Review*. Later contributors included

William Carlos Williams, Allen Ginsberg, and Terrence McNally.
18. *Columbia Spectator*, April 7, 1899.
19. *A History of Columbia College on Morningside* (New York: Columbia University Press, 1954), 22.
20. Henry Alsberg, "A Homely Tragedy," *Morningside*, March 23, 1899.
21. Anne Loftis, eulogy for Elsa Alsberg, Palo Alto Public Library Vertical File.
22. P.A. Kropotkin, *Selected Writings on Anarchism and Revolution* (Cambridge: MIT Press, 1970), 359.
23. Emma Goldman, "What I Believe," *New York World*, July 19, 1908.
24. Terence Kissack, *Free Comrades: Anarchism and Homosexuality in the United States, 1895–1917* (Oakland: AK Press, 2008), 3.
25. *Naughty Naughtian*, 12.
26. "Middies to Beat Columbia," *New York Tribune*, November 17, 1902.
27. Supreme Court, Appellate Term, New York, *Sling V. Cent. Union Gas Co.*, 144 N.Y.S. 740 (App. Term 1913.)
28. As quoted in Muriel Rukeyser, *Willard Gibbs* (Woodbridge, CT: Ox Bow Press, 1988), 378.
29. Jerre Mangione, *The Dream and the Deal: The Federal Writers' Project, 1935–1943* (Boston: Little, Brown, 1972), 54.
30. *Ibid.*, 57
31. "Recollections of Henry Alsberg by Alexander Bloch (From Interview by Janet Bloch Briggs)," recorded circa 1977. Personal email shared by Alexander Bloch's granddaughter, Meredith Briggs Skeath.
32. *Columbia Alumni News*, 8, no. 36, 1917. Erskine was a member of the Guilds' Committee for Federal Writers' Publications, Inc., which sponsored the *American Guide New York City Guide* book in 1939.
33. Biographical Note on Henry Alsberg, box 1, Katharine Amend Kellock Papers, Manuscript Division, Library of Congress, Washington, DC, WPA Federal Writers' Project, Reports and Correspondence, 1936–1942.

Chapter 2

1. U.S. House of Representatives, Special Committee on Un-American Activities, *Investigation of Un-American Propaganda Activities in the United States*; Executive Hearings on House Resolution 282, 78th Congress, First Session, 1943, volume 7, 3575.
2. "Author Henry Alsberg of Palo Alto Dies at 89," *Palo Alto Times*, November 4, 1970.
3. Henry Alsberg to Paul Kester, February 22, 1910, Paul Kester Papers. Manuscripts and Archives Division. The New York Public Library. Astor, Lenox, and Tilden Foundations.
4. C.D. af Wirsén, "Award Ceremony Speech,"

December 10, 1911. http://www.nobelprize.org/nobel_prizes/literature/laureates/1911/press.html.

5. Alsberg to Kester, February 22, 1910, Kester Papers, NYPL.

6. *Ibid.*, March 1, 1910.

7. *Ibid.*, December 6, 1910.

8. *Ibid.*

9. *Ibid.*

10. Henry G. Alsberg, "Soiree Kokimono," in *Forum Stories*, ed. Charles Vale (New York: Mitchell Kennerly, 1914), 197–215.

11. Abram Elkus, *The Memoirs of Abram Elkus: Lawyer, Ambassador, Statesman* (Princeton, NJ: Gomidas Institute, 2004), 41.

12. As quoted in *Ibid.*, 42–46.

13. This quote is generally attributed to the Women's International League for Peace and Freedom.

14. H.G. Alsberg, "Was It Something Like This," *The Masses* 5, no. 7 (April 1914): 14.

15. Terence Kissack, *Free Comrades: Anarchism and Homosexuality in the United States, 1895–1917* (Oakland: AK Press, 2008), 12.

16. *Ibid.*, 3.

17. *Ibid.*, 15.

18. Hippolyte Havel, as quoted in Allen Churchill, *Improper Bohemians* (New York: E.P. Dutton & Company, 1959), 35.

19. W.L. Holland and Paul F. Cooper, *Remembering the Institute of Pacific Relations: The Memoirs of William Lancelot Holland* (Tokyo: Ryukei Shyosha Publishing, 1995), 436.

20. Joseph Stancliffe Davis, ed., *Carl Alsberg, Scientist at Large* (Stanford, CA: Stanford University Press, 1948), 147.

21. Vincent McHugh to Jerre Mangione, August 8, 1969, box 179, folder 3, Jerre Mangione Papers, Rare Books Special Collections and Preservation Department, University of Rochester.

22. Henry Garfield Alsberg, Applications and Recommendations for Appointment to the Consular and Diplomatic Services, 1901–1924, Entry A1 764, box 4, General Records of the Department of State, Record Group 59, National Archives at College Park, MD.

23. *Ibid.*

24. "The Art of Blakelock," *The Nation*, May 4, 1916, 473.

25. Henry Morgenthau, *Ambassador Morgenthau's Story* (Detroit: Wayne State University Press, 2003), 264.

26. Elkus, *Memoirs*, 63.

27. *Ibid.*, 78.

28. Carl Alsberg to E.D. Adams, June 25, 1923, Henry Alsberg Collection, Hoover Institution Archives, Stanford University, Stanford, CA.

29. Elkus, *Memoirs*, 83.

30. JDC Archives, Records of the New York Office of the American Jewish Joint Distribution Committee, 1914–1918, folder 120.6, Secretary of State Washington Text Telegram as Published Local Press, May 16, 1917.

31. JDC Archives, Records of the New York Office of the American Jewish Joint Distribution Committee, 1914–1926, "A History of the JDC," by Henry Alsberg (manuscript), folder 3, 1914–1926. (Note: Alsberg's unpublished manuscript was revised by Isaac Don Levine in 1927 and by Herman Bernstein in 1928.)

32. Alsberg, "A History of the JDC."

33. Henry G. Alsberg, "Constantinople Memories—1917," *The Maccabean,* December 1918, 343.

34. *Ibid.*, 344.

35. Henry Garfield Alsberg, typescript, "Food Conditions in the Central Powers," 1919, Hoover Institution Archives, Stanford University, Stanford, CA.

36. Carl Alsberg to Adams, June 25, 1923, Henry Alsberg Collection, Hoover Institution Archives.

37. Arthur S. Link, ed., *Papers of Woodrow Wilson*, volume 42: *April 7–June 23, 1917* (Princeton, NJ: Princeton University Press, 1983).

38. *Ibid.*

39. Felix Frankfurter and Harlan B. Phillips, *Felix Frankfurter Reminisces* (New York: Reynal Company, 1960), 146–147.

40. "In the Co-Operators' World," *The Co-Operative Consumer* 4, no. 4 (1918): 76.

41. "Kerensky and Mirabeau," *The Nation*, June 28, 1917, 750.

42. Carl J. Richard, *When the United States Invaded Russia: Woodrow Wilson's Siberian Disaster* (Lanham, MD: Rowman & Littlefield, 2013), 23.

43. Henry Alsberg, "New Nations for Old," *Evening Post Magazine*, November 23, 1918.

44. Henry Alsberg, "Sky Comes Down, Up Go Earth and Sea," *New York Evening Post*, September 28, 1918.

45. Henry G. Alsberg, "It Happened in Armenia," *New York Evening Post Magazine*, July 6, 1918. In other records she has a different surname, so likely Alsberg gave her a pseudonym.

46. "Special Assembly of New England Zionists," *The Maccabaean* 31, no. 2 (February 1918), 66.

47. "Friends Speed Mr. Elkus, New U.S. Envoy to Turkey, Leaving for His Station," *Evening Telegram*, August 11, 1916.

48. Alsberg, "A History of the JDC."

49. Henry G. Alsberg, letter, "The Palestine Restoration Fund Campaign," *The Maccabaean* 31, no. 2 (February 1918), 34.

50. "Alumni Association Committee," Massachusetts Institute of Technology, *Technology's War Record 1919*, reprint (London: Forgotten Books, 2013), 322.

Chapter 3

1. Henry G. Alsberg, Passport Application. NARA Series: *Passport Applications*, January 2,

1906–March 31, 1925, December 12, 1918, National Archives, Washington, DC; attached letter: Oswald Garrison Villard to H.G. Alsberg, November 26, 1918.

2. Henry G. Alsberg, "An Interview with Lord Bryce," *The Nation*, February 22, 1919, 280.

3. Alsberg, "The Temper of Ireland," *The Nation*, March 22, 1919, 427–428.

4. Alsberg, "London Chill and Cheer," *The Nation*, March 1, 1919, 323–324.

5. "Delegates to the London Zionist Conference," *The Maccabaean*, February 1919, 51. Although he was listed here as a delegate, Alsberg may not have participated. He went to Paris the day after the conference started and was still there before it ended.

6. Telegram from Bernard Flexner, undated (but likely February 1919), file L8/171. Central Zionist Archives, Jerusalem. The delegation's aim, in addition to lobbying for a Jewish homeland in Palestine, was to secure in the final treaty full equality and safety for the Jews of the new Central and Eastern European nations.

7. Alsberg, "With Wilson Away," *The Nation*, March 15, 1919, 397.

8. Henry Alsberg, "Once a Jew, Always a Jew," *The Jewish Daily Forward*, December 12, 1926, English section, p. 1.

9. *Ibid.*

10. James N. Rosenberg, *Unfinished Business: James N. Rosenberg Papers*, ed. with preface by Maxwell Geismar (Mamaroneck, NY: Vincent Marasia Press, 1967), 266–267.

11. James N. Rosenberg Papers, 1911–1961, reel 874, Archives of American Art, Smithsonian Institution.

12. Theodora Kroeber, *Alfred Kroeber: A Personal Configuration* (Berkeley: University of California Press, 1970), 25.

13. Alsberg, "Once a Jew."

14. JDC Archives, Records of the New York Office of the American Jewish Joint Distribution Committee, 1914–1926, "A History of the JDC," by Henry Alsberg (manuscript), folder 3, 1914–1926.

15. JDC NY 1921–1932, folder 8.1, "Report on the Activities of the Joint Distribution Committee, Constructive Relief Conference," October 22–23, 1927.

16. JDC NY 1919–1921, folder 30, Lewis Strauss to Boris Bogen, February 25, 1919.

17. JDC NY 1919–1921, folder 126.2, Henry Alsberg to Lewis Strauss, March 5, 1919. The JDC made a number of appropriations, in 1919 and later years, to Czechoslovakia.

18. Alsberg, "A History of the JDC."

19. JDC NY 1919–1921, folder 126.2, Letter from United States Food Administration to Felix Warburg, March 10, 1919.

20. JDC NY 1919–1921, folder 126.2, Alsberg to Strauss, March 5, 1919.

21. Henry Alsberg to Lewis Strauss, March 11, 1919, box 8, folder 3, Admiral Lewis Lichtenstein Strauss Papers; P-632; American Jewish Historical Society New York, NY, and Boston, MA.

22. Alsberg, "A History of the JDC."

23. Alsberg to Strauss, March 23, 1919, box 8, folder 3, Strauss Papers, AJHS.

24. JDC NY 1919–1921, folder 126.2, Alsberg to Strauss, March 13, 1919.

25. Alsberg, "A History of the JDC."

26. JDC NY 1919–1921, folder 126.2, Alsberg to Strauss, March 16, 1919.

27. JDC NY 1919–1921, folder 126.2, Alsberg to Strauss, March 26, 1919.

28. Alsberg to Strauss, April 6, 1919, box 14, folder 3, Strauss Papers, AJHS.

29. JDC NY 1919–1921, folder 126.2, Alsberg to Strauss, March 23, 1919.

30. JDC NY 1919–1921, folder 126.2, Alsberg to Strauss, March 26, 1919.

31. Charles A. Selden, "Jews in Slovakia Appeal to Paris," *New York Times*, April 11, 1919.

32. Alsberg, "Four Capitals," *The Nation*, May 24, 1919, 831.

33. *Ibid.*

34. Alsberg, "The Plight of Czecho-Slovakia," *The Nation*, April 5, 1919, 497.

35. Alsberg, "Murderous Turks Find Safe Havens," special cable report, Press Publishing Company of the *New York World*, syndicated nationwide, May 5, 1919.

36. "Memorandum for Mr. Hoover: Harry G. Alsberg, Alias, Charles Alsberg, December 4, 1920; Alleged Bolshevik Activities, Henry G. Alsberg; M1085, roll 929; Bureau Section Files 1909–1921; Investigative Case Files of the Bureau of Investigation 1908–1922; RG 65; National Archives and Records Administration, Washington, DC. (The Bureau of Investigation preceded the FBI.)

37. Alsberg, "The Revolution in Hungary," *The Nation*, May 10, 1919, 736–737.

38. Harold Williams, "Denikin Scorns Parley with Reds," *New York Times*, December 19, 1919.

39. JDC NY 1919–1921, folder 126.2, Alsberg to Strauss, March 23, 1919.

40. JDC NY 1919–1921, folder 126.2, Alsberg to Strauss, April 12, 1919.

41. Alsberg, "A History of the JDC."

42. Alsberg to Strauss, March 19, 1919, box 8, folder 3, Strauss Papers, AJHS.

43. Alsberg to Strauss, April 6, 1919, box 14, folder 3, Strauss Papers, AJHS.

44. Alsberg to Strauss, April 29, 1919, box 14, folder 3, Strauss Papers, AJHS.

45. JDC 1919–1921, folder 129.5, Alsberg to Strauss, April 24, 1919.

46. JDC NY 1919–1921, folder 187.1, Strauss to Bogen, April 17, 1919.

47. Alsberg, "A History of the JDC."

48. JDC NY 1919–1921, folder 187.1, Bogen to Strauss, April 30, 1919.

49. "Pinsk," in Shmuel Spector, ed., *The Encyclopedia of Jewish Life Before and During the Holocaust* (New York: New York University Press, 2001). Also, Moshe Rosman, "Pinsk," YIVO Encyclopedia of Jews in Eastern Europe. http://www.yivoencyclopedia.org/article.aspx/Pinsk.

50. Strauss to Alsberg, May 6, 1919, box 10, folder 20, Strauss Papers, AJHS.

51. Alsberg, "A History of the JDC."

52. Alsberg to Strauss, May 19, 1919, box 8, folder 3, Strauss Papers, AJHS.

53. JDC NY 1919–1921, folder 30, Bogen to Strauss, May 14, 1919.

54. Alsberg to Strauss, May 19, 1919, box 8, folder 3, Strauss Papers, AJHS

55. *Ibid.*

56. Strauss to Alsberg, May 20, 1919, box 8, folder 3, Strauss Papers, AJHS.

57. Alsberg to Strauss, May 19, 1919, box 8, folder 3, Strauss Papers, AJHS.

58. Henry Alsberg to Felix Frankfurter, May 12, 1919, File A264/7, Central Zionist Archives.

59. Henry Morgenthau III, *Mostly Morgenthaus: A Family History* (New York: Ticknor & Fields, 1991), 196.

60. Boris David Bogen, *Born a Jew*, in collaboration with Alfred Segal (New York: Macmillan, 1930), 193.

61. JDC NY 1919–1921, folder 228.1, Jacob Billikopf Report, "Not for Publication," June 3, 1919.

62. JDC NY 1919–1921, folder 228.1, Bogen to Cyrus Adler, June 28, 1919.

63. Ella Winter, *And Not to Yield* (New York: Harcourt, Brace & World, 1963), 52.

64. Cyrus Adler, *I Have Considered the Days* (Philadelphia: Jewish Publication Society of America, 1941), 320–321.

65. JDC NY 1919–1921, folder 211.1, Bogen to Harriet Lowenstein, July 14, 1919.

66. Alsberg to Strauss, July 17, 1919, box 8, folder 3, Strauss Papers, AJHS.

67. *Ibid.*

68. Strauss to Alsberg, August 5, 1919, box 8, folder 3, Strauss Papers, AJHS.

69. Alsberg to Strauss, August 3, 1919, box 8, folder 3, Strauss Papers, AJHS.

70. Alsberg, "Party Politics in Rumania," *The Nation*, November 19, 1919, 697–698.

71. Alsberg, "The Dybbuk," *B'nai B'rith National Jewish Monthly*, January 1926, 133.

72. Alsberg, "Union in the Balkans," *The Nation*, October 4, 1919, 463.

73. Alsberg, "The Situation in Ukraine," *The Nation*, November 1, 1919, 569. There are various spellings for Kamenets-Podolski. This article was written in September, but not published until November. It was often the case that publication came months after he'd written the articles.

74. Alsberg, "In the Wake of Denikin," *The Nation*, January 10, 1920, 38–40.

75. *Ibid.*

76. JDC NY1919–1921, folder 126.2, Alsberg to Strauss, December 30, 1919.

77. JDC NY 1919–1921, folder 247.2, Alsberg to Strauss, December 30, 1919; folder 247.2, Alsberg to Lowenstein, December 31, 1919.

78. Alsberg, "A Dip into Russia," *The Nation*, March 20, 1920, 358.

79. U.S. House of Representatives, Special Committee on Un-American Activities, *Investigation of Un-American Propaganda Activities in the United States*, Hearings on House Resolution 282, 75th Congress, Third Session, volume 4, 1938 (Washington, DC: U.S. Government Printing Office, 1939), 2890.

80. William Ryall tells the story of his and Alsberg's visit to the British commissioner in "When the Red Flag Waved in the Ruhr Valley," *Dearborn Independent*, June 5, 1920.

81. Alsberg, "The Ruhr Revolution," *New York Call*, August 8, 1920.

Chapter 4

1. Alexander Berkman, *Bolshevik Myth* (New York: Boni and Liveright, 1925), 205.

2. Alsberg had spent some time with JDC commissioners, as confirmed by their report: JDC NY 1919–1921, folder 247, "Report from Judge Harry Fisher and Mr. Max Pine," April 6, 1920.

3. Marguerite E. Harrison, *Marooned in Moscow: The Story of an American Woman Imprisoned in Russia* (New York: George H. Doran), 170.

4. Emma Goldman, *Living My Life: An Autobiography* (Salt Lake City: Peregrine Smith, 1982), 794–95.

5. *Ibid.*, 733.

6. Harrison, *Marooned in Moscow*, 171.

7. Alsberg, "Will Russia Drive the British from Asia?," *The Nation*, August 14, 1920, 179–180.

8. Alsberg, "Russian Impressions," *The Nation*, August 21, 1920, 207–208. Nearly all foreign correspondents in the Soviet Union complained of heavy censorship imposed on them, with some articles rewritten, and others never making it past the telegraph office. Alsberg often sent his articles in packets along with his letters to Lewis Strauss via the JDC and ARA.

9. Alsberg, "Russia's Industrial Problem," *The Nation*, September 11, 1920, 293–294.

10. *Ibid.*

11. Alsberg, "Russian Impressions."

12. Alsberg's vacillation appeared throughout the summer in *Nation* articles: "The Soviet Domestic Program," August 28; "Tyranny by Prophets," September 4; and "Russian Impressions."

13. Peter Kropotkin, "L'ordre" (1881), translation by Nicolas Walter. Available at Anarchy Archives: http://dwardmac.pitzer.edu/Anarchist_Archives/kropotkin/freedompamphlet4.html.

14. Berkman, *Bolshevik Myth*, 158.

15. Goldman, *Living My Life*, 814.

16. *Ibid.*, 806.

17. Alsberg, "Social Reforms in Soviet Russia," *The Nation*, September 18, 1920, 320.

18. *Ibid.*

19. Michael Beizer, *Relief in Time of Need: Russian Jewry and the Joint, 1914–1924* (Bloomington, IN: Slavica Publishers, 2015), 86.

20. Lewis Strauss to Carl Alsberg, July 22, 1920, "Lewis L. Strauss Papers—Early Career Name and Subject Files—Alsberg, Carl," Herbert Hoover Presidential Library and Museum, West Branch, IA.

21. Goldman, *Living My Life*, 824.

22. *Ibid.*

23. "Fastoff: Extract of the Evidence of Different Witnesses," Henry Alsberg to Lewis L. Strauss, December 2, 1920, "Lewis L. Strauss Papers—Early Career Name and Subject Files—Alsberg, Henry," Herbert Hoover Presidential Library and Museum. Alsberg sent four single-spaced typed pages to Strauss. He also sent the information to *The Nation*. The news magazine published "The Fastov Pogrom," December 8, 1920, noting that an unnamed professor in Fastov (also called Fastoff) wrote the report and gave it to the Petrograd Museum of the Revolution. Likely it was Alsberg who passed this on to *The Nation*.

24. Goldman, *Living My Life*, 828.

25. *Ibid.*, 836.

26. Emma Goldman and Alexander Berkman to V.I. Lenin, September 12, 1920, reel 65, "Investigation of Henry Alsberg," *The Emma Goldman Papers: A Microfilm Edition* (Alexandria, VA: Chadwyck-Healey Inc., 1991).

27. While this diary no longer exists, Alsberg wrote about it in his article, "Russia: Smoked-Glass Vs. Rose-Tint," *The Nation*, June 15, 1921, 844–846.

28. Jerre Mangione, *The Dream and the Deal: The Federal Writers' Project, 1935–1943* (New York: Avon Books, 1972), 55.

29. U.S. House of Representatives, Special Committee on Un-American Activities, *Investigation of Un-American Propaganda Activities in the United States*, Hearings on House Resolution 282, 75th Congress, Third Session, volume 4, 1938 (Washington, DC: U.S. Government Printing Office, 1939), 2888.

30. Berkman, *Bolshevik Myth*, 245; Goldman, *Living My Life*, 846.

31. Alsberg, "The Russo-Polish Peace," *The Nation*, November 24, 1920, 587.

32. Suspect name Henry Garfield Alsberg; M1085, roll 581; Old German Files, 1909–1921; Alleged Bolshevik Activities, Henry G. Alsberg; M1085, roll 929; Bureau Section Files 1909–1921; Investigative Case Files of the Bureau of Investigation 1908–1922; RG 65; National Archives and Records Administration, Washington, DC.

33. As quoted in Zosa Szajkowski, *Jews, War and Communism, Volume 2: The Impact of the 1919–1920 Red Scare on American Jewish Life* (New York: KTAV Publishing, 1974), 320.

34. Emergency Passport Applications, Argentina thru Venezuela, 1906–1925: 1920–1921, volume 175: Paris, France. National Archives and Records Administration, Washington, DC.

35. JDC NY 1919–1921, folder 64, Conference of the Regional Directors and Representatives of the Joint Distribution Committee in Europe, Vienna, November 19, 1920.

36. *Ibid.*

37. "Report from Mr. Alsberg" (Alsberg to Boris Bogen), December 21, 1920, box 11, folder 2, Admiral Lewis Lichtenstein Strauss Papers; P-632; American Jewish Historical Society, New York and Boston.

38. Boris Bogen to Henry Alsberg, June 20, 1921, box 1, folder 1, MS-3, Boris D. Bogen Papers, American Jewish Archives, Cincinnati, Ohio.

39. This document was a statement regarding Soviet governance that Kropotkin wrote to anarchists in Europe. In Anthony D'Agostino, *Marxism and the Russian Anarchists* (San Francisco: Germinal Press, 1977), 107.

40. Goldman, *Living My Life*, 896.

41. *Ibid.*

42. HUAC 1938, 2891.

43. Goldman, *Living My Life*, 897.

44. *Ibid.*, 896.

45. Alsberg, "Russian Impressions,"

46. Alsberg, "Russia: Smoked-Glass Vs. Rose-Tint."

47. Bogen to Alsberg, June 30, 1921, Bogen Papers, AJA.

48. JDC NY 1919–1921, folder 65.2, Memorandum: "Left Paris Thursday, April 21st for Berlin. Arrived the following day at 6.30 P.M. Met Mr. Alsberg," April 27, 1921.

49. Bogen to Alsberg, June 30, 1921, Bogen Papers, AJA.

Chapter 5

1. Alleged Bolshevik Activities, Henry G. Alsberg; M1085, roll 929; Bureau Section Files 1909–1921; Investigative Case Files of the Bureau of Investigation 1908–1922; RG 65; National Archives.

2. Proceedings of Chicago Conference, American Jewish Relief Committee, September 24–25, 1921, 33, HathiTrust Digital Library, http://www.hathitrust.org.

3. JDC NY 1921–1932, folder 15.1, Dictation of Mr. Henry Alsberg to R. Frisch, Memorandum for Mr. Rosenberg, October 7, 1921.

4. Henry G. Alsberg, "A Polish Countess," *The Liberator* 5, no. 3 (March 1922): 10.

5. Alsberg, "I Own a Slave," *The Liberator* 5, no. 1 (January 1922): 24.

6. Alsberg, "Peace Conference of the Empruntos," *New York Call* magazine section, January 8, 1922.

7. Alsberg, "Mexico: The Price of Recognition," *The Nation*, May 10, 1922, 561–562.

8. "Alsberg's Bombshell," *Grand Rapids Press*, May 10, 1922; "Propaganda for Mexico Called a Batch of Lies," *Chicago Daily Tribune*, May 9, 1922; "Plan Commission to Study Mexican Recognition Issue," *New York Times*, May 9, 1922.

9. "Ten Questions to Secretary of State," *The Nation*, May 24, 1922, 614.

10. Alsberg, "Carlos Marx in Yucatan," *New York Call Magazine*, April 30, 1922, 3.

11. *Ibid.*

12. Henry Alsberg to Lewis Strauss, June 10, 1922, box 16, folder 4; Admiral Lewis Lichtenstein Strauss Papers; P-632; American Jewish Historical Society, New Yorkand Boston.

13. American Jewish Joint Distribution Committee, online exhibit. "Tumultuous Times— Great Needs (Averting Starvation)." Http://Archives.JDC.Org/Exhibits/Beyond-Relief/Tumultuous-Times-Great-Needs.Html.

14. Alsberg to Strauss, June 10, 1922, Box 16, Folder 4, Strauss Papers, AJHS.

15. *Ibid.*

16. *Ibid.*

17. *Ibid.*

18. JDC Ny 1921–1932, Folder 15.1, Felix M. Warburg to James Rosenberg, September 9, 1922.

19. Alsberg to Strauss, August 13, 1922, Box 16, Folder 4, Strauss Papers, AJHS.

20. Alice Wexler, *Emma Goldman in Exile: From the Russian Revolution to the Spanish Civil War* (Boston: Beacon Press, 1989), 103.

21. Henry Alsberg to Louise Bryant, September 17, 1922, Louise Bryant Papers (Ms 1840). Manuscripts and Archives, Yale University Library.

22. Strauss to Alsberg, October 15, 1922, Box 16, Folder 4, Strauss Papers, AJHS.

23. Alsberg to Strauss, October 22, 1922, Box 16, Folder 4, Strauss Papers, AJHS.

24. Alsberg to Strauss, November 12, 1922, "Lewis L. Strauss Papers—Early Career Name and Subject Files—Alsberg, Henry," Herbert Hoover Presidential Library and Museum, West Branch, IA.

25. *Ibid.*

26. *Ibid.*

27. Alsberg to Strauss, November 22, 1922, box 16, folder 4, Strauss Papers, AJHS.

28. Alsberg to Strauss, November 12, 1922, Strauss Papers, Hoover Presidential Library.

29. Henry G. Alsberg, "Letter from Abroad: 'Bourgwis' and Communist Jews," *Menorah Journal*, April 1924, 165.

30. Alsberg to Strauss, February 5, 1923, box 21, folder 9, Strauss Papers, AJHS.

31. Henry G. Alsberg, "Close Ups of New Life and New Hope," *The Sentinel: The American Jewish Weekly* (*Chicago*), February 16, 1923, and *Jewish Advocate*, February 8, 1923.

32. Evelyn Morrissey to Alsberg, February 19, 1923, box 21, folder 9, Strauss Papers, AJHS.

33. JDC NY 1921–1932, folder 449, Boris D. Bogen to Mr. Felix M. Warburg, January 30, 1923.

34. JDC NY 1921–1932, folder 449, Memo from Bogen, Subject: Crimea, March 5, 1923.

35. Alsberg, "Letter from Abroad: 'Bourgwis' and Communist Jews," 166.

36. *Ibid.*, 168.

37. JDC NY 1921–1932, folder 447, Publicity: "The Work of the American Joint Distribution Committee in the Famine District of the Crimea," April 11, 1923.

38. Boris Bogen to Alsberg, September 7, 1923, Boris D. Bogen Papers, MS-3, American Jewish Archives, Cincinnati, Ohio.

39. JDC NY 1921–1932, folder 47, Alsberg to James N. Rosenberg, October 8, 1923.

40. JDC NY 1921–1932, folder 47, Rosenberg to Alsberg, October 10, 1923.

41. Emma Goldman, *Living My Life: An Autobiography* (Salt Lake City: Peregrine Smith, 1982), 950.

42. JDC NY 1921–1932, folder 47, Carl L. Alsberg to Rosenberg, April 3, 1924.

43. JDC NY 1921–1932, folder 47, Henry Alsberg to Jacob Billikopf, August 29 1924.

44. JDC NY 1921–1932, folder 47, Alsberg to James W. Becker, December 20, 1924.

45. Michael Beizer, "American Jewish Joint Distribution Committee," YIVO Encyclopedia of Jews in Eastern Europe, http://www.yivoencyclopedia.org/article.aspx/American_Jewish_Joint_Distribution_Committee.

46. JDC NY 1921–1932, folder 3, "A History of the JDC," by Henry Alsberg (manuscript), 1921–1929; Alsberg to James Rosenberg, December 24, 1923.

47. Alsberg to Strauss, July 14, 1924, Strauss Papers, Hoover Presidential Library.

48. JDC NY 1921–1932, folder 3, "A History of the JDC"; Alsberg to Felix Warburg, October 29, 1924.

49. Alsberg to Bryant, December 19 1923, box 1, folder 4. Bryant Papers.

50. JDC NY 1921–1932, folder 3, "A History of the JDC"; Alsberg to Rosenberg, June 15 1927.

51. Carl Alsberg to Strauss, September 22, 1927, Strauss Papers, Hoover Presidential Library.

52. JDC NY 1921–1932, folder 3, "A History of the JDC"; Rosenberg to Warburg, August 27, 1927.

53. JDC NY 1921–1932, folder 3, "A History of the JDC"; Cyrus Adler to Warburg, September 19 1927. Adler saw the manuscript as a resource for a shorter book and suggested Herbert Hoover write the introduction.

54. JDC NY 1921–1932, folder 3, "A History of the JDC"; Evelyn M. Morrissey to Lewis L. Strauss, June 11, 1926.

55. JDC NY 1921–1932, folder 47, Alsberg to Bogen, December 4, 1924.

56. Alsberg to Walter Lippmann, November 11, 1925, Walter Lippmann Papers, Box 1 folder 29, Yale University Library.

Chapter 6

1. Henry Alsberg to Louise Bryant, December 19, 1923, Louise Bryant Papers (MS 1840). Manuscripts and Archives, Yale University Library.

2. Emma Goldman, *My Further Disillusionment in Russia* (Garden City, NY: Doubleday, Page, 1924), ix.

3. Henry G. Alsberg, "A Shattered Illusion," *Literary Review of the New York Evening Post,* March 29, 1924, 629.

4. Henry Alsberg, "Berkman and Bolshevism," *New York Herald Tribune Books,* April 26, 1925.

5. Henry G. Alsberg, "Son of the Prophet," *New York Herald Tribune* Books, August 16, 1925.

6. Henry Alsberg to Bertrand Russell, August 25, 1923, box 5.01, Bertrand Russell fonds, Bertrand Russell Archives, McMaster University, Hamilton, Ontario.

7. Alsberg to Russell, September 18, 1923, box 5.01, Bertrand Russell Archives.

8. Henry Alsberg to Roger Baldwin, February 20, 1924, Correspondence with Henry G. Alsberg, USSR country files. International Committee for Political Prisoners records (ICPP), Manuscripts and Archives Division, New York Public Library. Astor, Lenox, and Tilden Foundations.

9. *Ibid.*; Alice Wexler, *Emma Goldman in Exile: From the Russian Revolution to the Spanish Civil War* (Boston: Beacon Press, 1989), 103–105.

10. Alsberg to Baldwin, March 24, 1924, USSR country files, ICPP, NYPL.

11. Peggy Lamson, *Roger Baldwin, Founder of the American Civil Liberties Union: A Portrait* (Boston: Houghton Mifflin, 1976), 140.

12. Press release, March 7, 1925, Town Hall Protest meeting, box 1, folder 4, ICPP, NYPL.

13. Documents from the International Institute of Social History (IISH, Amsterdam) and the ICPP clearly show Alsberg as the initiator in 1924. They also show his various contributions to publications and group activities during its first few years of operation.

14. Alsberg to Baldwin, May 17, 1924, USSR country files, ICPP, NYPL.

15. Alsberg to Baldwin, June 9,1924, USSR country files, ICPP, NYPL.

16. Alsberg to Baldwin, September 26, 1924, USSR country files, ICPP, NYPL.

17. Emma Goldman to Roger Baldwin, November 26, 1924, folder 52, Emma Goldman Papers, International Institute of Social History (IISH), Amsterdam, The Netherlands, http://www.socialhistory.org.

18. Minutes of Executive Meetings, November 25, 1924, box 1, folder 2, ICPP, NYPL.

19. Alsberg to "Shapiro," March 14, 1925, Town Hall protest meeting, box 1, folder 4, ICPP, NYPL.

20. Emma Goldman to Harold Laski, January 9, 1925, quoted in Richard and Maria Drinnon, eds., *Nowhere at Home: Letters from Exile of Emma Goldman and Alexander Berkman* (New York: Schocken Books, 1975), 40.

21. Zosa Szajkowski, *Jews, Wars and Communism, Vol. 2: The Impact of the 1919–20 Red Scare on American Jewish Life* (New York: KTAV Publishing House, 1974), 103.

22. JDC NY 1921–1932, folder 30, Alsberg to Harlan F. Stone, November 10, 1924; Alsberg to Stone, December 29, 1924.

23. "Alsberg to Describe 'Misrule' of Soviets," *The Washington Post,* December 14, 1924.

24. JDC NY 1921–1932, folder 47, Alsberg to Boris Bogen, December 4, 1924.

25. Henry Alsberg, "Letters," *The Nation,* March 11, 1925, 266–267.

26. Alsberg to Goldman, May 13, 1925, folder 47, Goldman Papers, IISH.

27. Alsberg to Russell, August 25, 1923, box 5.01, Bertrand Russell Archives.

28. Pauline Turkel to Alexander Berkman, June 24, 1924, folder 61, Alexander Berkman Papers, International Institute of Social History, Amsterdam, The Netherlands. Isaac Don Levine and Reverend Ward were credited in some books over the years with gathering materials. In July 1925, Berkman wrote to Pauline Turkel that Levine "GOT NO DOCUMENTS whatsoever" (his emphasis) except what was already printed in the press. In Lamson, *Roger Baldwin,* p. 140, Baldwin recounted that Alsberg brought documents from Europe and translated them. In *Living My Life,* p. 976, Goldman credited Berkman first, then Alsberg and Levine for collecting the documents, including letters from twenty-two European and American writers and intellectuals.

29. Alsberg to Goldman, July 22, 1925, folder 47, Goldman Papers, IISH.

30. Alsberg to Baldwin, July 8, 1925, USSR country files, ICPP, NYPL.

31. *Letters from Russian Prisons,* introduction by Roger N. Baldwin (New York: Albert and Charles Boni, 1925), xiii–xix.

32. Simeon Strunsky, "About Books, More or Less: Russian Jails, New Style," *New York Times,* December 20, 1925.

33. Roderick Seidenberg, "Political Prisoners," *Saturday Review of Literature,* February 27 1926, 593.

34. Henry Alsberg to Emma Goldman, July 22, 1925, folder 47, Goldman Papers, IISH.

35. U.S. House of Representatives, Special Committee on Un-American Activities, *Investigation of Un-American Propaganda Activities in the United States,* Hearings on House Resolution 282,

75th Congress, Third Session, volume 4, 1938 (Washington, DC: U.S. Government Printing Office, 1939), 2887.

36. Woodrow Wilson International Center for Scholars Wilson Center, Digital Archive, http://www.wilsoncenter.org. Translation of original KGB notebooks by Alexander Vassiliev.

37. Turkel to Berkman, December 26, 1924, folder 61, Berkman Papers, IISH.

38. Wexler, *Emma Goldman in Exile*, 107.

39. Berkman to Alsberg, April 30 [no year indicated, but likely 1926], folder 8, Berkman Papers, IISH.

40. Minutes of Executive Meetings, December 10 and 31, 1925, box 1, folder 2, ICPP, NYPL; HUAC, volume 4, 1938, 2888.

41. Finding Aid, "Historical Note," ICPP Records, NYPL.

42. Lamson, *Roger Baldwin*, 140.

43. Alsberg, "Petlura," *The Nation*, August 11, 1926, 128.

44. Alsberg to Goldman, December 15, 1926, folder 47, Goldman Papers, IISH.

45. Alsberg to Goldman, May 13, 1925, folder 47, Goldman Papers, IISH.

46. Robert Aldrich, ed., *Gay Life and Culture: A World History* (New York: Universe Publishing, 2006), 179.

47. "Americans in Paris Protest," *New York Evening Post*, August 10, 1927.

48. Alsberg to Berkman, September 27, 1927, folder 8, Berkman Papers, IISH.

49. Berkman to Alsberg, October 21, 1927, folder 8, Berkman Papers, IISH.

50. Eugene Bloch to Alsberg, December 7, 1928, folder 47, Goldman Papers, IISH.

51. Emma Goldman to Alexander Berkman, November 23, 1928, quoted in Richard Drinnon and Maria Drinnon, eds., *Nowhere at Home: Letters from Exile of Emma Goldman and Alexander Berkman* (New York: Schocken Books, 1975), 94.

52. Emma Goldman, "An Unexpected Dash Through Spain," *The Road to Freedom* 5, no. 8 (April 1929).

53. HUAC, volume 4, 1938, 2893.

54. Alsberg to Goldman, March 22, 1929, folder 47, Goldman Papers, IISH.

55. Dorothy Commins, *What Is an Editor? Saxe Commins at Work* (Chicago: University of Chicago Press, 1978), 7–9. Commins later became a powerhouse editor at Random House, working with Eugene O'Neill, William Faulkner, Gertrude Stein, and Theodore Dreiser.

56. Alsberg to Goldman, January 24, 1929, folder 47, Goldman Papers, IISH.

57. Goldman to Berkman, November 23, 1928, in Drinnon and Drinnon, *Nowhere at Home*, 94.

58. Alsberg to Goldman, January 22, 1929, folder 47, Goldman Papers, IISH.

59. Alsberg to Goldman, March 22, 1929, folder 47, Goldman Papers, IISH.

60. Alsberg to Stella Bloch Hanau, April 16, 1929, Stella Hanau Papers, Sophia Smith Collection, Smith College, Northampton, MA.

61. http://www.bartleby.com/177/32.html, Margarete Münsterberg, ed. and trans., *A Harvest of German Verse* (1916).

62. Alsberg to Goldman, June 4, 1929, folder 47, Goldman Papers, IISH.

63. Alsberg to Goldman, June 18, 1929, folder 47, Goldman Papers, IISH.

Chapter 7

1. Henry G. Alsberg, "*The Dybbuk* Analyzed: Play's Translator Claims Spirit More Believable than Hamlet's Ghost," *New York Times*, October 31, 1954.

2. Cheryl Black's *Women of Provincetown*, 1915–1922 (Tuscaloosa: University of Alabama Press, 2002), covers this topic well.

3. The play's content disturbed critics and censors when it opened in 1922. Alsberg knew Sholem Asch from the Joint Distribution Committee and later hired his son, writer Nathan Asch, for the FWP.

4. Helen Deutsch and Stella Hanau, *The Provincetown: A Story of the Theatre* (New York: Farrar & Rinehart, 1931), 97.

5. *Ibid.*

6. C.W.E. Bigsby, *A Critical Introduction to Twentieth Century American Drama, Volume 1: 1900–1940* (Cambridge: Cambridge University Press, 1982), 305.

7. Deutsch and Hanau, *Provincetown*, 141.

8. *Ibid.*, 147.

9. J. Brooks Atkinson, "Folk Drama from the South," *New York Times*, February 20, 1927, X1.

10. Deutsch and Hanau, *Provincetown*, 154.

11. For a discussion on the controversy of black-themed plays written by white playwrights, see the entry on the Provincetown Players in the *Encyclopedia of the Harlem Renaissance*, ed. Cary D. Wintz and Paul Finkelman (New York: Routledge, 2004.)

12. Federal Writers' Project, *New York Panorama: A Comprehensive View of the Metropolis* (New York: Random House, 1938), 272–273.

13. Thomas N. Walters, "Paul Green's Transcendent Theater of the Imagination: In Abraham's Bosom," *Interpretations* 13, no. 1 (1981): 50.

14. Black, *Women of Provincetown*, 47.

15. Henry Alsberg to Stella Hanau, October 28, 1931, Stella Hanau Papers, Sophia Smith Collection, Smith College, Northampton, MA.

16. Edward Bloch (nephew of Stella Hanau) in discussion with author, May 2015, confirmed that the family was long aware and accepting of his sexuality.

17. Christopher Sawyer-Lauçanno, *E.E. Cummings: A Biography* (Naperville, IL: Sourcebooks,

2004), 311; Charles Norman, *E.E. Cummings: The Magic Maker* (Indianapolis: Bobbs-Merrill, 1972), 215.

18. William Warren Vilhauer, "A History and Evaluation of the Provincetown Players," Ph.D. dissertation, University of Iowa, 1965, 80–81.

19. Sawyer-Lauçanno, *E.E. Cummings*, 310.

20. Richard S. Kennedy, *Dreams in the Mirror: A Biography of E.E. Cummings* (New York: Liveright Publishing, 1980), 295 and 504. (Quote attributed to letter from author M.R. Werner to E.E. Cummings.)

21. Deutsch and Hanau, *Provincetown*, 158.

22. Norman, *Magic Maker*, 216.

23. *Ibid.*, 216, 228.

24. Deutsch and Hanau, *Provincetown*, 161.

25. Norman, *Magic Maker*, 216.

26. Stuart Chenoweth to Henry G. Alsberg, May 7, 1968, Henry Alsberg Papers, AX597, box 1, correspondence folder, Special Collections and University Archives, University of Oregon Libraries, Eugene, Oregon.

27. Although both Alsberg and Winifred Katzin shared credit and royalties for the book version of *The Dybbuk*, Alsberg was generally known and referred to as the play's adapter and held sole, exclusive English translation rights. Alsberg alone held the rights to dramatic productions. Because he'd worked with the Neighborhood Playhouse and other companies over the years to adapt the play to their needs, Alsberg saw himself as more than a translator. Writing in a 1961 letter to C.T. O'Leary at Samuel French, he said that "the acting version have made is entirely different in many ways, from the full-length translation" and "the result of a great deal of brain-sweat and the result of actual rehearsals of the play which I attended. It is practically a re written version, not at all a translation." Alsberg wrote that the acting version of the play that had evolved "with which Winifred Katzin had nothing to do" was "entirely my work." Alsberg to C.T. O'Leary, April 19, 1961, box 1, The Dybbuk folder, Alsberg Papers; alternatively, when publishers requested permission to reprint the play from the book version, Alsberg insisted that both he and Katzin receive translator credit and royalties.

28. H.I. Brock, "East Side, Too, Has 'Synthetic Theatre,'" *New York Times*, January 31, 1926.

29. Burns Mantle, ed., *The Best Plays of 1925–26 and the Year Book of the Drama in America* (New York: Dodd Mead, 1926).

30. There are various accepted spellings, including the commonly used An-ski.

31. Gabriella Safran, *Wandering Soul: The Dybbuk's Creator, S. Ansky* (Cambridge, MA: Harvard University Press, 2010), 94.

32. Memorandum of Agreement between Henry G. Alsberg and Chaim Zhitlovsky, executor of the estate of Ansky, May 9, 1924, box 1, The Dybbuk folder, Alsberg Papers.

33. Joseph Wood Krutch, Introduction to Alice Lewisohn Crowley, *The Neighborhood Playhouse: Leaves from a Theatre Scrapbook* (New York: Theatre Arts Books, 1959), xi.

34. *The Dybbuk* manuscript, undated, box 1, The Dybbuk folder, Alsberg Papers. This version appears to be the "acting" version worked on by Alsberg and differs from the book version.

35. Crowley, *The Neighborhood Playhouse*, 215.

36. *Ibid.*, 199.

37. *Ibid.*, 213.

38. Henry G. Alsberg, "The Play's Wider Appeal," Neighborhood Playbill No. 1, Season 1925–26.

39. Gilbert W. Gabriel, Introduction to *The Dybbuk*, by S. Ansky, translated by Henry G. Alsberg and Winifred Katzin (New York: Liveright Publishing, 1926), 6.

40. Edward Jablonski, *Gershwin* (New York: Doubleday, 1987), 195.

41. Charles Schwartz, *George Gershwin: His Life and Music* (Indianapolis: Bobbs-Merrill, 1973), 26.

42. Jablonski, *Gershwin*, 194.

43. Isaac Goldberg, *George Gershwin: A Study in American Music* (New York: Frederick Ungar Publishing, 1958), 39–40.

44. Alsberg to Louise Bryant, March 10, 1931, Louise Bryant Papers (MS 1840). Manuscripts and Archives, Yale University Library.

45. Howard Pollack, *Aaron Copland: The Life and Work of an Uncommon Man* (New York: Henry Holt, 1999), 142.

46. Alsberg, "The Dybbuk Analyzed."

Chapter 8

1. Henry Alsberg to Emma Goldman, December 22, 1929, folder 47, Emma Goldman Papers, International Institute of Social History (IISH), Amsterdam, The Netherlands. http://www.socialhistory.org.

2. Berkman to Goldman, April 11, 1929, in Emma Goldman et al., *Nowhere at Home: Letters from Exile of Emma Goldman and Alexander Berkman* (New York: Schocken Books, 1975), 201.

3. Goldman to Alsberg, November 26, 1929, folder 47, Goldman Papers.

4. Goldman to Alsberg, January 7, 1930, folder 47, Goldman Papers.

5. Alsberg to Goldman, January 18, 1930, folder 47, Goldman Papers.

6. Alsberg to Goldman, March 24, 1930, folder 47, Goldman Papers.

7. Alsberg to Alexander Berkman, March 3, 1930, folder 8, Alexander Berkman Papers, International Institute of Social History, Amsterdam, The Netherlands. http://www.socialhistory.org.

8. Berkman to Alsberg, March 16, 1930, folder 8, Berkman Papers.

9. "Book Review, the *Dissolution of the Hapsburg Monarchy*," *The Nation*, February 12, 1930, 204.

10. Henry Alsberg, "An Answer to Professor Carver," *Birth Control Review* 14, No. 8 (August 1930): 231.

11. Alsberg to Goldman, February 8, 1930, Folder 47, Goldman Papers.

12. Henry Alsberg, "Prisoners' Swaraj," *New Freeman*, May 10, 1930, 204–205.

13. Alsberg to Goldman, February 17, 1931, folder 47, Goldman Papers.

14. Berkman to Alsberg, undated, folder 8, Berkman Papers.

15. Alsberg, "Organize the Prisoners," *The Nation*, October 30, 1929, 493.

16. Alsberg to Goldman, May 14, 1930, folder 47, Goldman Papers.

17. Goldman to Alsberg, June 27, 1930, folder 47, Goldman Papers.

18. Alsberg's articles included "Book Review, *Psychology of Sex*," *Birth Control Review* 17, no. 7 (1933): 178; "We Still Challenge the Machine Age," *New York Times*, June 7, 1931; "Lacework of Bridges Over New York," *New York Times*, January 27, 1935; and "Book Review, *Toward a Science of Tyranny*," *The New Republic*, August 17, 1932, 24–25.

19. Alsberg to Goldman, February 17, 1931, folder 47, Goldman Papers.

20. Henry Alsberg, "Biographical Sketch of Alexander Berkman," *Alexander Berkman Sixtieth Birthday Celebration*, Pamphlet, 1930.

21. Berkman to Alsberg, December 7, 1930, folder 8, Berkman Papers.

22. Clifford McCarthy to Goldman, April 2, 1931, folder 121, Goldman Papers.

23. Alsberg to Berkman, August 20, 1931, folder 8, Berkman Papers.

24. Alsberg to Goldman, February 17, July 6, August 20, and December 30, 1931, folder 47, Goldman Papers.

25. Goldman to Alsberg, August 17, 1931, folder 47, Goldman Papers.

26. Berkman to Joseph Meyerovitch, April 5, 1931, folder 50, Berkman Papers.

27. Alsberg is listed as a delegate to the Amsterdam meeting of the World Congress Against War, August 27–29, 1932, in the pamphlet, *The World Congress Against War* (New York: American Committee for Struggle against War, 1932), 26. Tamiment Library and Robert F. Wagner Labor Archives Printed Ephemera Collection on Organizations, box 4; U.S. House of Representatives, Special Committee on Un-American Activities, *Investigation of Un-American Propaganda Activities in the United States*; Hearings on House Resolution 282, 75th Congress, Third Session, volume 4, 1938 (Washington, DC: U.S. Government Printing Office, 1939), 2894.

28. Berkman to Jimmie McGraw, December 12, 1932, folder 49, Berkman Papers.

29. Alsberg to Goldman, December 26, 1933, folder 47, Goldman Papers.

30. Alsberg to Goldman, January 6, 1934, folder 47, Goldman Papers.

31. *Ibid.*

32. Oz Frankel, "Whatever Happened to 'Red Emma'? Emma Goldman, from Alien Rebel to American Icon," *The Journal of American History* 83, no. 3 (1996): 914; Stella Ballantine to Berkman, February 10, 1934, folder 9, Berkman Papers; Alice Wexler, *Emma Goldman in Exile: From the Russian Revolution to the Spanish Civil War* (Boston: Beacon Press, 1989), 160.

33. Henry G. Alsberg, *America Fights the Depression: A Photographic Record of the Civil Works Administration* (New York: Coward-McCann, 1934).

34. Goldman to Alsberg, September 21, 1934, folder 47, Goldman Papers.

35. Alsberg to Goldman, April 16, 1935, folder 47, Goldman Papers.

36. Goldman to Alsberg, April 21, 1935, folder 47; Goldman to Emily Holmes, April 5, 1935, folder 66, Goldman Papers.

37. Alsberg to Goldman, January 22, 1939, folder 47, Goldman Papers.

Chapter 9

1. "Circus People," Terry Roth interview with Maude Cromwell, January 17, 1939, American Life Histories: Manuscripts from the Federal Writers' Project, 1936–1940. Library of Congress, Manuscript Division, WPA Federal Writers' Project Collection, http://www.loc.gov/collections/federal-writers-project/

2. Henry Alsberg to Emma Goldman, April 23, 1935, folder 47, Emma Goldman Papers, International Institute of Social History (IISH), Amsterdam, The Netherlands. http://www.socialhistory.org.

3. It was later changed to Work Projects Administration.

4. These included FERA, along with the Civil Works Administration (CWA), Public Works Administration (PWA), and the Civilian Conservation Corps (CCC).

5. Jerre Mangione, *The Dream and the Deal: The Federal Writers' Project, 1935–1943* (New York: Avon Books, 1972), 37.

6. June Hopkins, *Harry Hopkins: Sudden Hero, Brash Reformer* (New York: Palgrave Macmillan, 2009), 190. The provenance of this is dubious, but it is often quoted.

7. Hallie Flanagan, *Arena: The History of the Federal Theatre* (New York: Benjamin Blom, 1965), 18.

8. The Historical Records Survey, first part of the FWP, later branched off into a smaller agency under Federal One.

9. Unidentified WPA official quoted in Monty Noam Penkower, *The Federal Writers' Project: A Study in Government Patronage of the Arts* (Urbana: University of Illinois Press, 1977), 28.

10. William F. McDonald, *Federal Relief Administration and the Arts: The Origins and Administrative History of the Arts Projects of the Works Progress Administration* (Columbus: Ohio State University Press, 1969), 747.

11. Jacob Baker, Oral History Interview, September 25, 1963, Archives of American Art, Smithsonian Institution.

12. Essential works about the FWP are Jerre Mangione's *The Dream and the Deal*; Monty Noam Penkower's *The Federal Writers' Project: A Study in Government Patronage of the Arts*; Jerrold Hirsch's *Portrait of America: A Cultural History of the Federal Writers' Project*; Kathleen O'Connor McKinzie's *Writers on Relief*; and William Francis McDonald's *Federal Relief Administration and the Arts*. Benjamin Botkin's *Lay My Burden Down* and Norman Yetman's books introducing the slave narratives are similarly essential. These titles are well supplemented by the Library of Congress and other government websites, as well as numerous other worthy tracts by William Stott, Christine Bold, and others. See the Bibliography.

13. John Egerton, *Speak Now Against the Day: The Generation Before the Civil Rights Movement in the South* (New York: Knopf, 1994), 99.

14. Penkower, *Federal Writers' Project*, 29; "Hopkins New Aide Plans Jobs for 10,000 Writers on Relief," *Washington Evening Star*, July 28, 1935.

15. "Activities of the Federal Writers' Project," undated, Records of George Cronyn 1935–1939, Entry PI 57 3, box 1, miscellaneous folder, Records of the Federal Writers' Project, General Records of the Works Projects Administration, Record Group 69. National Archives at College Park, MD.

16. Penkower, *Federal Writers' Project*, 21.

17. "Hopkins New Aide," *Evening Star*, July 28, 1935.

18. Frank L. Kluckhohn, "Uncle Sam Expands as an Art Patron," *New York Times*, October 6, 1935.

19. Kathleen O'Connor McKinzie, "Writers on Relief: 1935–1942," Ph.D. dissertation, Indiana University, 1970, 19.

20. Mangione, *Dream and the Deal*, 72.

21. Robert Asure, Oral History Interview, October 7, 1965, Archives of American Art, Smithsonian Institution.

22. Thomas Gore is of dubious relation to former Vice-President Al Gore.

23. "Phone Conversation 10/4/35—Alsberg and Cronyn," box 1, folder 2, Cronyn Files, NARA.

24. "Telephone Conversation Between Mr. Alsberg and Mrs. Roosevelt," "Telephone Conversation Between Mr. H.J. Eckenrode and Mr. Alsberg," December 5, 1935, box 15, folder 2, Jerre Mangione Papers, Rare Books Special Collections and Preservation Department, University of Rochester.

25. Alsberg to Goldman, October 31, 1935, folder 47, Goldman Papers.

26. Goldman to Alsberg, November 19 and March 2, 1936, folder 47, Goldman Papers.

27. Ina Russell, ed., *Jeb and Dash: A Diary of Gay Life, 1918–1945* (Boston: Faber and Faber, 1993), 150.

28. Maurice L. Malkin, *Return to My Father's House: A Charter Member of the American Communist Party Tells Why He Joined, and Why He Later Left to Fight Communism* (New Rochelle, NY: Arlington House, 1972), 177.

29. McDonald, *Federal Relief*, 272–274; Mangione, *Dream and the Deal*, 229–238.

30. Jerrold Hirsch, *Portrait of America: A Cultural History of the Federal Writers' Project* (Chapel Hill: University of North Carolina Press, 2003), 8.

31. "Prepare Survey for Guide of U.S.," *The Pelham Sun*, November 15, 1935.

32. Blair Bolles, "The Federal Writers Project," *Saturday Review of Literature*, July 9, 1938.

33. Mangione, *Dream and the Deal*, 6.

34. Emma Goldman to Stella Ballantine, August 25 [no year given], folder 12, Goldman Papers.

35. "Alsberg to Eudora Ramsey Richardson," undated, Records of Henry Alsberg 1935–1939, Entry PI 57 2, box 2, folder 2, Records of the Federal Writers' Project, General Records of the Works Projects Administration, Record Group 69. National Archives at College Park, MD.

36. "Phrasing of Letters and Comments—Memorandum from Reed Harris to Katharine Kellock and Members of the Tour Section," February 17, 1937, box 1, folder 2, Cronyn Files, NARA. Alsberg instructed Reed Harris to send this memo.

37. *Idaho, a Guide in Word and Picture*, Works Progress Administration (Caldwell, ID: Caxton Printers, 1937), 287.

38. "Progress Report Memorandum from Henry Alsberg to Ellen Woodward and Aubrey Williams," July 29, 1936, box 2, miscellaneous folder, Alsberg Files, NARA.

39. Mangione, *Dream and the Deal*, 207.

40. "The First WPA Guide," *Saturday Review of Literature*, February 27, 1937, 8.

41. R.L. Duffus, "Uncle Sam Plays a Baedeker Role," *New York Times Magazine*, January 10, 1937.

42. "Hurley Given First Copy of WPA Book," *Daily Boston Globe*, August 18, 1937.

43. "Hopkins Jeers Book Critics," *Daily Boston Globe*, August 20, 1937.

44. "Protest Rises on Sacco Case in State Guide," *Christian Science Monitor*, August 19, 1937.

45. "Defends Writings of WPA Authors," *New York Times*, July 22, 1937.

46. "Alsberg Denies He Is a Red," *New York Times*, November 2, 1936.

47. "A Red Baedeker," reprinted from *New York American*, February 15, 1936. Ad sponsored by the National Republican Builders, Inc., box 1, "Dies Committee" folder, Katharine Amend Kellock Papers, Manuscript Division, Library of Congress.

48. Jay Du Von, Oral History Interview with Harry Hewes and Jay Du Von, October 1964, Archives of American Art, Smithsonian Institution.

49. Mangione, *Dream and the Deal*, 182.

50. Jack Conroy, "Writers Disturbing the Peace," *New Masses*, November 17, 1936, 13.

51. Henry Hart, ed., *Writer in a Changing World* (New York: Equinox Cooperative Press, 1937), 241–249.

52. Elsie Robinson, March 16, 1938, as quoted in E. Current-Garcia, "American Panorama (Federal Writers' Project)," *Prairie Schooner* 12, no. 2 (1938): 80.

53. "The Nation's Honor Roll for 1937," *The Nation*, January 1, 1938, 735.

54. "Mirror to America," *Time*, January 3, 1938, 65.

55. Lewis Mumford, "Writers' Project," *New Republic*, October 20, 1937, 306.

56. John Steinbeck, *Travels with Charley: In Search of America* (New York: Viking Press, 1974), 120–121.

Chapter 10

1. "Democracy and Particularism," *The Nation*, August 2, 1917, 114.

2. *American Guide Manual*, October 1935, page 54, box A7, Federal Writers' Project: Administrative File, 1935–1941, United States Work Projects Administration Records, Manuscript Division, Library of Congress, Washington, DC.

3. Henry Alsberg to Franz Boas, Franz Boas Papers, March 6, 1936, American Philosophical Society.

4. *Arizona: Grand Canyon State* (New York: Hastings House, 1968), 8.

5. *California: A Guide to the Golden State* (New York: Hastings House, 1939), 38–39, 5.

6. Alsberg to J. Harris, Cable, May 5, 1939, Records of Henry Alsberg 1935–1939, Entry PI 57 2, box 2, Records of the Federal Writers' Project, General Records of the Works Projects Administration, Record Group 69. National Archives at College Park, MD.

7. George Cronyn to Jacob Baker, November 30, 1935, Records of George Cronyn 1935–1939, Entry PI 57 3, box 2, Records of the Federal Writers' Project, General Records of the Works Projects Administration, Record Group 69. National Archives at College Park, MD; Alsberg to Aubrey Williams. December 16, 1935, box 1, Alsberg Files, NARA.

8. As quoted in Lauren Rebecca Sklaroff, *Black Culture and the New Deal: The Quest for Civil Rights in the Roosevelt Era* (Chapel Hill: University of North Carolina Press, 2009), 94. For more on Brown's work with Southern state editors and the FWP in general, see Joanne V. Gabbin, *Sterling A. Brown: Building the Black Aesthetic Tradition* (Westport, CT: Greenwood Press, 1985), and John Edgar Tidwell and Steven C. Tracy, eds., *After Winter: The Art and Life of Sterling A. Brown* (New York: Oxford University Press, 2009).

9. George Cronyn to Myrtle Miles, November 5, 1936, Reports and Records Pertaining to Negro Studies 1935–1940, Entry PI 57 27, box 1, Records of the Federal Writers' Project, General Records of the Works Projects Administration, Record Group 69. National Archives at College Park, MD.

10. *Mississippi: A Guide to the Magnolia State* (New York: Hastings House, 1959), 30.

11. Jared Putnam, "Guides to America," *The Nation*, December 24, 1938, 694–696.

12. *Washington: City and Capital* (Washington, DC: U.S. Government Printing Office, 1937), 68–90.

13. Monty Noam Penkower, *The Federal Writers' Project: A Study in Government Patronage of the Arts* (Urbana: University of Illinois Press, 1977), 203; and Tidwell and Tracy, *After Winter*, 301.

14. *Washington DC, a Guide to the Nation's Capital 1942* (New York: Hastings House, 1942), 51–59.

15. "Chicago Folkstuff," Betty Burke interview with Anna Novak, May 1, 1939, American Life Histories: Manuscripts from the Federal Writers' Project, 1936–1940, Library of Congress, Manuscript Division, WPA Federal Writers' Project Collection. http://www.loc.gov/collections/federal-writers-project/.

16. "Old Timers Dictionary in Detail," Marie Carter anonymous interview, March 8, 1937, American Life Histories: Manuscripts from the Federal Writers' Project, 1936–1940, Life Histories, FWP/LOC.

17. "Eddie's Bar," Ralph Ellison anonymous interview, May 10, 1939, American Life Histories: Manuscripts from the Federal Writers' Project, 1936–1940, Life Histories, FWP/LOC.

18. Henry Alsberg, undated speech, box 14, folder 3, Jerre Mangione Papers, Rare Books Special Collections and Preservation Department, University of Rochester.

19. William Couch, ed., *These Are Our Lives* (Chapel Hill: University of North Carolina Press, 1939).

20. Reminiscences of William Terry Couch (1970), Columbia Center for Oral History Archives, Rare Book and Manuscript Library, Columbia University in the City of New York.

21. Kevin Nance, "Roosevelt's Writers," Poets and Writers, July/August 2010, http://www.pw.org. Graham's quote is included in this review of the Smithsonian documentary by David A. Taylor, *Soul of a People: The WPA Writers' Project Uncovers Depression America*.

22. Pamela Bordelon, ed., *Go Gator and Muddy the Water: Writings by Zora Neale Hurston from the Federal Writers' Project* (New York: Norton, 1999), 35 and 48. According to Borden, the Florida FWP used only a fraction of Hurston's submitted writings and removed her essays from the published 1993 *Florida Negro*.

23. "America Learns of Negro from Books of

the Federal Writers' Project," Press Release, March 6, 1939, Records Pertaining to Negro Studies, NARA.

24. Alsberg, undated speech, box 14, folder 3, Mangione Papers. Although those three books and others would remain unpublished, much of the material collected eventually appeared in books and on websites.

25. "Born in Slavery: Slave Narratives from the Federal Writers' Project, 1936–1938," Manuscript Division, Library of Congress, http://lcweb2.loc.gov/ammem/snhtml/snhome.html.

26. Penkower, *Federal Writers' Project*, 144.

27. Norman R. Yetman, "The Background of the Slave Narrative Collection," *American Quarterly* 19, no. 3 (1967): 534–535.

28. Sharon Ann Musher, "Contesting: 'The Way the Almighty Wants It': Crafting Memories of Ex-Slaves in the Slave Narrative Collection," *American Quarterly* 53, no. 1 (2001): 5.

29. W.H. Auden, Introduction to Anzia Yezierska, *Red Ribbon on a White Horse* (New York: Persea Books, 1950), 18.

30. William F. McDonald, *Federal Relief Administration and the Arts: The Origins and Administrative History of the Arts Projects of the Works Progress Administration* (Columbus: Ohio State University Press, 1969), 697.

31. Frank L. Kluckhohn, "Uncle Sam Expands as an Art Patron," *New York Times*, October 6, 1935.

32. McDonald, *Federal Relief*, 697.

33. The FWP acquired *Cape Cod Pilot* after seeing the galleys and recognizing the writing quality. McDonald, *Federal Relief*, 703; Jerre Mangione, *The Dream and the Deal: The Federal Writers' Project, 1935–1943* (New York: Avon Books, 1972), 212–213 and 242–243.

34. McDonald, *Federal Relief*, 698–699.

35. "An Editorial Conference," broadcast transcript, April 13, 1938, box 3, folder 28, Richard Wright Papers. Yale Collection of American Literature, Beinecke Rare Book and Manuscript Library.

36. Henry Hart, ed., *The Writer in a Changing World* (New York: Equinox Cooperative Press, 1937), 244–247.

37. George Schuyler, "Writers on Relief," *Opportunity*, December 15, 1937, 378.

38. Eda Lou Walton, "A Federal Writers' Anthology," *New York Times Book Review*, August 29, 1937.

39. "An Editorial Conference," broadcast transcript, April 13, 1938, box 3, folder 28, Wright Papers, Yale.

40. "Headlines Bulletin," Constitutional Educational League, undated, box 119, folder 1922, Wright Papers, Yale.

41. Kathleen O'Connor McKinzie, "Writers on Relief: 1935–1942," Ph.D. dissertation, Indiana University, 1970, 97.

42. Franklin Folsom, *Days of Anger, Days of Hope: A Memoir of the League of American Writers, 1937–1942* (Niwot: University Press of Colorado,

1994), 240; Mangione, *Dream and the Deal*, 248; "American Stuff by Workers of Federal Writers' Project with Eight Prints by Federal Arts Project," *Direction* 3, no. 1 (1938).

43. *New York Panorama: A Comprehensive View of the Metropolis* (New York: Random House, 1938), 3.

44. Jared Putnam, "Guides to America," *The Nation*, December 24, 1938, 694–696.

45. Mangione, *Dream and the Deal*, 245; Penkower, *Federal Writers' Project*, 166; Yezierska, *Red Ribbon*, 168.

46. Harry Roskolenko, *When I Was Last on Cherry Street* (New York: Stein and Day, 1965), 153; Yezierska, *Red Ribbon*, 161.

47. Jerry W. Ward and Robert Butler, eds., *The Richard Wright Encyclopedia* (Westport, CT: Greenwood Press, 2008), 132.

48. McHugh to Jerre Mangione, , n.d., box 179, folder 3, Mangione Papers.

49. Alsberg to Richard Wright, April 9, 1938, box 97, folder 1331, Wright Papers, Yale.

50. Jerre Mangione, *An Ethnic at Large: A Memoir of America in the Thirties and Forties* (New York: Putnam, 1978), 237.

51. Mangione, *Dream and the Deal*, 227.

52. Jack Balch, *Lamps at High Noon* (Urbana: University of Illinois Press, 2000), 34.

53. Mangione, *Ethnic at Large*, 231; Mangione, *Dream and the Deal*, 223.

54. Mangione, *Dream and the Deal*, 225.

55. "White Miss. WPA Official Forgets Social Bugaboos," *Baltimore Afro American*, February 5, 1938.

56. Mangione, *Dream and the Deal*, 59.

57. Balch, *Lamps at High Noon*, 217.

58. Vincent McHugh to Jerre Mangione, September 5, 1978, box 179, folder 3, Mangione Papers.

59. Cora Alsberg to Roderick Seidenberg, June 12, 1932; Roderick Seidenberg and Mabel Dwight Papers; box 4, folder 13; University of Baltimore Langsdale Library Special Collections.

60. Michael Winkelmann, in collaboration with Katrin Burth, *Auf einmal sind sie weggemacht: Lebensbilder Arolser Juden im 20. Jahrhundert: eine dokumentation* [All at Once They Are Done Away With: Lebensbilder Arolser Jews in the 20th Century] (Kassel: Verlag Gesamthochschul-Bibliothek Kassel, 1992); Die Synagoge in Vöhl, www.synagoge-voehl.de/Juden_im_Landkreis/arolsen/personen/a/alsberg_frieda.htm; Central Database of Shoah Victims' Names, The Holocaust Martyrs' and Heroes' Remembrance Authority, Jerusalem, http://www.yadvashem.org; Bad Arolsen, Jewish History, http://www.alemannia-judaica.de/bad_arolsen_synagoge.htm; U.S. Holocaust Memorial Museum: Holocaust Survivors and Victims Database, http://www.ushmm.org.

61. Balch, *Lamps at High Noon*, 36–37.

Chapter 11

1. Dora Thea Hettwer to Henry Alsberg, August 15, 1939, box 14, folder 7, Jerre Mangione Papers, Rare Books Special Collections and Preservation Department, University of Rochester.

2. Jay Du Von, Oral History Interview with Harry Hewes and Jay Du Von, October 1964, Archives of American Art, Smithsonian Institution. Du Von referred here to a later FBI investigation.

3. D.A. Saunders, "Dies Committee: First Phase," *The Public Opinion Quarterly* 3, no. 4 (1939): 223–238.

4. William F. McDonald, *Federal Relief Administration and the Arts: The Origins and Administrative History of the Arts Projects of the Works Progress Administration* (Columbus: Ohio State University Press, 1969), 694–695.

5. "WPA Projects Proved to Be Red Rackets," *New York Sun*, July 19, 1937.

6. "Defends Writings of WPA Authors," *New York Times*, July 22, 1937.

7. Du Von, Oral History Interview, October 1964, Smithsonian.

8. U.S. House of Representatives, Special Committee on Un-American Activities, *Investigation of Un-American Propaganda Activities in the United States*, Hearings on House Resolution 282, 75th Congress, Third Session, 1938, volume 1 (Washington, DC: U.S. Government Printing Office, 1939), 1.

9. Du Von, Oral History Interview with Jay Du Von, 1963 November 7, Archives of American Art, Smithsonian Institution.

10. "Calls Brooklyn College Hotbed of Communism," *New York Herald Tribune*, July 31, 1938.

11. HUAC 1938, volume 1, 281.

12. Richard McKinzie, *The New Deal for Artists* (Princeton, NJ: Princeton University Press, 1973), 156.

13. "Links New Deal and Communism as Peril to U.S.," *Chicago Daily Tribune*, October 15, 1938.

14. Alsberg to Mary Maverick Lloyd, September 1938, box 18, Mary Maverick Lloyd papers, Manuscripts and Archives Division, the New York Public Library, Astor, Lenox, and Tilden Foundations.

15. Marcia Phelps to Lloyd, September 21, 1938, box 18, Lloyd Papers.

16. Jerre Mangione, *The Dream and the Deal: The Federal Writers' Project, 1935–1943* (New York: Avon Books, 1972), 289–290; *State Department Information Program—Voice of America*, Hearing before the Senate Permanent Subcommittee on Investigations of the Committee on Government Operations, 83rd Congress, First Session, Pursuant to S. Res. 40, Part 5, March 3, 1953 (Washington, DC: U.S. Government Printing Office, 1953), 385.

17. *Brief Containing Detailed Answers to the Federal Writers' Project Made by Witnesses Before the Committee to Investigate Un-American Activities* (Washington, DC, 1938), 2.

18. Mangione, *Dream and the Deal*, 302.

19. HUAC 1938, volume 4, 3109–3123. Lazelle's name in the HUAC hearings is misspelled as Lazell.

20. Mangione, *Dream and the Deal*, 306.

21. Clair Laning to Lloyd, November 11, 1938, box 17, Lloyd Papers.

22. Fleta Coe to Lloyd, November 7, 1938, box 18, Lloyd Papers.

23. Roderick Seidenberg to Lloyd, November 15, 1938, box 18, Lloyd Papers.

24. "Mr. Dies Goes to Town," *The Nation*, September 3, 1938, 216.

25. Dora Thea Hettwer to Laning, December 2, 1938, box 17, Lloyd Papers.

26. Hallie Flanagan, *Arena: The History of the Federal Theatre* (New York: Benjamin Blom, 1965), 339.

27. Jerrold Hirsch, *Portrait of America: A Cultural History of the Federal Writers' Project* (Chapel Hill: University of North Carolina Press, 2003), 206.

28. Flanagan, *Arena*, 201.

29. HUAC 1938, volume 4, 2857.

30. Christopher Vogler, *Hero's Journey*, www.thewritersjourney.com/hero's_journey.htm.

31. Mangione, *Dream and the Deal*, 309.

32. *Ibid.*, 315.

33. HUAC 1938, volume 4, 2888. The dialogue here is abridged.

34. *Ibid.*, 320.

35. Baker to Lloyd, box 16, n.d., Lloyd Papers.

36. Seidenberg to Lloyd, December 6, 1938, box 18, Lloyd Papers.

37. *Ibid.*

38. Baker to Lloyd, box 16, n.d., Lloyd Papers.

39. Alsberg to Lloyd, December 15, 1938, box 18, Lloyd Papers.

40. Laning to Lloyd, box 17, n.d., Lloyd Papers.

41. "Pen Project-America, the WPA, and 20,000,000 Words," *Pathfinder*, December 17, 1938.

42. Alsberg to Lloyd, December 15, 1938, box 18, Lloyd Papers.

43. "If Alsberg was the least concerned with self of all the directors of Federal One, he was also the most completely naive; and his failure to distinguish between friend and foe left him in the naked before his enemies." McDonald, *Federal Relief*, 665.

44. *Investigation of Un-American Activities and Propaganda; Report of the Special Committee on Un-American Activities* (Washington, DC: U.S. Government Printing Office, 1939).

45. Laning to Lloyd, January 9, 1939, box 20, Lloyd Papers.

46. Mangione, *Dream and the Deal*, 14.

47. Laning to Lloyd, February 29, 1939, box 20, Lloyd Papers.

48. *Ibid.*, February 26 and March 18, 1939.

49. "Urge WPA Restore 6000 to Art Rolls," *New York Times*, February 15, 1939.

50. Mangione, *Dream and the Deal*, 323 and 6.

51. Henry G. Alsberg, "Organize the Prisoners," *The Nation*, October 30, 1929, 493.

52. "Statement of Henry G. Alsberg," *Further Additional Appropriation for Work Relief and Relief, Fiscal Year 1939*, Hearings before the Subcommittee of the Committee on Appropriations, House of Representatives 76th Congress, First Session on H. J. Res. 209 and 246 (Washington, DC: U.S. Government Printing Office, 1939), 213.

53. *Ibid.*, 211–214.

54. "Summary of Contents in Mr. Henry Alsberg's Statement Refuting Charges Made Before the House Subcommittee on the Works Progress Administration on Monday, May 1, 1939," U.S. Senate Committee on Appropriations, *Work Relief and Public Works Appropriation Act of 1939*, Hearings on H.J. Res. 326, 76th Congress, First Session, 1939.

55. Hirsch, *Portrait of America*, 175.

56. Robert Cantwell, "America and the Writers' Project," *New Republic*, April 26, 1939, 323–325.

57. Mangione, *Dream and the Deal*, 15.

58. Alsberg to Carl Malmberg, June 6, 1939, box A5, Federal Writers' Project: Administrative File, 1935–1941; United States Work Projects Administration Records, Manuscript Division, Library of Congress, Washington, DC.

59. Laning to Lloyd, June 26, 1939, box 20, Lloyd Papers.

60. *Ibid.*, July 17, 1939.

61. Mari Tomasi and Roaldus Richmond, *Men Against Granite*, ed. Alfred F. Rosa and Mark Wanner, contains 55 of the original interviews (Shelburne, VT: New England Press, 2005); Mark Kurlansky, *Food of a Younger Land* (New York: Riverhead Books, 2009), and Pat Willard, *America Eats! On the Road with the WPA* (New York: Bloomsbury, 2008), make use of the FWP's *America Eats* documents.

62. Alsberg to John Frederick, July 22, 1939, box A6; Alsberg to Malmberg, August 1, 1939, box A6, Federal Writers' Project: Administrative File, 1935–1941; United States Work Projects Administration Records, Manuscript Division, Library of Congress, Washington, DC.

63. Although the timeline regarding circumstances of Alsberg's departure is muddied in various published accounts, it is certain that he did not leave of his own will, but was fired.

64. Florence Kerr, Oral History Interview, October 18–31, 1963, Archives of American Art, Smithsonian Institution. Kerr's talks with Alsberg about resigning likely came before the August date when he departed.

65. Laning to Lloyd, June 14, 1939, box 20, Lloyd Papers.

66. Leon [Dorais] to Katharine Kellock, August 10, 1939, box 1, Katharine Amend Kellock Papers, Manuscript Division, Library of Congress, Washington, DC.

67. Mangione, *Dream and the Deal*, 23 and 24.

68. *Ibid.*, 23.

69. Monty Noam Penkower, *The Federal Writers' Project: A Study in Government Patronage of the Arts* (Urbana: University of Illinois Press, 1977), 212.

70. "Alsberg Dismissed as Head of Writers' Project," *Publishers Weekly*, August 19, 1939. 513.

71. Walter White to Alsberg, August 10, 1939; Dora Thea Hettwer to Alsberg, August 15, 1939, Mangione Papers.

72. *Slave Narratives: A Folk History of Slavery in the United States from Interviews with Former Slaves*, Federal Writers' Project (Washington, DC, 1941).

73. Kellock to Harold Coy, May 14, 1942, box 1, Kellock Papers, LOC. The FWP's official demise came in 1943 with the end of the WPA.

74. These numbers are derived from "A Brief History of the Federal Writers' Project, July 1, 1935–August 31, 1939," box 1, Kellock Papers, LOC, and *FDR and the Arts: The WPA Arts Projects: An Exhibition in the Stokes Gallery, the New York Public Library, Astor, Lenox, and Tilden Foundations January Through March 1983* (New York: New York Public Library, 1983).

Chapter 12

1. Henry Alsberg to Richard Wright, March 5, 1940, box 97, folder 1331, Richard Wright Papers. Yale Collection of American Literature, Beinecke Rare Book and Manuscript Library.

2. Clair Laning to Mary Maverick Lloyd, June [n.d.] 1940, box 20, folder 1, Mary Maverick Lloyd Papers. Manuscripts and Archives Division. The New York Public Library. Astor, Lenox, and Tilden Foundations.

3. Laning to Lloyd, n.d., box 25, folder 4, Lloyd Papers.

4. Henry Alsberg, "War Aims," *The Antioch Review* 1, no. 1 (Spring 1941): 21–34.

5. Alsberg, "Post-War Apocalypse," *Decision*, September 1941, 10.

6. Alsberg, "What About the Federal Arts Projects?" *Decision*, May 1941, 9.

7. Laning to Lloyd, October 13, 1941, box 25, folder 4, Lloyd Papers.

8. Henry Alsberg, "The American Jew's Reaction to Anti-Semitism," July 21, 1941, Edward Weeks Papers, container 38.5, Harry Ransom Center, the University of Texas at Austin.

9. Laning to Lloyd, July 26 and May 2, 1941, box 26, folder 1; January 9, 1942, box 27, folder 6; Lloyd Papers.

10. U.S. Department of Justice, Federal Bureau of Investigation, Anna Rosenberg Files. Special Inquiry, New York, December 7 through December 9, 1950. "Allegation of Alleged Membership of Anna Rosenberg in the John Reed Club; re: Henry Garfield Alsberg." Bureau File 62-10641, sub A, serial 41, 56 and 67. Documents in this report refer to the 1942–1943 Civil Service investigation of Alsberg.

11. "Dies Denounces New List of Reds," *New York Times*, February 2, 1943; "Names and Records of 40 'Crackpots' Listed by Dies," *Chicago Daily Tribune*, February 2, 1943.

12. Martin Dies, February 1, 1943, House of Representatives, as quoted in Anna Rosenberg FBI Files.

13. Melchior Palyi, "Question of World Peace Is Analyzed," *Chicago Daily Tribune*, October 7, 1945; Albert Guerard, "Peace and Law," *The Nation*, November 10, 1945; T.V. Smith, "Making Peace by Impetuosity," *The Saturday Review*, September 29, 1945.

14. Henry Alsberg to Alfred Kroeber, May 22, 1948, folder 11, A.L. Kroeber Papers, BANC FILM 2049, the Bancroft Library, University of California, Berkeley.

15. Roger Baldwin to Alsberg, June 27, 1951; Lewis Mumford to Alsberg, June 26, 1950, correspondence folder, Henry Alsberg Papers, AX597. Special Collections and University Archives, University of Oregon Libraries, Eugene, Oregon.

16. Alsberg to Kroeber, April 13, 1948, folder 11, A.L. Kroeber Papers, BANC FILM 2049, the Bancroft Library, University of California, Berkeley.

17. Vincent McHugh to Jerre Mangione, August 8, 1969, box 179, folder 3, Jerre Mangione Papers, Rare Books Special Collections and Preservation Department, University of Rochester.

18. Robert Griffith, *The Politics of Fear: Joseph R. McCarthy and the Senate* (Amherst: University of Massachusetts, 1987), 135–139.

19. Anna Rosenberg FBI Files.

20. *State Department Information Program— Voice of America*, Hearing before the Senate Permanent Subcommittee on Investigations of the Committee on Government Operations, 83rd Congress, First Session, Pursuant to S. Res. 40, Part 5, March 3, 1953 (Washington, DC: U.S. Government Printing Office, 1953), 385–387.

21. Alsberg to Katharine Kellock, February 19, 1954, Alsberg Papers; Alsberg to Nathan Asch, September 3, 1954, Louis Pettus Archives and Special Collections, Winthrop University, Nathan Asch Papers—Accession 344.

22. Alsberg to [José Antonio] Villarreal, May 29, 1957, box 1, correspondence folder, Alsberg Papers.

23. "Ansky Play, in English, Opens Downtown," *The New York Times*, October 27, 1954.

24. Alsberg, "*The Dybbuk* Analyzed," *The New York Times*, October 31, 1954.

25. Alsberg registered a copyright on a new translation in 1953. On his death, it transferred to his niece. *The Dybbuk* folder, Alsberg Papers.

26. Alsberg to Vincent McHugh, August 25, 1957, box 1, correspondence folder, Alsberg Papers.

27. "Tres Marias" and "Unsuccesful Cain," box 1, Alsberg Papers.

28. McHugh to Mangione, August 8, 1969, box 179, folder 3, Mangione Papers.

29. Alsberg to "Robertson," October 12, 1956, box 1, correspondence folder, Alsberg Papers.

30. Alsberg to Vincent McHugh, July 29, 1957, box 1, correspondence folder, Alsberg Papers.

31. McHugh to Alsberg, June 23, 1957, box 1, correspondence folder, Alsberg Papers.

32. Alsberg to McHugh, November 24, 1958, box 1, correspondence folder, Alsberg Papers.

33. Alsberg to McHugh, October 25, 1957, and March 24, 1958, box 1, correspondence folder, Alsberg Papers.

34. Alsberg to McHugh, October 25, 1957, box 1, correspondence folder, Alsberg papers.

35. Alsberg to McHugh, June 15, 1961, box 4, Alsberg folder, Vincent McHugh Papers, Yale Collection of American Literature, Beinecke Rare Book and Manuscript Library.

36. Alsberg to McHugh, July 2, 1961, box 1, correspondence folder, Alsberg papers.

37. McHugh to Alsberg, July 6, 1961, box 1, correspondence folder, Alsberg Papers.

38. Stella Hanau to Alsberg, May 12, 1961; July 10 and September 24, 1962; box 1, correspondence folder, Alsberg Papers.

39. Alsberg to McHugh, April 4, 1962; October 3, 1963; June [n.d.] 1967; box 4, Alsberg folder March 24, 1966, box 7, "A" folder, McHugh Papers.

40. Alsberg to Hanau, July [n.d.] 1968, box 1, correspondence folder, Alsberg Papers.

41. Mary Maverick Lloyd to Mangione, May 19, 1969, box 177, folder 6, Mangione Papers.

42. Jerre Mangione to Joseph Gaer, August 7, 1968, box 172, folder 1, Mangione Papers.

43. McHugh to Mangione, May 11, 1968, box 179, folder 3, Mangione Papers.

44. Jim McGraw to Mangione, May 21, 1969; Mangione to McGraw, May 23, 1969; box 179, folder 2, Mangione Papers.

45. McHugh to Mangione, August 8, 1969, box 179, folder 3; Mangione to McHugh, August 29, 1969, box 179, folder 3, Mangione Papers.

46. McHugh to Mangione, May 5, 1972, box 179, folder 3, Mangione Papers.

47. Alsberg to Stella Hanau, July [n.d.], 1968, box 1, correspondence folder, Alsberg Papers.

48. Alsberg to McHugh, October 3, 1963, and July 14, 1961, box 4, McHugh Papers.

49. Dora Thea Hettwer, Walter Frese, and Isaac Don Levine to Elsa Alsberg; November 2, 3, and 4, respectively, 1970; box 1, letters of condolence folder, Alsberg Papers; Alfred Knopf to Julius Alsberg, November 4, 1970, Alfred A. Knopf, Inc. Records, Harry Ransom Center, the University of Texas at Austin.

50. McHugh to Mangione, August 8, 1969, box 179, folder 3, Mangione Papers.

Bibliography

All books referred to in the text or notes are included here, along with other significant works that relate to various aspects of Henry Alsberg's life. Additionally, a sampling of books that emanated from the Federal Writers' Project folklore, ethnic studies, and ex-slaves projects are also included, with some titles produced during the life of the project, and other, newer books and resources which have since been derived from original FWP source material.

Online sites listed below provide access to original books from the *American Guide* series and other FWP books. The Library of Congress, the National Archives, and other entities offer a wealth of textual and multimedia resources that may interest readers. The websites for the American Jewish Joint Distribution Committee and YIVO Institute for Jewish Research supply additional information concerning events covered in this book.

Books

Adler, Cyrus. *I Have Considered the Days*. Philadelphia: Jewish Publication Society of America, 1941.

_____. *With Firmness in the Right: American Diplomatic Action Affecting Jews, 1840–1945*. New York: American Jewish Committee, 1946.

Aldrich, Robert, ed. *Gay Life and Culture: A World History.* New York: Universe Publishing, 2006.

Alsberg, Henry. *America Fights the Depression: A Photographic Record of the Civil Works Administration.* New York: Coward-McCann, 1934.

_____, ed. *The American Guide: A Source Book and Complete Travel Guide for the United States.* New York: Hastings House, 1949.

_____, ed. *The American Guide: Four Volumes, New England and the Middle Atlantic States; the Lake States, the Plains States; the Mountain States, the West Coast; the South, the Southwest.* New York: Hastings House, 1949.

_____. *Let's Talk About the Peace.* New York: Hastings House, 1945.

_____, Errico Malatesta, Max Nettlau, Augustin Souchy, Erich Mühsam, and Bertrand Russell. *Alexander Berkman Sixtieth Birthday Celebration.* New York: N.p., 1930.

Ansky, S. *The Dybbuk: A Play in Four Acts.* Translated by Henry G. Alsberg and Winifred Katzin. New York: Liveright Publishing, 1926.

Arizona Writers' Program and Joseph Miller. *Arizona: Grand Canyon State.* New York: Hastings House, 1968.

Avrich, Paul, and Karen Avrich. *Sasha and Emma: The Anarchist Odyssey of Alexander Berkman and Emma Goldman*. Cambridge, MA: Belknap Press of Harvard University Press, 2012.

Balakian, Peter. *The Burning Tigris: The Armenian Genocide and America's Response*. New York: HarperCollins, 2003.

Balch, Jack S. *Lamps at High Noon*. Urbana: University of Illinois Press, 2000.

Banks, Ann, ed. *First Person America*. New York: Alfred A. Knopf, 1980.

Beizer, Michael. *Relief in Time of Need: Russian Jewry and the Joint, 1914–1924*. Bloomington, IN: Slavica Publishers, 2015.

Berger, Josef. *Cape Cod Pilot. Federal Writers' Project, Works Progress Administration for the State of Massachusetts*. Provincetown, MA: Modern Pilgrim Press, 1937.

Berkman, Alexander. *Bolshevik Myth*. New York: Boni and Liveright, 1925.

_____. *Prison Memoirs of an Anarchist*. New York: Schocken Books, 1970.

Bigsby, C.W.E. *A Critical Introduction to Twentieth Century American Drama. Volume 1: 1900–1940*. Cambridge: Cambridge University Press, 1982.

Black, Cheryl. *Women of Provincetown. 1915–1922*. Tuscaloosa: University of Alabama Press, 2002.

Bogen, Boris. *Born a Jew*. In collaboration with Alfred Segal. New York: Macmillan, 1930.

Bold, Christine. *The WPA Guides: Mapping America*. Jackson: University Press of Mississippi, 1999.

_____. *Writers, Plumbers and Anarchists: The WPA Writers' Project in Massachusetts*. Amherst: University of Massachusetts Press, 2006.

Botkin, Benjamin Albert. *Lay My Burden Down: A Folk History of Slavery*. Chicago: University of Chicago Press, 1945.

_____. *A Treasury of American Folklore: Stories, Ballads, and Traditions of the People*. New York: Crown Publishers, 1944.

Buhle, Mari Jo, Paul Buhle, and Dan Georgakas. *Encyclopedia of the American Left*. New York: Garland, 1990.

California: A Guide to the Golden State. New York: Hastings House, 1939.

Carter, David. *Stonewall: The Riots That Sparked the Gay Revolution*. New York: St. Martin's, 2004.

Cavalcade of the American Negro. Chicago: Diamond Jubilee Exposition Authority, 1940.

Chandler, Genevieve W., Kincaid Mills, Genevieve C. Peterkin, and Aaron McCollough. *Coming Through: Voices of a South Carolina Gullah Community from WPA Oral Histories*. Columbia: University of South Carolina Press, 2008.

Churchill, Allen. *Improper Bohemians*. New York: E.P. Dutton & Company, 1959.

Cohen, David Steven. *America, the Dream of My Life: Selections from the Federal Writers' Projects New Jersey Ethnic Survey*. New Brunswick, NJ: Rutgers University Press, 1990.

Commins, Dorothy. *What Is an Editor? Saxe Commins at Work*. Chicago: University of Chicago Press, 1978.

Couch, William, ed. *These Are Our Lives*. Chapel Hill: University of North Carolina Press, 1939.

Creel, George. *Rebel at Large: Recollections of Fifty Crowded Years*. New York, G. P. Putnam's Sons, 1947.

Crowley, Alice Lewisohn. *The Neighborhood Playhouse; Leaves from a Theatre Scrapbook*. New York: Theatre Arts Books, 1959.

D'Agostino, Anthony. *Marxism and the Russian Anarchists*. San Francisco: Germinal Press, 1977.

Davis, Joseph Stancliffe, ed. *Carl Alsberg, Scientist at Large*. Stanford: Stanford University Press, 1948.

Deutsch, Helen, and Stella Hanau. *The Provincetown: A Story of the Theatre*. New York: Farrar & Rinehart, 1931.

Dies, Martin. *Martin Dies' Story*. New York: Bookmailer, 1963.

_____. *The Trojan Horse in America*. New York: Arno Press, 1977.

Doty, C. Stewart, ed. *the First Franco-Americans: New England Life Histories from the Federal Writers' Project. 1938–1939*. Orono: University of Maine at Orono Press, 1985.

Drinnon, Richard. *Rebel in Paradise: A Biography of Emma Goldman*. Chicago: University of Chicago Press, 1961.

Drinnon, Richard, and Maria Drinnon, eds. *Nowhere at Home: Letters from Exile of Emma Goldman and Alexander Berkman*. New York: Schocken Books, 1975.

Egerton, John. *Speak Now Against the Day: The Generation Before the Civil Rights Movement in the South*. New York: Knopf, 1994.

Elkus, Abram I. *The Memoirs of Abram Elkus: Lawyer, Ambassador, Statesman*. With a commentary by Hilmar Kaiser. Princeton, NJ: Gomidas Institute, 2004.

Erskine, John. *the Memory of Certain Persons*. Philadelphia: Lippincott, 1947.

FDR and the Arts: The WPA Arts Projects: An Exhibition in the Stokes Gallery, the New York Public Library, Astor, Lenox, and Tilden Foundations January Through March 1983. New York: New York Public Library, 1983.

Forum Stories. Selected by Charles Vale. New York: Mitchell Kennerly, 1914.

Federal Writers' Project. *The Albanian Struggle in the Old World and New*. Boston: Writer, Inc., 1939.

_____. *American Stuff: An Anthology of Prose & Verse by Members of the Federal Writers' Project; with Sixteen Prints by the Federal Art Project*. New York: Viking Press, 1937.

_____. *Florida: A Guide to the Southern-Most State*. New York: Oxford University Press, 1939.

_____. *Massachusetts: A Guide to Its Places and People*. Cambridge, MA: Riverside Press, 1937.

_____. *Mississippi: A Guide to the Magnolia State*. New York: Hastings House, 1959.

_____. *New England Hurricane: A Factual Pictorial Record*. Boston: Hale Cushman & Flint, 1938.

_____. *New York Panorama: A Comprehensive View of the Metropolis*. New York: Random House, 1938.

_____. *Slave Narratives: A Folk History of Slavery in the United States from Interviews with Former Slaves*, Washington, D.C.: Library of Congress, 1941.

_____. *Washington: City and Capital*. Washington, D.C.: U.S. Government Printing Office, 1937.

_____. *Washington, D.C.: A Guide to the Nation's Capital*. New York: Hastings House, 1942.

_____. *The WPA Guide to New York City: The Federal Writers' Project Guide to 1930s New York*. New York: The New Press, 1995.

_____. *Wyoming Folklore: Reminisces, Folktales, Beliefs, Customs, and Folk Speech*. Edited by James R. Dow, Roger L. Welsch, and Susan D. Dow. Lincoln: University of Nebraska, 2010.

Flanagan, Hallie. *Arena: The History of the Federal Theatre*. New York: Benjamin Blom, 1965.

Folsom, Franklin. *Days of Anger, Days of Hope: A Memoir of the League of American Writers, 1937–1942*. Niwot: University Press of Colorado, 1994.

Frankfurter, Felix, and Harlan B. Phillips. *Felix Frankfurter Reminisces*. New York: Reynal Company, 1960.

Gabbin, Joanne V. *Sterling A. Brown: Building the Black Aesthetic Tradition*. Westport, CT: Greenwood Press, 1985.

Glover, Jacqueline, and Thomas Lennon. *Unchained Memories: Readings from the Slave Narratives*. DVD. 2003. HBO Documentary Films.

Goldberg, Isaac. *George Gershwin: A Study in American Music*. New York: Frederick Ungar Publishing, 1958.

Goldman, Emma. *Anarchism and Other Essays*. New York: Dover Publications, 1969.

_____. *Living My Life: An Autobiography*. Salt Lake City: Peregrine Smith, 1982.

_____. *My Disillusionment in Russia*. Garden City, NY: Doubleday, Page, 1923.

_____. *My Further Disillusionment in Russia*. Garden City, NY: Doubleday, Page, 1924.

Goodman, Walter. *The Committee: The Extraordinary Career of the House Committee on Un-American Activities.* New York: Farrar, Straus, and Giroux, 1968.

Govenar, Alan B. *African American Frontiers: Slave Narratives and Oral Histories.* Santa Barbara, CA: ABC-CLIO, 2000.

Griffith, Robert. *The Politics of Fear: Joseph R. McCarthy and the Senate.* Amherst: University of Massachusetts, 1987.

Handlin, Oscar. *A Continuing Task; the American Jewish Joint Distribution Committee, 1914–1964.* New York: Random House, 1964.

Harrison, Marguerite E. *Marooned in Moscow: The Story of an American Woman Imprisoned in Russia.* New York: George H. Doran, 1921.

Hart, Henry, ed. *Writer in a Changing World.* New York: Equinox Cooperative Press, 1937.

Hirsch, Jerrold. *Portrait of America: A Cultural History of the Federal Writers' Project.* Chapel Hill: University of North Carolina Press, 2003.

A History of Columbia College on Morningside. New York: Columbia University Press, 1954.

Hobson, Archie, and Bill Stott. *Remembering America: A Sampler of the WPA American Guide Series.* New York: Columbia University Press, 1985.

Holland, W.L., and Paul F. Hooper. *Remembering the Institute of Pacific Relations: The Memoirs of William L. Holland.* Tokyo: Ryukei Shyosha, 1995.

Hopkins, June. *Harry Hopkins: Sudden Hero. Brash Reformer.* New York: Basingstoke; Palgrave Macmillan, 2009.

Hurston, Zora Neale, and Pamela Bordelon. *Go Gator and Muddy the Water: Writings by Zora Neale Hurston from the Federal Writers' Project.* New York: Norton, 1999.

Idaho, a Guide in Word and Picture. Works Progress Administration. Caldwell, ID: Caxton Printers, 1937.

Jablonski, Edward. *Gershwin.* New York: Doubleday, 1987.

Kalin, Andrea, David A. Taylor, James Mirabello, Olive Bucklin, David Alan Taylor, Richard Ford, Jonathan Holloway, et al. *Soul of a People: Writing America's Story.* DVD. 2009. Smithsonian Networks.

Kennedy, Richard S. *Dreams in the Mirror: A Biography of E.E. Cummings.* New York: Liveright Publishing, 1980.

Kipen, David, Federal Writers' Project. *Los Angeles in the 1930s: The WPA Guide to the City of Angels.* Berkeley: University of California Press. 2011.

_____, Federal Writers' Project. *San Francisco in the 1930s: The WPA Guide to the City by the Bay.* Berkeley: University of California Press. 2011.

Kissack, Terence. *Free Comrades: Anarchism and Homosexuality in the United States, 1895–1917.* Oakland, CA: AK Press, 2008.

Kroeber, Theodora. *Alfred Kroeber: A Personal Configuration.* Berkeley: University of California Press, 1970.

Kropotkin, P.A. *Selected Writings on Anarchism and Revolution.* Cambridge: MIT Press, 1970.

Kropotkin, Peter. "L'ordre" (1881), translation, Nicolas Walter. Available at Anarchy Archives: http://dwardmac.pitzer.edu/Anarchist_Archives/kropotkin/freedompamphlet4.html.

Kurlansky, Mark. *Food of a Younger Land.* New York: Riverhead Books, 2009.

Lamson, Peggy. *Roger Baldwin, Founder of the American Civil Liberties Union: A Portrait.* Boston: Houghton Mifflin, 1976.

Letters from Russian Prisons. Introduction by Roger N. Baldwin. New York: Albert and Charles Boni, 1925.

Link, Arthur S., ed. *Papers of Woodrow Wilson. Volume 42: April 7–June 23, 1917.* Princeton, NJ: Princeton University Press, 1983.

Malkin, Maurice L. *Return to My Father's House: A Charter Member of the American Communist Party Tells Why He Joined, and Why He Later Left to Fight Communism.* New Rochelle, NY: Arlington House, 1972.

Mangione, Jerre. *The Dream and the Deal: The Federal Writers' Project, 1935–1943.* New York: Avon Books, 1972.

_____. *An Ethnic at Large: A Memoir of America in the Thirties and Forties.* New York: Putnam, 1978.

Mantle, Burns, ed. *The Best Plays of 1925–26 and the Year Book of the Drama in America.* New York: Dodd Mead, 1926.

McDonald, William F. *Federal Relief Administration and the Arts: The Origins and Administrative History of the Arts Projects of the Works Progress Administration.* Columbus: Ohio State University Press, 1969.

McKinzie, Richard. *The New Deal for Artists.* Princeton, NJ: Princeton University Press, 1973.

Morgan, Ted. *Reds: McCarthyism in 20th Century America.* New York: Random House, 2003.

Morgenthau, Henry. *Ambassador Morgenthau's Story.* Detroit: Wayne State University Press, 2003.

Morgenthau III, Henry. *Mostly Morgenthaus: A Family History.* New York: Ticknor & Fields, 1991.

Norman, Charles. *E.E. Cummings: The Magic Maker.* Indianapolis: Bobbs-Merrill, 1972.

O'Connor McKinzie, Kathleen. "Writers on Relief: 1935–1942," Ph.D. dissertation, Indiana University, 1970.

O'Neill, William L. *The Last Romantic: A Life of Max Eastman.* New York: Oxford University Press, 1978.

Penkower, Monty Noam. *The Federal Writers' Project: A Study in Government Patronage of the Arts.* Urbana: University of Illinois Press, 1977.

Pollack, Howard. *Aaron Copland: The Life and Work of an Uncommon Man.* New York: Henry Holt, 1999.

Quinn, Susan. *Furious Improvisation: How the WPA and a Cast of Thousands Made High Art Out of Desperate Times.* New York: Walker and Company, 2008.

Rebolledo, Tey Diana, and María Teresa Márquez. *Women's Tales from the New Mexico WPA: La Diabla a Pie.* Houston: Arte Público Press, 2000.

Richard, Carl J. *When the United States Invaded Russia: Woodrow Wilson's Siberian Disaster.* Lanham, MD: Rowman & Littlefield, 2013.

Robbins, Tim. *Cradle Will Rock.* Film. 1999. Cradle Productions, Havoc, Touchstone Productions.

Rodgers, Lawrence R., and Jerrold Hirsch. *America's Folklorist: B.A. Botkin and American Culture.* Norman: University of Oklahoma Press, 2010.

Rosenberg, James N. *On the Steppes; a Russian Diary.* New York: Alfred Knopf, 1927.

_____. *Unfinished Business: James N. Rosenberg Papers.* Edited and with a preface by Maxwell Geismar. Mamaroneck, NY: Vincent Marasia Press, 1967.

Roskolenko, Harry. *When I Was Last on Cherry Street.* New York. Stein and Day, 1965.

Rukeyser, Muriel. *Willard Gibbs.* Woodbridge, CT: Ox Bow Press, 1988.

Russell, Ina, ed. *Jeb and Dash: A Diary of Gay Life, 1918–1945.* Boston: Faber and Faber, 1993.

Safran, Gabriella. *Wandering Soul: The Dybbuk's Creator, S. Ansky.* Cambridge, MA: Harvard University Press, 2010.

Sawyer-Lauçanno, Christopher. *E.E. Cummings: A Biography.* Naperville, IL: Sourcebooks, 2004.

Schwartz, Charles. *George Gershwin: His Life and Music.* Indianapolis: Bobbs-Merrill, 1973.

Sklaroff, Lauren Rebecca. *Black Culture and the New Deal: The Quest for Civil Rights in the Roosevelt Era.* Chapel Hill: University of North Carolina Press, 2009.

Spector, Shmuel, ed. *The Encyclopedia of Jewish Life Before and During the Holocaust.* New York: New York University Press, 2001.

Sporn, Paul. *Against Itself: The Federal Theatre and Writers' Projects in the Midwest.* Detroit: Wayne State University Press, 1995.

Steinbeck, John. *Travels with Charley.* New York: Viking Press, 1962.

Steward, Julian. *Alfred Kroeber*. New York: Columbia University Press, 1973.

Stott, William. *Documentary Expression and Thirties America*. Chicago: University of Chicago Press, 1986.

Szajkowski, Zosa. *Jews, War and Communism, Volume 2: the Impact of the 1919–1920 Red Scare on American Jewish Life*. New York: KTAV Publishing, 1974.

Taylor, David A. *Soul of a People: The WPA Writers' Project Uncovers Depression America*. Hoboken: John Wiley and Sons, 2009.

Taylor, Nick. *American-Made: The Enduring Legacy of the WPA: When FDR Put the Nation to Work*. New York: Bantam Book, 2008.

Terrill, Tom E., and Jerrold Hirsch. *Such as Us: Southern Voices of the Thirties*. Chapel Hill: University of North Carolina Press, 1978.

Tidwell, John Edgar, and Steven C. Tracy, eds. *After Winter: The Art and Life of Sterling A. Brown*. New York: Oxford University Press, 2009.

Tomasi, Mari, and Roaldus Richmond. *Men Against Granite*. Edited by Alfred F. Rosa and Mark Wanner. Shelburne, VT: New England Press, 2003.

Virginia Writers' Project. *The Negro in Virginia*. New York: Hastings House, 1940.

Ward, Jerry W., and Robert Butler, eds. *The Richard Wright Encyclopedia*. Westport, CT: Greenwood Press, 2008.

Weisberger, Bernard A. *The WPA Guide to America: The Best of 1930s America as Seen by the Federal Writers' Project*. New York: Pantheon Books, 1985.

Wexler, Alice. *Emma Goldman in Exile: From the Russian Revolution to the Spanish Civil War*. Boston: Beacon Press, 1989.

Whealdon, Bon. I., and Robert Bigart. *I Will Be Meat for My Salish: Montana Writers' Project and the Buffalo of the Flathead Indian Reservation*. Helena: Montana Historical Society Press, 2001.

Willard, Pat. *America Eats! On the Road with the W.P.A.: The Fish Fries, Box Supper Socials, and Chitlin Feasts That Define Real American Food*. New York: Bloomsbury, 2008.

Winkelmann, Michael, in collaboration with Katrin Burth. *Auf einmal sind sie weggemacht: Lebensbilder Arolser Juden im 20. Jahrhundert: eine Dokumentation*. Kassel: Verlag Gesamthochschul-Biblikothek Kassel, 1992.

Winter, Ella. *And Not to Yield*. New York: Harcourt, Brace & World, 1963.

Wintz, Cary D., and Paul Finkelman, eds. *Encyclopedia of the Harlem Renaissance*. New York: Routledge, 2004.

Wright, Richard. *Native Son*. New York: Harper & Bros., 1940.

Writers' Program of New York. *The Italians of New York*. New York: Arno Press, 1969.

Yetman, Norman R. *Voices from Slavery: 100 Authentic Slave Narratives*. Mineola, NY: Dover, 2000.

_____. *When I Was a Slave: Memoirs from the Slave Narrative Collection*. Mineola, NY: Dover, 2002.

Yezierska, Anzia. *Red Ribbon on a White Horse*. New York: Persea Books, 1950.

Yiddish Writers' Group of the Federal Writers' Project. *The Jewish Landsmanschaften of New York*. New York: I.L. Peretz Yiddish Writers' Union, 1938.

Zweig, Stefan, Friderike Maria Burger Winternitz Zweig, and Henry G. Alsberg. *Stefan and Friderike Zweig: Their Correspondence, 1912–1942*. New York: Hastings House, 1954.

Selected Online Resources

American Jewish Joint Distribution Committee: http://www.jdc.org

American Life Histories: Manuscripts from the Federal Writers' Project, 1936–1940: https://www.loc.gov/collections/federal-writers-project/

Born in Slavery: Slave Narratives from the Federal Writers' Project, 1936–1938 http://memory.loc.gov/ammem/snhtml/snhome.html

Digital Book Index. *American Guide* Books: http://www.digitalbookindex.com/_search/search010histus20fedwriproja.asp

Federal Writers' Project: http://www.loc.gov/rr/program/bib/newdeal/fwp.html

Internet Archive. Government documents and *American Guide* series books: http://www.archive.org

Living New Deal, University of California, Berkeley: http://www.livingnewdeal.org

The National Archives: A New Deal for the Arts: http://www.archives.gov/exhibits/new_deal_for_the_arts

New Deal: http://www.loc.gov/rr/program/bib/newdeal/index.html

New Deal Network: http://newdeal.feri.org

WPA Children's Books, Digital Archives of Broward County Library: http://digitalarchives.broward.org/cdm/landingpage/collection/WPAChildren

YIVO Institute for Jewish Research: http://www.yivo.org

Index

Numbers in **bold italics** refer to pages with photographs.